INTRODUCTION TO DIGITAL SIGNAL PROCESSING AND FILTER DESIGN

INTRODUCTION TO DIGITAL SIGNAL PROCESSING AND FILTER DESIGN

B. A. Shenoi

WILEY-
INTERSCIENCE

A JOHN WILEY & SONS, INC., PUBLICATION

Published by John Wiley & Sons, Inc., Hoboken, New Jersey.
Published simultaneously in Canada.

For general information on our other products and services or for technical support, please contact our Customer Care Department within the United States at (800) 762-2974, outside the United States at (317) 572-3993 or fax (317) 572-4002.

Wiley also publishes its books in a variety of electronic formats. Some content that appears in print may not be available in electronic formats. For more information about Wiley products, visit our web site at www.wiley.com.

Library of Congress Cataloging-in-Publication Data:

ISBN-13 978-0-471-65442-1 (cloth)
ISBN-10 0-471-65442-6 (cloth)

Printed in the United States of America.

10 9 8 7 6 5 4 3 2 1

◼◼◼ CONTENTS

■■■■■■ PREFACE

This preface is addressed to instructors as well as students at the junior–senior level for the following reasons. I have been teaching courses on digital signal processing, including its applications and digital filter design, at the undergraduate and the graduate levels for more than 25 years. One common complaint I have heard from undergraduate students in recent years is that there are not enough numerical problems worked out in the chapters of the book prescribed for the course. But some of the very well known textbooks on digital signal processing have more problems than do a few of the books published in earlier years. However, these books are written for students in the senior and graduate levels, and hence the junior-level students find that there is too much of mathematical theory in these books. They also have concerns about the advanced level of problems found at the end of chapters. I have not found a textbook on digital signal processing that meets these complaints and concerns from junior-level students. So here is a book that I have written to meet the junior students' needs and written with a student-oriented approach, based on many years of teaching courses at the junior level.

Network Analysis is an undergraduate textbook authored by my Ph.D. thesis advisor Professor M. E. Van Valkenburg (published by Prentice-Hall in 1964), which became a world-famous classic, not because it contained an abundance of all topics in network analysis discussed with the rigor and beauty of mathematical theory, but because it helped the students understand the basic ideas in their simplest form when they took the first course on network analysis. I have been highly influenced by that book, while writing this textbook for the first course on digital signal processing that the students take. But I also have had to remember that the generation of undergraduate students is different; the curriculum and the topic of digital signal processing is also different. This textbook does not contain many of the topics that are found in the senior–graduate-level textbooks mentioned above. One of its main features is that it uses a very large number of numerical problems as well as problems using functions from MATLAB® (MATLAB is a registered trademark of The MathWorks, Inc.) and Signal Processing Toolbox, worked out in every chapter, in order to highlight the fundamental concepts. These problems are solved as examples after the theory is discussed or are worked out first and the theory is then presented. Either way, the thrust of the approach is that the students should understand the basic ideas, using the worked, out problems as an instrument to achieve that goal. In some cases, the presentation is more informal than in other cases. The students will find statements beginning with "Note that. . .," "Remember. . .," or "It is pointed out," and so on; they are meant to emphasize the important concepts and the results stated in those sentences. Many of the important results are mentioned more than once or summarized in order to emphasize their significance.

The other attractive feature of this book is that all the problems given at the end of the chapters are problems that can be solved by using only the material discussed in the chapters, so that students would feel confident that they have an understanding of the material covered in the course when they succeed in solving the problems. Because of such considerations mentioned above, the author claims that the book is written with a student-oriented approach. Yet, the students should know that the ability to understand the solution to the problems is important but understanding the theory behind them is far more important.

The following paragraphs are addressed to the instructors teaching a junior-level course on digital signal processing. The first seven chapters cover well-defined topics: (1) an introduction, (2) time-domain analysis and z-transform, (3) frequency-domain analysis, (4) infinite impulse response filters, (5) finite impulse response filters, (6) realization of structures, and (7) quantization filter analysis. Chapter 8 discusses hardware design, and Chapter 9 covers MATLAB. The book treats the mainstream topics in digital signal processing with a well-defined focus on the fundamental concepts.

Most of the senior–graduate-level textbooks treat the theory of finite wordlength in great detail, but the students get no help in analyzing the effect of finite word-length on the frequency response of a filter or designing a filter that meets a set of frequency response specifications with a given wordlength and quantization format. In Chapter 7, we discuss the use of a MATLAB tool known as the "FDA Tool" to thoroughly investigate the effect of finite wordlength and different formats of quantization. This is another attractive feature of the textbook, and the material included in this chapter is not found in any other textbook published so far.

When the students have taken a course on digital signal processing, and join an industry that designs digital signal processing (DSP) systems using commercially available DSP chips, they have very little guidance on what they need to learn. It is with that concern that additional material in Chapter 8 has been added, leading them to the material that they have to learn in order to succeed in their professional development. It is very brief but important material presented to guide them in the right direction. The textbooks that are written on DSP hardly provide any guidance on this matter, although there are quite a few books on the hardware implementation of digital systems using commercially available DSP chips. Only a few schools offer laboratory-oriented courses on the design and testing of digital systems using such chips. Even the minimal amount of information in Chapter 8 is not found in any other textbook that contains "digital signal processing" in its title. However, Chapter 8 is not an exhaustive treatment of hardware implementation but only as an introduction to what the students have to learn when they begin a career in the industry.

Chapter 1 is devoted to discrete-time signals. It describes some applications of digital signal processing and defines and, suggests several ways of describing discrete-time signals. Examples of a few discrete-time signals and some basic operations applied with them is followed by their properties. In particular, the properties of complex exponential and sinusoidal discrete-time signals are described. A brief history of analog and digital filter design is given. Then the advantages of digital signal processing over continuous-time (analog) signal processing is discussed in this chapter.

Chapter 2 is devoted to discrete-time systems. Several ways of modeling them and four methods for obtaining the response of discrete-time systems when excited by discrete-time signals are discussed in detail. The four methods are (1) recursive algorithm, (2) convolution sum, (3) classical method, and (4) z-transform method to find the total response in the time domain. The use of z-transform theory to find the zero state response, zero input response, natural and forced responses, and transient and steady-state responses is discussed in great detail and illustrated with many numerical examples as well as the application of MATLAB functions. Properties of discrete-time systems, unit pulse response and transfer functions, stability theory, and the Jury–Marden test are treated in this chapter. The amount of material on the time-domain analysis of discrete-time systems is a lot more than that included in many other textbooks.

Chapter 3 concentrates on frequency-domain analysis. Derivation of sampling theorem is followed by the derivation of the discrete-time Fourier transform (DTFT) along with its importance in filter design. Several properties of DTFT and examples of deriving the DTFT of typical discrete-time signals are included with many numerical examples worked out to explain them. A large number of problems solved by MATLAB functions are also added. This chapter devoted to frequency-domain analysis is very different from those found in other textbooks in many respects.

The design of infinite impulse response (IIR) filters is the main topic of Chapter 4. The theory of approximation of analog filter functions, design of analog filters that approximate specified frequency response, the use of impulse-invariant transformation, and bilinear transformation are discussed in this chapter. Plenty of numerical examples are worked out, and the use of MATLAB functions to design many more filters are included, to provide a hands-on experience to the students.

Chapter 5 is concerned with the theory and design of finite impulse response (FIR) filters. Properties of FIR filters with linear phase, and design of such filters by the Fourier series method modified by window functions, is a major part of this chapter. The design of equiripple FIR filters using the Remez exchange algorithm is also discussed in this chapter. Many numerical examples and MATLAB functions are used in this chapter to illustrate the design procedures.

After learning several methods for designing IIR and FIR filters from Chapters 4 and 5, the students need to obtain as many realization structures as possible, to enable them to investigate the effects of finite wordlength on the frequency response of these structures and to select the best structure. In Chapter 6, we describe methods for deriving several structures for realizing FIR filters and IIR filters. The structures for FIR filters describe the direct, cascade, and polyphase forms and the lattice structure along with their transpose forms. The structures for

IIR filters include direct-form and cascade and parallel structures, lattice–ladder structures with autoregressive (AR), moving-average (MA), and allpass structures as special cases, and lattice-coupled allpass structures. Again, this chapter contains a large number of examples worked out numerically and using the functions from MATLAB and Signal Processing Toolbox; the material is more than what is found in many other textbooks.

The effect of finite wordlength on the frequency response of filters realized by the many structures discussed in Chapter 6 is treated in Chapter 7, and the treatment is significantly different from that found in all other textbooks. There is no theoretical analysis of finite wordlength effect in this chapter, because it is beyond the scope of a junior-level course. I have chosen to illustrate the use of a MATLAB tool called the "FDA Tool" for investigating these effects on the different structures, different transfer functions, and different formats for quantizing the values of filter coefficients. The additional choices such as truncation, rounding, saturation, and scaling to find the optimum filter structure, besides the alternative choices for the many structures, transfer functions, and so on, makes this a more powerful tool than the theoretical results. Students would find experience in using this tool far more useful than the theory in practical hardware implementation.

Chapters 1–7 cover the core topics of digital signal processing. Chapter 8, on hardware implementation of digital filters, briefly describes the simulation of digital filters on Simulink®, and the generation of C code from Simulink using Real-Time Workshop® (Simulink and Real-Time Workshop are registered trademarks of The MathWorks, Inc.), generating assembly language code from the C code, linking the separate sections of the assembly language code to generate an executable object code under the Code Composer Studio from Texas Instruments is outlined. Information on DSP Development Starter kits and simulator and emulator boards is also included. Chapter 9, on MATLAB and Signal Processing Toolbox, concludes the book.

The author suggests that the first three chapters, which discuss the basics of digital signal processing, can be taught at the junior level in one quarter. The prerequisite for taking this course is a junior-level course on linear, continuous-time signals and systems that covers Laplace transform, Fourier transform, and Fourier series in particular. Chapters 4–7, which discuss the design and implementation of digital filters, can be taught in the next quarter or in the senior year as an elective course depending on the curriculum of the department. Instructors must use discretion in choosing the worked-out problems for discussion in the class, noting that the real purpose of these problems is to help the students understand the theory. There are a few topics that are either too advanced for a junior-level course or take too much of class time. Examples of such topics are the derivation of the objective function that is minimized by the Remez exchange algorithm, the formulas for deriving the lattice–ladder realization, and the derivation of the fast Fourier transform algorithm. It is my experience that students are interested only in the use of MATLAB functions that implement these algorithms, and hence I have deleted a theoretical exposition of the last two topics and also a description of the optimization technique in the Remez exchange algorithm. However, I have included many examples using the MATLAB functions to explain the subject matter.

Solutions to the problems given at the end of chapters can be obtained by the instructors from the Website `http://www.wiley.com/WileyCDA/WileyTitle/productCd-0471464821.html`. They have to access the solutions by clicking "Download the software solutions manual link" displayed on the Webpage. The author plans to add more problems and their solutions, posting them on the Website frequently after the book is published.

As mentioned at the beginning of this preface, the book is written from my own experience in teaching a junior-level course on digital signal processing. I wish to thank Dr. M. D. Srinath, Southern Methodist University, Dallas, for making a thorough review and constructive suggestions to improve the material of this book. I also wish to thank my colleague Dr. A. K. Shaw, Wright State University, Dayton. And I am most grateful to my wife Suman, who has spent hundreds of lonely hours while I was writing this book. Without her patience and support, I would not have even started on this project, let alone complete it. So I dedicate this book to her and also to our family.

B. A. SHENOI

May 2005

CHAPTER 1

Introduction

1.1 INTRODUCTION

We are living in an age of information technology. Most of this technology is based on the theory of digital signal processing (DSP) and implementation of the theory by devices embedded in what are known as *digital signal processors* (DSPs). Of course, the theory of digital signal processing and its applications is supported by other disciplines such as computer science and engineering, and advances in technologies such as the design and manufacturing of very large scale integration (VLSI) chips. The number of devices, systems, and applications of digital signal processing currently affecting our lives is very large and there is no end to the list of new devices, systems, and applications expected to be introduced into the market in the coming years. Hence it is difficult to forecast the future of digital signal processing and the impact of information technology. Some of the current applications are described below.

1.2 APPLICATIONS OF DSP

Digital signal processing is used in several areas, including the following:

1. *Telecommunications*. Wireless or mobile phones are rapidly replacing wired (landline) telephones, both of which are connected to a large-scale telecommunications network. They are used for voice communication as well as data communications. So also are the computers connected to a different network that is used for data and information processing. Computers are used to generate, transmit, and receive an enormous amount of information through the Internet and will be used more extensively over the same network, in the coming years for voice communications also. This technology is known as *voice over Internet protocol* (VoIP) or *Internet telephony*. At present we can transmit and receive a limited amount of text, graphics, pictures, and video images from

mobile phones, besides voice, music, and other audio signals—all of which are classified as multimedia—because of limited hardware in the mobile phones and not the software that has already been developed. However, the computers can be used to carry out the same functions more efficiently with greater memory and large bandwidth. We see a seamless integration of wireless telephones and computers already developing in the market at present. The new technologies being used in the abovementioned applications are known by such terms as CDMA, TDMA,[1] spread spectrum, echo cancellation, channel coding, adaptive equalization, ADPCM coding, and data encryption and decryption, some of which are used in the software to be introduced in the third-generation (G3) mobile phones.

2. *Speech Processing*. The quality of speech transmission in real time over telecommunications networks from wired (landline) telephones or wireless (cellular) telephones is very high. Speech recognition, speech synthesis, speaker verification, speech enhancement, text-to-speech translation, and speech-to-text dictation are some of the other applications of speech processing.

3. *Consumer Electronics*. We have already mentioned cellular or mobile phones. Then we have HDTV, digital cameras, digital phones, answering machines, fax and modems, music synthesizers, recording and mixing of music signals to produce CD and DVDs. Surround-sound entertainment systems including CD and DVD players, laser printers, copying machines, and scanners are found in many homes. But the TV set, PC, telephones, CD-DVD players, and scanners are present in our homes as separate systems. However, the TV set can be used to read email and access the Internet just like the PC; the PC can be used to tune and view TV channels, and record and play music as well as data on CD-DVD in addition to their use to make telephone calls on VoIP. This trend toward the development of fewer systems with multiple applications is expected to accelerate in the near future.

4. *Biomedical Systems*. The variety of machines used in hospitals and biomedical applications is staggering. Included are X-ray machines, MRI, PET scanning, bone scanning, CT scanning, ultrasound imaging, fetal monitoring, patient monitoring, and ECG and EEC mapping. Another example of advanced digital signal processing is found in hearing aids and cardiac pacemakers.

5. *Image Processing*. Image enhancement, image restoration, image understanding, computer vision, radar and sonar processing, geophysical and seismic data processing, remote sensing, and weather monitoring are some of the applications of image processing. Reconstruction of two-dimensional (2D) images from several pictures taken at different angles and three-dimensional (3D) images from several contiguous slices has been used in many applications.

6. *Military Electronics*. The applications of digital signal processing in military and defense electronics systems use very advanced techniques. Some of the applications are GPS and navigation, radar and sonar image processing, detection

---

[1]Code- and time-division multiple access. In the following sections we will mention several technical terms and well-known acronyms without any explanation or definition. A few of them will be described in detail in the remaining part of this book.

and tracking of targets, missile guidance, secure communications, jamming and countermeasures, remote control of surveillance aircraft, and electronic warfare.

7. *Aerospace and Automotive Electronics*. Applications include control of aircraft and automotive engines, monitoring and control of flying performance of aircraft, navigation and communications, vibration analysis and antiskid control of cars, control of brakes in aircrafts, control of suspension, and riding comfort of cars.

8. *Industrial Applications*. Numerical control, robotics, control of engines and motors, manufacturing automation, security access, and videoconferencing are a few of the industrial applications.

Obviously there is some overlap among these applications in different devices and systems. It is also true that a few basic operations are common in all the applications and systems, and these basic operations will be discussed in the following chapters. The list of applications given above is not exhaustive. A few applications are described in further detail in [1]. Needless to say, the number of new applications and improvements to the existing applications will continue to grow at a very rapid rate in the near future.

1.3   DISCRETE-TIME SIGNALS

A signal defines the variation of some physical quantity as a function of one or more independent variables, and this variation contains information that is of interest to us. For example, a continuous-time signal that is periodic contains the values of its fundamental frequency and the harmonics contained in it, as well as the amplitudes and phase angles of the individual harmonics. The purpose of signal processing is to modify the given signal such that the quality of information is improved in some well-defined meaning. For example, in mixing consoles for recording music, the frequency responses of different filters are adjusted so that the overall quality of the audio signal (music) offers as high fidelity as possible. Note that the contents of a telephone directory or the encyclopedia downloaded from an Internet site contains a lot of useful information but the contents do not constitute a signal according to the definition above. It is the functional relationship between the function and the independent variable that allows us to derive methods for modeling the signals and find the output of the systems when they are excited by the input signals. This also leads us to develop methods for designing these systems such that the information contained in the input signals is improved.

We define a *continuous-time signal* as a function of an independent variable that is continuous. A one-dimensional continuous-time signal $f(t)$ is expressed as a function of time that varies continuously from $-\infty$ to ∞. But it may be a function of other variables such as temperature, pressure, or elevation; yet we will denote them as continuous-time signals, in which time is continuous but the signal may have discontinuities at some values of time. The signal may be a

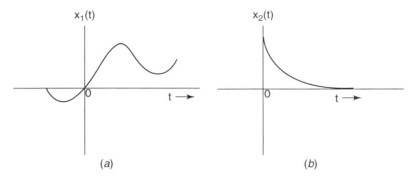

Figure 1.1   Two samples of continuous-time signals.

real- or complex-valued function of time. We can also define a continuous-time signal as a mapping of the set of all values of time to a set of corresponding values of the functions that are subject to certain properties. Since the function is well defined for all values of time in $-\infty$ to ∞, it is differentiable at all values of the independent variable t (except perhaps at a finite number of values). Two examples of continuous-time functions are shown in Figure 1.1.

A *discrete-time signal* is a function that is defined only at discrete instants of time and undefined at all other values of time. Although a discrete-time function may be defined at arbitrary values of time in the interval $-\infty$ to ∞, we will consider only a function defined at equal intervals of time and defined at $t = nT$, where T is a fixed interval in seconds known as the *sampling period* and n is an integer variable defined over $-\infty$ to ∞. If we choose to sample $f(t)$ at equal intervals of T seconds, we generate $f(nT) = f(t)|_{t=nT}$ as a sequence of numbers. Since T is fixed, $f(nT)$ is a function of only the integer variable n and hence can be considered as a function of n or expressed as $f(n)$. The continuous-time function $f(t)$ and the discrete-time function $f(n)$ are plotted in Figure 1.2.

In this book, we will denote a discrete-time (DT) function as a DT sequence, DT signal, or a DT series. So a DT function is a mapping of a set of all integers to a set of values of the functions that may be real-valued or complex-valued. Values of both $f(t)$ and $f(n)$ are assumed to be continuous, taking any value in a continuous range; hence can have a value even with an infinite number of digits, for example, $f(3) = 0.4\sqrt{2}$ in Figure 1.2.

A zero-order hold (ZOH) circuit is used to sample a continuous signal $f(t)$ with a sampling period T and hold the sampled values for one period before the next sampling takes place. The DT signal so generated by the ZOH is shown in Figure 1.3, in which the value of the sample value during each period of sampling is a constant; the sample can assume any continuous value. The signals of this type are known as *sampled-data signals*, and they are used extensively in sampled-data control systems and switched-capacitor filters. However, the duration of time over which the samples are held constant may be a very small fraction of the sampling period in these systems. When the value of a sample

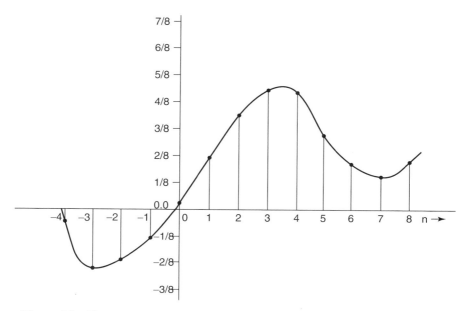

Figure 1.2   The continuous-time function $f(t)$ and the discrete-time function $f(n)$.

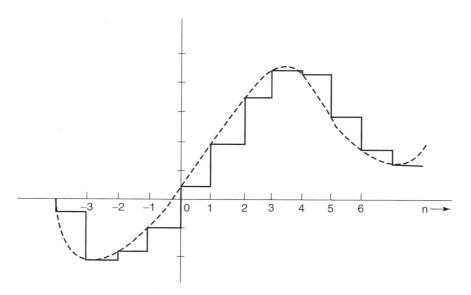

Figure 1.3   Sampled data signal.

is held constant during a period T (or a fraction of T) by the ZOH circuit as its output, that signal can be converted to a value by a quantizer circuit, with finite levels of value as determined by the binary form of representation. Such a process is called *binary coding* or *quantization*. A This process is discussed in full detail in Chapter 7. The precision with which the values are represented is determined by the number of bits (binary digits) used to represent each value. If, for example, we select 3 bits, to express their values using a method known as "signed magnitude fixed-point binary number representation" and one more bit to denote positive or negative values, we have the finite number of values, represented in binary form and in their equivalent decimal form. Note that a 4-bit binary form can represent values between $-\frac{7}{8}$ and $\frac{7}{8}$ at 15 distinct levels as shown in Table 1.1. So a value of $f(n)$ at the output of the ZOH, which lies between these distinct levels, is rounded or truncated by the quantizer according to some rules and the output of the quantizer when coded to its equivalent binary representation, is called the *digital signal*. Although there is a difference between the discrete-time signal and digital signal, in the next few chapters we assume that the signals are discrete-time signals and in Chapter 7, we consider the effect of quantizing the signals to their binary form, on the frequency response of the

TABLE 1.1   4 Bit Binary Numbers and their Decimal Equivalents

Binary Form	Decimal Value
$0_\triangle 111$	$\frac{7}{8} = 0.875$
$0_\triangle 110$	$\frac{6}{8} = 0.750$
$0_\triangle 101$	$\frac{5}{8} = 0.625$
$0_\triangle 100$	$\frac{4}{8} = 0.500$
$0_\triangle 011$	$\frac{3}{8} = 0.375$
$0_\triangle 010$	$\frac{2}{8} = 0.250$
$0_\triangle 001$	$\frac{1}{8} = 0.125$
$0_\triangle 000$	$0.0 = 0.000$
$1_\triangle 000$	$-0.0 = -0.000$
$1_\triangle 001$	$-\frac{1}{8} = -0.125$
$1_\triangle 010$	$-\frac{2}{8} = -0.250$
$1_\triangle 011$	$-\frac{3}{8} = -0.375$
$1_\triangle 100$	$-\frac{4}{8} = -0.500$
$1_\triangle 101$	$-\frac{5}{8} = -0.625$
$1_\triangle 110$	$-\frac{6}{8} = -0.750$
$1_\triangle 111$	$-\frac{7}{8} = -0.875$

filters. However, we use the terms *digital filter* and *discrete-time system* interchangeably in this book. Continuous-time signals and systems are also called *analog signals* and *analog systems*, respectively. A system that contains both the ZOH circuit and the quantizer is called an *analog-to digital converter* (ADC), which will be discussed in more detail in Chapter 7.

Consider an analog signal as shown by the solid line in Figure 1.2. When it is sampled, let us assume that the discrete-time sequence has values as listed in the second column of Table 1.2. They are expressed in only six significant decimal digits and their values, when truncated to four digits, are shown in the third column. When these values are quantized by the quantizer with four binary digits (bits), the decimal values are truncated to the values at the finite discrete levels. In decimal number notation, the values are listed in the fourth column, and in binary number notation, they are listed in the fifth column of Table 1.2. The binary values of $f(n)$ listed in the third column of Table 1.2 are plotted in Figure 1.4.

A continuous-time signal $f(t)$ or a discrete-time signal $f(n)$ expresses the variation of a physical quantity as a function of one variable. A black-and-white photograph can be considered as a two-dimensional signal $f(m, r)$, when the intensity of the dots making up the picture is measured along the horizontal axis (x axis; abscissa) and the vertical axis (y axis; ordinate) of the picture plane and are expressed as a function of two integer variables m and r, respectively. We can consider the signal $f(m, r)$ as the discretized form of a two-dimensional signal $f(x, y)$, where x and y are the continuous spatial variables for the horizontal and vertical coordinates of the picture and T_1 and T_2 are the sampling

TABLE 1.2 Numbers in Decimal and Binary Forms

n	Decimal Values of $f(n)$	Values of $f(n)$ Truncated to Four Digits	Quantized Values of $f(n)$	Binary Number Form
-4	-0.054307	-0.0543	0.000	$1_\triangle000$
-3	-0.253287	-0.2532	-0.250	$1_\triangle010$
-2	-0.236654	-0.2366	-0.125	$1_\triangle001$
-1	-0.125101	-0.1251	-0.125	$1_\triangle001$
0	0.522312	0.5223	0.000	$0_\triangle000$
1	0.246210	0.2462	0.125	$0_\triangle001$
2	0.387508	0.3875	0.375	$0_\triangle011$
3	0.554090	0.5540	0.500	$0_\triangle100$
4	0.521112	0.5211	0.500	$0_\triangle100$
5	0.275432	0.2754	0.250	$0_\triangle010$
6	0.194501	0.1945	0.125	$0_\triangle001$
7	0.168887	0.1687	0.125	$0_\triangle001$
8	0.217588	0.2175	0.125	$0_\triangle001$

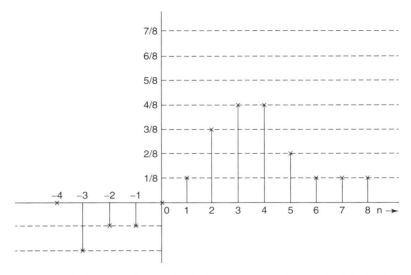

Figure 1.4   Binary values in Table 1.2, after truncation of $f(n)$ to 4 bits.

periods (measured in meters) along the x and y axes, respectively. In other words, $f(x, y)|_{x=mT_1, y=rT_2} = f(m, r)$.

A black-and-white video signal $f(x, y, t)$ is a 3D function of two spatial coordinates x and y and one temporal coordinate t. When it is discretized, we have a 3D discrete signal $f(m, p, n)$. When a color video signal is to be modeled, it is expressed by a vector of three 3D signals, each representing one of the three primary colors—red, green, and blue—or their equivalent forms of two luminance and one chrominance. So this is an example of multivariable function or a multichannel signal:

$$\mathbf{F}(m, r, n) = \begin{bmatrix} f_r(m, p, n) \\ f_g(m, p, n) \\ f_b(m, p, n) \end{bmatrix} \tag{1.1}$$

1.3.1   Modeling and Properties of Discrete-Time Signals

There are several ways of describing the functional relationship between the integer variable n and the value of the discrete-time signal $f(n)$: (1) to plot the values of $f(n)$ versus n as shown in Figure 1.2, (2) to tabulate their values as shown in Table 1.2, and (3) to define the sequence by expressing the sample values as elements of a set, when the sequence has a finite number of samples.

For example, in a sequence $x_1(n)$ as shown below, the arrow indicates the value of the sample when $n = 0$:

$$x_1(n) = \left\{ 2 \quad 3 \quad 1.5 \quad \underset{\uparrow}{0.5} \quad -1 \quad 4 \right\} \tag{1.2}$$

We denote the DT sequence by $x(n)$ and also the value of a sample of the sequence at a particular value of n by $x(n)$. If a sequence has zero values for $n < 0$, then it is called a *causal sequence*. It is misleading to state that the causal function is a sequence defined for $n \geq 0$, because, strictly speaking, a DT sequence has to be defined for all values of n. Hence it is understood that a causal sequence has zero-valued samples for $-\infty < n < 0$. Similarly, when a function is defined for $N_1 \leq n \leq N_2$, it is understood that the function has zero values for $-\infty < n < N_1$ and $N_2 < n < \infty$. So the sequence $x_1(n)$ in Equation (1.2) has zero values for $2 < n < \infty$ and for $-\infty < n < -3$. The discrete-time sequence $x_2(n)$ given below is a causal sequence. In this form for representing $x_2(n)$, it is implied that $x_2(n) = 0$ for $-\infty < n < 0$ and also for $4 < n < \infty$:

$$x_2(n) = \left\{ \underset{\uparrow}{1} \quad -2 \quad 0.4 \quad 0.3 \quad 0.4 \quad 0 \quad 0 \quad 0 \right\} \tag{1.3}$$

The length of a finite sequence is often defined by other authors as the number of samples, which becomes a little ambiguous in the case of a sequence like $x_2(n)$ given above. The function $x_2(n)$ is the same as $x_3(n)$ given below:

$$x_3(n) = \left\{ \underset{\uparrow}{1} \quad -2 \quad 0.4 \quad 0.3 \quad 0.4 \quad 0 \quad 0 \quad 0 \quad 0 \quad 0 \quad 0 \right\} \tag{1.4}$$

But does it have more samples? So the length of the sequence $x_3(n)$ would be different from the length of $x_2(n)$ according to the definition above. When a sequence such as $x_4(n)$ given below is considered, the definition again gives an ambiguous answer:

$$x_4(n) = \left\{ \underset{\uparrow}{0} \quad 0 \quad 0.4 \quad 0.3 \quad 0.4 \right\} \tag{1.5}$$

The definition for the length of a DT sequence would be refined when we define the degree (or order) of a polynomial in z^{-1} to express the z transform of a DT sequence, in the next chapter.

To model the discrete-time signals mathematically, instead of listing their values as shown above or plotting as shown in Figure 1.2, we introduce some basic DT functions as follows.

1.3.2   Unit Pulse Function

The unit pulse function $\delta(n)$ is defined by

$$\delta(n) = \begin{cases} 1 & n = 0 \\ 0 & n \neq 0 \end{cases} \tag{1.6}$$

and it is plotted in Figure 1.5a. It is often called the *unit sample function* and also the *unit impulse function*. But note that the function $\delta(n)$ has a finite numerical

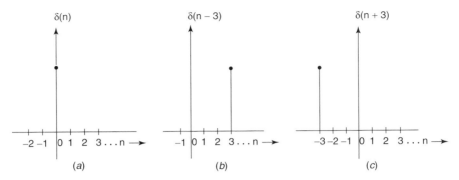

Figure 1.5   Unit pulse functions $\delta(n)$, $\delta(n-3)$, and $\delta(n+3)$.

value of one at $n = 0$ and zero at all other values of integer n, whereas the unit impulse function $\delta(t)$ is defined entirely in a different way.

When the unit pulse function is delayed by k samples, it is described by

$$\delta(n-k) = \begin{cases} 1 & n = k \\ 0 & n \neq k \end{cases} \tag{1.7}$$

and it is plotted in Figure 1.5b for $k = 3$. When $\delta(n)$ is advanced by $k = 3$, we get $\delta(n+k)$, and it is plotted in Figure 1.5c.

1.3.3   Constant Sequence

This sequence $x(n)$ has a constant value for all n and is therefore defined by $x(n) = K; -\infty < n < \infty$.

1.3.4   Unit Step Function

The unit step function $u(n)$ is defined by

$$u(n) = \begin{cases} 1 & n \geq 0 \\ 0 & n < 0 \end{cases} \tag{1.8}$$

and it is plotted in Figure 1.6a.

When the unit step function is delayed by k samples, where k is a positive integer, we have

$$u(n-k) = \begin{cases} 1 & n \geq k \\ 0 & n < k \end{cases} \tag{1.9}$$

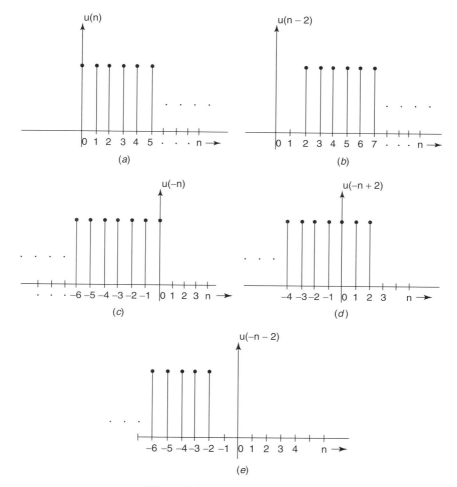

Figure 1.6 Unit step functions.

The sequence $u(n + k)$ is obtained when $u(n)$ is advanced by k samples. It is defined by

$$u(n + k) = \begin{cases} 1 & n \geq -k \\ 0 & n < -k \end{cases} \tag{1.10}$$

We also define the function $u(-n)$, obtained from the time reversal of $u(n)$, as a sequence that is zero for $n > 0$. The sequences $u(-n + k)$ and $u(-n - k)$, where k is a positive integer, are obtained when $u(-n)$ is delayed by k samples and advanced by k samples, respectively. In other words, $u(-n + k)$ is obtained by delaying $u(-n)$ when k is positive and obtained by advancing $u(-n)$ when k is a negative integer. Note that the effect on $u(-n-k)$ is opposite that on $u(n-k)$, when k is assumed to take positive and negative values. These functions are shown in Figure 1.6, where $k = 2$. In a strict sense, all of these functions are defined implicitly for $-\infty < n < \infty$.

1.3.5 Real Exponential Function

The real exponential function is defined by

$$x(n) = a^n; \qquad -\infty < n < \infty \qquad (1.11)$$

where a is real constant. If a is a complex constant, it becomes the complex exponential sequence. The real exponential sequence or the complex exponential sequence may also be defined by a more general relationship of the form

$$x(n) = \begin{cases} a^n & k \le n < \infty \\ b^n & -\infty < n < k \end{cases} \qquad (1.12)$$

A special discrete-time sequence that we often use is the function defined for $n \ge 0$:

$$x(n) = a^n u(n) \qquad (1.13)$$

An example of $x_1(n) = (0.8)^n u(n)$ is plotted in Figure 1.7a. The function $x_2(n) = x_1(n-3) = (0.8)^{(n-3)} u(n-3)$ is obtained when $x_1(n)$ is delayed by three samples. It is plotted in Figure 1.7b. But the function $x_3(n) = (0.8)^n u(n-3)$ is obtained by chopping off the first three samples of $x_1(n) = (0.8)^n u(n)$, and as shown in Figure 1.7c, it is different from $x_2(n)$.

1.3.6 Complex Exponential Function

The complex exponential sequence is a function that is complex-valued as a function of n. The most general form of such a function is given by

$$x(n) = A\alpha^n, \qquad -\infty < n < \infty \qquad (1.14)$$

where both A and α are complex numbers. If we let $A = |A| e^{j\phi}$ and $\alpha = e^{(\sigma_0 + j\omega_0)}$, where σ_0, ω_0, and ϕ are real numbers, the sequence can be expanded to the form

$$\begin{aligned} x(n) &= |A| e^{j\phi} e^{(\sigma_0 + j\omega_0)n} \\ &= |A| e^{\sigma_0 n} e^{j(\omega_0 n + \phi)} \\ &= |A| e^{\sigma_0 n} \cos(\omega_0 n + \phi) + j |A| e^{\sigma_0 n} \sin(\omega_0 n + \phi) \qquad (1.15) \\ &= x_{\text{re}}(n) + j x_{\text{im}}(n) \end{aligned}$$

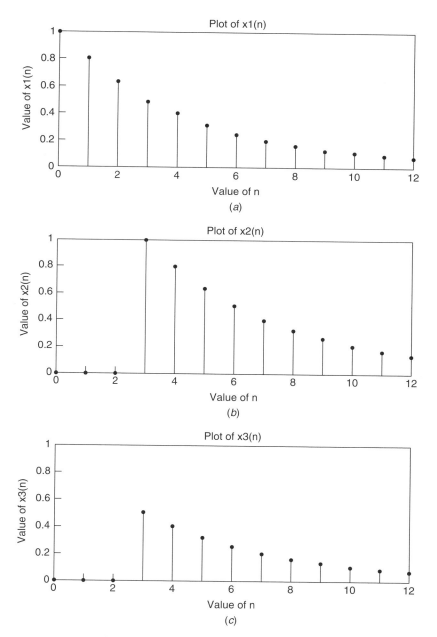

Figure 1.7   Plots of $x_1(n)$, $x_2(n)$, and $x_3(n)$.

When $\sigma_0 = 0$, the real and imaginary parts of this complex exponential sequence are $|A|\cos(\omega_0 n + \phi)$ and $|A|\sin(\omega_0 n + \phi)$, respectively, and are real sinusoidal sequences with an amplitude equal to $|A|$. When $\sigma_0 > 0$, the two sequences increase as $n \to \infty$ and decrease when $\sigma_0 < 0$ as $n \to \infty$. When $\omega_0 = \phi = 0$, the sequence reduces to the real exponential sequence $|A|e^{\sigma_0 n}$.

1.3.7   Properties of cos($\omega_0 n$)

When $A = 1$, and $\sigma_0 = \phi = 0$, we get $x(n) = e^{j\omega_0 n} = \cos(\omega_0 n) + j\sin(\omega_0 n)$. This function has some interesting properties, when compared with the continuous-time function $e^{j\omega_0' t}$ and they are described below.

First we point out that ω_0 in $x(n) = e^{j\omega_0 n}$ is a frequency normalized by $f_s = 1/T$, where f_s is the sampling frequency in hertz and T is the sampling period in seconds, specifically, $\omega_0 = 2\pi f_0'/f_s = \omega_0' T$, where $\omega_0' = 2\pi f_0'$ is the actual real frequency in radians per second and f_0' is the actual frequency in hertz. Therefore the unit of the normalized frequency ω_0 is radians. It is common practice in the literature on discrete-time systems to choose ω as the normalized frequency variable, and we follow that notation in the following chapters; here we denote ω_0 as a constant in radians. We will discuss this normalized frequency again in a later chapter.

Property 1.1   In the complex exponential function $x(n) = e^{j\omega_0 n}$, two frequencies separated by an integer multiple of 2π are indistinguishable from each other. In other words, it is easily seen that $e^{j\omega_0 n} = e^{j(\omega_0 n + 2\pi r)}$. The real part and the imaginary part of the function $x(n) = e^{j\omega_0 n}$, which are sinusoidal functions, also exhibit this property. As an example, we have plotted $x_1(n) = \cos(0.3\pi n)$ and $x_2(n) = \cos(0.3\pi + 4\pi)n$ in Figure 1.8. In contrast, we know that two continuous-time functions $x_1(t) = e^{j\omega_1 t}$ and $x_2(t) = e^{j\omega_2 t}$ or their real and imaginary parts are different if ω_1 and ω_2 are different. They are different even if they are separated by integer multiples of 2π. From the property $e^{j\omega_0 n} = e^{j(\omega_0 n + 2\pi r)}$ above, we arrive at another important result, namely, that the output of a discrete-time system has the same value when these two functions are excited by the complex exponential functions $e^{j\omega_0 n}$ or $e^{j(\omega_0 n + 2\pi r)}$. We will show in Chapter 3 that this is true for all frequencies separated by integer multiples of 2π, and therefore the frequency response of a DT system is periodic in ω.

Property 1.2   Another important property of the sequence $e^{j\omega_0 n}$ is that it is periodic in n. A discrete-time function $x(n)$ is defined to be periodic if there exists an integer N such that $x(n + rN) = x(n)$, where r is any arbitrary integer and N is the period of the periodic sequence. To find the value for N such that $e^{j\omega_0 n}$ is periodic, we equate $e^{j\omega_0 n}$ to $e^{j\omega_0(n+rN)}$. Therefore $e^{j\omega_0 n} = e^{j\omega_0 n}e^{j\omega_0 rN}$, which condition is satisfied when $e^{j\omega_0 rN} = 1$, that is, when $\omega_0 N = 2\pi K$, where

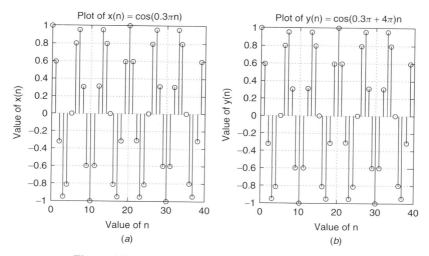

Figure 1.8   Plots of $\cos(0.3\pi n)$ and $\cos(0.3\pi + 4\pi)n$.

K is any arbitrary integer. This condition is satisfied by the following equation:

$$\frac{\omega_0}{2\pi} = \frac{K}{N} \tag{1.16}$$

In words, this means that the ratio of the given normalized frequency ω_0 and 2π must be a rational number. The period of the sequence N is given by

$$N = \frac{2\pi K}{\omega_0} \tag{1.17}$$

When this condition is satisfied by the smallest integer K, the corresponding value of N gives the fundamental period of the periodic sequence, and integer multiples of this frequency are the harmonic frequencies.

Example 1.1

Consider a sequence $x(n) = \cos(0.3\pi n)$. In this case $\omega_0 = 0.3\pi$ and $\omega_0/2\pi = 0.3\pi/2\pi = \frac{3}{20}$. Therefore the sequence is periodic and its period N is 20 samples. This periodicity is noticed in Figure 1.8a and also in Figure 1.8b.

Consider another sequence $x(n) = \cos(0.5n)$, in which case $\omega_0 = 0.5$. Therefore $\omega_0/2\pi = 0.5/2\pi = 1/4\pi$, which is not a rational number. Hence this is not a periodic sequence.

When the given sequence is the sum of several complex exponential functions, each of which is periodic with different periods, it is still periodic. We consider an example to illustrate the method to find the fundamental period in this case.

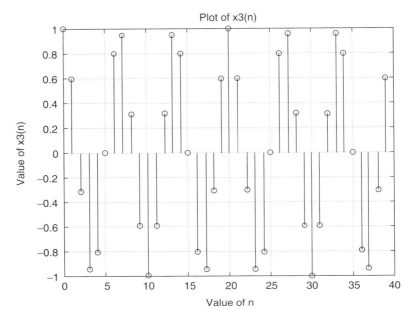

Figure 1.9   Plot of $x_3(n)$.

Suppose $x_3(n) = \cos(0.2\pi n) + \cos(0.5\pi n) + \cos(0.6\pi n)$. Its fundamental period N must satisfy the condition

$$N = \frac{2\pi K_1}{0.2\pi} = \frac{2\pi K_2}{0.5\pi} = \frac{2\pi K_3}{0.6\pi} \tag{1.18}$$

$$= 10K_1 = 4K_2 = \frac{10K_3}{3} \tag{1.19}$$

where K_1, K_2, and K_3 and N are integers. The value of N that satisfies this condition is 20 when $K_1 = 2$, $K_2 = 5$, and $K_3 = 6$. So $N = 20$ is the fundamental period of $x_3(n)$. The sequence $x_3(n)$ plotted in Figure 1.9 for $0 \leq n \leq 40$ shows that it is periodic with a period of 20 samples.

Property 1.3   We have already observed that the frequencies at ω_0 and at $\omega_0 + 2\pi$ are the same, and hence the frequency of oscillation are the same. But consider the frequency of oscillation as ω_0 changes between 0 and 2π. It is found that the frequency of oscillation of the sinusoidal sequence $\cos(\omega_0 n)$ increases as ω_0 increases from 0 to π and the frequency of oscillation decreases as ω_0 increases from π to 2π. Therefore the highest frequency of oscillation of a discrete-time sequence $\cos(\omega_0 n)$ occurs when $\omega_0 = \pm\pi$. When the normalized frequency $\omega_0 = 2\pi f_0'/f_s$ attains the value of π, the value of $f_0' = f_s/2$. So the highest frequency of oscillation occurs when it is equal to half the sampling

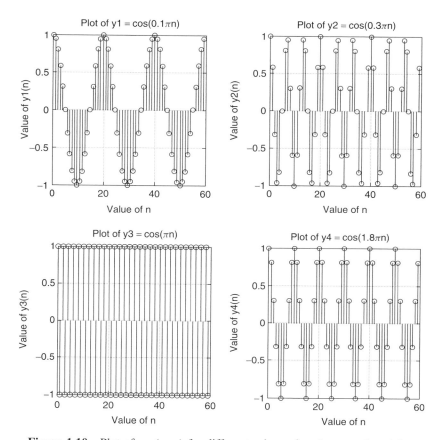

Figure 1.10 Plot of $\cos(\omega_0 n)$ for different values of ω_0 between 0 and 2π.

frequency. In Figure 1.10 we have plotted the DT sequences as ω_0 attains a few values between 0 and 2π, to illustrate this property. We will elaborate on this property in later chapters of the book.

Since frequencies separated by 2π are the same, as ω_0 increases from 2π to 3π, the frequency of oscillation increases in the same manner as the frequency of oscillation when it increases from 0 to π. As an example, we see that the frequency of $v_0(n) = \cos(0.1\pi n)$ is the same as that of $v_1(n) = \cos(2.1\pi n)$. It is interesting to note that $v_2(n) = \cos(1.9\pi n)$ also has the same frequency of oscillation as $v_1(n)$ because

$$v_2(n) = \cos(1.9\pi n) = \cos(2\pi - 0.1\pi n) \tag{1.20}$$

$$= \cos(2\pi n)\cos(0.1\pi n) + \sin(2\pi n)\sin(0.1\pi n) \tag{1.21}$$

$$= \cos(0.1\pi n)$$

$$= v_0(n)$$

$$v_1(n) = \cos(2.1\pi n) = \cos(2\pi n + 0.1\pi n) \tag{1.22}$$

$$= \cos(2\pi n)\cos(0.1\pi n) - \sin(2\pi n)\sin(0.1\pi n) \tag{1.23}$$

$$= \cos(0.1n)$$

$$= v_0(n)$$

We have plotted the sequences $v_1(n)$ and $v_2(n)$ in Figure 1.11, to verify this property.

Remember that in Chapter 3, we will use the term "folding" to describe new implications of this property. We will also show in Chapter 3 that a large class of discrete-time signals can be expressed as the weighted sum of exponential sequences of the form $e^{j\omega_0 n}$, and such a model leads us to derive some powerful analytical techniques of digital signal processing.

We have described several ways of characterizing the DT sequences in this chapter. Using the unit sample function and the unit step function, we can express the DT sequences in other ways as shown below.

For example, $\delta(n) = u(n) - u(n-1)$ and $u(n) = \sum_{m=-\infty}^{m=n} \delta(m)$. A mathematical way of modeling a sequence

$$x(n) = \left\{ 2 \quad 3 \quad 1.5 \quad \underset{\uparrow}{0.5} \quad -1 \quad 4 \right\} \tag{1.24}$$

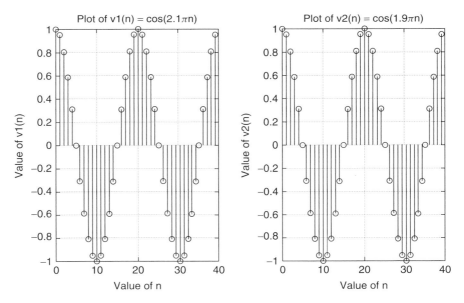

Figure 1.11   Plots of $\cos(2.1\pi n)$ and $\cos(1.9\pi n)$.

is the weighted sum of shifted unit sample functions, as given by

$$x(n) = 2\delta(n+3) + 3\delta(n+2) + 1.5\delta(n+1) + 0.5\delta(n) - \delta(n-1) + 4\delta(n-2)$$
$$(1.25)$$

If the sequence is given in an analytic form $x(n) = a^n u(n)$, it can also be expressed as the weighted sum of impulse functions:

$$x(n) = \sum_{m=0}^{\infty} x(m)\delta(n-m) = \sum_{m=0}^{\infty} a^m \delta(n-m) \qquad (1.26)$$

In the next chapter, we will introduce a transform known as the *z transform*, which will be used to model the DT sequences in additional forms. We will show that this model given by (1.26) is very useful in deriving the z transform and in analyzing the performance of discrete-time systems.

1.4 HISTORY OF FILTER DESIGN

Filtering is the most common form of signal processing used in all the applications mentioned in Section 1.2, to remove the frequencies in certain parts and to improve the magnitude, phase, or group delay in some other part(s) of the spectrum of a signal. The vast literature on filters consists of two parts: (1) the theory of approximation to derive the transfer function of the filter such that the magnitude, phase, or group delay approximates the given frequency response specifications and (2) procedures to design the filters using the hardware components. Originally filters were designed using inductors, capacitors, and transformers and were terminated by resistors representing the load and the internal resistance of the source. These were called the *LC* (inductance × capacitance) filters that admirably met the filtering requirements in the telephone networks for many decades of the nineteenth and twentieth centuries. When the vacuum tubes and bipolar junction transistors were developed, the design procedure had to be changed in order to integrate the models for these active devices into the filter circuits, but the mathematical theory of filter approximation was being advanced independently of these devices. In the second half of the twentieth century, operational amplifiers using bipolar transistors were introduced and filters were designed without inductors to realize the transfer functions. The design procedure was much simpler, and device technology also was improved to fabricate resistors in the form of thick-film and later thin-film depositions on ceramic substrates instead of using printed circuit boards. These filters did not use inductors and transformers and were known as *active-RC* (resistance × capacitance) filters. In the second half of the century, switched-capacitor filters were developed, and they are the most common type of filters being used at present for audio applications. These filters contained only capacitors and operational amplifiers using complementary metal oxide semiconductor (CMOS) transistors. They used no resistors and inductors, and the whole circuit was fabricated by the very large scale integration (VLSI) technology. The analog signals were converted to sampled data signals by these filters and the signal processing was treated as analog signal processing. But later, the signals were transitioned as discrete-time signals, and the theory of discrete-time systems is currently used to analyze and design these filters. Examples of an *LC* filter, an active-*RC* filter, and a switched-capacitor filter that realize a third-order lowpass filter function are shown in Figures 1.12–1.14.

The evolution of digital signal processing has a different history. At the beginning, the development of discrete-time system theory was motivated by a search for numerical techniques to perform integration and interpolation and to solve differential equations. When computers became available, the solution of physical systems modeled by differential equations was implemented by the digital

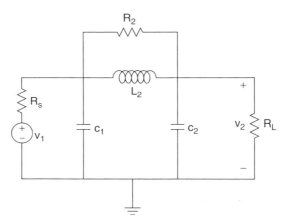

Figure 1.12   A lowpass analog *LC* filter.

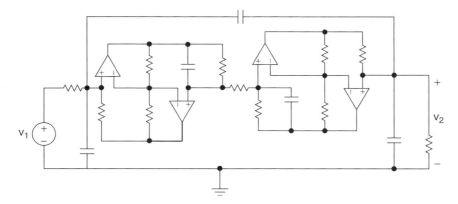

Figure 1.13   An active-*RC* lowpass analog filter.

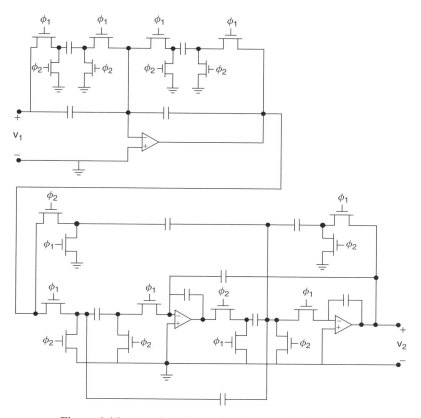

Figure 1.14   A switched-capacitor lowpass (analog) filter.

computers. As the digital computers became more powerful in their computational power, they were heavily used by the oil industry for geologic signal
processing and by the telecommunications industry for speech processing. The
theory of digital filters matured, and with the advent of more powerful computers
built on integrated circuit technology, the theory and applications of digital signal
processing has explosively advanced in the last few decades. The two revolutionary results that have formed the foundations of digital signal processing are the
Shannon's sampling theorem and the Cooley–Tukey algorithm for fast Fourier
transform technique. Both of them will be discussed in great detail in the following chapters. The Shannon's sampling theorem proved that if a continuous-time
signal is bandlimited (i.e., if its Fourier transform is zero for frequencies above
a maximum frequency f_m) and it is sampled at a rate that is more than twice
the maximum frequency f_m in the signal, then no information contained in the
analog signal is lost in the sense that the continuous-time signal can be exactly
reconstructed from the samples of the discrete-time signal. In practical applications, most of the analog signals are first fed to an analog lowpass filter—known

as the *preconditioning filter* or *antialiasing filter*—such that the output of the lowpass filter attenuates the frequencies considerably beyond a well-chosen frequency so that it can be considered a bandlimited signal. It is this signal that is sampled and converted to a discrete-time signal and coded to a digital signal by the analog-to-digital converter (ADC) that was briefly discussed earlier in this chapter. We consider the discrete-time signal as the input to the digital filter designed in such a way that it improves the information contained in the original analog signal or its equivalent discrete-time signal generated by sampling it. A typical example of a digital lowpass filter is shown in Figure 1.15.

The output of the digital filter is next fed to a digital-to-analog converter (DAC) as shown in Figure 1.17 that also uses a lowpass analog filter that smooths the sampled-data signal from the DAC and is known as the "smoothing filter." Thus we obtain an analog signal $y_d(t)$ at the output of the smoothing filter as shown. It is obvious that compared to the analog filter shown in Figure 1.16, the circuit shown in Figure 1.17 requires considerably more hardware or involves a lot more signal processing in order to filter out the undesirable frequencies from the analog signal $x(t)$ and deliver an output signal $y_d(t)$. It is appropriate to compare these two circuit configurations and determine whether it is possible to get the output $y_d(t)$ that is the same or nearly the same as the output $y(t)$ shown in Figure 1.16; if so, what are the advantages of digital signal processing instead of analog signal processing, even though digital signal processing requires more circuits compared to analog signal processing?

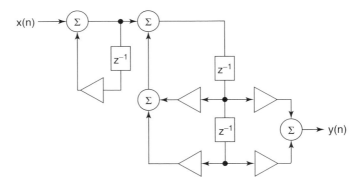

Figure 1.15   A lowpass third-order digital filter.

Figure 1.16   Example of an analog signal processing system.

Figure 1.17 Example of a digital signal processing system.

1.5 ANALOG AND DIGITAL SIGNAL PROCESSING

The basic elements in digital filters are the multipliers, adders, and delay elements, and they carry out multiplication, addition, and shifting operations on numbers according to an algorithm determined by the transfer function of the filters or their equivalent models. (These models will be discussed in Chapter 3 and also in Chapter 7.) They provide more flexibility and versatility compared to analog filters. The coefficients of the transfer function and the sample values of the input signal can be stored in the memory of the digital filter hardware or on the computer (PC, workstation, or the mainframe computer), and by changing the coefficients, we can change the transfer function of the filter, while changing the sample values of the input, we can find the response of the filter due to any number of input signals. This flexibility is not easily available in analog filters.

The digital filters are easily programmed to do time-shared filtering under time-division multiplexing scheme, whereas the analog signals cannot be interleaved between timeslots. Digital filters can be designed to serve as time-varying filters also by changing the sampling frequency and by changing the coefficients as a function of time, namely, by changing the algorithm accordingly.

The digital filters have the advantage of high precision and reliability. Very high precision can be obtained by increasing the number of bits to represent the coefficients of the filter transfer function and the values of the input signal. Again we can increase the dynamic range of the signals and transfer function coefficients by choosing floating-point representation of binary numbers. The values of the inductors, capacitors, and the parameters of the operational amplifier parameters and CMOS transistors, and so on used in the analog filters cannot achieve such high precision. Even if the analog elements can be obtained with high accuracy, they are subject to great drift in their value due to manufacturing tolerance, temperature, humidity, and other parameters—depending on the type of device technology used—over long periods of service, and hence their filter response degrades slowly and eventually fails to meet the specifications. In the case of digital filters, such effects are nonexistent because the wordlength of the transfer coefficients as well as the product of addition and multiplication within the filter do not change with respect to time or any of the environmental conditions that plague the analog circuits. Consequently, the reliability of digital filters is much higher than that of analog filters, and this means that they are more economical in application. Of course, catastrophic failures due to unforeseen factors are equally possible in both cases. If we are using computers to analyze, design, and simulate these filters, we can assume even double-precision format for the numbers that represent filter coefficients and signal samples. We point out that we can carry out the simulation, analysis, and design of any number of filters and under many conditions, for example, Monte Carlo analysis, worst-case analysis, or iterative optimization to test the design before we build the hardware and test it again and again. Of course, we can do the same in the case of analog filters or continuous-time systems also (e.g., analog control systems) using such software as MATLAB and Simulink.[2] During the manufacture of analog filters, we may have to tune each of them to correct for manufacturing tolerances, but there is no such need to test the accuracy of the wordlength in digital filters.

Data on digital filters can be stored on magnetic tapes, compact disks(CDs), digital videodisks (DVDs), and optical disks for an indefinite length of time. They can be retrieved without any degradation or loss of data; a good example is the music recorded on CDs. In contrast, analog signals deteriorate slowly as time passes and cannot be retrieved easily without any loss. There is no easy way of storing the transfer function coefficients that defines the analog system and feeding the input signals stored on these storage devices to the analog system.

By using digital filters, we can realize many transfer functions that cannot be realized by analog filters. For example, in addition to those already mentioned above, we can realize the following characteristics from digital filters:

1. Transition bands much smaller than what can be achieved from analog filters; an example would be a lowpass filter with a bandwidth of 5000 Hz and a passband ripple of 0.5 dB, and 100 dB attenuation above 5010 Hz. In spectrum analyzers and synthesizers, vocoders (voice recorders), and similar devices, extremely low tolerances on the magnitude and phase responses over adjacent passbands are required, and digital filters can be designed to meet these specifications.

2. Finite duration impulse response and filters with linear phase. Neither of these characteristics can be achieved by analog filters. Digital filters with these characteristics are used extensively in many applications.

3. Bandwidth of the order 5 Hz or even a fraction thereof that are commonly required to process biomedical or seismic signals.

4. Programmable filters, multirate filters, multidimensional filters, and adaptive filters. Programmable filters are used to adjust the frequency-selective properties of the filters. Multirate filters are used in the processing of many complex signals with different rates of fluctuation, whereas two-dimensional digital filters are the filters used in image processing. Adaptive filters are used invariably when the transmission medium between the transmitter and receiver changes—either as the transmission line is switched to

---

[2]MATLAB and Simulink are registered trademarks of The MathWorks, Inc. Natick, MA. The software is available from The MathWorks, Inc.

different receivers or as it changes continuously between the transmitter and the receiver. For example, when a telephone conversation is switched from one point to another and the cable or the microwave link changes, or when the mobile phone moves as the talker moves over a wide territory, adaptive filters are absolutely necessary to compensate for the distortion of the signal as it passes through the transmission link.

5. We have chosen filters only as an example to compare digital and analog signal processors. There are many other types of digital signal processing that are feasible and are being used, and these are not possible or very efficient in analog filters. For example, error detection in transmitted signals and correction to reduce the error rate is an advanced technique used in many applications. Another example is our ability to compress the data by a significant factor and receive the input signal at lower cost and very good quality. To point out the power of digital signal processing theory and the digital signal processors available, let us again consider the mobile phone. Bateman and Patterson-Stephans state that "Within the phone, a single DSP device may be performing real-time speech compression, video compression, echo cancellation, noise cancellation, voice recognition, waveform coding, modulation/demodulation, interleaving, multipath equalization, soft decision decoding, convolution, automatic frequency-, power- and gain-control" [3], and all of them done in a triband phone with TDMA, CDMA, and analog signal processing! The mobile phone is just an example to illustrate the large number of digital signal processing techniques that are built into any of the applications described above. But an application such as the mobile phone implements other functions also, and their features are briefly described given below.

1.5.1   Operation of a Mobile Phone Network

Consider a geographic area in which a part of the mobile phone network operates. It is divided into cells as indicated in Figure 1.18. The cells are not really equal in area but could be as small as 300 m where the telephone traffic is high and as large as 35 km in rural areas. The size and shape of each cell is determined by the radiation pattern and the power output of the antenna (and is not hexagonal of equal shape and size) serving the mobile phones. A base station controller (BSC), usually installed on a tower, serves as many as 124 base transceiver stations (BTSs). These stations communicate with all the cell phones that are known to be located within the area covered by the cell. The BTSs operate on different frequencies, also called "channels," to transmit to and receive signals from the cell phones. Global System for Mobile Communication (GSM) is one of the most widely used mobile cellular phone network systems in the world, and in that system, the frequencies for transmitting from the mobile phone and receiving by the BTS lie in the band 890–915 MHz, and the frequencies for transmitting from the BTS and receiving by the mobile phone lie in the band 935–960 MHz. But in order to utilize the frequency spectrum efficiently, cells

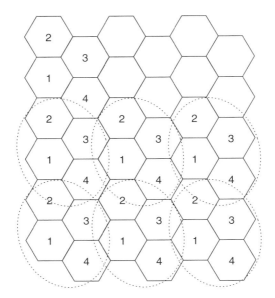

Figure 1.18   Cell repeat pattern in a mobile network coverage area.

using the same frequency are kept sufficiently apart so that there is no cochannel interference; also the frequencies used in a BTS are separated by 200 kHz. The base transceiver stations located on towers over a coverage area are connected by fixed digital lines to a mobile switching center (MSC), and the mobile switching center is connected to the public switched telephone network (PSTN) as shown in Figure 1.19 as well as the Internet, to which other MSCs are also connected.

When a phone initiates a call to send voice, text, an instant message, or other media, it registers with the network via the BTS closest to its location and the BTS tracks its location and passes this information to the mobile switching center (MSC) over fixed digital lines, which updates this information continuously as received from the BTS. Each mobile phone has a home location register (HLR) and a visitor location register (VLR) assigned to it. The HLR contains information such as the identity of the user and phone number assigned to the user in the user's home network, the services to which the user has subscribed, whereas the VLR contains information about the mobile phone when it is used outside the home network. So when a mobile phone initiates a call, it sends the information to the BTS about its identity and so on from the VLR or the HLR depending on the location of the phone at the time the call originates. The mobile switching center checks the data from its HLR or VLR to authenticate the call and gives permission for the phone to access the network. As the caller moves within the cell, the BTS monitors the strength of the signal between the phone and the receiver, and if this falls below a certain level, it may transfer control of the phone to the BTS in the next cell, which may offer a stronger signal. If no such cell is nearby, the caller is cut off (i.e., will not be able to receive or to send

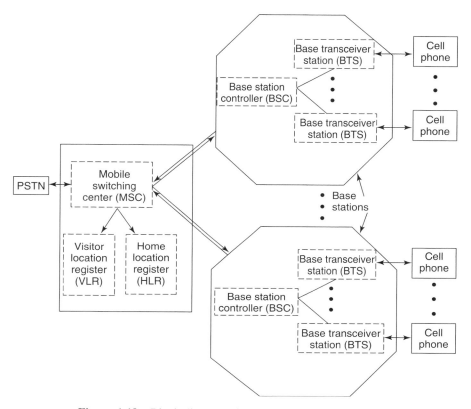

Figure 1.19   Block diagram of a mobile cell phone network.

a call). As the caller moves from one cell to another cell, the BTS serving it will transfer control to the BTS in the cell that it has moved to. This is the main feature that makes mobile telephony possible. All of these operations are carried out by the computers serving the mobile cellular phone network, and that technology is known as *computer networking technology*. It is different from the theory of digital signal processing. This textbook offers an introduction to the fundamental theory of digital signal processing, which is used in such techniques as speech compression, multipath equalization, and echo cancellation, mentioned in the previous section.

There are some disadvantages and limitations in digital signal processing in comparison with analog signal processing. By looking at the two circuit configurations in Figures 1.16 and 1.17, it is obvious that the digital signal processor is a more complex system, because of the additional components of analog low-pass filters (ADC and DAC) on either side of the digital signal processor besides the additional control and programming circuits, which are not shown in the figures. Another disadvantage is that the digital signal processor can process signals within a range of frequencies that is limited mainly by the highest sampling

TABLE 1.3 ADCs Currently Available

Sampling Rate (samples per second)	Resolution (bits)	Maximum Frequency in Input Signal	Power
96,000	24	48 kHz	90 mW
96,000	18	48 kHz	60 mW
96,000	16	48 kHz	40 mW
65,000,000	14	500 MHz	0.6 W
400,000,000	8	1 GHz	3 W

frequency of the ADC and DAC that are available. As the frequency is increased, the wordlength of these devices decreases and therefore the accuracy and dynamic range of the input and output data decrease.

For example, data on a few ADCs currently available are given in Table 1.3 [3].

Hence digital signal processing is restricted to approximately one megahertz, and analog signal processors are necessary for processing signals above that frequency, for example, processing of radar signals. In such applications, analog signal processing is a more attractive and viable choice, and currently a lot of research is being directed toward what is known as mixed-signal processing. Note in Table 1.3, that as the resolution (wordlength) for a given signal decreases, the power consumption also decreases, but that is just the power consumed by the ADCs; the power increases as the sampling frequency increases, even when the resolution is decreased. The digital signal processor itself consumes a lot more power, and hence additional power management circuits are added to the whole system. In contrast, the analog signal processors consume less power. The *LC* filters consume almost negligible power and can operate at frequencies in the megahertz range. The active-*RC* filters and switched-capacitor filters are restricted to the audiofrequency range, but they consume more power than do the *LC* filters. It is expected that mixed-signal processing carried out on a single system or a single chip will boost the maximum frequency of the signal that can be processed, by a significant range, beyond what is possible with a strictly digital signal processing system. Therefore we will see more and more applications of DSP with increasing frequencies because the advantages of DSP outweigh the disadvantages in analog signal processing.

1.6 SUMMARY

In this introductory chapter, we defined the *discrete-time signal* and gave a few examples of these signals, along with some simple operations that can be applied with them. In particular, we pointed out the difference between a sinusoidal signal, which is a continuous-time signal, and a discrete-time signal. We discussed the basic procedure followed to sample and quantize an analog signal and compared the advantages and disadvantages of digital signal processing with those of directly processing the analog signal through an analog system, taking a filter as an example. In doing so, we introduced many terms or acronyms that we have not explained. Some of them will be explained in great detail in the following chapter. In Chapter 2 we will discuss several ways of modeling a *discrete-time system* and the methods used to find the response in the time domain, when excitation is effected by the discrete-time signals.

PROBLEMS

1.1 Given two discrete-time signals $x_1(n) = \{0.9 \quad 0.5 \quad 0.8 \quad \underset{\uparrow}{1.0} \quad 1.5 \quad 2.0$
$0.2\}$ and $x_2(n) = \{\underset{\uparrow}{1.0} \quad 0.3 \quad 0.6 \quad 0.4\}$, sketch each of the following:

(a) $y_1(n) = x_1(n) + 3x_2(n)$
(b) $y_2(n) = x_1(n) - x_2(n - 5)$
(c) $y_3(n) = x_1(n)x_2(n)$
(d) $y_4(n) = x_1(-n + 4)$
(e) $y_5(n) = y_4(n)x_2(n)$
(f) $y_6(n) = x_2(-n - 3)$
(g) $y_7(n) = y_4(n)y_6(n)$

1.2 Sketch each of the following, where $x_1(n)$ and $x_2(n)$ are the DT sequences given in Problem 1.1:

(a) $v_1(n) = x_1(n)x_2(4 - n)$
(b) $v_2(n) = \sum_{k=-\infty}^{\infty} x_1(k)x_2(n - k)$
(c) $v_3(n) = \sum_{k=-\infty}^{\infty} x_2(k)x_1(n - k)$
(d) $v_4(n) = \sum_{n=0}^{n=10} x_2^2(n)$
(e) $v_5(n) = x_1(2n)$

1.3 Repeat Problem 1.1 with $x_1(n) = \{1.0 \quad 0.8 \quad 0.2 \quad \underset{\uparrow}{-0.2} \quad -0.5$
$-0.7\}$ and $x_2(n) = \{0.5 \quad 0.2 \quad 0.1 \quad \underset{\uparrow}{0.2} \quad 0.6\}$.

1.4 Repeat Problem 1.2 with $x_1(n)$ and $x_2(n)$ as given in Problem 1.3.

1.5 Find the even and odd parts of $x_1(n)$ and $x_2(n)$ given in Problem 1.1. Even part of $x_1(n)$ is defined as $[x_1(n) + x_1(-n)]/2$, and the odd part as $[x_1(n) - x_1(-n)]/2$

1.6 Repeat Problem 1.5 with $x_1(n)$ and $x_2(n)$ as given in Problem 1.3.

1.7 Find $S_1(k) = \sum_{n=0}^{n=k} n$ and sketch it, for $k = 0, 1, \ldots 5$.

1.8 Find and sketch $S_2(k) = \sum_{n=-\infty}^{k} x_1(n)$ and $S_3(k) = \sum_{n=-\infty}^{k} x_2(n)$, where $x_1(n)$ and $x_2(n)$ are as given in Problem 1.1.

1.9   Repeat Problem 1.8 with $x_1(n)$ and $x_2(n)$ as given in Problem 1.3.

1.10   Express the sequences $x_1(n)$ and $x_2(n)$ as a summation of weighted and shifted unit step functions, where $x_1(n)$ and $x_2(n)$ are as given in Problem 1.1.

1.11   Repeat Problem 1.10 with the sequences $x_1(n)$ and $x_2(n)$ given in Problem 1.3.

1.12   Given $x(n) = [0.5e^{j(\pi/6)}]^n [u(n) - u(n - 4)]$, calculate the values of $|x(n)|$ and sketch them. What are the real and imaginary parts of $x(n)$?

1.13   Express the real and imaginary parts of $x(n) = \sum_{k=0}^{4}[0.5e^{j(\pi/6)}]^k \delta(n - k)$.

1.14   What are the real and imaginary parts of $q(n) = \sum_{n=0}^{\infty}(0.3 - j0.4)^n$?

1.15   What is the fundamental period of $p_1(n) = e^{j0.3\pi n}$?

1.16   Find the fundamental period of $p_2(n) = e^{j0.4\pi n} + 2e^{j0.6\pi n}$.

1.17   Find the fundamental period of $p_3(n) = \cos(0.5\pi n) + 4\cos(2.5\pi n)$.

1.18   What is the fundamental period of $p_4(n) = \cos(0.2\pi n) + \cos(0.7\pi n) + \cos(\pi n)$?

1.19   Find the fundamental period of $p_5(n) = \cos(0.5n) + 3\cos(0.2n)$.

1.20   Find the fundamental period of $p_6(n) = p_1(n)p_2(n)$, where $p_1(n)$ and $p_2(n)$ are as given above.

1.21   Find the fundamental period of $p_7(n) = \cos(1.2\pi n) + 4\sin(0.2\pi n)$.

1.22   What is the fundamental period of $p_8(n) = \cos(0.1\pi n)p_3(n)$?

1.23   The sinusoidal sequence $h(n) = A\cos(\omega_0 n + \phi)$ has the following values over one period; find the values of A, ω_0 and ϕ:

$$h(n) = \{2.00 \quad 0.00 \quad -2.00 \quad -0.00\}$$

REFERENCES

1. S. K. Mitra and J. F. Kaiser, *Handbook for Digital Signal Processing*, Wiley-Interscience, 1993, Chapter 1.
2. J. G. Proakis and D. G. Manolakis, *Digital Signal Processing*, Prentice-Hall, 1996.
3. A. Bateman and I. Patterson-Stephans, *The DSP Handbook, Algorithms, Applications and Design Techniques*, Prentice-Hall, 2000.
4. S. K. Mitra, *Digital Signal Processing, A Computer-Based Approach*, McGraw-Hill, 1998.
5. A. V. Oppenheim and R. W. Schafer, *Discrete-Time Signal Processing*, Prentice-Hall, 1989.

6. R. D. Strum and D. E. Kirk, *Discrete Systems and Digital Signal Processing*, Addison-Wesley, 1989.

7. S. S. Soliman and M. D. Srinath, *Continuous and Discrete Signals and Systems*, Prentice-Hall, 1990.

8. L. R. Rabiner and B. Gold, *Theory and Application of Digital Signal Processing*, Prentice-Hall, 1975.

9. E. C. Ifeachor and B. W. Jervis, *Digital Signal Processing*, Prentice-Hall, 2002.

10. V. K. Ingle and J. G. Proakis, *Digital Signal Processing Using MATLAB*$^{(R)}$ *V.4*, PWS Publishing, 1997.

CHAPTER 2

Time-Domain Analysis and z Transform

2.1 A LINEAR, TIME-INVARIANT SYSTEM

The purpose of analysis of a discrete-time system is to find the output in either the time or frequency domain of the system due to a discrete-time input signal. In Chapter 1, we defined the *discrete-time signal* as a function of the integer variable n, which represents discrete time, space, or some other physical variable. Given any integer value in $-\infty < n < \infty$, we can find the value of the signal according to some well-defined relationship. This can be described as a mapping of the set of integers to a set of values of the discrete-time signal. Description of this relationship varied according to the different ways of modeling the signal. In this chapter, we define the *discrete-time system* as a mapping of the set of discrete-time signals considered as the input to the system, to another set of discrete-time signals identified as the output of the system. This mapping can also be defined by an analytic expression, formula, algorithm, or rule, in the sense that if we are given an input to the system, we can find the output signal. The mapping can therefore be described by several models for the system. The mapping or the input–output relationship may be linear, nonlinear, time-invariant, or time-varying. The system defined by this relationship is said to be linear if it satisfies the following conditions.

Assume that the output is $y(n)$ due to an input $x(n)$ according to this relationship. If an input $Kx(n)$ produces an output $Ky(n)$, the system satisfies the condition of homogeneity, where K is any arbitrary constant. Let $K_1 y_1(n)$ and $K_2 y_2(n)$ be the outputs due to the inputs $K_1 x_1(n)$ and $K_2 x_2(n)$, respectively, where K_1 and K_2 are arbitrary constants. If the output is $K_1 y_1(n) + K_2 y_2(n)$ when the input is $K_1 y_1(n) + K_2 y_2(n)$, then the system satisfies the superposition property. A system that satisfies both homogeneity and superposition is defined as a *linear system*. If the output is $y(n - M)$ when the input is delayed by M samples, that is, when the input is $x(n - M)$, the system is said to be *time-invariant* or *shift-invariant*. If the output is determined by the weighted sum of only the previous values of the output and the weighted sum of the current and previous

Introduction to Digital Signal Processing and Filter Design, by B. A. Shenoi
Copyright © 2006 John Wiley & Sons, Inc.

values of the input, then the system is defined as a *causal* system. This means that the output does not depend on the future values of the input. We will discuss these concepts again in more detail in later sections of this chapter. In this book, we consider only discrete-time systems that are linear and time-invariant (LTI) systems.

Another way of defining a system in general is that it is an interconnection of components or subsystems, where we know the input–output relationship of these components, and that it is the way they are interconnected that determines the input–output relationship of the whole system. The model for the DT system can therefore be described by a circuit diagram showing the interconnection of its components, which are the delay elements, multipliers, and adders, which are introduced below. In the following sections we will use both of these definitions to model discrete-time systems. Then, in the remainder of this chapter, we will discuss several ways of analyzing the discrete-time systems in the time domain, and in Chapter 3 we will discuss frequency-domain analysis.

2.1.1 Models of the Discrete-Time System

First let us consider a discrete-time system as an interconnection of only three basic components: the delay elements, multipliers, and adders. The input–output relationships for these components and their symbols are shown in Figure 2.1. The fourth component is the modulator, which multiplies two or more signals and hence performs a nonlinear operation.

A simple discrete-time system is shown in Figure 2.2, where input signal $x(n) = \{x(0), x(1), x(2), x(3)\}$ is shown to the left of $v_0(n) = x(n)$. The signal

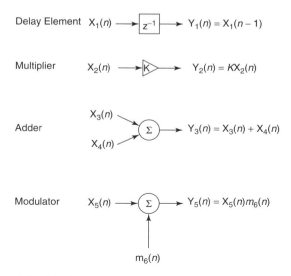

Figure 2.1 The basic components used in a discrete-time system.

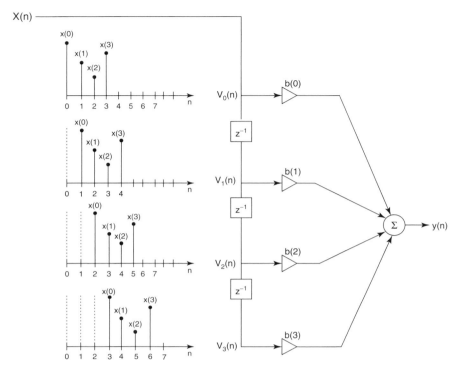

Figure 2.2   Operations in a typical discrete-time system.

$v_1(n)$ shown on the left is the signal $x(n)$ delayed by T seconds or one sample, so, $v_1(n) = x(n-1)$. Similarly, $v(2)$ and $v(3)$ are the signals obtained from $x(n)$ when it is delayed by $2T$ and $3T$ seconds: $v_2(n) = x(n-2)$ and $v_3(n) = x(n-3)$. When we say that the signal $x(n)$ is delayed by T, $2T$, or $3T$ seconds, we mean that the samples of the sequence are present T, $2T$, or $3T$ seconds *later*, as shown by the plots of the signals to the left of $v_1(n)$, $v_2(n)$, and $v_3(n)$. But at any given time $t = nT$, the samples in $v_1(n)$, $v_2(n)$, and $v_3(n)$ are the samples of the input signal that occur T, $2T$, and $3T$ seconds *previous* to $t = nT$. For example, at $t = 3T$, the value of the sample in $x(n)$ is $x(3)$, and the values present in $v_1(n)$, $v_2(n)$ and $v_3(n)$ are $x(2)$, $x(1)$, and $x(0)$, respectively. A good understanding of the operation of the discrete-time system as illustrated above is essential in analyzing, testing, and debugging the operation of the system when available software is used for the design, simulation, and hardware implementation of the system.

It is easily seen that the output signal in Figure 2.2 is

$$y(n) = b(0)v(0) + b(1)v(1) + b(2)v(2) + b(3)v(3)$$
$$= b(0)x(n) + b(1)x(n-1) + b(2)x(n-2) + b(3)x(n-3)$$

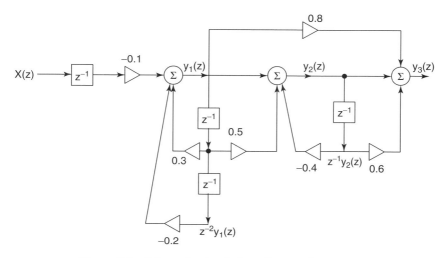

Figure 2.3 Schematic circuit for a discrete-time system.

where $b(0), b(1), b(2), b(3)$ are the gain constants of the multipliers. It is also easy to see from the last expression that the output signal is the weighted sum of the current value and the previous three values of the input signal. So this gives us an input–output relationship for the system shown in Figure 2.2.

Now we consider another example of a discrete-time system, shown in Figure 2.3. Note that a fundamental rule is to express the output of the adders and generate as many equations as the number of adders found in this circuit diagram for the discrete-time system. (This step is similar to writing the node equations for an analog electric circuit.) Denoting the outputs of the three adders as $y_1(n)$, $y_2(n)$, and $y_3(n)$, we get

$$y_1(n) = 0.3y_1(n-1) - 0.2y_1(n-2) - 0.1x(n-1)$$
$$y_2(n) = y_1(n) + 0.5y_1(n-1) - 0.4y_2(n-1)$$
$$y_3(n) = y_2(n) + 0.6y_2(n-1) + 0.8y_1(n) \qquad (2.1)$$

These three equations give us a mathematical model derived from the model shown in Figure 2.3 that is schematic in nature. We can also derive (draw the circuit realization) the model shown in Figure 2.3 from the model given in Equations (2.1). We will soon describe a method to obtain a single input–output relationship between the input $x(n)$ and the output $y(n) = y_3(n)$, after eliminating the internal variables $y_1(n)$ and $y_2(n)$; that relationship constitutes the third model for the system. The general form of such an input–output relationship is

$$y(n) = -\sum_{k=1}^{N} a(k)y(n-k) + \sum_{k=0}^{M} b(k)x(n-k) \qquad (2.2)$$

or in another equivalent form

$$\sum_{k=0}^{N} a(k)y(n-k) = \sum_{k=0}^{M} b(k)x(n-k); \qquad a(0) = 1 \qquad (2.3)$$

Equation (2.2) shows that the output $y(n)$ is determined by the weighted sum of the previous N values of the output and the weighted sum of the current and previous $M+1$ values of the input. Very often the coefficient $a(0)$ as shown in (2.3) is normalized to unity.

Soon we will introduce the z transform to represent the discrete-time signals in the set of equations above, thereby generating more models for the system, and from these models in the z domain, we will derive the transfer function $H(z^{-1})$ and the unit sample response or the unit impulse response $h(n)$ of the system. From any one of these models in the z domain, we can derive the other models in the z domain and also the preceding models given in the time domain. It is very important to know how to obtain any one model from any other given model so that the proper tools can be used efficiently, for analysis of the discrete-time system. In this chapter we will elaborate on the different models of a discrete-time system and then discuss many tools or techniques for finding the response of discrete-time systems when they are excited by different kinds of input signals.

2.1.2   Recursive Algorithm

Let us consider an example of Equation (2.2) as $y(n) = y(n-1) - 0.25y(n-2) + x(n)$, where the input sequence $x(n) = \delta(n)$, and the two initial conditions are $y(-1) = 1.0$ and $y(-2) = 0.4$.

We compute $y(0)$, $y(1)$, $y(2)$, ... in a recursive manner as follows: $y(0) = y(-1) - 0.25y(-2) + x(0)$. Since $x(n) = \delta(n)$, we substitute $x(0) = 1$ and get $y(0) = 1.0 - 0.25(0.4) + 1 = 1.9$. Next $y(1) = y(0) - 0.25y(-1) + x(1)$. We know $y(0) = 1.9$ from the step shown above, and also that $x(1) = 0$. So we get $y(1) = 1.9 - 0.25(1.0) + 0 = 1.65$. Next, for $n = 2$, when we compute $y(2) = y(1) - 0.25y(0) + x(2)$. Substituting the known values from above, we get $y(2) = 1.65 - 0.25(1.9) + 0 = 1.175$.

Next, when $n = 3$, we obtain

$$y(3) = y(2) - 0.25y(1) + x(3)$$

$$= 1.175 - 0.25(1.65) + 0 = 0.760$$

We can continue to calculate the values of the output $y(n)$ for $n = 4, 5, 6, 7, \ldots$.

This is known as the *recursive algorithm*, which we use to calculate the output when we are given an equation of the form (2.2); it can be used when there is any other input. For a system modeled by an equation of the form (2.2), the output is infinite in length in general. As a special case, when the input is the unit impulse function $\delta(n)$, and the initial conditions are assumed to be zero, the resulting output is called the *unit impulse response h(n)* (or more appropriately the *unit sample response*) and is infinite in length.

Consider a system in which the multiplier constants $a(k) = 0$ for $k = 1, 2, 3, \ldots, N$. Then Equation (2.2) reduces to the form

$$y(n) = \sum_{k=0}^{M} b(k)x(n-k) \qquad (2.4)$$

$$= b(0)x(n) + b(1)x(n-1) + b(2)x(n-2) + \cdots + b(M)x(n-M)$$

Let us find the unit impulse response of this system, using the recursive algorithm, as before:

$$y(0) = b(0)(1) + 0 + 0 + 0 + \cdots = b(0)$$
$$y(1) = b(0)x(1) + b(1)x(0) + b(2)x(-1) + 0 + 0 + \cdots = b(1)$$
$$y(2) = b(0)x(2) + b(1)x(1) + b(2)x(0) + 0 + 0 + 0 + \cdots = b(2)$$

Continuing this procedure recursively, we would get

$$y(3) = b(3)$$
$$y(4) = b(4)$$
$$\cdot$$
$$\cdot$$
$$\cdot$$
$$y(M) = b(M)$$

This example leads to the following two observations: (1) the samples of the unit impulse response are the same as the coefficients $b(n)$, and (2) therefore the unit impulse response $h(n)$ of the system is finite in length.

So we have shown without proof but by way of example that the unit impulse response of the system modeled by an equation of the form (2.2) is infinite in length, and hence such a system is known as an *infinite impulse response* (IIR) filter, whereas the system modeled by an equation of the form (2.4), which has an unit impulse response that is finite in length, is known as the *finite impulse response (FIR)* filter. We will have a lot more to say about these two types of filters later in the book. Equation (2.3) is the ordinary, linear, time-invariant, difference equation of Nth order, which, if necessary, can be rewritten in the recursive difference equation form (2.2). The equation can be solved in the time domain, by the following four methods:

1. The recursive algorithm as explained above
2. The convolution sum, to get the zero state response, as explained in the next section

3. The classical method of solving a difference equation

4. The analytical solution using the z transform.

We should point out that methods 1–3 require that the DT system be modeled by a single-input, single-output equation. If we are given a large number of difference equations describing the DT system, then methods 1–3 are not suitable for finding the output response in the time domain. Method 4, using the z transform, is the only powerful and general method to solve such a problem, and hence it will be treated in greater detail and illustrated by several examples in this chapter. Given a model in the z-transform domain, we will show how to derive the recursive algorithm and the unit impulse response $h(n)$ so that the convolution sum can be applied. So the z-transform method is used most often for time-domain analysis, and the frequency-domain analysis is closely related to this method, as will be discussed in the next chapter.

2.1.3 Convolution Sum

In the discussion above, we have assumed that the unit impulse response of a discrete-time system when it is excited by a unit impulse function $\delta(n)$, exists (or is known), and we denote it as $h(n)$. Instead of using the recursive algorithm to find the response due to any input, let us represent the input signal $x(n)$ not by its values in a sequence $\{x(0), x(1), x(2), x(3), \ldots\}$ but as the values of impulse function at the corresponding instants of time. In other words, we consider the sequence of impulse functions $x(0)\delta(n), x(1)\delta(n-1), x(2)\delta(n-2), \ldots$ as the input—and not the sequence of values $\{x(0), x(1), x(2), x(3), \ldots\}$. The difference between the values of the samples as a sequence of numbers and the sequence of impulse functions described above should be clearly understood. The first operation is simple sampling operation, whereas the second is known as *impulse sampling*, which is a mathematical way to represent the same data, and we represent the second sequence in a compact form: $x(n) = \sum_{k=0}^{\infty} x(k)\delta(n-k)$. The mathematical way of representing impulse sampling is a powerful tool that is used to analyze the performance of discrete-time systems, and the values of the impulse functions at the output are obtained by analytical methods. These values are identified as the numerical values of the output signal.

Since $h(n)$ is the response due to the input $\delta(n)$, we have $x(0)h(n)$ as the response due to $x(0)\delta(n)$ because we have assumed that the system is linear. Assuming that the system is time-invariant as well as linear, we get the output due to an input $x(1)\delta(n-1)$ to be $x(1)h(n-1)$. In general, the output due to an input $x(k)\delta(n-k)$ is given by $x(k)h(n-k)$. Adding the responses due to all the impulses in $x(n) = \sum_{k=0}^{\infty} x(k)\delta(n-k)$, we get the total output as the sum

$$y(n) = \sum_{k=0}^{\infty} x(k)h(n-k) \tag{2.5}$$

This is known as the *convolution sum*, denoted by a compact notation $y(n) = x(n) * h(n)$. The summation formula can be used to find the response due to any input signal. So if we know the unit impulse response $h(n)$ of the system, we can find the output $y(n)$ due to any input $x(n)$—therefore it is another model for the discrete-time system. In contrast to the recursive algorithm, however, note that the convolution sum cannot be used to find the response due to given initial conditions. When and if the input signal is defined for $-\infty < n < \infty$ or $-M \leq n < \infty$, obviously the lower index of summation is changed to $-\infty$. In this case the convolution sum formula takes the general form

$$y(n) = \sum_{k=-\infty}^{\infty} x(k)h(n - k) \qquad (2.6)$$

For example, even though we know that $h(n) = 0$ for $-\infty < n < 0$, if the input sequence $x(n)$ is defined for $-M < n < \infty$, then we have to use the formula $y(n) = \sum_{k=-\infty}^{\infty} x(k)h(n - k)$. If $x(n) = 0$ for $-\infty < n < 0$, then we have to use the formula $y(n) = \sum_{k=0}^{\infty} x(k)h(n - k)$.

To understand the procedure for implementing the summation formula, we choose a graphical method in the following example. Remember that the recursive algorithm cannot be used if the DT system is described by more than one difference equation, and the convolution sum requires that we have the unit pulse response of the system. We will find that these limitations are not present when we use the z-transform method for analyzing the DT system performance in the time domain.

Example 2.1

Given an $h(n)$ and $x(n)$, we change the independent variable from n to k and plot $h(k)$ and $x(k)$ as shown in Figure 2.4a,b. Note that the input sequence is defined for $-2 \leq k \leq 5$ but $h(k)$ is a causal sequence defined for $0 \leq k \leq 4$. Next we do a time reversal and plot $h(-k)$ in Figure 2.4c. When $n \geq 0$, we obtain $h(n - k)$ by delaying (or shifting to the right) $h(-k)$ by n samples; when $n < 0$, the sequence $h(-k)$ is advanced (or shifted to the left). For every value of n, we have $h(n - k)$ and $x(k)$ and we multiply the samples of $h(n - k)$ and $x(k)$ at each value of k and add the products.

For our example, we show the summation of the product when $n = -2$ in Figure 2.4d, and show the summation of the product when $n = 3$ in Figure 2.4e. The output $y(-2)$ has only one nonzero product $= x(-2)h(0)$. But the output sample $y(3)$ is equal to $x(0)h(3) + x(1)h(2) + x(2)h(1) + x(3)h(0)$.

But note that when $n > 9$, and $n < -2$, the sequences $h(n - k)$ and $x(k)$ do not have overlapping samples, and therefore $y(n) = 0$ for $n > 9$ and $n < -2$.

Example 2.2

As another example, let us assume that the input sequence $x(n)$ and also the unit impulse response $h(n)$ are given for $0 \leq n < \infty$. Then output $y(n)$ given

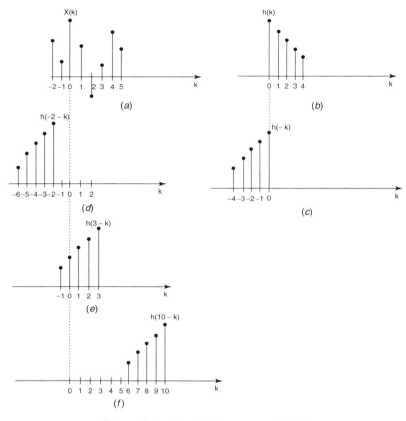

Figure 2.4   Convolution sum explained.

by (2.5) can be computed for each value of n as shown below:

$y(0) = x(0)h(0)$

$y(1) = x(0)h(1) + x(1)h(0)$

$y(2) = x(0)h(2) + x(1)h(1) + x(2)h(0)$

$y(3) = x(0)h(3) + x(1)h(2) + x(2)h(1) + x(3)h(0)$

$y(4) = x(0)h(4) + x(1)h(3) + x(2)h(2) + x(3)h(1) + x(4)h(0)$

$\cdot$

$\cdot$

$\cdot$

$y(n) = x(0)h(n) + x(1)h(n-1) + x(2)h(n-2) + x(3)h(n-3) + \cdots + x(n)h(0)$

$\cdot$ (2.7)

$\cdot$

$\cdot$

It is interesting to note the following pattern. In the expressions for each value of the output $y(n)$ above, we have $x(0), x(1), x(2) \ldots$ and $h(n), h(n-1)$, $h(n-2) \ldots$ multiplied term by term in order and the products are added, while the indices of the two samples in each product always add to n.

Convolution is a fundamental operation carried out by digital signal processors in hardware and in the processing of digital signals by software. The design of digital signal processors and the software to implement the convolution sum have been developed to provide us with very efficient and powerful tools. We will discuss this subject again in Section 2.5, after we learn the theory and application of z transforms.

2.2   z TRANSFORM THEORY

2.2.1   Definition

In many textbooks, the z transform of a sequence $x(n)$ is simply defined as

$$\mathcal{Z}[x(n)] = X(z) = \sum_{n=-\infty}^{\infty} x(n)z^{-n} \tag{2.8}$$

and the inverse z transform defined as

$$\mathcal{Z}^{-1}[X(z)] = x(n) = \frac{1}{2\pi j} \int_C X(z)z^{n-1}dz \tag{2.9}$$

Equation (2.8) represents the (double-sided or) bilateral z transform of a sequence $x(n)$ defined for $-\infty < n < \infty$. The inverse z transform given in (2.9) is obtained by an integration in the complex z plane, and this integration in the z plane is beyond the scope of this book.

We prefer to consider signals that are of interest in digital signal processing and hence consider a sequence obtained by sampling a continuous-time signal $x(t)$ with a constant sampling period T (where T is the sampling period), and generate a sequence of numbers $x(nT)$. Remember that according to the sifting theorem, we have $x(t)\delta(t) = x(0)\delta(t)$. We use this result to carry out a procedure called *impulse sampling* by multiplying $x(t)$ with an impulse train $p(t) = \sum_{n=0}^{\infty} \delta(t-nT)$. Consequently we consider a sequence of delayed impulse functions weighted by the strength equal to the numerical values of the signal instead of a sequence of numbers. By doing so, we express the discrete sequence as a function of the continuous variable t, which allows us to treat signal processing mathematically. The product is denoted as

$$x^*(t) = \sum_{n=0}^{\infty} x(t)\delta(t-nT)$$

$$= \sum_{n=0}^{\infty} x(nT)\delta(t-nT) \tag{2.10}$$

This expression has a Laplace transform denoted as

$$X^*(s) = \sum_{n=0}^{\infty} x(nT)e^{-snT} \tag{2.11}$$

Now we use a frequency transformation $e^{sT} = z$, (where z is a complex variable), and substituting it in expression (2.11), we get

$$X^*(s)\big|_{e^{sT}=z} = \sum_{n=0}^{\infty} x(nT)z^{-n}$$

Since T is a constant, we consider the samples $x(nT)$ as a function of n and obtain the z transform of $x(n)$ as

$$X^*(s)\big|_{e^{sT}=z} = \sum_{n=0}^{\infty} x(nT)z^{-n}$$

$$X(z) = \sum_{n=0}^{\infty} x(n)z^{-n} \tag{2.12}$$

Although the first definition of a discrete sequence given in (2.8) is devoid of any signal concepts, soon concepts such as frequency response and time-domain response are used in the analysis of discrete-time systems and signal processing. Our derivation of the z transform starts with a continuous-time signal that is sampled by impulse sampling and introduces the transformation $e^{sT} = z$ to arrive at the same definition. In Chapter 3, we will study the implication of this transformation in more detail and get a fundamental understanding of the relationship between the frequency responses of the continuous-time systems and those of the discrete-time systems. Note that we consider in this book only the unilateral z transform as defined by (2.12), so we set the lower index in the infinite sum as $n = 0$.

Example 2.3

Let us derive the z transform of a few familiar discrete-time sequences. Consider the unit pulse

$$\delta(n) = \begin{cases} 1 & n = 0 \\ 0 & n \neq 0 \end{cases}$$

There is only term in the z transform of $\delta(n)$, which is one when $n = 0$. Hence $\mathcal{Z}[\delta(n)] = 1$.

Example 2.4

Consider the unit sample sequence $u(n)$

$$u(n) = \begin{cases} 1 & \text{for } n \geq 0 \\ 0 & \text{for } n < 0 \end{cases} \tag{2.13}$$

From the definition of the z transform, we get

$$\mathcal{Z}[u(n)] = 1 + z^{-1} + z^{-2} + z^{-3} + \cdots \tag{2.14}$$

$$= \sum_{n=0}^{\infty} z^{-n} \tag{2.15}$$

This is an infinite series that converges to a closed-form expression (2.16), only when $\left|z^{-1}\right| < 1$, or $|z| > 1$. This represents the region outside the unit circle in the z plane and it is called the *region of convergence* (ROC). This means that the closed-form expression exists only for values of z that lie in this region:

$$\sum_{n=0}^{\infty} z^{-n} = \frac{1}{1 - z^{-1}} = \frac{z}{z - 1} \tag{2.16}$$

It is obvious that the region of convergence for the z transform of $\delta(n)$ is the entire z plane.

Example 2.5

Let $x(n) = \alpha^n u(n)$, where α is assumed to be a complex number in general. From the definition for the z transform, we obtain

$$X(z) = \sum_{n=0}^{\infty} \alpha^n z^{-n} = \sum_{n=0}^{\infty} \left(\alpha z^{-1}\right)^n \tag{2.17}$$

This power series converges to (2.18), when $\left|\alpha z^{-1}\right| < 1$, that is, when $|z| > |\alpha|$. This shows that the region of convergence for the power series is outside the circle of radius $R = \alpha$. It is important to know the region of convergence in which the closed-form expression for the z transform of a sequence of infinite length is valid.[1]

$$X(z) = \frac{1}{1 - \alpha z^{-1}} = \frac{z}{z - \alpha} \tag{2.18}$$

---

[1]It can be shown that the z transform for the anticausal sequence $f(n) = -\alpha^n u(-n - 1)$ is $F(z) = \sum_{n=-\infty}^{-1} \alpha^n z^{-n}$, which also converges to $z/(z - \alpha)$, which is the same as $X(z)$ in (2.18), but its ROC is $|z| < \alpha$. So the inverse z transform of a function is not unique; only when we know its ROC does the inverse z transform become unambiguous.

Example 2.6

Let us consider another example, $x(n) = e^{j\theta n}u(n)$, which is a complex-valued sequence. Its z transform is

$$X(z) = \sum_{n=0}^{\infty} e^{j\theta n} z^{-n} = \frac{1}{1 - e^{j\theta}z^{-1}} = \frac{z}{z - e^{j\theta}} \tag{2.19}$$

and its region of convergence is the region outside the unit circle in the z plane: $|z| > 1$.

Example 2.7

Given a sequence $x(n) = r^n \cos(\theta n)u(n)$, where $0 < r \leq 1$, to derive its z transform, we express it as follows:

$$x(n) = r^n \left[\frac{e^{j\theta n} + e^{-j\theta n}}{2} \right] u(n)$$

$$= \left[\frac{r^n e^{j\theta n}}{2} + \frac{r^n e^{-j\theta n}}{2} \right] u(n)$$

$$= \frac{\left(re^{j\theta}\right)^n}{2} u(n) + \frac{\left(re^{-j\theta}\right)^n}{2} u(n) \tag{2.20}$$

Now one can use the previous results and obtain the z transform of $x(n) = r^n \cos(\theta n)u(n)$ as

$$X(z) = \frac{z(z - r\cos(\theta))}{z^2 - (2r\cos(\theta))z + r^2} \tag{2.21}$$

and its region of convergence is given by $|z| > r$. Of course, if the sequence given is $x(n) = e^{-an} \cos(\omega_0 n)u(n)$, we simply substitute e^{-a} for r in (2.21), to get the z transform of $x(n)$. It is useful to have a list of z transforms for discrete-time sequences that are commonly utilized; they are listed in Table 2.1. It is also useful to know the properties of z transforms that can be used to generate and add more z transforms to Table 2.1, as illustrated by the following example.

Property 2.1: Differentiation   If $X(z)$ is the z transform of $x(n)u(n)$, $-z[dX(z)]/dz$ is the z transform of $nx(n)u(n)$. We denote this property by

$$nx(n)u(n) \iff -z\frac{dX(z)}{dz} \tag{2.22}$$

TABLE 2.1   List of z-Transform Pairs

	$x(n)$, for $n \geq 0$	$X(z)$
1	$\delta(n)$	1
2	$\delta(n-m)$	z^{-m}
3	$u(n)$	$\dfrac{z}{z-1}$
4	$au(n)$	$\dfrac{az}{z-1}$
5	a^n	$\dfrac{z}{z-a}$
6	na^n	$\dfrac{az}{(z-a)^2}$
7	n^2	$\dfrac{z(z+1)}{(z-1)^3}$
8	n^3	$\dfrac{z(z^2+4z+1)}{(z-1)^4}$
9	$n^2 a^n$	$\dfrac{az(z+a)}{(z-a)^3}$
10	$\dfrac{n(n-1)}{2!}a^{n-2}$	$\dfrac{z}{(z-a)^3}$
11	$\dfrac{n(n-1)(n-2)\cdots\cdots(n-m+2)}{(m-1)!}a^{n-m+1}$	$\dfrac{z}{(z-a)^m}$
12	$r^n e^{j\theta n}$	$\dfrac{z}{z-re^{j\theta}}$
13	$r^n \cos(\theta n)$	$\dfrac{z(z-r\cos(\theta))}{z^2-(2r\cos(\theta))z+r^2}$
14	$r^n \sin(\theta n)$	$\dfrac{rz\sin(\theta)}{z^2-(2r\cos(\theta))z+r^2}$
15	$e^{-\alpha n}\cos(\theta n)$	$\dfrac{z(z-e^{-\alpha}\cos(\theta))}{z^2-(2e^{-\alpha}\cos(\theta))z+e^{-2\alpha}}$

Proof: $X(z) = \sum_{n=0}^{\infty} x(n)z^{-n}$. Differentiating both sides with respect to z, we get

$$\frac{dX(z)}{dz} = \sum_{n=0}^{\infty} x(n)\left[-nz^{-n-1}\right] = -z^{-1}\sum_{n=0}^{\infty} nx(n)z^{-n}$$

$$-z\frac{dX(z)}{dz} = \sum_{n=0}^{\infty} nx(n)z^{-n} = \mathcal{Z}[nx(n)u(n)]$$

Now consider the z transform given by (2.18) and also listed in Table 2.1:

$$x(n) = a^n u(n) \Longleftrightarrow \frac{z}{z - a} = X(z) \tag{2.23}$$

Using this differentiation property recursively, we can show that

$$na^n u(n) \Longleftrightarrow \frac{az}{(z - a)^2} \tag{2.24}$$

and

$$n^2 a^n u(n) \Longleftrightarrow \frac{az(z + a)}{(z - a)^3} \tag{2.25}$$

From these results, we can find the z transform of $\frac{1}{2}(n + 1)(n + 2)a^n u(n) = \frac{1}{2}(n^2 + 3n + 2)a^n u(n)$ as follows:

$$\frac{1}{2}(n + 1)(n + 2)a^n u(n) \Longleftrightarrow \frac{z^3}{(z - a)^3} \tag{2.26}$$

The transform pair given by (2.26) is an addition to Table 2.1. Indeed, we can find the z transforms of $n^3 a^n u(n)$, $n^4 a^n u(n)$, ..., using (2.22) and then find the z transforms of

$$\frac{1}{3!}(n + 1)(n + 2)(n + 3)a^n u(n)$$

$$\frac{1}{4!}(n + 1)(n + 2)(n + 3)(n + 4)a^n u(n) \tag{2.27}$$

$$.$$
$$.$$
$$.$$

which can be added to Table 2.1.

Properties of z transform are useful for deriving the z transform of new sequences. Also they are essential for solving the linear difference equations and finding the response of discrete-time systems when the input function and initial conditions are given. Instead of deriving all the properties one after another, as is done in many textbooks, we derive one or two at a time and immediately show their applications.

Property 2.2: Delay   Let the z transform of $x(n)u(n)$ be $X(z) = \sum_{n=0}^{\infty} x(n)z^{-n} = x(0) + x(1)z^{-1} + x(2)z^{-2} + x(3)z^{-3} + \cdots$.

Then the z transform of $x(n - 1)u(n - 1)$ is $z^{-1}X(z) + x(-1)$:

$$x(n - 1)u(n - 1) \Longleftrightarrow z^{-1}X(z) + x(-1) \tag{2.28}$$

Proof: The z transform of $x(n-1)u(n-1)$ is obtained by shifting to the right or delaying $x(n)u(n)$ by one sample, and if there is a sample $x(-1)$ at $n = -1$, it will be shifted to the position $n = 0$. The z transform of this delayed sequence is therefore given by

$$x(-1) + x(0)z^{-1} + x(1)z^{-2} + x(2)z^{-3} + \cdots$$
$$= x(-1) + z^{-1}\left[x(0) + x(1)z^{-1} + x(2)z^{-2} + \cdots\right]$$
$$= x(-1) + z^{-1}X(z)$$

By repeated application of this property, we derive

$$x(n-2)u(n-2) \Longleftrightarrow z^{-2}X(z) + z^{-1}x(-1) + x(-2) \tag{2.29}$$

$$x(n-3)u(n-3) \Longleftrightarrow z^{-3}X(z) + z^{-2}x(-1) + z^{-1}x(-2) + x(-3) \tag{2.30}$$

and

$$x(n-m)u(n-m) \Longleftrightarrow z^{-m}X(z^{-1}) + z^{-m+1}x(-1) + z^{-m+2}x(-2)$$
$$+ \cdots + x(-m)$$

or

$$x(n-m)u(n-m) \Longleftrightarrow z^{-m}X(z) + \sum_{n=0}^{m-1} x(n-m)z^{-n} \tag{2.31}$$

If the initial conditions are zero, we have the simpler relationship

$$x(n-m)u(n-m) \Longleftrightarrow z^{-m}X(z) \tag{2.32}$$

Example 2.8

Let us consider an example of solving a first-order linear difference equation using the results obtained above. We have

$$y(n) - 0.5y(n-1) = 5x(n-1) \tag{2.33}$$

where

$$x(n) = (0.2)^n u(n)$$
$$y(-1) = 2$$

Let $\mathcal{Z}[y(n)] = Y(z)$. From (2.28), we have $\mathcal{Z}[y(n-1)] = z^{-1}Y(z) + y(-1)$ and $\mathcal{Z}[x(n-1)] = z^{-1}X(z) + x(-1)$ where $X(z) = z/(z-0.2)$ and $x(-1) = 0$, since $x(n)$ is zero for $-\infty < n < 0$. Substituting these results, we get

$$Y(z) - 0.5\left[z^{-1}Y(z) + y(-1)\right] = 5\left[z^{-1}X(z) + x(-1)\right]$$
$$Y(z) - 0.5\left[z^{-1}Y(z) + y(-1)\right] = 5z^{-1}X(z)$$

$$Y(z)\left[1 - 0.5z^{-1}\right] = 0.5y(-1) + 5z^{-1}X(z) \qquad (2.34)$$

$$Y(z) = \frac{0.5y(-1)}{(1 - 0.5z^{-1})} + \frac{5z^{-1}}{(1 - 0.5z^{-1})}X(z)$$

$$Y(z) = \frac{0.5y(-1)z}{(z - 0.5)} + \frac{5}{(z - 0.5)}X(z)$$

Substituting $y(-1) = 2$ and $X(z) = z/(z - 0.2)$ in this last expression, we get

$$Y(z) = \frac{z}{(z - 0.5)} + \frac{5z}{(z - 0.5)(z - 0.2)} \qquad (2.35)$$

$$= Y_{0i}(z) + Y_{0s}(z) \qquad (2.36)$$

where $Y_{0i}(z)$ is the z transform of the zero input response and $Y_{0s}(z)$ is the z transform of the zero state response as explained below.

Now we have to find the inverse z transform of the two terms on the right side of (2.35). The inverse transform of the first term $Y_{0i}(z) = z/(z - 0.5)$ is easily found as $y_{0i}(n) = (0.5)^n u(n)$. Instead of finding the inverse z transform of the second term by using the complex integral given in (2.9), we resort to the same approach as used in solving differential equations by means of Laplace transform, namely, by decomposing $Y_{0s}(z)$ into its partial fraction form to obtain the inverse z transform of each term. We have already derived the z transform of $Ra^n u(n)$ as $Rz/(z - a)$, and it is easy to write the inverse z transform of terms like $R_k z/(z - a_k)$. Hence we should expand the second term in the form

$$Y_{0s}(z) = \frac{R_1 z}{z - 0.5} + \frac{R_2 z}{z - 0.2} \qquad (2.37)$$

by a slight modification to the partial fraction expansion procedure that we are familiar with. Dividing $Y_{0s}(z)$ by z, we get

$$\frac{Y_{0s}(z)}{z} = \frac{5}{(z - 0.5)(z - 0.2)} = \frac{R_1}{z - 0.5} + \frac{R_2}{z - 0.2}$$

Now we can easily find the residues R_1 and R_2 using the normal procedure and get

$$R_1 = \left.\frac{Y_{0s}(z)}{z}(z - 0.5)\right|_{z=0.5} = \left.\frac{5}{(z - 0.2)}\right|_{z=0.5} = 16.666$$

$$R_2 = \left.\frac{Y_{0s}(z)}{z}(z - 0.2)\right|_{z=0.2} = \left.\frac{5}{(z - 0.5)}\right|_{z=0.2} = -16.666$$

Therefore

$$\frac{Y_{0s}(z)}{z} = \frac{5}{(z - 0.5)(z - 0.2)} = \frac{16.666}{z - 0.5} - \frac{16.666}{z - 0.2}$$

Multiplying both sides by z, we get

$$Y_{0s}(z) = \frac{16.666z}{z - 0.5} - \frac{16.666z}{z - 0.2} \tag{2.38}$$

Now we obtain the inverse z transform $y_{0s}(n) = 16.666[(0.5)^n - (0.2)^n]u(n)$. The total output satisfying the given difference equation is therefore given as

$$y(n) = y_{0i}(n) + y_{0s}(n) = \left\{(0.5)^n + 16.666[(0.5)^n - (0.2)^n]\right\}u(n)$$
$$= \left\{17.6666(0.5)^n - 16.666(0.2)^n\right\}u(n)$$

Thus the modified partial fraction procedure to find the inverse z transform of any function $F(z)$ is to divide the function $F(z)$ by z, expand $F(z)/z$ into its normal partial fraction form, and then multiply each of the terms by z to get $F(z)$ in the form $\sum_{k=1} R_k z/(z - a_k)$. From this form, the inverse z transform $f(n)$ is obtained as $\sum_{k=1} R_k (a_k)^n u(n)$.

However, there is an alternative method, to expand a transfer function expressed in the form, when it has only simple poles

$$H(z^{-1}) = \frac{N(z^{-1})}{\prod_{k=1}(1 - a_k z^{-1})}$$

to its partial fraction form

$$H(z^{-1}) = \sum_{k=1} \frac{R_k}{(1 - a_k z^{-1})} \tag{2.39}$$

where

$$R_k = H(z^{-1})(1 - a_k z^{-1})\big|_{z=a_k}$$

Then the inverse z transform is the sum of the inverse z transform of all the terms in (2.39): $h(n) = \sum_{k=1}^{K} R_k (a_k)^n u(n)$. We prefer the first method because we are already familiar with the partial fraction expansion of $H(s)$ and know how to find the residues when it has multiple poles in the s plane. This method will be illustrated by several examples that are worked out in the following pages.

2.2.2 Zero Input and Zero State Response

In Section 2.2.1, the total output $y(n)$ was obtained as the sum of two outputs $y_{0i}(n) = (0.5)^n u(n)$ and $y_{0s}(n) = 16.666[(0.5)^n - (0.2)^n]u(n)$.

If the input function $x(n)$ is zero, then $X(z) = 0$, and $Y(s)$ in (2.34) will contain only the term $Y_{0i}(z) = 0.5y(-1)z/(z - 0.5) = z/(z - 0.5)$; therefore the response $y(n) = (0.5)^n u(n)$ when the input is zero. The response of a system described by a linear difference equation, when the input to the system is assumed to be zero is called the *zero input response* and is determined only by the initial conditions given. The initial conditions specified with the difference equation are better known as *initial states*. (But the term *state* has a specific definition in the theory of linear discrete-time systems, and the terminology of initial states is consistent with this definition.) When the initial state $y(-1)$ in the problem presented above is assumed to be zero, the z transform of the total response $Y(z)$ contains only the term $Y_{0s}(z) = 5/(z - 0.5)X(z) = 5/[(z - 0.5)(z - 0.2)]$, which gives a response $y_{0s}(n) = 16.666[(0.5)^n - (0.2)^n]u(n)$. This is the response $y(n)$ when the initial condition or the initial state is zero and hence is called the *zero state response*. The zero state response is the response due to input only, and the zero input response is due to the initial states (initial conditions) only. We repeat it in order to avoid the common confusion that occurs among students! The zero input response is computed by neglecting the input function and computing the response due to initial states only, and the zero state response is computed by neglecting the initial states (if they are given) and computing the response due to input function only. Students are advised to know the exact definition and meaning of the zero input response and zero state response, without any confusion between these two terms.

2.2.3 Linearity of the System

If the input $x(n)$ to the discrete-time system described by (2.33) is multiplied by a constant, say, $K = 10$, the total response of the system $y(n)$ is given as $y_{0i}(n) + 10y_{0s}(n)$, which is not 10 times the total response $y_{0i}(n) + y_{0s}(n)$. This may give rise to the incorrect inference that the system described by the difference equation (2.33) above, is not linear. The correct way to test whether a system is linear is to apply the test on the zero state response only or to the zero input response only as explained below.

   Let the zero state response of a system defined by a difference equation be $y_1(n)$ when the input to the system is $x_1(n)$ and the zero state response be $y_2(n)$ when the input is $x_2(n)$, where the inputs are arbitrary. Here we emphasize that the definition should be applied to the zero state response only or to the zero input only. So the definition of a linear system given in Section 2.1 is repeated below, emphasizing that the definition should be applied to the zero input response or zero state response only.

   Given a system $x(n) \Rightarrow y(n)$, if $Kx(n) \Rightarrow Ky(n)$ and $K_1x_1(n) + K_2x_2(n) \Rightarrow K_1y_1(n) + K_2y_2(n)$, then the system is linear, provided $y(n)$ is the zero state response due to an input signal $x(n)$ or the zero input response due to initial states. Now it should be easy to verify that the system described by (2.33) is a linear system.

2.2.4 Time-Invariant System

Let a discrete-time system be defined by a linear difference equation of the general form (2.3), which defines the input–output relationship of the system.

Let us denote the solution to this equation as the output $y(n)$ when an input $x(n)$ is applied. Such a system is said to be time-invariant if the output is $y(n - N)$ when the input is $x(n - N)$, which means that if the input sequence is delayed by N samples, the output also is delayed by N samples. For this reason, a time-invariant discrete-time system is also called a *shift-invariant* system. Again from the preceding discussion about linearity of a system, it should be obvious the output $y(n)$ and $y(n - N)$ must be chosen as the zero state response only or the zero input response only, when the abovementioned test for a system to be time-invariant is applied.

2.3   USING z TRANSFORM TO SOLVE DIFFERENCE EQUATIONS

We will consider a few more examples to show how to solve a linear shift-invariant difference equation, using the z transform in this section, and later we show how to solve a single-input, single-output difference equation using the classical method. Students should be familiar with the procedure for decomposing a proper, rational function of a complex variable in its partial fraction form, when the function has simple poles, multiple poles, and pairs of complex conjugate poles. A "rational" function in a complex variable is the ratio between two polynomials with real coefficients, and a "proper" function is one in which the degree of the numerator polynomial is less than that of the denominator polynomial. It can be shown that the degree of the numerator in the transfer function $H(s)$ of a continuous-time system is at most equal to that of its denominator. In contrast, it is relevant to point out that the transfer function of a discrete-time system when expressed in terms of the variable z^{-1} need not be a proper function. For example, let us consider the following example of an improper function of the complex variable z^{-1}:

$$H(z^{-1}) = \frac{z^{-4} - 0.8z^{-3} - 2.2z^{-2} - 0.4z^{-1}}{z^{-2} - z^{-1} + 2.0} \tag{2.40}$$

In this equation, the coefficients of the two polynomials are arranged in descending powers of z^{-1}, and when we carry out a long division of the numerator by the denominator, until the remainder is a polynomial of a degree lower than that in the denominator, we get the quotient $(z^{-2} + 0.2z^{-1} - 4.0)$ and a remainder $(-4.8z^{-1} + 8.0)$:

$$H(z^{-1}) = z^{-2} + 0.2z^{-1} - 4.0 + \frac{-4.8z^{-1} + 8.0}{z^{-2} - z^{-1} + 2.0} \tag{2.41}$$

$$= z^{-2} + 0.2z^{-1} - 4.0 + H_1(z^{-1}) \tag{2.42}$$

Since the inverse z transform of z^{-m} is $\delta(n - m)$, we get the inverse z transform of the first three terms as $\delta(n - 2) + 0.2\delta(n - 1) - 4.0\delta(n)$, and we add it to the inverse z transform of the $H_1(z^{-1})$, which will be derived below.

Example 2.9: Complex Conjugate Poles

Let us choose the second term on the right side of (2.41) as an example of a transfer function with complex poles:

$$H_1(z^{-1}) = \frac{-4.8z^{-1} + 8.0}{z^{-2} - z^{-1} + 2.0}$$

Multiplying the numerator and denominator by z^2, and factorizing the denominator, we find that $H_1(z^{-1})$ has a complex conjugate pair of poles at $0.25 \pm j0.6614$:

$$H_1(z) = \frac{8(z^2 - 0.6z)}{2z^2 - z + 1}$$

$$= \frac{8(z^2 - 0.6z)}{2(z^2 - 0.5z + 0.5)}$$

$$= 4\frac{(z^2 - 0.6z)}{(z - 0.25 - j0.6614)(z - 0.25 + j06614)}$$

Let us expand $H_1(z)/z$ into its modified partial fraction form:

$$\frac{H_1(z)}{z} = \frac{2 + j1.0583}{z - 0.25 - j0.6614} + \frac{2 - j1.0583}{z - 0.25 + j0.6614}.$$

It is preferable to express the residues and the poles in their exponential form and then multiply by z to get

$$H_1(z) = \frac{(2.2627e^{j0.4867})\,z}{z - 0.7071e^{j1.209}} + \frac{(2.2627e^{-j0.4867})\,z}{z - 0.7071e^{-j1.209}}$$

The inverse z transform of $H_1(z)$ is given by

$$h_1(n) = \{(2.2627e^{j0.4867})\,(0.7071e^{j1.209})^n$$

$$+ (2.2627e^{-j0.4867})\,(0.7071e^{-j1.209})^n\}\,u(n)$$

$$= \{2.2627(0.7071)^n e^{j1.209n} e^{j0.4867}$$

$$+ 2.2627(0.7071)^n e^{-j1.209n} e^{-j0.4867}\}\,u(n)$$

$$= 2.2627(0.7071)^n \{e^{j(1.209n+0.4867)} + e^{-j(1.209n+0.4867)}\}\,u(n)$$

$$= 2.2627(0.7071)^n \{2\cos(1.209n + 0.4867)\}\,u(n)$$

$$= 4.5254(0.7071)^n \{\cos(1.209n + 0.4867)\}\,u(n).$$

Adding these terms, we get the inverse z transform of

$$H(z^{-1}) = z^{-2} + 0.2z^{-1} - 4.0 + \frac{(2.2627e^{j0.4867})\,z}{z - 0.7071e^{j1.209}} + \frac{(2.2627e^{-j0.4867})\,z}{z - 0.7071e^{-j1.209}}$$

$$h(n) = \delta(n-2) + 0.2\delta(n-1) - 4.0\delta(n) + 2.2627e^{j0.4867}(0.7071e^{j1.209})^n$$
$$+ 2.2627e^{j-0.4867}(0.7071e^{-j1.209})^n u(n)$$
$$= \delta(n-2) + 0.2\delta(n-1) - 4.0\delta(n) + 2.2627(0.7071)^n$$
$$\times \{e^{j(1.209n+0.4867)} + e^{-j(1.209n+0.4867)}\}u(n)$$
$$= \delta(n-2) + 0.2\delta(n-1) - 4.0\delta(n) + 2.2627(0.7071)^n$$
$$\times \{2\cos(1.209n + 0.4867)\}u(n)$$
$$= \delta(n-2) + 0.2\delta(n-1) - 4.0\delta(n)$$
$$+ 4.5254(0.7071)^n \{\cos(1.209n + 0.4867)\}\,u(n)$$

Note that the angles in this solution are expressed in radians.

Example 2.10

Let us consider a discrete-time system described by the linear shift-invariant difference equation of second order given below

$$y(n) = 0.3y(n-1) - 0.02y(n-2) + x(n) - 0.1x(n-1)$$

where

$$x(n) = (-0.2)^n u(n)$$
$$y(-1) = 1.0$$
$$y(-2) = 0.6$$

Using the z transform for each term in this difference equation, we get

$$Y(z) = 0.3[z^{-1}Y(z) + y(-1)] - 0.02[z^{-2}Y(z) + z^{-1}y(-1) + y(-2)]$$
$$+ X(z) - 0.1[z^{-1}X(z) + x(-1)]$$

We know $X(z) = z/(z+0.2)$ and $x(-1) = 0$. Substituting these and the given initial states, we get

$$Y(z)[1 - 0.3z^{-1} + 0.02z^{-2}] = [0.3y(-1) - 0.02z^{-1}y(-1) - 0.02y(-2)]$$
$$+ X(z)[1 - 0.1z^{-1}]$$
$$Y(z) = \frac{[0.3y(-1) - 0.02z^{-1}y(-1) - 0.02y(-2)]}{[1 - 0.3z^{-1} + 0.02z^{-2}]}$$
$$+ \frac{X(z)[1 - 0.1z^{-1}]}{[1 - 0.3z^{-1} + 0.02z^{-2}]}$$

When the input $x(n)$ is zero, $X(z) = 0$; hence the second term on the right side is zero, leaving only the first term due to initial conditions given. It is the z transform of the zero input response $y_{0i}(n)$.

The inverse z transform of this first term on the right side

$$Y_{0i}(z) = \frac{[0.3y(-1) - 0.02z^{-1}y(-1) - 0.02y(-2)]}{[1 - 0.3z^{-1} + 0.02z^{-2}]}$$

gives the response when the input is zero, and so it is the zero input response $y_{0i}(n)$. The inverse z transform of

$$\frac{X(z)[1 - 0.1z^{-1}]}{[1 - 0.3z^{-1} + 0.02z^{-2}]} = Y_{0s}(z)$$

gives the response when the initial conditions (also called the initial states) are zero, and hence it is the zero state response $y_{0s}(n)$.

Substituting the values of the initial states and for $X(z)$, we obtain

$$Y_{0i}(z) = \frac{[0.288 - 0.02z^{-1}]}{[1 - 0.3z^{-1} + 0.02z^{-2}]} = \frac{[0.288z^2 - 0.02z]}{z^2 - 0.3z + 0.02} = \frac{z[0.288z - 0.02]}{(z - 0.1)(z - 0.2)}$$

and

$$Y_{0s}(z) = \frac{X(z)[1 - 0.1z^{-1}]}{[1 - 0.3z^{-1} + 0.02z^{-2}]} = \left[\frac{z}{z + 0.2}\right]\frac{[1 - 0.1z^{-1}]}{[1 - 0.3z^{-1} + 0.02z^{-2}]}$$

$$= \frac{z[z^2 - 0.1z]}{(z + 0.2)(z^2 - 0.3z + 0.02)} = \frac{z^2(z - 0.1)}{(z + 0.2)(z - 0.1)(z - 0.2)}$$

We notice that there is a pole and a zero at $z = 0.1$ in the second term on the right, which cancel each other, and $Y_{0s}(z)$ reduces to $z^2/[(z + 0.2)(z - 0.2)]$. We divide $Y_{0i}(z)$ by z, expand it into its normal partial fraction form

$$\frac{Y_{0i}(z)}{z} = \frac{[0.288z - 0.02]}{(z - 0.1)(z - 0.2)} = \frac{0.376}{(z - 0.2)} - \frac{0.088}{(z - 0.1)}$$

and multiply by z to get

$$Y_{0i}(z) = \frac{0.376z}{(z - 0.2)} - \frac{0.088z}{(z - 0.1)}$$

Similarly, we expand $Y_{0s}(z)/z = z/[(z + 0.2)(z - 0.2)]$ in the form $-0.5/(z + 0.2) + 0.5/(z - 0.2)$ and get

$$Y_{0s}(z) = \frac{z^2}{(z + 0.2)(z - 0.2)} = \frac{-0.5z}{(z + 0.2)} + \frac{0.5z}{(z - 0.2)}$$

Therefore, the zero input response is $y_{0i}(n) = [0.376(0.2)^n - 0.088(0.1)^n]u(n)$ and the zero state response is $y_{0s}(n) = 0.5[-(-0.2)^n + (0.2)^n]u(n)$.

Example 2.11: Multiple Poles

Here we discuss the case of a function that has multiple poles and expand it into its partial fraction form. Let

$$\frac{G(z)}{z} = \frac{N(z)}{(z - z_0)^r (z - z_1)(z - z_2)(z - z_3) \cdots (z - z_m)}$$

Its normal partial fraction is in the form

$$\frac{G(z)}{z} = \frac{C_0}{(z - z_0)^r} + \frac{C_1}{(z - z_0)^{r-1}} + \cdots + \frac{C_{r-1}}{(z - z_0)}$$

$$+ \frac{k_1}{(z - z_1)} + \frac{k_2}{(z - z_2)} + \cdots + \frac{k_m}{(z - z_m)}$$

The residues $k_1, k_2, \ldots, k_m$ for the simple poles at $z_1, z_2, \ldots$ are obtained by the normal method of multiplying $G(z)/z$ by $(z - z_i)$, $i = 1, 2, 3, \ldots, m$ and evaluating the product at $z = z_i$. The residue C_0 is also found by the same method:

$$C_0 = \left\{ (z - z_0)^r \frac{G(z)}{z} \right\}\Big|_{z=z_0}$$

The coefficient C_1 is found from

$$\frac{d}{dz} \left\{ (z - z_0)^r \frac{G(z)}{z} \right\}\Big|_{z=z_0}$$

and the coefficient C_2 is found from

$$\frac{1}{2} \frac{d^2}{dz^2} \left\{ (z - z_0)^r \frac{G(z)}{z} \right\}\Big|_{z=z_0}$$

The general formula for finding the coefficients C_j, $j = 1, 2, 3, \ldots, (r - 1)$ is

$$C_j = \frac{1}{j!} \frac{d^j}{dz^j} \left\{ (z - z_0)^r \frac{G(z)}{z} \right\}\Big|_{z=z_0} \tag{2.43}$$

After obtaining the residues and the coefficients, we multiply the expansion by z:

$$G(z) = \frac{C_0 z}{(z - z_0)^r} + \frac{C_1 z}{(z - z_0)^{r-1}} + \cdots + \frac{C_{r-1} z}{(z - z_0)}$$

$$+ \frac{k_1 z}{(z - z_1)} + \frac{k_2 z}{(z - z_2)} + \cdots + \frac{k_m z}{(z - z_m)}$$

Then we find the inverse z transform of each term to get $g(n)$, using the z transform pairs given in Table 2.1. To illustrate this method, we consider the function $G(z)$, which has a simple pole at $z = 1$ and a triple pole at $z = 2$:

$$G(z) = \frac{z(2z^2 - 11z + 12)}{(z - 1)(z - 2)^3} \tag{2.44}$$

$$\frac{G(z)}{z} = \frac{(2z^2 - 11z + 12)}{(z - 1)(z - 2)^3} = \frac{C_0}{(z - 2)^3} + \frac{C_1}{(z - 2)^2} + \frac{C_2}{(z - 2)} + \frac{k}{(z - 1)}$$

$$k = \frac{(2z^2 - 11z + 12)}{(z - 2)^3}\bigg|_{z=1} = -3$$

$$C_0 = \frac{(2z^2 - 11z + 12)}{(z - 1)}\bigg|_{z=2} = -2$$

$$C_1 = \frac{d}{dz}\left(\frac{(2z^2 - 11z + 12)}{(z - 1)}\right)\bigg|_{z=2} = \left\{\frac{2z^2 - 4z - 1}{(z - 1)^2}\right\}\bigg|_{z=2} = -1$$

$$C_2 = \frac{1}{2}\frac{d^2}{dz^2}\left(\frac{(2z^2 - 11z + 12)}{(z - 1)}\right)\bigg|_{z=2} = \frac{1}{2}\frac{d}{dz}\left\{\frac{2z^2 - 4z - 1}{(z - 1)^2}\right\}\bigg|_{z=2} = 3$$

Therefore we have

$$G(z) = \frac{-2z}{(z - 2)^3} + \frac{-z}{(z - 2)^2} + \frac{3z}{(z - 2)} + \frac{-3z}{(z - 1)} \tag{2.45}$$

Now note that the inverse z transform of $az/(z - a)^2$ is easily obtained from Table 2.1, as $na^n u(n)$. We now have to reduce the term $-z/(z - 2)^2$ to $-(\frac{1}{2})2z/(z - 2)^2$ so that its inverse z transform is correctly written as $-(\frac{1}{2})n2^n u(n)$. From the transform pair 6 in Table 2.1, we get the inverse z transform of $z/(z - a)^3$ as $n(n - 1)/2!a^{n-2}u(n)$.

Therefore the inverse z transform of $-2z/(z - 2)^3$ is obtained as

$$\frac{-2n(n - 1)}{2!}(2)^{n-2}u(n) = \frac{-n(n - 1)}{4}(2)^n u(n)$$

Finally, we get the inverse z transform of $G(z)$ as

$$\left[\frac{-n(n - 1)}{4}(2)^n - \frac{n}{2}(2)^n - 3(2)^n - 3\right]u(n)$$

2.3.1   More Applications of z Transform

In this section, we consider the circuit shown in Figure 2.5 and model it by equations in the z domain, instead of the equivalent model given by equations (2.1) in the time domain. This example is chosen to illustrate the analysis of a discrete-time system that has a large number of adders and hence gives rise to a large number of difference equations in the z domain. Writing the z transform

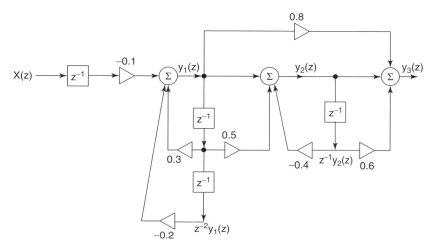

Figure 2.5   A discrete-time system.

for each of the equations in (2.1), we get

$$Y_1(z) = 0.3[z^{-1}Y_1(z) + y_1(-1)] - 0.2[z^{-2}Y_1(z) + z^{-1}y_1(-1) + y_1(-2)]$$
$$- 0.1z^{-1}X(z)$$

$$Y_2(z) = Y_1(z) + 0.5[z^{-1}Y_1(z) + y_1(-1)] - 0.4[z^{-1}Y_2(z) + y_2(-1)]$$

$$Y_3(z) = Y_2(z) + 0.6[z^{-1}Y_2(z) + y_2(-1)] + 0.8Y_1(z) \qquad (2.46)$$

Note that these are linear algebraic equations—three equations in three unknown functions $Y_1(z)$, $Y_2(z)$, and $Y_3(z)$, where the initial states and $X(z)$ are known. After rearranging these equations as follows

$$Y_1(z)[1 - 0.3z^{-1} + 0.2z^{-2}] = 0.3y_1(-1) - 0.2z^{-1}y_1(-1)$$
$$+ y_1(-2) - 0.1z^{-1}X(z)$$

$$Y_1(z)[-1 - 0.5z^{-1}] + Y_2(z)[1 + 0.4z^{-2}] = 0.5y_1(-1) - 0.4y_2(-1)$$

$$0.8Y_1(z) + Y_2(z)[1 + 0.6z^{-1}] - Y_3(z) = -0.6y_2(-1) \qquad (2.47)$$

we express them in a matrix form as

$$\begin{bmatrix} (1 - 0.3z^{-1} + 0.2z^{-2}) & 0 & 0 \\ (-1 - 0.5z^{-1}) & (1 + 0.4z^{-2}) & 0 \\ 0.8 & (1 + 0.6z^{-1}) & -1 \end{bmatrix} \begin{bmatrix} Y_1(z) \\ Y_2(z) \\ Y_3(z) \end{bmatrix}$$

$$= \begin{bmatrix} 0.3y_1(-1) - 0.2z^{-1}y_1(-1) + y_1(-2) - 0.1z^{-1}X(z) \\ 0.5y_1(-1) - 0.4y_2(-1) \\ -0.6y_2(-1) \end{bmatrix} \qquad (2.48)$$

By use of matrix algebra, we can now find any one or all three unknown functions $Y_1(z)$, $Y_2(z)$, and $Y_3(z)$, when the input $X(z)$ is zero—their inverse z transforms yield zero input responses. We can find them when all the initial states are zero—their inverse z transform will yield zero state responses. Of course we can find the total responses $y_1(n)$, $y_2(n)$, and $y_3(n)$, under the given initial states and the input function $x(n)$. This outlines a powerful algebraic method for the analysis of discrete-time systems described by any large number of equations in either the discrete-time domain or the z-transform domain. We use this method to find the zero input response and the zero state response and their sum, which is the total response denoted as $y_1(n)$, $y_2(n)$, and $y_3(n)$.

2.3.2 Natural Response and Forced Response

It is to be pointed out that the total response can also be expressed as the sum of the natural response and forced response of the system. First let us make it clear that the natural response is not the same as the zero input response of the system. The natural response is defined as the component of the total response, which consists of all terms displaying the natural frequencies of the system. Natural frequencies are also known as the "characteristic roots" of the system, eigenvalues of the system determinant, and poles of the transfer function.

A few methods are used to find the natural frequencies of a system. Suppose that the system is described by its single input–output relationship as $a_0 y(n) + a_1 y(n-1) + a_2 y(n-2) + \cdots + a_N y(n-N) = b_0 x(n) + b_1 x(n-1) + \cdots + b_M x(n-M)$.

If we assume the solution to the homogeneous equation to be of the form $y_c(n) = A(c)^n$, and substitute it as well as its delayed sequences, we get the following characteristic equation:

$$A(c)^n [a_0 + a_1(c)^{-1} + a_2(c)^{-2} + \cdots + a_N(c)^{-N}]$$
$$= A(c)^{n-N} [a_0(c)^N + a_1(c)^{N-1} + \cdots + a_{N-1}(c) + a_N] = 0.$$

Let the N roots of the characteristic polynomial

$$[a_0(c)^N + a_1(c)^{N-1} + \cdots + a_{N-1}(c) + a_N]$$

be denoted by (c_1), (c_2), ..., (c_N), which are the natural frequencies. Assuming that all the roots are distinct and separate, the natural response assumes the form

$$y_c(n) = A_1(c_1)^n + A_2(c_2)^n + \cdots + A_N(c_N)^n$$

which in classical literature is known as the *complementary function* or *complementary solution*.

If, however, the characteristic polynomial has a repeated root (c_r) with a multiplicity of R, then the R terms in $y_c(n)$ corresponding to this natural frequency (c_r) are assumed to be of the form

$$[B_0 + B_1 n + B_2 n^2 + \cdots + B_R n^R](c_r)^n$$

Suppose that the system is described by a set of linear difference equations such as (2.47). When we solve for $Y_1(z)$, $Y_2(z)$, or $Y_3(z)$, we get the determinant of the system matrix shown in (2.48) as the denominator in $Y_1(z)$, $Y_2(z)$, and $Y_3(z)$. The roots of this system determinant are the poles of the z transform $Y_1(z)$, $Y_2(z)$, $Y_3(z)$ and appear in the partial fraction expansion for these functions. The inverse z transform of each term in the partial fraction expansion will exhibit the corresponding natural frequency. All terms containing the natural frequencies make up the natural response of the system. The important observation to be made is that terms with these natural frequencies appear in the zero input response as well as the zero state response; hence the amplitudes A_j of the term with the natural frequency (c_j) have to be computed as the sum of terms with the natural frequency (c_j) found in both the zero input and zero state response. It follows, therefore, that the natural response is not the same as the zero input response and the forced response is not the same as the zero state response. Computation of these different components in the total response must be carried out by using the correct definition of these terms.

2.4 SOLVING DIFFERENCE EQUATIONS USING THE CLASSICAL METHOD

Now that we have described the method for finding the complementary function for a system described by an nth linear ordinary difference equation, we discuss the computation of the particular function or particular solution, due to the specified input function. Note that this classical method can be used when there is only one such equation, and it is not very easy when there are many equations describing the given discrete-time system. Also, when the order of the characteristic polynomial or the system determinant is more than 3, finding the zeros of the characteristic polynomial or the system determinant analytically is not possible. We have to use numerical techniques to find these zeros, which are the natural frequencies of the system. If and when we have found the natural frequencies, the natural response can be identified as the function $y_c(n)$ given in the preceding section. Next we have to choose the form of the particular function that depends on the form of the input or the forcing function. Hence it is the forced response, and the sum of the natural response (complementary function) and the forced response (particular function) is the total response. The form of the particular function is chosen as listed in Table 2.2.

We substitute the particular function in the nonhomogeneous difference equation, and by comparing the coefficients on both sides of the resulting

TABLE 2.2   Form of Input Function and Forced Response

	Input or Forcing Function	Particular Function or Forced Response
1	$A(\alpha)^n, \alpha \neq c_1 (i = 1, 2, \ldots)$	$B(\alpha)^n$
2	$A(\alpha)^n, \alpha = c_i$	$[B_0 + B_1 n](\alpha)^n$
3	$A\cos(\omega_0 n + \theta)$	$B\cos(\omega_0 n + \phi)$
4	$\left(\sum_{i=0}^{m} A_i n^i\right)\alpha^n$	$\left(\sum_{i=0}^{m} B_i n^i\right)\alpha^n$

equation, we compute the coefficient B or the coefficients B_i. Next we apply the given initial conditions on the sum of the complementary function and the particular function, in which there are n unknown constants of the complementary function. When we obtain these constants that satisfy the initial conditions, and substitute them, the solution for the total output is complete. Example 2.12 illustrates the classical method of solving a difference equation.

Example 2.12

Solve the linear difference equation given below, using the classical method:

$$y(n) - 0.5y(n - 1) + 0.06y(n - 2) = 2(0.1)^n \tag{2.49}$$

$$y(-1) = 1 \quad \text{and} \quad y(-2) = 0 \tag{2.50}$$

The characteristic polynomial is $z^2 - 0.5z + 0.06 = (z - 0.3)(z - 0.2)$, which has the characteristic roots at $z_1 = 0.3$ and $z_2 = 0.2$. Since these are simple zeros, the complementary function $y_c(n) = A_1(0.3)^n + A_2(0.2)^n$. Since the input $x(n)$ is given as $2(0.1)^n$, we choose from Table 2.2, the particular function y_p to be of the form $y_p(n) = B(0.1)^n$. Thus we substitute $y_p(n - 1) = B(0.1)^{n-1}$ and $y_p(n - 2) = B(0.1)^{n-2}$ and get the following:

$$B(0.1)^n - 0.5B(0.1)^{n-1} + 0.06B(0.1)^{n-2} = 2(0.1)^n$$

$$B(0.1)^n - 0.5(10)B(0.1)^n + 0.06(100)B(0.1)^n = 2(0.1)^n$$

$$[1.0 - 5 + 6]B(0.1)^n = 2(0.1)^n$$

Therefore $B = 1$ and the particular function $y_p(n) = (0.1)^n$. So the total solution is

$$y(n) = y_c(n) + y_p(n)$$

$$= A_1(0.3)^n + A_2(0.2)^n + (0.1)^n$$

When we apply the initial conditions on this total response, we get

$$y(-1) = 3.3333A_1 + 5A_2 + 10 = 1$$

$$y(-2) = 11.111A_1 + 25A_2 + 100 = 0$$

Solving these two equations, we get $A_1 = 9.903$ and $A_2 = -8.4$. So the total response is

$$y(n) = 9.903(0.3)^n - 8.4(0.2)^n + (0.1)^n$$

Example 2.13

Let us reconsider Example 2.10. The zero input response and the zero state response in this example were found to be

$$y_{0i}(n) = [0.376(0.2)^n - 0.088(0.1)^n]u(n)$$

$$y_{0s}(n) = 0.5[-(-0.2)^n + (0.2)^n]u(n) = [0.5(0.2)^n - 0.5(-0.2)^n]u(n)$$

The characteristic polynomial for the system given in Example 2.10 is easily seen as $[1 - 0.3z^{-1} + 0.02z^{-2}]$. After multiplying it by z^2, we find the natural frequencies as the zeros of $[z^2 - 0.3z + 0.02] = [(z - 0.2)(z - 0.1)]$ to be $(c_1) = (0.2)$ and $(c_2) = (0.1)$. Note that the zero input response $y_{0i}(n)$ has a term $0.376(0.2)^n u(n)$, which has the natural frequency equal to (0.2) and the term $-0.088(0.1)^n u(n)$ with the natural frequency of (0.1), while the zero state response $y_{0s}(n)$ also contains the term $0.5(0.2)^n u(n)$ with the natural frequency of (0.2). We also noticed that the pole of $Y_{0s}(z)$ at $z = 0.1$ was canceled by a zero at $z = 0.1$. Therefore there is no term in the zero state response $y_{0s}(n)$ with the natural frequency of (0.1). So the term containing the natural frequency of (0.2) is the sum $0.5(0.2)^n u(n) + 0.376(0.2)^n u(n) = 0.876(0.2)^n u(n)$, whereas the other term with the natural frequency of (0.1) is $-0.088(0.1)^n u(n)$. Consequently, the natural response of the system is $0.876(0.2)^n u(n) - 0.088(0.1)^n u(n)$.

The remaining term $-0.5(-0.2)^n u(n)$ is the forced response with the frequency (-0.2), which is found in the forcing function or the input function $x(n) = (-0.2)^n u(n)$. Thus the total response of the system is now expressed as the sum of its natural response $0.876(0.2)^n u(n) - 0.088(0.1)^n u(n)$ and forced response $-0.5(-0.2)^n u(n)$. We repeat that in the zero state response, there are terms with natural frequencies of the system, besides terms with input frequencies; hence it is erroneous to state that the zero input response is equal to the natural response or that the zero state response is the forced response.

Example 2.14

As another example, let us analyze the discrete-time system model shown in Figure 2.6. Assuming the initial states are zero, we get the equations for the outputs of the two adders as

$$y_1(n) = x(n - 1) - 0.2y_1(n - 1) - 0.4y_1(n - 2)$$

$$y_2(n) = 2y_1(n - 1) - 0.1y_2(n - 1)$$

When a discrete-time system is described by several linear difference equations like the equations above, it is difficult to derive a single-input, single-output

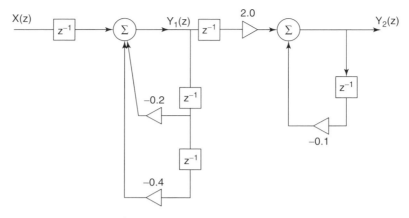

Figure 2.6   Example of a discrete-time system.

equation, and hence solving for output by using the recursive algorithm or the classical method is not possible. However, we can transform the difference equations to their equivalent z-transform equations. They become linear, algebraic equations that can be solved to find the z transform of the output using matrix algebra. The inverse z transform of the output function gives us the final solution in the time domain. So it is the z-transform method that is the more powerful method for time-domain analysis. To illustrate this method, let us transform the two equations above in the time domain to get the following:

$$Y_1(z) = z^{-1}X(z) - 0.2z^{-1}Y_1(z) - 0.4z^{-2}Y_1(z)$$

$$Y_2(z) = 2z^{-1}Y_1(z) - 0.1z^{-1}Y_2(z)$$

Rearranging these equations in the form

$$Y_1(z)[1 + 0.2z^{-1} + 0.4z^{-2}] + Y_2(z)[0] = z^{-1}X(z)$$

$$Y_1(z)[-2z^{-1}] + Y_2(z)[1 + 0.1z^{-1}] = 0$$

and expressing them in a matrix equation as

$$\begin{bmatrix} (1 + 0.2z^{-1} + 0.4z^{-2}) & 0 \\ -2z^{-1} & (1 + 0.1z^{-1}) \end{bmatrix} \begin{bmatrix} Y_1(z) \\ Y_2(z) \end{bmatrix} = \begin{bmatrix} z^{-1}X(z) \\ 0 \end{bmatrix}$$

from Cramer's rule, we find the z transform of the output $y_2(n)$:

$$Y_2(z) = \frac{\begin{Vmatrix} (1 + 0.2z^{-1} + 0.4z^{-2}) & z^{-1}X(z) \\ -2z^{-1} & 0 \end{Vmatrix}}{\begin{Vmatrix} (1 + 0.2z^{-1} + 0.4z^{-2}) & 0 \\ -2z^{-1} & (1 + 0.1z^{-1}) \end{Vmatrix}}$$

$$= \left[\frac{2z^{-2}}{1 + 0.3z^{-1} + 0.42z^{-2} + 0.04z^{-3}} \right] X(z)$$

$$= \left[\frac{2z}{z^3 + 0.3z^2 + 0.42z + 0.04} \right] X(z)$$

When we substitute the z transform of the given input above and find the inverse z transform, we get the output $y_2(n)$.

In this example, the natural frequencies of the system are computed as the zeros of the system determinant

$$\left\| \begin{matrix} (1 + 0.2z^{-1} + 0.4z^{-2}) & 0 \\ -2z^{-1} & (1 + 0.1z^{-1}) \end{matrix} \right\|$$

which is $1 + 0.21z^{-1} + 0.42z^{-2} + 0.04z^{-3} = z^{-3}[z^3 + 0.3z^2 + 0.42z + 0.04]$. It is obvious that the zeros of this determinant are the same as the poles of the transfer function

$$H(z) = \frac{Y_2(z)}{X(z)} = \left[\frac{2z}{z^3 + 0.3z^2 + 0.42z + 0.04} \right]$$

As long as these poles of $H(z)$ are not canceled by its zeros, that is, if there are no common factors between its numerator and the denominator, its inverse z transform will display all three natural frequencies. If some poles of the transfer function are canceled by its zeros, and it is therefore given in its reduced form, we may not be able to identify all the natural frequencies of the system. Therefore the only way to find all the natural frequencies of the system is to look for the zeros of the system determinant or the characteristic polynomial. We see that in this example, the system response does contain three terms in its natural response, corresponding to the three natural frequencies of the system. But if and when there is a cancellation of its poles by some zeros, the natural response components corresponding to the canceled poles will not be present in the zero state response $h(n)$. So we repeat that in some cases, the poles of the transfer function may not display all the natural frequencies of the system.

Note that the inverse z transform of $Y_2(z)$ is computed from $Y_2(z) = H(z)X(z)$ when the initial states are zero. Therefore the response $y_2(n)$ is just the zero state response of the system, for the given input $x(n)$.

2.4.1   Transient Response and Steady-State Response

The total response can also be expressed as the sum of its transient response and steady-state response. But there is again a misconception that the natural response of a system is the same as the transient response, and hence an explanation is given below to clarify this misconception.

The transient response is the component of the total response, which approaches zero as $n \to \infty$, whereas the steady-state response is the part that is left as the nonzero component. All terms with their frequencies that lie within the unit circle of the z plane approach zero as $n \to \infty$, and terms with simple poles that lie on the unit circle contribute to the steady-state response.

For example, let us consider a function

$$Y(z) = \frac{0.5z}{z-1} + \frac{z}{(z-0.2)^2} + \frac{0.4z}{(z+0.4)} + \frac{0.5e^{j40^\circ}z}{(z-e^{j50^\circ})} + \frac{0.5e^{-j40^\circ}z}{(z-e^{-j50^\circ})}$$

The response $y(n)$ is obtained as

$$y(n) = \left[0.5 + 5n(0.2)^n + 0.4(-0.4)^n + \cos(50^\circ n + 40^\circ)\right]u(n)$$

In this example, $Y(z)$ has a double pole at $z = 0.2$ and a simple pole at $z = -0.4$, and the terms $[5n(0.2)^n + 0.4(-0.4)^n]u(n)$ corresponding to these frequencies inside the unit circle constitute the transient response in $y(n)$ since these terms approach zero as $n \to \infty$. The other terms in $Y(z)$ have a pole at $z = 1$ and another one at $z = \pm e^{j50^\circ}$. These are frequencies that lie on the unit circle, and their inverse z transform is $[0.5 + \cos(50^\circ n + 40^\circ)]u(n)$, which remains bounded and is nonzero as $n \to \infty$. It is the steady-state component in $y(n)$, and obviously the sum of the transient response and steady-state response is the total response $y(n)$ of the system. The frequencies at $z = \pm e^{j50^\circ}$ may be the natural frequencies of the system or may be the frequencies of the forcing function; this also applies for the other frequencies that show up as the poles of $Y(z)$. The natural response and forced response are therefore not necessarily the same as the transient response and the steady-state response. Only by using the different definitions of these terms should one determine the different components that add up to the total response. In summary, we have shown how to express the total response as the sum of two terms in the following three different ways:

- The zero state response and the zero input response
- The natural response and the forced response
- The transient response and the steady-state response

2.5 z TRANSFORM METHOD REVISITED

The transfer function $H(z)$ of a system is defined as the ratio of the z transform of the output and the z transform of the input, under the condition that all initial states are zero and there are no other independent sources within the system. For the system described in Figure 2.6, the ratio

$$\frac{Y_2(z)}{X(z)} = \frac{2z}{z^3 + 0.3z^2 + 0.02z + 0.8} = H(z)$$

is the transfer function. So we can also use the relationship $Y_2(z) = H(z)X(z)$. That means that when $X(z) = 1$ and when the initial states are zero, we have

$Y_2(z) = H(z)$, or the output response of a system when it is excited by a unit pulse function $\delta(n)$, under zero initial states, is given by the inverse z transform of $H(z)$. Thus the unit pulse response denoted by $h(n)$ is given by $\mathcal{Z}^{-1}[H(z)]$. So $h(n)$ is the response of the system due to an excitation $\delta(n)$ only. However, from the general relationship $Y_2(z) = H(z)X(z)$, we observe that if we know the transfer function $H(z)$ or if we know the unit pulse response $h(n)$ of the system, we can find the response due to any other input $x(n)$. Therefore $H(z)$ or the unit impulse response $h(n)$ constitutes another model for the system. If we have derived or have been given $H(z)$ or $h(n)$, next we find the z transform $X(z)$ of the given input, and multiply $H(z)$ and $X(z)$ to get $Y(z) = H(z)X(z)$ as the z transform of the output. Then we find the inverse z transform of $Y(z)$ to get the output $y(n)$. For these operations, which are algebraic in nature, finding the output $y(n)$ as the inverse z transform of $H(z)X(z)$ is an efficient method for finding the system output. It is this z-transform method that is used extensively in system analysis, but it depends on the satisfaction of two conditions: (1) we can find the z transform of the input sequence and (2) we know or can find the transfer function of the system under investigation. Students should be aware that in practice, either one or both of these conditions may not be satisfied and other methods of analysis or design of systems are called for. For example, finding a closed-form expression for a discrete-time signal obtained by sampling a speech is not easy. Finding the transfer function of physical systems may not be as easy and straightforward as the one shown in (2.46). In this book, we assume that these conditions are always satisfied.

2.6 CONVOLUTION REVISITED

In a previous section on convolution, we had shown that the output $y(n)$ of a linear, shift-invariant, discrete-time system is obtained by convolution of $x(n)$ and $h(n)$, specifically, $y(n) = x(n) * h(n) = \sum_{k=0}^{\infty} x(k)h(n-k)$.

Since $Y(z) = H(z)X(z) = X(z)H(z)$, we now conclude that convolution sum operation is commutative:

$$x(n) * h(n) = h(n) * x(n)$$

Therefore $y(n) = \sum_{k=0}^{\infty} x(k)h(n-k) = \sum_{k=0}^{\infty} h(k)x(n-k)$.

Another way of proving this result is as follows. Let

$$y(n) = \sum_{k=0}^{\infty} x(k)h(n-k).$$

Then

$$Y(z) = \sum_{n=0}^{\infty} y(n)z^{-n} = \sum_{n=0}^{\infty} \left[\sum_{k=0}^{\infty} x(k)h(n-k) \right] z^{-n}$$

Interchanging the order of summation, we obtain

$$Y(z) = \sum_{k=0}^{\infty} x(k) \sum_{n=0}^{\infty} h(n-k)z^{-n}$$

Let us make a substitution $m = n - k$, and now we have

$$Y(z) = \sum_{k=0}^{\infty} x(k) \sum_{m=-k}^{\infty} h(m)z^{-(m+k)}$$

$$= \sum_{k=0}^{\infty} x(k)z^{-k} \sum_{m=-k}^{\infty} h(m)z^{-m}$$

But $h(m) = 0$ for $-k \le m \le -1$, so that

$$Y(z) = \sum_{k=0}^{\infty} x(k)z^{-k} \sum_{m=0}^{\infty} h(m)z^{-m}$$

$$= X(z)H(z) = H(z)X(z)$$

So we have proved that

1. $x(n) * h(n) = h(n) * x(n)$, which means that the convolution sum is *commutative*. It is now easy to prove that this satisfies the following additional properties, by using the algebraic relationships for the z transforms of the discrete-time sequences.
2. $KX_1(z)X_2(z) = X_1(z)K X_2(z)$. Hence convolution sum operation is *linear*: $Kx_1(n) * x_2(n) = x_1(n) * Kx_2(n)$.
3. $[X_1(z)X_2(z)]X_3(z) = X_1(z)[X_2(z)X_3(z)]$. Hence convolution sum operation is *associative*:

$$[x_1(n) * x_2(n)] * x_3(n) = x_1(n) * [x_2(n) * x_3(n)]$$

4. $X_1(z)[X_2(z)+X_3(z)] = X_1(z)X_2(z)+X_1(z)X_3(z)$. Convolution sum operation is *distributive*:

$$x_1(n) * [x_2(n) + x_3(n)] = x_1(n) * x_2(n) + x_1(n) * x_3(n)$$

It is interesting to make a new interpretation of the convolution sum operation as explained below. Let the z transforms $X(z)$, $H(z)$, and $Y(z)$ be expressed in their power series expansion:

$$X(z) = x_0 + x_1 z^{-1} + x_2 z^{-2} + x_3 z^{-3} + \cdots$$

$$H(z) = h_0 + h_1 z^{-1} + h_2 z^{-2} + h_3 z^{-3} + \cdots$$

$$Y(z) = y_0 + y_1 z^{-1} + y_2 z^{-2} + y_3 z^{-3} + y_4 z^{-4} + y_5 z^{-5} + y_6 z^{-6} + \cdots$$

The coefficients $x_0, x_1, x_2, \ldots$ and $h_0, h_1, h_2, h_3, \ldots$ are the known samples of the input $x(n)$ and the unit sample response $h(n)$. Either one or both sequences may be finite or infinite in length. If we multiply the polynomial or the power series for $X(z)$ and $H(z)$, and group all the terms for the coefficients of z^{-n}, in the polynomial or the power series, we get

$$
\begin{aligned}
X(z)H(z) &= (x_0 + x_1 z^{-1} + x_2 z^{-2} + x_3 z^{-3} + \cdots) \\
&\quad \times (h_0 + h_1 z^{-1} + h_2 z^{-2} + h_3 z^{-3} + \cdots) \\
&= (x_0 h_0) + (x_0 h_1 + x_1 h_0) z^{-1} + (x_0 h_2 + x_1 h_1 + x_2 h_0) z^{-2} \\
&\quad + (x_0 h_3 + x_1 h_2 + x_2 h_1 + x_3 h_0) z^{-3} + \cdots
\end{aligned}
$$

By comparing the coefficients of z^{-n} in $Y(z)$ and those in this expression, we notice that

$$
\begin{aligned}
y_0 &= (x_0 h_0) \\
y_1 &= (x_0 h_1 + x_1 h_0) \\
y_2 &= (x_0 h_2 + x_1 h_1 + x_2 h_0) \\
y_3 &= (x_0 h_3 + x_1 h_2 + x_2 h_1 + x_3 h_0)
\end{aligned}
$$

$$\vdots \tag{2.51}$$

$$
y_n = (x_0 h_n + x_1 h_{n-1} + x_2 h_{n-2} + x_3 h_{n-3} + \cdots + x_n h_0)
$$

$$\vdots$$

These are the same results as given in (2.7), which are obtained by expanding the convolution sum $y_n = \sum_{k=-\infty}^{\infty} x(k)h(n-k)$. We can multiply the polynomial or the power series as $H(z)X(z)$ and identify the coefficients of the resulting polynomial as $y_n = \sum_{k=-\infty}^{\infty} h(k)x(n-k)$. [We can also find the coefficients of $H(z)X(z)$ by computing the convolution of the coefficients of $H(z)$ and $X(z)$.]

Then we would get the following expressions for the coefficients, which are the same as those given in (2.51):

$$
\begin{aligned}
y_0 &= (h_0 x_0) \\
y_1 &= (h_0 x_1 + h_1 x_0) \\
y_2 &= (h_0 x_2 + h_1 x_1 + h_2 x_0) \\
y_3 &= (h_0 x_3 + h_1 x_2 + h_2 x_1 + h_3 x_0)
\end{aligned}
$$

$$\vdots \tag{2.52}$$

$$y_n = (h_0 x_n + h_1 x_{n-1} + h_2 x_{n-2} + h_3 x_{n-3} + \cdots + h_n x_0)$$

.

.

.

One can store the coefficients $h(n)$ and $x(n)$ for a system being investigated, on a personal computer or workstation, do the time reversal off line, delay the time-reversed sequence, and multiply the terms and add the products as explained in Figure 2.4. Computer software has been developed to perform the convolution of two sequences in a very rapid and efficient manner—even when the sequences are very long.[2] But a real hardware that contains the electronic devices such as the delay element, multiplier, and the adder cannot reverse a sequence in real time, but it operates on the incoming samples of the input as follows. When the sample x_0 enters the system at $t = 0$, it launches the sequence $x_0 h(nT)$, which appears at the output; when the next sample x_1 enters the system at $t = T$, it launches the sequence $x_1 h(nT - T)$, which appears at the output, and when the next sample x_2 enters the system, the sequence at the output is $x_2 h(nT - 2T)$, and so on. At any time $t = mT$, the value of the output sample is

$$y(mT) = x_0 h(mT) + x_1 h(mT - T) + x_2 h(mT - 2T) + x_3 h(mT - 3T) + \cdots$$

This is the physical process being implemented by the real hardware; an example of this process was described in Figure 2.2. However, a real hardware can be programmed to store the input data $x(n)$ and $h(n)$ in its memory registers and to implement the convolution sum.

It is important to remember that convolution can be used to find the output, even when the input sequence does not have a z transform, that is, when we cannot use the z-transform approach. This makes convolution a very fundamental operation for signal processing and is one of the most powerful algorithms implemented by the electronic hardware as it does not know what z transform is!

Example 2.15

Suppose that the input sequence is $x(n) = (0.1)^{n^2} u(n)$ and the unit impulse response $h(n) = \{0.2 \quad 0.4 \quad 0.6 \quad 0.8 \quad 1.0\}$.

The z transform $X(z)$ for the infinite sequence $x(n)$ does not have a closed-form expression, whereas it is easy to write the z transform $H(z) = 0.2 + 0.4z^{-1} + 0.6z^{-2} + 0.8z^{-3} + z^{-4}$. Therefore we cannot find $X(z)H(z) = Y(z)$ as a rational function and invert to get $y(n)$. However, the polynomial $H(z)$ can be multiplied by the power series $X(z) = \sum_{n=0}^{\infty} (0.1)^{n^2} z^{-n}$ to get $y(n)$, according

---

[2]Two methods used to improve the efficiency of computation are known as the *overlap-add* and *overlap-save* methods. Students interested in knowing more details of these methods may refer to other books.

to either one of the algorithms $x(n) * h(n)$ or $h(n) * x(n)$. For example

$$y(0) = 0.2$$

$$y(1) = 0.4 + 0.1(0.2)$$

$$y(2) = 0.6 + (0.1)(0.4) + (0.1)^4(0.2)$$

$$y(3) = 0.8 + (0.1)(0.6) + (0.1)^4(0.4) + (0.1)^9(0.2)$$

$$.$$
$$.$$
$$.$$

Recollect that we have obtained two different equations for finding the output due to a given input. They are the convolution sum (2.6) and the linear difference equation (2.2), which are repeated below.

$$y(n) = \sum_{k=0}^{\infty} x(k)h(n-k) \tag{2.53}$$

$$y(n) = -\sum_{k=1}^{N} a(k)y(n-k) + \sum_{k=0}^{M} b(k)x(n-k) \tag{2.54}$$

In Equation (2.53), the product of the input sequence and the current and previous values of the unit impulse response are added, whereas in Equation (2.54) the previous values of the output and present and past values of the input are multiplied by the fixed coefficients and added. The transfer function $H(z)$ for the first case is given by $H(z) = \sum_{n=0}^{\infty} h(n)z^{-n}$, and for the second case, we use the z transform for both sides to get

$$Y(z) = -\sum_{k=1}^{N} a(k)z^{-k}Y(z) + \sum_{k=0}^{M} b(k)z^{-k}X(z)$$

$$Y(z)\left[1 + \sum_{k=1}^{N} a(k)z^{-k}\right] = \sum_{k=0}^{M} b(k)z^{-k}X(z)$$

$$H(z) = \frac{Y(z)}{X(z)} = \frac{\sum_{k=0}^{M} b(k)z^{-k}}{\left[1 + \sum_{k=1}^{N} a(k)z^{-k}\right]}$$

So we can derive the transfer function $H(z)$ from the linear difference equation (2.54), which defines the input–output relationship.

We can also obtain the linear difference equation defining the input–output relationship, from the transfer function $H(z)$, simply by reversing the steps as follows. Given the transfer function $H(z)$, we get $Y(z)[1 + \sum_{k=1}^{N} a(k)z^{-k}] =$

$\sum_{k=0}^{M} b(k)z^{-k} X(z)$. Finding the inverse z transform for each term, we arrive at the input–output relationship for the system, as shown by the following example.

Example 2.16

Let us assume that we are given a transfer function

$$H(z) = \frac{0.2 + 0.1z}{0.8 + 0.6z + 0.2z^2 + z^3}$$

We rewrite it as a transfer function in inverse powers of z, by dividing both the numerator and denominator by z^3 to get

$$H(z^{-1}) = \frac{0.1z^{-2} + 0.2z^{-3}}{1 + 0.2z^{-1} + 0.6z^{-2} + 0.8z^{-3}} = \frac{Y(z^{-1})}{X(z^{-1})}$$

Therefore

$$Y(z^{-1})\left[1 + 0.2z^{-1} + 0.6z^{-2} + 0.8z^{-3}\right] = X(z^{-1})\left[0.1z^{-2} + 0.2z^{-3}\right]$$

By expressing the inverse z transform of each term, we get the linear difference equation or the input–output relationship

$$y(n) + 0.2y(n-1) + 0.6y(n-2) + 0.8y(n-3) = 0.1x(n-2) + 0.2x(n-3)$$

Since the transfer function has been defined and derived by setting the initial conditions to zero , one may assert that from the transfer function we cannot find the response due to initial conditions, but this is not true. In the preceding example, after we have derived the input–output relationship from the given transfer function, we write the corresponding z-transform equation including the terms containing the initial conditions, in the form

$$Y(z) + 0.2[z^{-1}Y(z) + y(-1)] + 0.6[z^{-2}Y(z) + z^{-1}y(-1) + y(-2)]$$
$$+ 0.8[z^{-3}Y(z) + z^{-2}y(-1) + z^{-1}y(-2) + y(-3)]$$
$$= 0.1z^{-2}X(z) + 0.2z^{-3}X(z)$$

We substitute the initial conditions $y(-1)$, $y(-2)$ and $y(-3)$, in these equations and obtain the zero input response as well as the zero state response of the system. Therefore the transfer function $H(z)$ constitutes a complete model of the discrete-time system.

2.7 A MODEL FROM OTHER MODELS

In this section, we review the important concepts and techniques that we have discussed so far. For this purpose, we select one more example below.

Example 2.17

The circuit for a discrete-time system is shown in Figure 2.7. The equations that describe it are.

$$y_1(n) = -x(n) + y_3(n-2)$$
$$y_2(n) = d_2 y_1(n) + x(n-1) - y_3(n-1) \qquad (2.55)$$
$$y_3(n) = x(n-2) + d_1 y_2(n)$$

Let us try to eliminate the internal variables $y_1(n)$ and $y_2(n)$ and get a difference equation relating the output $y_3(n)$ and $x(n)$:

$$y_3(n) = x(n-2) + d_1 \left[d_2 y_1(n) + x(n-1) - y_3(n-1) \right]$$
$$= x(n-2) + d_1 \left[d_2 \{-x(n) + y_3(n-2)\} + x(n-1) - y_3(n-1) \right]$$

The difference equation given below is the input–output relationship obtained by substituting the expression for $y_2(n)$ and $y_1(n)$ successively in the expression for $y_3(n)$:

$$y_3(n) + d_1 y_3(n-1) - d_1 d_2 y_3(n-2) = x(n-2) + d_1 x(n-1) - d_1 d_2 x(n) \qquad (2.56)$$

But remember that in general, it may not be so easy to obtain the single-input, single-output relationship from the many equations written in the time domain, by successive elimination. It is always easier to z-transform Equations (2.55) or write them directly from the circuit diagram, use matrix algebra to obtain the transfer function $H(z)$ and then obtain the difference equation as shown below:

$$Y_1(z) = -X(z) + z^{-2} Y_3(z)$$

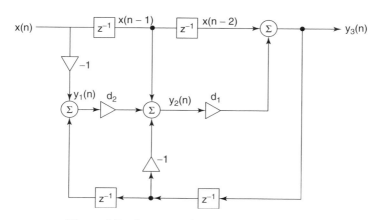

Figure 2.7   Structure of a discrete-time system.

$$Y_2(z) = d_2 Y_1(z) + z^{-1} X(z) - z^{-1} Y_3(z) \qquad (2.57)$$

$$Y_3(z) = z^{-2} X(z) + d_1 Y_2(z)$$

Solving these algebraic equations, by using matrix algebra, we get

$$\frac{Y_3(z)}{X(z)} = H(z) = \frac{z^{-2} + d_1 z^{-1} - d_1 d_2}{1 + d_1 z^{-1} - d_1 d_2 z^{-2}} \qquad (2.58)$$

Now we can derive the difference equation relating the input and output, in the form of (2.56).

Let us choose $d_1 = 0.5$ and $d_2 = -0.5$. Then the preceding transfer function reduces to

$$H(z) = \frac{z^{-2} + 0.5 z^{-1} + 0.25}{1 + 0.5 z^{-1} + 0.25 z^{-2}}$$

$$= \frac{1 + 0.5 z + 0.25 z^2}{z^2 + 0.5 z + 0.25} \qquad (2.59)$$

The unit impulse response $h(n)$ is computed as the inverse z transform of $H(z)$:

$$\frac{H(z)}{z} = 4 + \frac{k_1}{(z + 0.25 - j0.433)} + \frac{k_1^*}{(z + 0.25 + j0.433)}$$

$$= \frac{4}{z} + \frac{(1.9843 e^{j160.9^\circ})}{(z - 0.5 e^{j120^\circ})} + \frac{(1.9843 e^{-j160.9^\circ})}{(z - 0.5 e^{-j120^\circ})}$$

Therefore we have

$$H(z) = 4 + \frac{(1.9843 e^{j160.9^\circ})z}{(z - 0.5 e^{j120^\circ})} + \frac{(1.9843 e^{-j160.9^\circ})z}{(z - 0.5 e^{-j120^\circ})}$$

$$h(n) = 4\delta(n) + 1.9843 \left[e^{160.9^\circ} (0.5 e^{j120^\circ})^n + e^{-160.9^\circ} (0.5 e^{-j120^\circ})^n \right]$$

$$= 4\delta(n) + \left[3.9686(0.5)^n \cos(120^\circ n + 160.9^\circ) \right] u(n) \qquad (2.60)$$

2.7.1 Review of Model Generation

Using the example above, we review the different models derived for the system and show how we can obtain one model from the other models. Recollect the two definitions for a model of the discrete-time system given in Section 2.1:

1. The circuit shown in Figure 2.7 is model 1, in a block diagram representation.
2. The equations in the discrete-time domain is model 2—an example is Equation (2.55).

3. The single difference equation for the input–output relationship is model 3—an example is Equation (2.56).
4. The equations in the z domain is model 4—an example is Equation (2.57).
5. The z transform for model 3 or the transfer function $H(z)$ is model 5—an example is Equation (2.59).
6. The unit impulse response $h(n)$ is model 6—an example is Equation (2.60).

The first model is a circuit diagram, whereas the remaining ones are mathematical models describing the discrete-time system.

In the example worked out above, we have shown how to derive model 2 from model 1, model 3 from model 2, to model 6 from model 5. It is easy to see that we can get model 5 from model 6 and model 3 from model 5. But when we get a model 2 or 4 from model 3 or 4, the result is not unique. We will show that getting a circuit model from model 5 is not unique, either. Yet the flexibility to generate one model from many of the other models makes the analysis of discrete-time systems very versatile and requires that we learn how to choose the most appropriate model to find the output of a system for a given input, with initial states also given. Even when the transfer function of a system is derived under zero initial states, we can get model 3 and then can include the previous values of the output as the initial states and obtain the total output.

Property 2.3: Time Reversal If $X(z)$ is the z transform of a causal sequence $x(n)$, $n \geq 0$, then the z transform of the sequence $x(-n)$ is $X(z^{-1})$. The sequence $x(-n)$ is obtained by reversing the sequence of time, which can be done only by storing the samples of $x(n)$ and generating the sequence $x(-n)$ by reversing the order of the sequence. If a discrete-time sequence or data $x(n)$ is recorded on an audiocassette or a magnetic tape, it has to be played in reverse to generate $x(-n)$. The sequence $x(-n)$ and its z transform $X(z^{-1})$ are extensively used in the simulation and analysis of digital signal processing for the purpose of designing digital signal processors, although the sequence $x(-n)$ cannot be generated in real time, by actual electronic signal processors.

Let $X(z) = \sum_{n=0}^{\infty} x(n)z^{-n}$. Then, $\sum_{n=-\infty}^{0} x(-n)z^n = \sum_{n=0}^{\infty} x(n)z^n = X(z^{-1})$.

Example 2.18

$$\mathcal{Z}[(0.5)^n u(n)] = \sum_{n=0}^{\infty} (0.5)^n z^{-n} = \frac{1}{1 - 0.5z^{-1}} = \frac{z}{z - 0.5} = X(z)$$

Then

$$\mathcal{Z}[(0.5)^{-n} u(-n)] = \sum_{n=-\infty}^{0} (0.5)^{-n} z^n = X(z^{-1}) = \frac{z^{-1}}{z^{-1} - 0.5} = \frac{1}{1 - 0.5z}$$

If

$$F(z) = \frac{0.1 + 0.25z^{-1} + 0.6z^{-2}}{1.0 + 0.4z^{-1} + 0.5z^{-2} + 0.3z^{-3} + 0.08z^{-4}} \qquad (2.61)$$

is the z transform of $f(n)u(n)$, multiplying both the numerator and denominator polynomial by z^4, we can express $F(z)$ in the form

$$F(z) = \frac{0.1z^4 + 0.25z^3 + 0.6z^2}{z^4 + 0.4z^3 + 0.5z^2 + 0.3z + 0.08} \tag{2.62}$$

The z transform of $f(-n)u(-n)$ is obtained by replacing z by z^{-1} in (2.62) for $F(z)$, and therefore the z transform of $f(-n)u(-n)$ is

$$F(z^{-1}) = \frac{0.1z^{-4} + 0.25z^{-3} + 0.6z^{-2}}{z^{-4} + 0.4z^{-3} + 0.5z^{-2} + 0.3z^{-1} + 0.08} \tag{2.63}$$

$$= \frac{0.1 + 0.25z + 0.6z^2}{1.0 + 0.4z + 0.5z^2 + 0.3z^3 + 0.08z^4} \tag{2.64}$$

which is different from either (2.61) or (2.62) for $F(z)$ given above.

Property 2.4: Initial Value   If the z transform of a sequence $x(n)$ is known as $X(z)$, the value of its sample $x(0)$ is called the *initial value* and is easily found from

$$x(0) = \lim_{z \to \infty} X(z)$$

We prove this result by expressing $X(z) = x(0) + x(1)z^{-1} + x(2)z^{-2} + \cdots$ and noting that all terms except the first term $x(0)$ go to zero as $z \to \infty$. If, however, we are interested in finding a few samples $x(0), x(1), x(2), \ldots, x(k)$ at the beginning, and not just the initial value $x(0)$, then we use long division to get a few samples of the quotient as illustrated below.

Consider, for example, the transfer function

$$
\begin{array}{r}
0.1 + 0.21z^{-1} - 0.134z^{-2} - 0.0514z^{-3} + \cdots \\
1.0 + 0.4z^{-1} + 0.5z^{-2} \overline{\smash{\big)}\, 0.1 + 0.25z^{-1} } \\
0.1 + 0.04z^{-1} + 0.05z^{-2} \\
\hline
0.21z^{-1} - 0.05z^{-2} \\
0.21z^{-1} + 0.084z^{-2} + 0.105z^{-3} \\
\hline
-0.134z^{-2} - 0.105z^{-3} \\
-0.134z^{-2} - 0.0536z^{-3} - 0.067z^{-4} \\
\hline
-0.0514z^{-3} + 0.067z^{-4} \\
\ddots
\end{array}
$$

$$\tag{2.65}$$

From the coefficients in the quotient, we see that $x(0) = 0.1$, $x(1) = 0.21$, $x(2) = -0.134$, $x(3) = -0.0514$ and by continuing this procedure, we can get $x(4)$, $x(5)$, ...

The method of finding the few coefficients of the inverse z transform of a transfer function $X(z)$ can be shown to have a recursive formula [1,6] which is given as follows. Let the transfer function $X(z)$ be expressed in the form

$$\frac{\sum_{n=0}^{M} b_n z^{-n}}{\sum_{n=0}^{N} a_n z^{-n}} = x_0 + x_1 z^{-1} + x_2 z^{-2} + x_3 z^{-3} + \cdots \tag{2.66}$$

The samples of the inverse z transform are given by the recursive formula

$$x_n = \frac{1}{a_0} \left[b_n - \sum_{i=1}^{n} x(n-i)a_i \right], \quad n = 1, 2, \ldots. \tag{2.67}$$

where $x_0 = b_0/a_0$.

Property 2.5: Final Value   To find the value of $x(n)$, as $n \to \infty$, we use

$$\lim_{N \to \infty} x(N) = \lim_{z \to 1} (z-1)X(z)$$

when and if $(z-1)X(z)$ has all its poles inside the unit circle.

Proof: Consider $X(z) = x(0) + x(1)z^{-1} + x(2)z^{-2} + \cdots$. If we shift the sequence $x(0), x(1), x(2), \ldots$ to the left (i.e., advance it) by one sample, we have the sequence of values $x(1)$ at $n = 0$, $x(2)$ at $n = 1$, $x(3)$ at $n = 2$, and so on. This sequence is represented as $x(n+1)$, and the unilateral z transform of this sequence is

$$\begin{aligned}
\mathcal{Z}[x(n+1)] &= x(1) + x(2)z^{-1} + x(3)z^{-2} + x(4)z^{-3} + \cdots \\
&= z\left[x(1)z^{-1} + x(2)z^{-2} + x(3)z^{-3} + x(4)z^{-4} + \cdots \right] \\
&= z\left[-x(0) + x(0) + x(1)z^{-1} + x(2)z^{-2} + x(3)z^{-3} \right. \\
&\qquad \left. + x(4)z^{-4} + \cdots \right] \\
&= z\left[-x(0) + X(z) \right]
\end{aligned}$$

Let us express

$$\mathcal{Z}[x(n)] = \lim_{N \to \infty} \sum_{n=0}^{N} x(n)z^{-N} \quad \text{and} \quad \mathcal{Z}[x(n+1)] = \lim_{N \to \infty} \sum_{n=0}^{N} x(n+1)z^{-N}$$

Then

$$\mathcal{Z}[x(n+1)] - \mathcal{Z}[x(n)]$$

$$= \lim_{N \to \infty} \left[\sum_{n=0}^{N} \{x(n+1) - x(n)\} z^{-N} \right] = z\left[-x(0) + X(z)\right] - X(z)$$

$$= [(z-1)X(z) - zx(0)]$$

Letting $z \to 1$, we get

$$\lim_{N \to \infty} \left[\sum_{n=0}^{N} \{x(n+1) - x(n)\} \right] = \lim_{z \to 1} [(z-1)X(z) - zx(0)]$$

$$= \lim_{N \to \infty} [\{x(N+1) - x(0)\}]$$

$$= \lim_{z \to 1} [(z-1)X(z) - x(0)]$$

$$= x(\infty) - x(0)$$

where we have assumed that $\lim_{N \to \infty} [\{x(N+1)\}] = x(\infty)$ has a finite or zero value. This condition is satisfied when $(z-1)X(z)$ has all its poles inside the unit circle. Under this condition, we have proved that

$$x(\infty) = \lim_{z \to 1} [(z-1)X(z)]$$

Property 2.6: Multiplication by r^n If we have $\mathcal{Z}[x(n)u(n)] = X(z)$, then $\mathcal{Z}[r^n x(n)u(n)] = X(z/r)$.

Proof:

$$\mathcal{Z}[r^n x(n)u(n)] = \sum_{n=0}^{\infty} r^n x(n) z^{-n} = \sum_{n=0}^{\infty} x(n) \left(\frac{z}{r}\right)^{-n} = X\left(\frac{z}{r}\right)$$

We have already used this property in deriving a few z transforms shown in Table 2.1. As another example, let $\mathcal{Z}[a^n u(n)] = z/(z-a)$. Then

$$\mathcal{Z}[r^n a^n u(n)] = \frac{\left(\frac{z}{r}\right)}{\left(\frac{z}{r}\right) - a} = \frac{z}{z - ra}$$

A few other properties have already been discussed in this chapter, and Table 2.3 summarizes the properties of z transforms.

TABLE 2.3   Properties of z Transforms

Operation	$x(n)u(n)$	$X(z)$
Addition	$x_1(n) + x_2(n)$	$X_1(z) + X_2(z)$
Scalar multiplication	$Kx(n)$	$KX(z)$
Delay	$x(n-1)u(n-1)$	$z^{-1}X(z) + x(-1)$
	$x(n-2)u(n-2)$	$z^{-2}X(z) + z^{-1}x(-1) + x(-2)$
	$x(n-3)u(n-3)$	$z^{-3}X(z) + z^{-2}x(-1) +$
		$z^{-1}x(-2) + x(-3)$
	$x(n-m)u(n-m)$	$z^{-m}X(z) + \sum_{n=0}^{m-1} x(n-m)z^{-n}$
Time reversal	$x(-n)u(-n)$	$X(z^{-1})$
Multiplication by n	$nx(n)$	$-z\dfrac{dX(z)}{dz}$
Multiplication by r^n	$r^n x(n)$	$X(r^{-1}z)$
Time convolution	$x_1(n) * x_2(n)$	$X_1(z)X_2(z)$
Modulation	$x_1(n)x_2(n)$	$(1/2\pi j) \int_C X_1(z)X_2\left(\dfrac{z}{u}\right)u^{-1}du$
Initial value	$x(0)$	$\lim_{z\to\infty} X(z)$
Final value	$\lim_{N\to\infty} x(N)$	$\lim_{z\to 1}(z-1)X(z)$, when poles of $(z-1)X(z)$ are inside the unit circle

2.8   STABILITY

It is essential that every system designed by an engineer be extremely stable in practical use. Hence we must always analyze the stability of the system under various operating conditions and environments. The basic requirement is that when it is disturbed by a small input, the response of the system will eventually attain a zero or a constant value or at most be bounded within a finite limit. There are definitions for various kinds of stability, but the definition used most often is that the output asymptotically approaches a constant or bounded value when a bounded input is applied. This is known as the *bounded input–bounded output* (BIBO) stability condition. It satisfies the condition when the unit impulse response $h(n)$ satisfies the condition $\sum_{n=0}^{\infty} |h(n)| < M < \infty$. To prove this result, let us assume that $H(z) = z/z - \gamma_i$, where γ_i is the pole of $H(z)$. The unit impulse response is γ_i^n for $n \geq 0$:

$$\sum_{n=0}^{\infty} |h(n)| = \sum_{n=0}^{\infty} |\gamma_i|^n$$

$$= \frac{1}{1 - |\gamma_i|} \quad \text{when} \quad |\gamma_i| < 1$$

When $H(z) = N(z)/\prod_{i=1}^{K}(z - \gamma_i)$, where γ_i are the poles of $H(z)$ such that $|\gamma_i| < 1$ for $i = 1, 2, 3, \ldots, K$, we get

$$\sum_{n=0}^{\infty} |h(n)| \leq \sum_{i=1}^{K} \frac{1}{1 - |\gamma_i|} < \infty$$

Next consider an input $x(n)$ that is bounded in magnitude:

$$|x(n)| < B \text{ for all } n$$

From the convolution property, we get

$$|y(n)| = \left| \sum_{k=-\infty}^{\infty} h(k)x(n - k) \right| \leq \left| \sum_{k=-\infty}^{\infty} |h(k)| \, |x(n - k)| \right|$$

Since $|x(n)| < B$ for all values of n and k, we get

$$|y(n)| \leq B \sum_{k=0}^{\infty} |h(k)| \text{ for all } n$$

Therefore, we conclude that if the impulse response is absolutely summable, that is, if

$$\sum_{n=0}^{\infty} |h(n)| < \infty$$

then the output $y(n)$ is bounded in magnitude when the input $x(n)$ is bounded and the system is BIBO-stable.

There are a few tests that we can use to determine whether the poles of a transfer function

$$H(z) = \frac{b_0 + b_1 z^{-1} + b_2 z^{-2} + \cdots + b_M z^{-M}}{a_0 + a_1 z^{-1} + a_2 z^{-2} + a_3 z^{-3} + a_4 z^{-4} + \cdots + a_N z^{-N}}$$

$$= \frac{b_0 z^N + b_1 z^{N-1} + \cdots + b_M z^{N-M}}{a_0 z^N + a_1 z^{N-1} + a_2 z^{N-2} + \cdots + a_N}$$

are inside the unit circle in the z plane.

2.8.1 Jury–Marden Test

To determine whether the poles are inside the unit circle in the z plane, we choose the Jury–Marden test [1,4] because it has some similarity with the

TABLE 2.4   The Jury–Marden Array of Coefficients

Row	Coefficients			
1	a_0	a_1	$a_2 \ldots a_{N-1}$	a_N
2	a_N	a_{N-1}	$a_{N-2} \ldots a_1$	a_0
3	c_0	c_1	$c_2 \ldots$	c_{N-1}
4	c_{N-1}	c_{N-2}	$\ldots c_1$	c_0
5	d_0	d_1	$d_2 \ldots d_{N-2}$	
6	d_{N-2}	d_{N-3}	$\ldots d_0$	
7				
8				
$\vdots$				
$2N-3$	r_0	r_1	r_2	

Routh–Hurwitz test that the students have learned from an earlier course, and it is easier than the other tests that are available.[3]

We consider the coefficients of the denominator arranged in descending powers of z, specifically $D(z) = a_0 z^N + a_1 z^{N-1} + a_2 z^{N-2} + \cdots + a_N$ where $a_0 > 0$. The first row of the Jury–Marden array lists the coefficients $a_0, a_1, a_2, \ldots, a_N$ (see Table 2.4), and the second row lists these coefficients in the reverse order, $a_N, a_{N-1}, a_{N-2}, \ldots, a_2, a_1, a_0$ So we start with the two rows with elements chosen directly from the given polynomial as follows:

$$
\begin{matrix}
a_0 & a_1 & a_2 \ldots a_{N-1} & a_N \\
a_N & a_{N-1} & a_{N-2} \ldots a_1 & a_0
\end{matrix}
$$

The elements of the third row are computed as second-order determinants according to the following rule:

$$c_i = \begin{vmatrix} a_0 & a_{N-i} \\ a_N & a_i \end{vmatrix} \quad \text{for } i = 0, 1, 2, \ldots, (N-1)$$

For example

$$c_0 = \begin{vmatrix} a_0 & a_N \\ a_N & a_0 \end{vmatrix}$$

$$c_1 = \begin{vmatrix} a_0 & a_{N-1} \\ a_N & a_1 \end{vmatrix}$$

$$c_2 = \begin{vmatrix} a_0 & a_{N-2} \\ a_N & a_2 \end{vmatrix}$$

[3]However, in Chapter 6 we describe the use of a MATLAB function `tf2latc`, which is based on the Schur–Cohn test.

Note that the entries in the first column of the determinants do not change as i changes in computing c_i. The coefficients of the fourth row are the coefficients of the third row in reverse order, as shown in the array below. The elements of the fifth row are computed by

$$d_i = \begin{vmatrix} c_0 & c_{N-1-i} \\ c_{N-1} & c_i \end{vmatrix} \quad \text{for } i = 0, 1, 2, \ldots, (N-2)$$

For example

$$d_0 = \begin{vmatrix} c_0 & c_{N-1} \\ c_{N-1} & c_0 \end{vmatrix}$$

$$d_1 = \begin{vmatrix} c_0 & c_{N-2} \\ c_{N-1} & c_1 \end{vmatrix}$$

$$d_2 = \begin{vmatrix} c_0 & c_{N-3} \\ c_{N-1} & c_2 \end{vmatrix}$$

and the elements of the sixth row are those of the fifth row in reverse order. Note that the number of elements in these rows are one less than those in the two rows above. As we continue this procedure, the number of elements in each successive pair of rows decreases by one, until we construct $(2N-3)$ rows and end up with the last row having three elements. Let us denote them as r_0, r_1, r_2.

The Jury–Marden test states that the denominator polynomial $D(z) = a_0 z^n + a_1 z^{n-1} + \cdots + a_N$ has roots inside the unit circle in the z plane if and only if the following three conditions are satisfied. Note here that we need to express the denominator polynomial in positive powers of z, because we have to evaluate it at $z = \pm 1$ in the first two criteria shown below:

1. $D(1) = D(z)|_{z=1} > 0$
2. $(-1)^N D(-1) > 0$
3. $a_0 > |a_N|$

Also

$$|c_0| > |c_{N-1}|$$
$$|d_0| > |d_{N-2}|$$
$$\vdots$$
$$|r_0| > |r_2|$$

Example 2.19

Let us consider the denominator polynomial $D(z) = 5z^5 + 4z^4 + 3z^3 + z^2 + z + 1$. We construct the Jury–Marden array following the method described above:

Row			Coefficients			
1	5	4	3	1	1	1
2	1	1	1	3	4	5
3	24	19	14	2	1	
4	1	2	14	19	24	
5	575	454	322	29		
6	29	322	454	575		
7	329784	251712	171984			

Check whether the three test criteria are satisfied:

$$D(1) = D(z)|_{z=1} = 15(-1)^5 R(-1) = 3$$

$a_0 = 5;$	$a_5 = 1;$	$a_0 > |a_5|$
$c_0 = 24;$	$c_4 = 1;$	$|c_0| > |c_4|$
$d_0 = 575;$	$d_3 = 29;$	$|d_0| > |d_3|$
$r_0 = 329784;$	$r_2 = 171984;$	$|r_0| > |r_2|$

All criteria are satisfied, and therefore the $D(z)$ above has its five zeros inside the unit circle.

Example 2.20

Now consider another example: $D(z) = 3z^4 + 5z^3 + 3z^2 + 2z + 1$. The Jury–Marden array is constructed as shown below:

JURY–MARDEN ARRAY

Row 1	3	5	3	2	1
2	1	2	3	5	3
3	8	13	6	1	
4	1	6	13	8	
5	63	98	35		

Although we have calculated all the entries in the array, we find that the second criterion is not satisfied because $(-1)^4 D(-1) = 0$. We conclude that there is at least one zero of $D(z)$ that is not *inside* the unit circle. Indeed, it is found that there is one zero at $z = -1.000$. It is a good idea to check at the beginning, whether the first two criteria are satisfied, because if one or both of these two criteria (which are easy to check) fail, there is no need to compute the entries in the rows after the first two rows of the Jury–Marden array.

2.9 SOLUTION USING MATLAB FUNCTIONS

In the previous sections, we have described many models for the discrete-time system and discussed three methods of finding the output of the system when the input sequence is given, along with initial conditions in some cases.

The three methods are

1. Recursive algorithm
2. Convolution sum
3. z-Transform method

In this section, we illustrate the use of MATLAB functions to implement some of the algorithms discussed in the previous sections. At this point it is strongly suggested that the students review the MATLAB primer in Chapter 9 to refresh their understanding of MATLAB, although it is only an introduction to the software.

First let us consider the case of a system described by the linear shift-invariant difference equation

$$y(n) = 0.4y(n-1) + 0.05y(n-2) + x(n)$$

where the initial states are given as $y(-1) = 2$ and $y(-2) = 1.0$. We learned how to find the output of this system for any given input, by using the recursive algorithm. Assuming $x(n) = \delta(n)$ and the initial two states in this example to be zero, we found the unit impulse response $h(n)$. Knowing the unit impulse response, we can find the response when any input is given, by using the convolution algorithm. It was pointed out that convolution algorithm can be used to find only the zero state response since it uses $h(n)$, whereas the recursive algorithm computes the total response due to the given input and the initial states.

Now we use the z transform to convert the difference equation above to get

$$Y(z)[1 - 0.4z^{-1} - 0.05z^{-2}] = 0.4y(-1) + 0.05[z^{-1}y(-1) + y(-2)] + X(z)$$
$$= [0.8 + 0.1z^{-1} + 0.05] + X(z)$$

Therefore

$$Y(z) = \frac{0.85 + 0.1z^{-1}}{[1 - 0.4z^{-1} - 0.05z^{-2}]} + \frac{X(z)}{[1 - 0.4z^{-1} - 0.05z^{-2}]} \qquad (2.68)$$
$$= Y_{0i}(z) + Y_{0s}(z) \qquad (2.69)$$
$$= Y_{0i}(z) + H(z)X(z)$$

We obtain the transfer function $H(z) = 1/[1 - 0.4z^{-1} - 0.05z^{-2}]$ from the given linear difference equation describing the discrete-time system.

But when we decide to use MATLAB functions, note that if the given input is a finite-length sequence $x(n)$, we can easily find the coefficients of the polynomial in the descending powers of z as the entries in the row vector that will be required for defining the polynomial $X(z)$. But if the input $x(n)$ is infinite in length, MATLAB cannot find a closed-form expression for the infinite power series $X(z) = \sum_{n=0}^{\infty} x(n)z^{-n}$; we have to find the numerator and denominator coefficients of $X(z)$.

Example 2.21

As an example, let us assume that $x(n) = [(-0.2)^n + 0.5(0.3)^n]u(n)$. We have to derive its z transform as

$$X(z) = \frac{z}{z + 0.2} + \frac{0.5z}{z - 0.3} \tag{2.70}$$

$$= \frac{1.5z^2 - 0.2z}{z^2 - 0.1z - 0.06} \tag{2.71}$$

$$= \frac{1.5 - 0.2z^{-1}}{1 - 0.1z^{-1} - 0.06z^{-2}} \tag{2.72}$$

Using (2.70), we have

$$Y(z) = \frac{0.85 + 0.1z^{-1}}{[1 - 0.4z^{-1} - 0.05z^{-2}]}$$
$$+ \frac{1.5 - 0.2z^{-1}}{[1 - 0.4z^{-1} - 0.05z^{-2}][1 - 0.1z^{-1} - 0.06z^{-2}]} \tag{2.73}$$

We illustrate the use of MATLAB function `conv` to find the product of two polynomials in the denominator of $Y_{0i}(z)$

```
den2=conv(d1,d2)
```

where the entries for the row vectors `d1` and `d2` are the coefficients in ascending powers of z^{-1} for the two polynomials $[1 - 0.4z^{-1} - 0.05z^{-2}]$ and $[1 - 0.1z^{-1} - 0.06z^{-2}]$.

So we use the following MATLAB statements to find the coefficients of their product by convolution:

```
d1= [1 -0.4 -0.05];
d2= [1 -0.1 -0.06];
den2=conv(d1,d2).
```

MATLAB gives us the vector `den2` = [1.00 -0.50 -0.07 0.029 0.003].

Example 2.22

We introduce three MATLAB functions `residuez`, `impz`, and `filter`, which are very useful in time domain analysis of discrete-time systems:

```
[r,p,k]=residuez(num,den)
```

This function gives us the partial fraction expansion of the z transform

$$Y(z^{-1}) = \frac{B(z^{-1})}{A(z^{-1})} = \frac{b_0 + b_1 z^{-1} + b_2 z^{-2} + \cdots + b_M z^{-M}}{1 + a_1 z^{-1} + a_2 z^{-2} + a_3 z^{-3} + \cdots + b_N z^{-N}} \tag{2.74}$$

in the form

$$k_1 + k_2 z^{-1} + k_2 z^{-2} + \cdots + \frac{r(1)}{1 - p(1)z^{-1}} + \frac{r(2)}{1 - p(2)z^{-1}} + \cdots + \frac{r(N)}{1 - p(N)z^{-1}} \tag{2.75}$$

which can be expressed in a more familiar form:

$$k_1 + k_2 z^{-1} + k_2 z^{-2} + \cdots + \frac{r(1)z}{z - p(1)} + \frac{r(2)z}{z - p(2)} + \cdots + \frac{r(N)z}{z - p(N)}$$

The vector num $= [b_0 \quad b_1 \quad b_2 \ldots b_M]$ and the vector den $= [1 \quad a_1 \quad a_2 \quad a_3 \ldots a_N]$ list the coefficients of the numerator and denominator polynomial in ascending powers of z^{-1}. In the output, the vectors r and p list the residues and corresponding poles, while k is the vector of gain constants which are present when $M > N$. If there is a pole $p(j)$ of multiplicity m, then the partial fraction expansion will show terms in the form

$$\frac{r(j)}{[1 - p(j)z^{-1}]} + \frac{r(j+1)}{[1 - p(j)z^{-1}]^2} + \frac{r(j+2)}{[1 - p(j)z^{-1}]^3} + \cdots + \frac{r(j+m-1)}{[1 - p(j)z^{-1}]^m} \tag{2.76}$$

After we have obtained the partial fraction expansion, we can express the inverse z transform for each of its terms to get $y(n)$ for all $n \geq 0$. This is one method for finding the response of the discrete-time system.

Instead of this procedure, we can use the MATLAB function impz to obtain the response $y(n)$, but this procedure yields the value of the response $y(n)$ for only a finite number of samples $n = 0, 1, 2, 3, \ldots, K$:

```
[y,T]=impz(num,den,K)
```

In this function, the column vector $T = [0 \quad 1 \quad 2 \quad 3 \quad \ldots \quad K]'$ and the column vector y gives us the K samples of the inverse z transform of $Y(z^{-1}) = y(n)$. We can then plot the samples in $y(n)$ using the function stem(T,y). If we use only the command impz(num,den,K), without the output arguments, we will get the plot of $y(n)$ immediately.

The third MATLAB function that we use is filter, which gives us the output $y(n)$ of the system with a transfer function $H(z^{-1})$ when its input is a finite sequence $x(n)$:

```
y =filter(num,den,x)
```

So we enter the samples of the input in the row vector x, besides the vectors for the coefficients of num and den of $H(z^{-1})$. When the vector x is simply 1, the output vector y is obviously the unit sample response $h(n)$. This function even allows us to find the output when initial states are given, if we use

```
[y, F]=filter(num, den, x, I₀)
```

where I_0 is the vector listing the initial conditions and F is the final value. It is important to know that although the transfer function $H(z^{-1})$ is the z transform of the zero state response, the function filter implements the recursive algorithm based on the transfer function and can find the total response when initial states are also given. So this function is a more useful function in signal processing applications.

Example 2.23

Let us consider the z transform of the zero input function found in (2.73):

$$Y_{0i}(z^{-1}) = \frac{0.85 + 0.1z^{-1}}{[1 - 0.4z^{-1} - 0.05z^{-2}]} \tag{2.77}$$

To find the partial fraction expansion, we use the following MATLAB script:

```
num=[0.85 0.1];
den=[1 -0.4 -0.05] ;
[r,p,k]=residuez(num,den)
```

and we get

$$r = \begin{matrix} 0.8750 \\ -0.0250 \end{matrix}$$

$$p = \begin{matrix} 0.5000 \\ -0.1000 \end{matrix}$$

$$k = [\ ]$$

So the partial fraction expansion of $Y_{0i}(z^{-1}) = 0.8750z/(z - 0.5) - 0.025z/(z + 0.1)$. Therefore the zero input response $y_{0i}(n) = [0.8750(0.5)^n - 0.025(-0.1)^n]u(n)$.

Example 2.24

To find the 20 samples of the zero input response $y_{0i}(n)$ directly from (2.77), we use the function impz in the following script:

```
num=[0.85 0.1];
den=[1 -0.4 -0.05];
[y,T]=impz (num,den,20)
```

and we get the samples of output $y_{0i}(n)$ as

$$y = 0.8500$$
$$0.4400$$
$$0.2185$$
$$0.1094$$
$$0.0547$$
$$0.0273$$
$$0.0137$$
$$0.0068$$
$$0.0034$$
$$0.0017$$
$$0.0009$$
$$0.0004$$
$$0.0002$$
$$0.0001$$
$$0.0001$$
$$0.0000$$
$$0.0000$$
$$0.0000$$
$$0.0000$$
$$0.0000$$

Example 2.25

As the second example, we consider the z transform of the zero state response $Y_{0s}(z^{-1})$ in (2.73) and use the following MATLAB program to find the partial fraction expansion:

$$Y_{0s}(z^{-1}) = \frac{1.5 - 0.2z^{-1}}{[1 - 0.4z^{-1} - 0.05z^{-2}][1 - 0.1z^{-1} - 0.06z^{-2}]}$$

```
d1=[1 -0.4 -0.05];
d2=[1 -0.1 -0.06];
den2=conv(d1,d2).
num=[1.5 -0.2];
[r,p.k]=residuez(num,den2);
```

The output from the program is

$$r = \quad 1.6369$$
$$-0.5625$$
$$0.5714$$
$$-0.1458$$
$$p = \quad 0.5000$$
$$0.3000$$
$$-0.2000$$
$$-0.1000$$
$$k = [\,]$$

Therefore the partial fraction expansion is given by

$$Y_{0s}(z^{-1}) = \frac{1.6369z}{z - 0.5} - \frac{0.5625z}{z - 0.3} + \frac{0.5714z}{z + 0.2} - \frac{0.1458z}{z + 0.1} \tag{2.78}$$

and the zero state response

$$y_{0s}(n) = \left[1.6369(0.5)^n - 0.5625(0.3)^n + 0.5714(-0.2)^n - 0.1458(-0.1)^n\right]u(n)$$

Example 2.26

To find the zero state response by using the function `filter`, we choose an input of finite length, say, 10 samples of

$$x(n) = [(-0.2)^n + 0.5(0.3)^n] \text{ for } n = 0, 1, \ldots, 9$$

we use the following script:

```
n=(0:9);
x=[(-0.2).^n+0.5*(0.3).^n];
y=filter(b,a,x)
```

The output $y_{0s}(n)$ is

$\quad$ y = columns 1–7:

$\qquad$ 1.5000   0.5500   0.3800   0.1850   0.0987   0.0496   0.0252

$\quad$ columns 8–10:

$\qquad$ 0.0127   0.0064   0.0032

We compute 10 samples of the response obtained from the partial fraction expansion method:

$$y_{0s}(n) = \left[1.6369(0.5)^n - 0.5625(0.3)^n + 0.5714(-0.2)^n - 0.1458(-0.1)^n\right]$$

for $n = 0, 1, 2, \ldots 9$, using the following program and find that the result agrees with that obtained by the function `filter`:

```
n=(0:9);
y=[1.6369*(0.5).^n-0.5625*(0.3).^n+0.5714*(-0.2).^n-0.1458*(
    -0.1).^n]
```

The output is

$\quad$ y = columns 1–7:

$\qquad$ 1.5000   0.5500   0.3800   0.1850   0.0986   0.0496   0.0252

$\quad$ columns 8–10:

$\qquad$ 0.0127   0.0064   0.0032

Example 2.27

Now let us verify whether the result from the function `impz` also agrees with the results above. We use the script

```
d1=[1 -0.4 -0.05];
d2=[1 -0.1 -0.06];
den2=conv(d1,d2).
num=[1.5 -0.2];
[y,T]=impz(num,den2)
```

We get the following result, which also agrees with the results from the preceding two methods:

$$y = 1.5000$$
$$0.5500$$
$$0.3800$$

0.1850

0.0986

0.0496

0.0252

0.0127

0.0064

0.0032

0.0016

0.0008

0.0004

0.0002

Example 2.28

To find the unit impulse response $h(n)$ using the function `filter`, we identify the transfer function $H(z^{-1})$ in (2.73) as $1/[1 - 0.4z^{-1} - 0.05z^{-2}]$.
From the MATLAB program

```
b=[1];
a=[1 -0.4 -0.05];
[r,p,k]=residuez(b,a),
```

we get

$$r = \quad 0.8333$$
$$0.1667$$
$$p = \quad 0.5000$$
$$-0.1000$$
$$k = [\ ]$$

From this data output, we express the transfer function

$$H(z^{-1}) = \frac{0.8333z}{z - 0.5} - \frac{0.1667z}{z + 0.1}$$

and the unit impulse response of the system is

$$h(n) = \left[0.8333(0.5)^n - 0.1667(-0.1)^n\right]u(n)$$

To find the unit impulse response using the function `impz`, we use

```
b=[1];
a=[1 -0.4 -0.05];
[y,T]=impz(b,a,20)
```

and get

$$
\begin{aligned}
y = \; &1.0000 \\
&0.4000 \\
&0.2100 \\
&0.1040 \\
&0.0521 \\
&0.0260 \\
&0.0130 \\
&0.0065 \\
&0.0033 \\
&0.0016 \\
&0.0008 \\
&0.0004 \\
&0.0002 \\
&0.0001 \\
&0.0001 \\
&0.0000 \\
&0.0000 \\
&0.0000 \\
&0.0000 \\
&0.0000
\end{aligned}
$$

Example 2.29

To get the same result, using the function `filter`, we use `x =[1 zeros(1, 19)]` which creates a vector [1 0 0 0 0 0 0 0 0 0 0 0 0 0 0 0 0 0 0 0]:

```
b=[1 0 0];
a=[1 -0.4 -0.05];
```

```
x=[1 zeros(1,19];
y=filter(b,a,x)
```

The output is

$y = $ columns 1–7:

   1.0000   0.4000   0.2100   0.1040   0.0521   0.0260   0.0130

   columns 8–14:

   0.0065   0.0033   0.0016   0.0008   0.0004   0.0002   0.0001

   columns 15–20:

   0.0001   0.0000   0.0000   0.0000   0.0000   0.0000

Example 2.30

Now we consider the use of the function `residuez` when the transfer function has multiple poles. Let us choose $G(z)$ from (2.44) and (2.45) and also reduce it to a rational function in ascending powers of z^{-1} as shown in (2.80):

$$G(z) = \frac{z(2z^2 - 11z + 12)}{(z-1)(z-2)^3}$$

$$G(z) = \frac{-2z}{(z-2)^3} + \frac{-z}{(z-2)^2} + \frac{3z}{(z-2)} + \frac{-3z}{(z-1)} \qquad (2.79)$$

$$= \frac{2z^3 - 11z^2 + 12z}{z^4 - 7z^3 + 18z^2 - 20z + 8}$$

$$= \frac{2z^{-1} - 11z^{-2} + 12z^{-3}}{1 - 7z^{-1} + 18z^{-2} - 20z^{-3} + 8z^{-4}} \qquad (2.80)$$

The program used to obtain the partial fraction expansion is

```
b=[0 2 -11 12];
a=[1 -7 18 -20 8];
[r,p,k]=residuez(b,a)
```

and the following is the output data we get:

$$r = \quad 3.0000 + 0.0000i$$
$$0.5000 - 0.0000i$$
$$- 0.5000$$
$$- 3.0000$$

$$p = \begin{aligned} & 2.0000 + 0.0000i \\ & 2.0000 - 0.0000i \\ & 2.0000 \\ & 1.0000 \end{aligned}$$

$$k = [\ ]$$

From these data, we construct the partial fraction expansion as

$$G_1(z) = \frac{3}{(1 - 2z^{-1})} + \frac{0.5}{(1 - 2z^{-1})^2} - \frac{0.5}{(1 - 2z^{-1})^3} - \frac{3}{(1 - z^{-1})}$$

which can be reduced to the equivalent expression

$$G(z) = \frac{3z}{(z - 2)} + \frac{0.5z^2}{(z - 2)^2} - \frac{0.5z^3}{(z - 2)^3} - \frac{3z}{(z - 1)}$$

which differs from the partial fraction expansion shown in (2.45) or (2.79). But let us expand

$$\frac{0.5z^2}{(z - 2)^2} = \left[\frac{z}{(z - 2)^2} + \frac{0.5z}{(z - 2)} \right]$$

and

$$-\frac{0.5z^3}{(z - 2)^3} = \frac{-2z}{(z - 2)^3} - \frac{2z}{(z - 2)^2} - \frac{0.5z}{(z - 2)}$$

Substituting these expressions in the preceding form for $G(z)$, we get

$$G(z) = \frac{-2z}{(z - 2)^3} - \frac{z}{(z - 2)^2} + \frac{3z}{(z - 2)} - \frac{3z}{(z - 1)}$$

which is exactly the same as the form obtained in (2.79).

Example 2.31

We can use a MATLAB function deconv(b,a) to find a few values in the inverse z transform of a transfer function, and it is based on the recursive formula given by (2.65). Let us select the transfer function (2.67) to illustrate this function.

%MATLAB program to find a few samples of the inverse z transform

```
b  = [0.1 0.25 0];
a  = [1 0.4 0.5];
n  = 5;
b= [b zeros(1, n-1)];
[x,r]  = deconv(b,a)
```

where

$$x = 0.1000 \quad 0.2100 \quad -0.1340 \quad -0.0514$$

$$r = 0 \quad 0 \quad 0 \quad 0 \quad 0.0876 \quad 0.0257$$

From these output data, we get

$$X(z) = \frac{0.1 + 0.25z^{-1}}{1 + 0.4z^{-1} + 0.5z^{-2}} = 0.1 + 0.21z^{-1} - 0.134z^{-2} - 0.0514z^{-3}$$
$$+ \frac{0.086z^{-4} - 0.0257z^{-5}}{1 + 0.4z^{-1} + 0.5z^{-2}}.$$

Therefore we get $x_0 = 0.1$, $x_1 = 0.21$, $x_2 = -0.134$, $x_3 = -0.0514$, which agrees with the result obtained from long division, by hand calculation. Note that the vector b has to be augmented by $(n - 1)$ zeros in the above program above, as pointed out by Ifeachor and Jervis [6].

Students may find it useful to know the following additional MATLAB functions in their analysis of discrete-time systems, in addition to those used in the examples above presented. Given a vector of zeros, the coefficients of the polynomial having these zeros is obtained by the function `poly`. A complex number entered as a zero must be accompanied by its conjugate so that the coefficients become real. Given the coefficients of the polynomial in a row vector, its zeros are found from the function `roots`. The poles and zeros of a rational function $F(z)$ are plotted in the z plane by the function `zplane`. Two other functions that may be interesting to the students are `tfdata` and `tf`. Typing the commands `help poly`, `help roots`, `help zplane`, `help tfdata`, and `help tf` will display the details for using these commands. A list of all MATLAB functions available in the Signal Processing Toolbox is displayed when the command `help signal` is typed in the command window and is given in the MATLAB primer in Chapter 9. Typing `Type functionname` displays the MATLAB code as well as the help manual for the function where `functionname` is the name of the function. Using the `help` command, students become familiar with and proficient in the use of MATLAB functions that are available for conducting many tasks in the analysis and design of discrete-time systems. It is only by trying as many functions in MATLAB and the Signal Processing Toolbox as possible that one becomes familiar with and proficient in their use, and the books by Ingle and Proakis [9] and Mitra [10] are highly recommended for this purpose, in addition to the functions we have included in this textbook.

2.10   SUMMARY

In this chapter, we have described several ways of modeling linear shift-invariant discrete-time systems, highlighting that we should learn how to obtain the one model from other models that is appropriate for solving a given problem in the time-domain analysis of the system. The recursive algorithm and the convolution sum were described first; then the theory and application of z transform was discussed in detail, for finding the response of the system in the time domain. In this process, many properties of the z transform of discrete-time signals were introduced. Some fundamental concepts and applications that we discussed in this chapter are (1) using a recursive algorithm to find the output in the time domain, due to a given input and initial conditions; (2) finding the output (zero input response, zero state response, natural response, forced response, transient response, steady-state response, etc.) of a discrete-time system from a linear difference equation (or set of equations), using the z transform; (3) finding the transfer function and the unit impulse response of the system; and (4) finding the output due to any input by means of convolution sum. We also showed the method for obtaining the single input–output relation from the transfer function and then solving for the zero input and zero state response by introducing the initial conditions of the output into the linear difference equation.

The concept of stability and a procedure for testing the stability of a discrete-time system was discussed in detail and followed by a description of many MATLAB functions that facilitate the time-domain analysis of such systems. In the next chapter, we consider the analysis of these systems in the frequency domain, which forms the foundation for the design of digital filters.

PROBLEMS

2.1   Given a linear difference equation as shown below, find the output $y(n)$ for $0 \leq n \leq 5$, using the recursive algorithm

$$y(n) = 0.3y(n-1) + y(n-2) + x(n)$$

where $y(-1) = 1.0$, $y(-2) = 0$ and $x(n) = (0.1)^n u(n)$.

2.2   An LTI-DT system is described by the following equation

$$y(n) = 0.3y(n-1) + y(n-2) - 0.2y(n-3) + x(n)$$

where $y(-1) = 1$, $y(-2) = 0$, $y(-3) = 2$, and $x(n) = (0.5)^n u(n)$. Find the output samples $y(n)$ for $0 \leq n \leq 5$, using the recursive algorithm.

2.3   An LTI-DT system is described by the recursive equation

$$y(n) = -0.5y(n-1) + 0.06y(n-2) + x(n)$$

where $y(-1) = 0$; $y(-2) = 0$ and $x(n) = \cos(0.5\pi n)u(n)$. Find the output $y(n)$ for $0 \leq n \leq 5$, using the recursive algorithm.

2.4   An LTI-DT system is described by the difference equation

$$y(n) + 0.5y(n-1) + 0.06y(n-2) = 2x(n) - x(n-1)$$

where $y(-1) = 1.5$, $y(-2) = -1.0$, and $x(n) = (0.2)^n u(n)$. Find the output sample $y(4)$ using the recursive algorithm.

2.5   What are the **(a)** zero state response, **(b)** zero input response, **(c)** natural response, **(d)** forced response, **(e)** transient response, **(f)** steady-state response, and **(g)** unit impulse response of the system described in Problem 2.4?

2.6   Given an input sequence $x(-3) = 0.5$, $x(-2) = 0.1$, $x(-1) = 0.9$, $x(0) = 1.0$, $x(1) = 0.4$, $x(2) = -0.6$, and $h(n) = (0.8)^n u(n)$, find the output $y(n)$ for $-5 \le n \le 5$, using the convolution sum.

2.7   Find the samples of the output $y(n)$ for $0 \le n \le 4$, using the convolution sum $y(n) = x(n) * h(n)$, where $x(n) = \{1.0 \quad 0.5 \quad -0.2 \quad 0.4 \quad 0.4\}$
$\underset{\uparrow}{}$
and $h(n) = (0.8)^n u(n)$.

2.8   Given an input sequence $x(n) = \{-0.5 \quad 0.2 \quad 0.0 \quad 0.2 \quad -0.5\}$ and
$\underset{\uparrow}{}$
the unit impulse response $h(n) = \{0.1 \quad -0.1 \quad 0.1 \quad -0.1\}$, find the
$\underset{\uparrow}{}$
output using the convolution sum, for $0 \le n \le 6$.

2.9   Given an input $x(n) = (0.5)^n u(n)$ and $h(n) = (0.8)^n u(n)$, find the output $y(n)$ for $0 \le n \le 4$, using the convolution sum formula and verify that answer by using the z transforms $X(z)$ and $H(z)$.

2.10   When $x(n) = \{1.0 \quad 0.5 \quad -0.2 \quad 0.4 \quad 0.4\}$, and $h(n) = (0.8)^n u(n)$,
$\underset{\uparrow}{}$
find the output $y(n)$ for $0 \le n \le 6$, using the convolution formula.

2.11   Find the output $y(n)$ using the convolution sum formula, $y(n) = v(n) * x(n)$, where $v(n) = (-1)^n u(n)$ and $x(n) = (-1)^n u(n)$.

2.12   Find the output sample $y(3)$, using the convolution sum formula for $y(n) = x(n) * h(n)$, where $x(n) = e^{0.5n} u(n)$ and $h(n) = e^{-0.5n} u(n)$.

2.13   Find the output $y(5)$, using the convolution sum, when an LTI-DT system defined by $h(n) = (0.5)^n u(n)$ is excited by an input $x(n) = (0.2)^n$; $2 \le n \le \infty$.

2.14   Given $h(n) = (-1)^n u(n)$ and $x(n) = \{0.1 \quad 0.2 \quad 0.3 \quad 0.4 \quad 0.5 \quad 0.6\}$,
$\underset{\uparrow}{}$
find the value of $y(n) = x(n) * h(n)$ at $n = 3$, from the convolution sum.

2.15   An LTI, discrete-time system is defined by its $h(n) = (0.8)^n u(n)$. Find the output $y(n)$ for $n = 1, 2, 3, 4$, when the input is given by $x(n) = \{1.0 \quad 0.5 \quad -0.5 \quad 0.2 \quad 0.2 \quad 0.4 \quad 0.6 \quad 0.8\}$, using the convolution
$\underset{\uparrow}{}$
sum.

2.16   **(a)** Plot the output $y(n)$ for $-3 \leq n \leq 3$, when $x(n) = \{1.0 \quad 0.5 \quad \underset{\uparrow}{0.0}$
$0.5 \quad 1.0\}$ is convolved with $h(n) = (-1)^n u(n)$.

(b) Plot the output $y(n)$ for $-4 \leq n \leq 4$, when $x(n) = (-1)^n u(-n+3)$ is convolved with $h(n) = (-1)^n u(n-2)$.

2.17   The input sequence is $x(n) = \{1.0 \quad -0.5 \quad \underset{\uparrow}{1.0} \quad -0.5 \quad 1.0 \quad -0.5$
$1.0 \quad -0.5\}$ and the unit pulse response $h(n) = \{0.1 \quad 0.2 \quad 0.3\}$. Find the output sample $y(1)$ and $y(4)$, using the convolution sum formula.

2.18   Show that the z transform of $x(n) = (n+1)a^n u(n)$ is $X(z) = z^2/(z-a)^2$

2.19   Find the z transform of the following sequences:
(a) $x_1(n) = (0.1)^{n-3} u(n)$
(b) $x_2(n) = (0.1)^n u(n-3)$
(c) $x_3(n) = e^{-j\pi n} \cos(0.5\pi n) u(n)$

2.20   Find the z transform of the following two functions:
(a) $x_1(n) = n(0.5)^{n-2} u(n)$
(b) $x_2(n) = (0.5)^n u(n-2)$

2.21   Find the z transform of the following two functions:
(a) $x_1(n) = -na^n u(-n-1)$
(b) $x_2(n) = (-1)^n \cos(\frac{\pi}{3}n) u(n)$

2.22   Find the z transform of the following functions:
(a) $x_1(n) = (-1)^n 2^{-n} u(n)$
(b) $x_2(n) = na^n \sin(\omega_0 n) u(n)$
(c) $x_3(n) = (n^2 + n)a^{n-1} u(n-1)$
(d) $x_4(n) = (0.5)^n [u(n) - u(n-5)]$

2.23   Show that

$$X(z) = 1 + z^{-1} + z^{-2} + \cdots + z^{-(N-1)} = \begin{cases} N & \text{when } z = 1 \\ \dfrac{1 - z^{-N}}{1 - z^{-1}} & \text{when } z \neq 1 \end{cases}$$

2.24   Find the z transform of an input $x(n) = (-1)^n [u(n-4) - u(n-8)]$. When an LTI, discrete-time system, defined by its $h(n) = \{1.0 \quad 0.8 \quad 0.6 \quad \underset{\uparrow}{0.4}\}$, is excited by this $x(n)$, what is the output $y(n)$; $n \geq 0$?

2.25   An LTI discrete-time system has an unit pulse response $h(n) = (0.1)^n u(n)$. What is its output $y(n)$ when it is excited by an input $x(n) = (n+1)(0.5)^n u(n)$?

2.26   Find the inverse z transform of $H(z) = 0.3z + 1.0/[(z+0.5)(z+0.2)^2(z+0.3)]$.

2.27 Find the inverse z transform of $H(z) = 0.6z/[(z+0.1)(z-0.5)^3]$.

2.28 Find $f(n)$ from $F(z) = (z+0.3)/z(z+0.5)^2$.

2.29 Find the inverse z transform of $X(z) = z(z+0.5)/(z^2+0.6z+0.5)$.

2.30 Find the inverse z transform of $X(z) = (z+0.2)/[(z+0.5)(z-1)(z-0.1)]$.

2.31 Find the inverse z transform of $Y(z^{-1}) = (z^{-1}+0.4z^{-2})/(1+z^{-1}+0.25z^{-2})$.

2.32 Find the inverse z transforms of the following two transfer functions:

$$H_1(z) = \frac{z+0.6}{(z^2+0.8z+0.5)(z-0.4)}$$

$$H_2(z) = \frac{(z+0.4)(z+1)}{(z-0.5)^2}$$

2.33 Find the inverse z transform of $H(z) = z/[(z+0.5)^2(z^2+0.25)]$.

2.34 Find the inverse z transform of $H(z) = [0.1z(z+1)]/[(z-1)(z^2-z+0.9)]$.

2.35 Find the inverse z transform of $F(z) = (z+0.5)/z(z^2+0.2z+0.02)$.

2.36 Find the inverse z transform of the following two functions:

$$G_1(z) = \frac{1+0.1z^{-1}+0.8z^{-2}}{(1+z^{-1})}$$

$$G_2(z) = \frac{0.2z^2+z+1.0}{(z+0.2)(z+0.1)}$$

2.37 Find the inverse z transform of $X(z) = (3.0+1.35z^{-1}+0.28z^{-2}+0.03z^{-3})/(1.0+0.5z^{-1}+0.06z^{-2})$.

2.38 Show that the inverse z transform of $H(z) = 1/[1-2r(\cos\theta)z^{-1}+r^2z^{-2}]$ is given by

$$h(n) = \frac{r^n \sin(n+1)\theta}{\sin\theta} u(n)$$

2.39 Show that the inverse z transform of $H(z) = z/(z-a)^3$ is given by

$$h(n) = \frac{n(n-1)a^{n-2}}{2} u(n-2)$$

2.40   Given an LTI-DT system described by

$$y(n) + 0.25y(n - 2) = x(n - 6)$$

where $y(-1) = 1$, $y(-2) = 0$, and $x(n) = u(n)$, find the **(a)** zero state response, **(b)** zero input response, **(c)** natural response, **(d)** forced response, **(e)** transient response, and **(f)** steady-state response of the system.

2.41   Given an LTI discrete-time system described by

$$y(n) + 0.2y(n - 1) + 0.2y(n - 2) = 0.5x(n - 1)$$

where $y(-1) = 1$, $y(-2) = -2$, and $x(n) = (-0.3)^n u(n)$, find the **(a)** zero state response, **(b)** zero input response, **(c)** natural response, **(d)** forced response, **(e)** transient response, and **(f)** steady-state response of the system above. What is the unit pulse response $h(n)$ of this system?

2.42   An LTI discrete-time system is described by its difference equation $y(n) - 0.09y(n - 2) = u(n)$, where $y(-1) = 1$ and $y(-2) = 0$. Find its **(a)** zero state response, **(b)** zero input response, **(c)** natural response, **(d)** forced response, **(e)** transient response, and **(f)** steady-state response, and **(g)** the unit pulse response.

2.43   Given an LTI discrete-time system described by

$$y(n) = -0.2y(n - 1) + 0.3y(n - 2) + 0.1y(n - 3) + 0.5x(n) + x(n - 1)$$

where $y(-1) = 1$, $y(-2) = 1$, $y(-3) = 2$, and $x(n) = (0.5)^n u(n)$, find its transfer function $H(z)$.

2.44   Given an LTI discrete-time system described by the difference equation

$$y(n) + 0.6y(n - 1) + 0.25y(n - 2) = x(n) + 0.04x(n - 2)$$

where $y(-1) = 0$, $y(-2) = 0.4$, and $x(n) = (-1)^n u(n)$, find the **(a)** natural response, **(b)** forced response, **(c)** transient response, and **(d)** steady-state response of the system.

2.45   Given an LTI-DT system defined by the difference equation

$$y(n) - 0.5y(n - 1) + 0.06y(n - 2) = u(n)$$

and $y(-1) = y(-2) = 0$, find its **(a)** natural response, **(b)** forced response, **(c)** transient response, and **(d)** steady-state response, when it is excited by $x(n) = u(n)$. What is its unit impulse response $h(n)$?

2.46   Find the total response $y(n)$ of the LTI-DT system defined by the following difference equation

$$y(n) + 0.25y(n - 1) + y(n - 2) = (0.5)^n u(n)$$

where $y(-1) = 1$ and $y(-2) = -1$

2.47   Find the total response $y(n)$ for the LTI system given by $y(n) + 1.4y(n - 1) + 0.44y(n - 2) = 0.5\delta(n - 2)$, where $y(-1) = 1$ and $y(-2) = 0.5$ are the initial states.

2.48   Repeat Problem 2.47 for the system described by the difference equation

$$y(n) + 0.5y(n - 1) + 0.04y(n - 2) = x(n)$$

where $y(-1) = 0$, $y(-2) = 0$, and $x(n) = \{1.0 \; 0.5 - 1.0\}$.
$\uparrow$

2.49   Solve the following difference equation for $y(n), n \geq 0$

$$y(n) + 0.6y(n - 1) - 0.4y(n - 2) = 2x(n - 2)$$

where $y(-1) = 1$, $y(-2) = 0.5$, and $x(n) = (0.1)^n u(n)$.

2.50   Given an LTI, discrete-time system described by the difference equation

$$y(n) + 0.4y(n - 1) + 0.04y(n - 2) = x(n) - 0.5x(n - 1)$$

where $y(-1) = 2$, $y(-2) = 2$, and $x(n) = (e^{-0.1n})u(n)$, find its unit pulse response $h(n)$.

2.51   The difference equation describing an LTI discrete-time system is given below. Solve for $y(n)$

$$y(n) + 0.4y(n - 1) + 0.03y(n - 2) = x(n - 2)$$

where $y(-1) = 1$, $y(-2) = 1$, and $x(n) = (0.5)^n u(n)$.

2.52   Find the total response $y(n)$ of the discrete-time system described by the following difference equation

$$y(n) - 0.3y(n - 1) + 0.02y(n - 2) = x(n) - 0.1x(n - 1)$$

where $y(-1) = 0$, $y(-2) = 0$, and $x(n) = (-0.2)^n u(n)$.

2.53   Repeat Problem 2.52, assuming that the system is described by the difference equation

$$y(n) - 0.04y(n - 2) = x(n - 1)$$

where $y(-1) = -0.2$, $y(-2) = 1.0$, and $x(n) = (0.2)^n u(n)$.

2.54   An LTI discrete-time system is described by the following difference equation

$$y(n) + 0.25y(n - 2) = x(n - 1)$$

where $y(-1) = 0$, $y(-2) = 2$, and $x(n) = (0.5)^n u(n)$. Calculate the **(a)** zero state response, **(b)** zero input response, **(c)** natural response, **(d)** forced response, **(e)** transient response, and **(f)** steady-state response of the system.

2.55   Given an LTI discrete-time system described by the difference equation

$$y(n) - 0.5y(n - 1) = x(n) + 0.5x(n - 1)$$

where $y(-1) = 2$ and $x(n) = (0.5)^n u(n)$, find $y(n)$ and also the unit impulse response $h(n)$.

2.56   Given the transfer function $H(z) = z/[(z - 1)^2(z + 1)]$ of a digital filter, compute and plot the values of $h(n)$ for $n = 0, 1, 2, 3, 4, 5$. What is the value of $\lim_{n \to \infty} h(n)$?

2.57   Given the input $X(z^{-1}) = 1.0 + 0.1z^{-1} + 0.2z^{-2}$ and the transfer function $H(z) = z/[(z - 0.2)(z + 0.3)]$, find the output $y(n)$.

2.58   If the z transform of $y(n) = x(n) * h(n)$ is $X(z)H(z)$, what is the convolution sum formula for $x(-n) * h(n)$? What is the z transform of $x(-n) * h(n)$?

2.59   Given an LTI discrete-time system described by the difference equation

$$y(n) = 4\cos(0.4)y(n - 1) - 4y(n - 2) + x(n)$$

find $h(n)$ and the zero state response when $x(n) = u(n)$.

2.60   Derive the transfer function $H(z)$ of the LTI discrete-time system described by the circuit shown in Figure 2.8.

2.61   Derive the transfer function $H(z)$ of the LTI-DT system described by the circuit given in Figure 2.9. Obtain the difference equation relating the input $x(n)$ to the output $y(n)$.

2.62   Derive the single input–single output relationship as a difference equation for the LTI-DT system shown in Figure 2.10.

2.63   Obtain the transfer function $H(z) = Y_3(z)/X(z)$ as the ratio of polynomials, for the discrete-time system shown in Figure 2.11.

2.64   Write the equations in the z domain to describe the LTI-DT system shown in Figure 2.12. and find the z transform $Y_2(z)$.

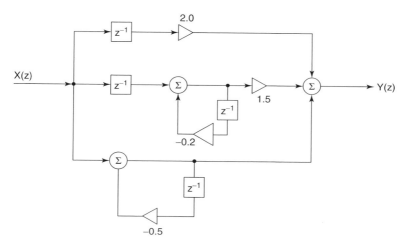

Figure 2.8   Problem 2.60.

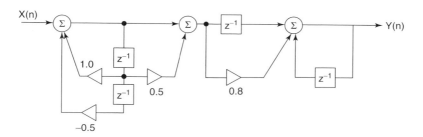

Figure 2.9   Problem 2.61.

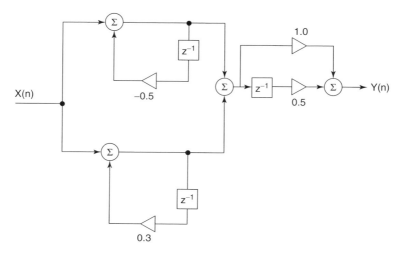

Figure 2.10   Problem 2.62.

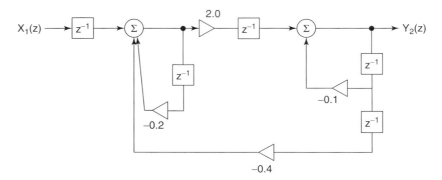

Figure 2.11   Problem 2.63.

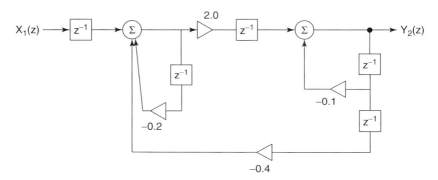

Figure 2.12   Problem 2.64.

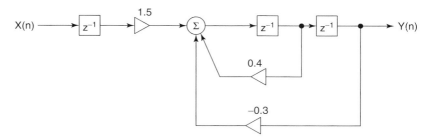

Figure 2.13   Problem 2.65.

2.65   Derive the transfer function $H(z)$ for the circuit shown in Figure 2.13 and find its unit impulse response $h(n)$.

2.66   Write the equations in the z domain to describe the LTI-DT system given in Figure 2.14 and derive the transfer function $H(z) = Y_3(z)/X(z)$, as a ratio of two polynomials.

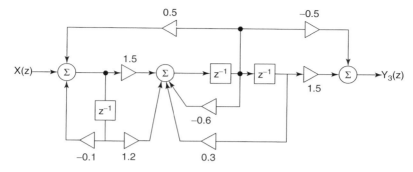

Figure 2.14   Problem 2.66.

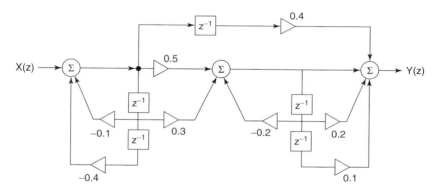

Figure 2.15   Problem 2.67.

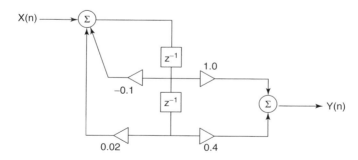

Figure 2.16   Problem 2.68.

2.67   Repeat Problem 2.66 for the circuit given in Figure 2.15.

2.68   Find the unit pulse response of the LTI-DT system shown in Figure 2.16.

2.69   Find the unit pulse response $h(n)$ of the discrete-time system shown in Figure 2.17.

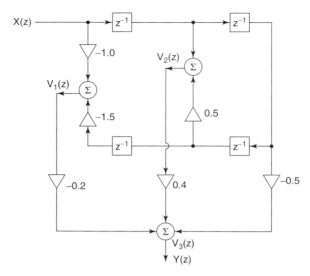

Figure 2.17   Problem 2.69.

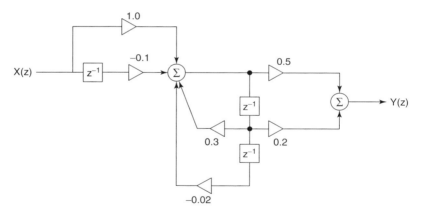

Figure 2.18   Problem 2.70.

2.70   Find the transfer function $H(z)$ of the discrete-time system given in Figure 2.18.

2.71   Derive the transfer function of the digital filter shown in Figure 2.19 and find the samples $h(0), h(1),$ and $h(2)$.

2.72   Derive the transfer function $H(z)$ for the digital filter shown in Figure 2.20 and find its unit impulse response $h(n)$.

2.73   Find the unit sample response $h(n)$ of the discrete-time system shown in Figure 2.21.

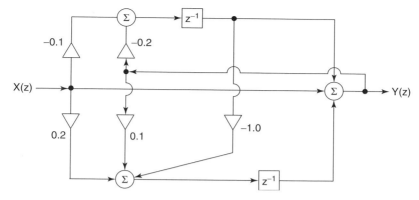

Figure 2.19   Problem 2.71.

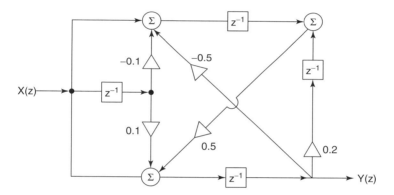

Figure 2.20   Problem 2.72.

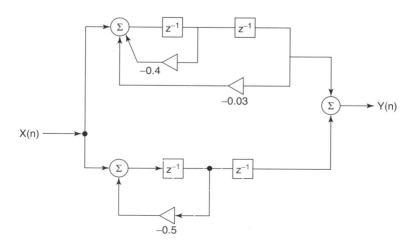

Figure 2.21   Problem 2.73.

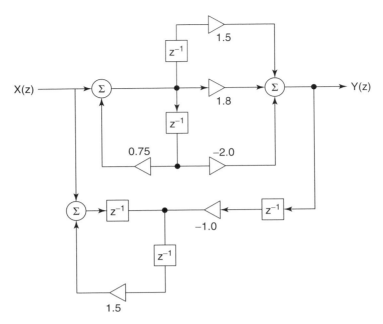

Figure 2.22   Problem 2.74.

2.74   Derive the transfer function $H(z) = Y(z)/X(z)$ for the LTI-DT system shown in Figure 2.22.

2.75   A moving-average filter is defined by $y(n) = 1/N \sum_{k=0}^{N-1} y(n-k)$. Find the transfer function of the filter when $N = 10$.

2.76   In the partial fraction expansion of $H(z) = N(z)/\prod_{k=1}^{K}(z - z_k) = \sum_{k=1}^{K} R_k/(z - z_k)$, which has simple poles at $z = z_k$, show that the residues R_k can be found from the formula $R_k = N(z_k)/D'(z_k)$, where $D'(z) = dD(z)/dz$.

2.77   The transfer function $H(z)$ is expanded into its partial fraction form as shown below:

$$H(z) = \frac{z}{(z - 0.1)(z - 0.2)(1 - 0.3z^{-1})(1 - 0.5z^{-1})}$$

$$= \frac{K_1 z}{(z - 0.1)} + \frac{K_2 z}{(z - 0.2)} + \frac{R_3}{(1 - 0.3z^{-1})} + \frac{R_4}{(1 - 0.5z^{-1})}$$

Find the values of K_1, K_2, R_3, R_4.

2.78   (a) If the transfer function $H(z^{-1})$ is expanded into the form as shown below, find the values of R_1 and R_2:

$$H(z^{-1}) = \frac{1}{(1 - 0.5z^{-1})(1 - 0.1z^{-1})}$$

$$= \frac{R_1}{(1 - 0.5z^{-1})} + \frac{R_2}{(1 - 0.1z^{-1})}$$

(b) If we are given a general transfer function of the form

$$H(z^{-1}) = \frac{N(z^{-1})}{\prod_{n=1}^{N}(1 - a_n z^{-1})} = \sum_{n=1}^{N} \frac{R_n}{(1 - a_n z^{-1})}$$

what is the general method for finding the residues R_n? What is the unit impulse response $h(n)$ of this system?

2.79   **(a)** In the expression given below, find the values of K_1 and K_2 and find $h(n)$:

$$H(z^{-1}) = \frac{1}{(z^{-1} - 0.5)(z^{-1} - 0.1)} = \frac{K_1}{(z^{-1} - 0.5)} + \frac{K_2}{(z^{-1} - 0.1)}$$

(b) If we are given a transfer function of the form

$$H(z^{-1}) = \frac{N(z^{-1})}{\prod_{n=1}^{N}(z^{-1} - a_n)} = \sum_{n=1}^{N} \frac{K_n}{(z^{-1} - a_n)}$$

what is the general expression for finding K_n?

2.80   Given the three difference equations describing an LTI discrete-time system, find $Y_2(z)$

$y_1(n) = 0.1x(n) + 0.2y_1(n - 1) + 0.3y_2(n - 2)$
$y_2(n) = 0.2y_1(n) + 0.4y_3(n)$
$y_3(n) = y_1(n - 1) + y_3(n - 1)$
and $x(n) = \delta(n)$.

2.81   Derive the linear difference equation for the input–output relationship for the discrete-time system described by its transfer function

$$H(z) = \frac{z + 0.1}{z^2 + 0.5z + 0.4}$$

2.82   Derive the linear difference equation for the input–output relationship for the system with its transfer function $H(z)$

$$H(z) = \frac{z(z + 0.4)}{z^3 + 0.2z^2 - 0.4z + 0.05}$$

2.83   Given the transfer function for an LTI-DT system as

$$H(z^{-1}) = \frac{z^{-1}}{(1 + 0.3z^{-1} + 0.02z^{-2})}$$

find the zero state response when the input is a unit step function. What is the zero input response that satisfies the initial conditions $y(-1) = 2$ and $y(-2) = 4$?

2.84   Use the Jury–Marden test to determine whether the discrete-time system defined by the following transfer function is stable:

$$H(z) = \frac{z + 0.5}{z^3 + z^2 + 2z + 5}$$

2.85   Determine whether the polynomial $D(z) = 2 + 2z^{-1} + 1.7z^{-2} + 0.6z^{-3} + 0.1z^{-4}$ has all four zeros inside the unit circle $|z| = 1$, using the Jury–Marden test.

2.86   Determine whether all the zeros of the poiynomial

$$Q(z) = 2 + 5z + 8z^2 + 7z^3 + 2z^4$$

are inside the unit circle $|z| = 1$, using the Jury–Marden test.

2.87   Determine whether the three zeros of the polynomial

$$P(z) = z^3 + 2z^2 + 4z + 6$$

are inside the unit circle $|z| = 1$, using the Jury–Marden test.

2.88   Apply the Jury–Marden test to determine whether the polynomial has its zeros inside the unit circle in the z plane:

$$R(z) = 1 - 1.5z^{-1} - 0.5z^{-2} + z^{-3}.$$

MATLAB Problems

2.89   Find the roots of the following two polynomials:

$$N_1(z) = 1 - 0.7z^{-1} +)0.1725z^{-2} + 0.1745z^{-3} - 0.4425z^{-4}$$

$$D_1(z) = 1 + 0.8z^{-1}0.8775z^{-2} + 0.4333z^{-3} - 0.1808z^{-4} - 0.6639z^{-5}$$

2.90   Plot the poles and zeros of the transfer function $H_1(z) = N_1(z)/D_1(z)$, where $N_1(z)$ and $D_1(Z)$ are the polynomials given above.

2.91   Find the polynomials that have the zeros given below and also the product of the two polynomials $N_2(z)D_2(z)$:

$$\text{Zeros of } N_2(z) : -0.2 \quad 0.3 + j0.4 \quad 0.3 - j0.4 \quad 0.5$$

$$\text{Zeros of } D_2(z) : 0.4 \quad 0.4 \quad 0.2 + j0.2 \quad 0.0 - j0.2$$

2.92   Plot the poles and zeros of $H_2(z) = N_2(z)/D_2(z)$ in the z plane.

2.93   Find the values of R_1, R_2, and R_3 in the expansion of the transfer function $G(z)$, using the MATLAB function `residuez`:

$$G(z) = \frac{(1+0.6z)}{(z-0.8)(z+0.5)^2} = \frac{R_1z}{(z-0.8)} + \frac{R_2z}{(z+0.5)^2} + \frac{R_3z}{(z+0.5)}$$

2.94   Find the values of K_1, K_2, K_3, K_4, K_5 in the expansion of the following transfer functions, using the MATLAB function `residuez`:

$$H_1(z) = \frac{(z-0.3)}{(z-0.2)^3(z+0.4)(z+0.5)}$$

$$= \frac{K_1z}{(z-0.2)^3} + \frac{K_2z}{(z-0.2)^2} + \frac{K_3z}{(z-0.2)} + \frac{K_4z}{(z+0.4)} + \frac{K_5z}{(z+0.5)}$$

$$H_2(z) = \frac{(z)^2}{(z+0.5)^2(z+0.1)^2(z-0.2)}$$

$$= \frac{K_1z}{(z+0.5)^2} + \frac{K_2z}{(z+0.5)} + \frac{K_3z}{(z+0.1)^2} + \frac{K_4z}{(z+0.1)} + \frac{K_5z}{(z-0.2)}$$

2.95   Plot the magnitude, phase, and group delay of the transfer function $H_1(z^{-1})$ given below:

$$H_1(z^{-1}) = \frac{0.20 - 0.45z^{-1}}{1 - 1.3z^{-1} + 0.75z^{-2}}$$

$$+ \frac{2.1 + 1.45z^{-1}}{1 - 1.07z^{-1} + 0.30z^{-2}} + \frac{1.8 - 0.60z^{-1}}{1 - z^{-1} + 0.25z^{-2}}$$

2.96   Given $H_2(z) = (1 - z^{-1})/(1 - 0.9z^{-1})$, plot the magnitude of $H_3(z) = H_2(ze^{j1.5})H_2(ze^{-j1.5})$ and the magnitude of $H_4(z) = H_2(ze^{j1.5}) + H_2(ze^{-j1.5})$.

2.97   Find the partial fraction expansion of the following two transfer functions and evaluate their unit pulse response for $0 \le n \le 10$:

$$H_1(z) = \frac{z(z-0.5)}{(z-0.8)(z-+0.6)}$$

$$H_2(z) = \frac{(z-0.6)}{(z+0.6)(z^2+0.8z+0.9)}$$

2.98   Repeat Problem 2.97 with $H_3(z)$ as follows:

$$H_3(z) = \frac{(z - 0.5)}{(z + 0.4)(z + 0.2)^2}$$

2.99   Find the output $y_1(n)$, $y_2(n)$, and $y_3(n)$ for $0 \leq n \leq 15$ of the LTI-DT systems defined by the preceding transfer functions $H_1(z)$, $H_2(z)$, and $H_3(z)$, respectively, assuming that they are excited by an input sequence $x(n) = \{0.5 \quad 0.2 \quad -0.3 \quad 0.1\}$.

Write your code using the MATLAB function `filter`, and submit it with the computer output.

2.100   An LTI-DT system is described by the following difference equation

$$y(n) + 3y(n - 1) + 2y(n - 2) + y(n - 3) = x(n) + 3x(n - 2)$$

where $y(-1) = 1$, $y(-2) = 2$, $y(-3) = 1$, and $x(n) = (0.5)^n u(n)$. Find the total response $y(n)$ for $0 \leq n \leq 20$ and plot $y(n)$.

2.101   Find the pulse responses $x_1(n)$ of $X_1(z)$, $h_2(n)$ of $H_2(z)$, and $y_3(n)$ of $Y_3(z) = X_1(z)H_2(z)$. Convolve the first 9 samples of $x_1(n)$ with the 9 samples of $h_2(n)$ and compare the result with the first 9 samples of $y_3(n)$:

$$X_1(z) = \frac{z}{(z + 0.2)(z + 0.5)}$$

$$H_2(z) = \frac{(z + 0.2)}{z(z + 0.1)}$$

REFERENCES

1. E. I. Jury, *Theory and Applications of the z-Transform Method*, Wiley, 1964.
2. S. K. Mitra, *Digital Signal Processing—A Computer-Based Approach*, McGraw-Hill, 2001.
3. B. P. Lathi, *Signal Processing and Linear Systems*, Berkeley Cambridge Press, 1998.
4. A. Antoniou, *Digital Filters, Analysis, Design and Applications*, McGraw-Hill, 1993.
5. A. V. Oppenheim and R. W. Schafer, *Discrete-Time Signal Processing*, Prentice-Hall, 1989.
6. E. C. Ifeachor and B. W. Jervis, *Digital Signal Processing, A Practical Approach*, Prentice-Hall, 2002.
7. S. K. Mitra and J. F. Kaiser, eds., *Handbook for Digital Signal Processing*, Wiley-Interscience, 1993.
8. B. A. Shenoi, *Magnitude and Delay Approximation of 1-D and 2-D Digital Filters*, Springer-Verlag, 1999.

9. V. K. Ingle and J. G. Proakis, *Digital Signal Processing Using MATLAB$^{(R)}$ V.4*, PWS Publishing, 1997.

10. S. K. Mitra, *Digital Signal Processing Laboratory Using MATLAB*, McGraw-Hill, 1999.

11. J. G. Proakis and D. G. Manolakis, *Digital Signal Processing*, Prentice-Hall, 1996.

CHAPTER 3

Frequency-Domain Analysis

3.1 INTRODUCTION

In the previous chapter, we derived the definition for the z transform of a discrete-time signal by impulse-sampling a continuous-time signal $x_a(t)$ with a sampling period T and using the transformation $z = e^{sT}$. The signal $x_a(t)$ has another equivalent representation in the form of its Fourier transform $X(j\omega)$. It contains the same amount of information as $x_a(t)$ because we can obtain $x_a(t)$ from $X(j\omega)$ as the inverse Fourier transform of $X(j\omega)$. When the signal $x_a(t)$ is sampled with a sampling period T, to generate the discrete-time signal represented by $\sum_{k=0}^{\infty} x_a(kT)\delta(nT - kT)$, the following questions need to be answered:

Is there an equivalent representation for the discrete-time signal in the frequency domain?

Does it contain the same amount of information as that found in $x_a(t)$? If so, how do we reconstruct $x_a(t)$ from its sample values $x_a(nT)$?

Does the Fourier transform represent the frequency response of the system when the unit impulse response $h(t)$ of the continuous-time system is sampled? Can we choose any value for the sampling period, or is there a limit that is determined by the input signal or any other considerations?

We address these questions in this chapter, arrive at the definition for the discrete-time Fourier transform (DTFT) of the discrete-time system, and describe its properties and applications. In the second half of the chapter, we discuss another transform known as the *discrete-time Fourier series* (DTFS) for periodic, discrete-time signals. There is a third transform called *discrete Fourier transform* (DFT), which is simply a part of the DTFS, and we discuss its properties as well as its applications in signal processing. The use of MATLAB to solve many of the problems or to implement the algorithms will be discussed at the end of the chapter.

3.2 THEORY OF SAMPLING

Let us first choose a continuous-time (analog) function $x_a(t)$ that can be represented by its Fourier transform $X_a(j\Omega)$[1]

$$X_a(j\Omega) = \int_{-\infty}^{\infty} x_a(t)e^{-j\Omega t}\,dt \tag{3.1}$$

whereas the inverse Fourier transform of $X_a(j\Omega)$ is given by[2]

$$x_a(t) = \frac{1}{2\pi} \int_{-\infty}^{\infty} X_a(j\Omega)e^{j\Omega t}\,d\Omega \tag{3.2}$$

Now we generate a discrete-time sequence $x(nT)$ by sampling $x_a(t)$ with a sampling period T. So we have $x(nT) = x_a(t)|_{t=nT}$, and substituting $t = nT$ in (3.2), we can write

$$x_a(nT) = x(nT) = \frac{1}{2\pi} \int_{-\infty}^{\infty} X_a(j\Omega)e^{j\Omega nT}\,d\Omega \tag{3.3}$$

The z transform of this discrete-time sequence is[3]

$$X(z) = \sum_{n=-\infty}^{\infty} x(nT)z^{-n} \tag{3.4}$$

and evaluating it on the unit circle in the z plane; thus, when $z = e^{j\omega T}$, we get

$$X(e^{j\omega T}) = \sum_{n=-\infty}^{\infty} x(nT)e^{-j\omega nT} \tag{3.5}$$

Next we consider $h(nT)$ as the unit impulse response of a linear, time-invariant, discrete-time system and the input $x(nT)$ to the system as $e^{j\omega nT}$. Then the output $y(nT)$ is obtained by convolution as follows:

$$y(nT) = \sum_{k=-\infty}^{\infty} e^{j\omega(nT-kT)}h(kT)$$

$$= e^{j\omega nT} \sum_{k=-\infty}^{\infty} e^{-j\omega kT}h(kT) = e^{j\omega nT} \sum_{k=-\infty}^{\infty} h(kT)e^{-j\omega kT} \tag{3.6}$$

---

[1]The material in this section is adapted from a section with the same heading, in the author's book *Magnitude and Delay Approximation of 1-D and 2-D Digital Filters* [1], with permission from the publisher, Springer-Verlag.

[2]We have chosen Ω (measured in radians per second) to denote the frequency variable of an analog function in this section and will choose the same symbol to represent the frequency to represent the frequency response of a lowpass, normalized, prototype analog filter in Chapter 5.

[3]Here we have used the bilateral z transform of the DT sequence, since we have assumed that it is defined for $-\infty < n < \infty$ in general. But the theory of bilateral z transform is not discussed in this book.

Note that the signal $e^{j\omega nT}$ is assumed to have values for $-\infty < n < \infty$ in general, whereas $h(kT)$ is a causal sequence: $h(kT) = 0$ for $-\infty < k < 0$. Hence the summation $\sum_{k=-\infty}^{\infty} h(kT)e^{-j\omega kT}$ in (3.6) can be replaced by $\sum_{k=0}^{\infty} h(kT)e^{-j\omega kT}$. It is denoted as $H(e^{j\omega T})$ and is a complex-valued function of ω, having a magnitude response $|H(e^{j\omega T})|$ and phase response $\theta(e^{j\omega T})$. Thus we have the following result

$$y(nT) = e^{j\omega nT}\left|H(e^{j\omega T})\right|e^{j\theta(e^{j\omega T})} \tag{3.7}$$

which shows that when the input is a complex exponential function $e^{j\omega nT}$, the magnitude of the output $y(nT)$ is $|H(e^{j\omega T})|$ and the phase of the output $y(nT)$ is $(\omega nT + \theta)$. If we choose a sinusoidal input $x(nT) = \text{Re}(Ae^{j\omega nT}) = A\cos(\omega nT)$, then the output $y(nT)$ is also a sinusoidal function given by $y(nT) = A\left|H(e^{j\omega T})\right|\cos(\omega nt + \theta)$. Therefore we multiply the amplitude of the sinusoidal input by $|H(e^{j\omega T})|$ and increase the phase by $\theta(e^{j\omega T})$ to get the amplitude and phase of the sinusoidal output. For the reason stated above, $H(e^{j\omega T})$ is called the *frequency response* of the discrete-time system. We use a similar expression $\sum_{k=-\infty}^{\infty} x(kT)e^{-j\omega kT} = X(e^{j\omega T})$ for the frequency response of any input signal $x(kT)$ and call it the *discrete-time Fourier transform* (DTFT) of $x(kT)$.

To find a relationship between the Fourier transform $X_a(j\Omega)$ of the continuous-time function $x_a(t)$ and the Fourier transform $X(e^{j\omega T})$ of the discrete-time sequence, we start with the observation that the DTFT $X(e^{j\omega T})$ is a periodic function of ω with a period $\omega_s = 2\pi/T$, namely, $X(e^{j\omega T + jr\omega_s T}) = X(e^{j\omega T + jr2\pi}) = X(e^{j\omega T})$, where r is any integer. It can therefore be expressed in a Fourier series form

$$X(e^{j\omega T}) = \sum_{n=-\infty}^{\infty} C_n e^{-j\omega nT} \tag{3.8}$$

where the coefficients C_n are given by

$$C_n = \frac{T}{2\pi} \int_{-(\pi/T)}^{\pi/T} X(e^{j\omega T})e^{j\omega T}\,d\omega \tag{3.9}$$

By comparing (3.5) with (3.8), we conclude that $x(nT)$ are the Fourier series coefficients of the periodic function $X(e^{j\omega T})$, and these coefficients are evaluated from

$$C_n = x(nT) = \frac{T}{2\pi} \int_{-(\pi/T)}^{\pi/T} X(e^{j\omega T})e^{j\omega nT}\,d\omega \tag{3.10}$$

Therefore

$$X(e^{j\omega T}) = \sum_{n=-\infty}^{\infty} x(nT)e^{-j\omega nT} \tag{3.11}$$

Let us express (3.3), which involves integration from $\Omega = -\infty$ to $\Omega = \infty$ as the sum of integrals over successive intervals each equal to one period $2\pi/T = \omega_s$:

$$x(nT) = \frac{1}{2\pi} \sum_{r=-\infty}^{\infty} \int_{\frac{(2r-1)\pi}{T}}^{\frac{(2r+1)\pi}{T}} X_a(j\Omega) e^{j\Omega nT} \, d\Omega \tag{3.12}$$

However, each term in this summation can be reduced to an integral over the range $-(\pi/T)$ to π/T by a change of variable from Ω to $\Omega + 2\pi r/T$, to get

$$x(nT) = \frac{T}{2\pi} \sum_{r=-\infty}^{\infty} \frac{1}{T} \int_{-(\pi/T)}^{\pi/T} X_a\left(j\Omega + j\frac{2\pi r}{T}\right) e^{j\Omega nT} e^{j2\pi rn} \, d\Omega \tag{3.13}$$

Note that $e^{j2\pi rn} = 1$ for all integer values of r and n. By changing the order of summation and integration, this equation can be reduced to

$$x(nT) = \frac{T}{2\pi} \int_{-(\pi/T)}^{\pi/T} \left[\frac{1}{T} \sum_{r=-\infty}^{\infty} X_a\left(j\Omega + j\frac{2\pi r}{T}\right) \right] e^{j\Omega nT} \, d\Omega \tag{3.14}$$

Without loss of generality, we change the frequency variable Ω to ω, thereby getting

$$x(nT) = \frac{T}{2\pi} \int_{-(\pi/T)}^{\pi/T} \left[\frac{1}{T} \sum_{r=-\infty}^{\infty} X_a\left(j\omega + j\frac{2\pi r}{T}\right) \right] e^{j\omega nT} \, d\omega \tag{3.15}$$

Comparing (3.10) with (3.15), we get the desired relationship:

$$X(e^{j\omega T}) = \left[\frac{1}{T} \sum_{r=-\infty}^{\infty} X_a\left(j\omega + j\frac{2\pi r}{T}\right) \right] \tag{3.16}$$

This shows that the discrete-time Fourier transform (DTFT) of the sequence $x(nT)$ generated by sampling the continuous-time signal $x_a(t)$ with a sampling period T is obtained by a periodic duplication of the Fourier transform $X_a(j\omega)$ of $x_a(t)$ with a period $2\pi/T = \omega_s$ and scaled by T. To illustrate this result, a typical analog signal $x_a(t)$ and the magnitude of its Fourier transform are sketched in Figure 3.1. In Figure 3.2a the discrete-time sequence generated by sampling $x_a(t)$ is shown, and in Figure 3.2b, the magnitude of a few terms of (3.16) as well as the magnitude $|X(e^{j\omega T})|$ are shown.

Ideally the Fourier transform of $x_a(t)$ approaches zero only as the frequency approaches ∞. Hence it is seen that, in general, when $X_a(j\omega)/T$ is duplicated and added as shown in Figure 3.2b, there is an overlap of the frequency responses at all frequencies. The frequency responses of the individual terms in (3.16) add up, giving the actual response as shown by the curve for $|X(e^{j\omega})|$. [We have

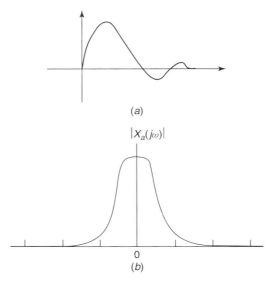

Figure 3.1   An analog signal $x_a(t)$ and the magnitude of its Fourier transform $X(j\omega)$.

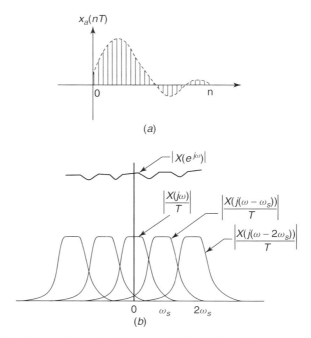

Figure 3.2   The discrete-time signal $x_a(nT)$ obtained from the analog signal $x_a(t)$ and the discrete-time Fourier transform $H(e^{j\omega})$.

disregarded the effect of phase in adding the duplicates of $X(j\omega)$.] Because of this overlapping effect, more commonly known as "aliasing," there is no way of retrieving $X(j\omega)$ from $X(e^{j\omega})$ by any linear operation; in other words, we have lost the information contained in the analog function $x_a(t)$ when we sample it. Aliasing of the Fourier transform can be avoided if and only if (1) the function $x_a(t)$ is assumed to be bandlimited—that is, if it is a function such that its Fourier transform $X_a(j\omega) \equiv 0$ for $|\omega| > \omega_b$; and (2) the sampling period T is chosen such that $\omega_s = 2\pi/T > 2\omega_b$. When the analog signal $x_b(t)$ is bandlimited as shown in Figure 3.3b and is sampled at a frequency $\omega_s \geq 2\omega_b$, the resulting discrete-time signal $x_b(nT)$ and its Fourier transform $X(e^{j\omega})$ are as shown in Figure 3.4a,b, respectively.

If this bandlimited signal $x_b(nT)$ is passed through an ideal lowpass filter with a bandwidth of $\omega_s/2$, the output will be a signal with a Fourier transform equal to $X(e^{j\omega T})H_{lp}(j\omega) = X_b(j\omega)/T$. The unit impulse response of the ideal lowpass filter with a bandwidth ω_b obtained as the inverse Fourier transform of $H_{lp}(j\omega)$ is given by

$$h_{lp}(t) = \frac{1}{2\pi} \int_{-\infty}^{\infty} H_{lp}(j\omega)e^{j\omega t}\,d\omega$$

$$= \frac{1}{2\pi} \int_{-\frac{\omega_s}{2}}^{\frac{\omega_s}{2}} Te^{j\omega t}\,d\omega \tag{3.17}$$

$$= \frac{\sin\left(\dfrac{\omega_s t}{2}\right)}{\left(\dfrac{\omega_s t}{2}\right)} = \frac{\sin\left(\dfrac{\pi t}{T}\right)}{\left(\dfrac{\pi t}{T}\right)} \tag{3.18}$$

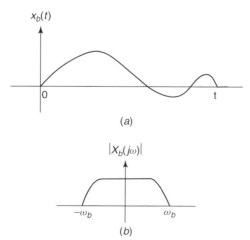

(a)

(b)

Figure 3.3   A bandlimited analog signal and the magnitude of its Fourier transform.

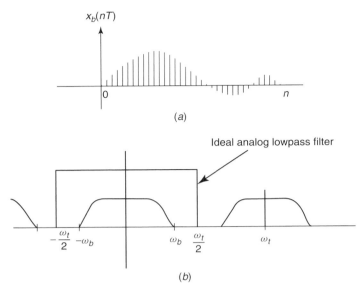

(a)

(b)

Figure 3.4   The discrete-time signal obtained from the bandlimited signal and the magnitude of its Fourier transform.

The output signal will be the result of convolving the discrete input sequence $x_b(nT)$ with the unit impulse response $h_{lp}(t)$ of the ideal analog lowpass filter. But we have not defined the convolution between a continuous-time signal and samples of discrete-time sequence. Actually it is the superposition of the responses due to the delayed impulse responses $h_{lp}(t - nT)$, weighted by the samples $x_b(nT)$, which gives the output $x_b(t)$. Using this argument, Shannon [2] derived the formula for reconstructing the continuous-time function $x_b(t)$, from only the samples $x(n) = x_b(nT)$—under the condition that $x_b(t)$ be bandlimited up to a maximum frequency ω_b and be sampled with a period $T < \pi/\omega_b$. This formula (3.19) is commonly called the *reconstruction formula*, and the statement that the function $x_b(t)$ can be reconstructed from its samples $x_b(nT)$ under the abovementioned conditions is known as *Shannon's sampling theorem*:

$$x_b(t) = \sum_{n=-\infty}^{\infty} x_b(nT) \frac{\sin\left[\frac{\pi}{T}(t - nT)\right]}{\left[\frac{\pi}{T}(t - nT)\right]} \tag{3.19}$$

The reconstruction process is indicated in Figure 3.5a. An explanation of the reconstruction is also given in Figure 3.5b, where it is seen that the delayed impulse response $\sin\left[\frac{\pi}{T}(t - nT)\right] / \left[\frac{\pi}{T}(t - nT)\right]$ has a value of $x_b(nT)$ at $t = nT$ and contributes zero value at all other sampling instants $t \neq nT$ so that the reconstructed analog signal interpolates exactly between these sample values of the discrete samples.

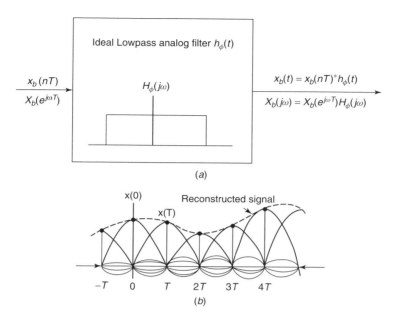

Figure 3.5   Reconstruction of the bandlimited signal from its samples, using an ideal lowpass analog filter.

This revolutionary theorem implies that the samples $x_b(nT)$ contain all the information that is contained in the original analog signal $x_b(t)$, if it is bandlimited and if it has been sampled with a period $T < \pi/\omega_b$. It lays the necessary foundation for all the research and developments in digital signal processing that is instrumental in the extraordinary progress in the information technology that we are witnessing.[4] In practice, any given signal can be rendered almost bandlimited by passing it through an analog lowpass filter of fairly high order. Indeed, it is common practice to pass an analog signal through an analog lowpass filter before it is sampled. Such filters used to precondition the analog signals are called as *antialiasing filters*. As an example, it is known that the maximum frequency contained in human speech is about 3400 Hz, and hence the sampling frequency is chosen as 8 kHz. Before the human speech is sampled and input to telephone circuits, it is passed through a filter that provides an attenuation of at least 30 dB at 4000 Hz. It is obvious that if there is a frequency above 4000 Hz in the speech signal, for example, at 4100 Hz, when it is sampled at 4000 Hz, due to aliasing of the spectrum of the sampled signal, there will be a frequency at 4100 Hz as well as 3900 Hz. Because of this phenomenon, we can say that the frequency of 4100 Hz is folded into 3900 Hz, and 4000 Hz is hence called the "folding frequency." In general, half the sampling frequency is known as the folding frequency (expressed in radians per second or in hertz).

---

[4]This author feels that Shannon deserved an award (such as the Nobel prize) for his seminal contributions to sampling theory and information theory.

There is some ambiguity in the published literature regarding the definition of what is called the *Nyquist frequency*. Most of the books define half the sampling frequency as the Nyquist frequency and $2f_b$ as the Nyquist rate, which is the minimum sampling rate required to avoid aliasing. Because of this definition for the Nyquist rate, some authors erroneously define f_b as the Nyquist frequency. In our example, when the signal is sampled at 8 kHz, we have 4 kHz as the Nyquist frequency (or the folding frequency) and 6.8 kHz as the Nyquist rate. If we sample the analog signal at 20 kHz, the Nyquist frequency is 10 kHz, but the Nyquist rate is still 6.8 kHz. We will define half the sampling frequency as the Nyquist frequency throughout this book. Some authors define the Nyquist frequency as the bandwidth of the corresponding analog signal, whereas some authors define $2f_b$ as the bandwidth.

3.2.1 Sampling of Bandpass Signals

Suppose that we have an analog signal that is a bandpass signal (i.e., it has a Fourier transform that is zero outside the frequency range $\omega_1 \leq \omega \leq \omega_2$); the bandwidth of this signal is $B = \omega_2 - \omega_1$, and the maximum frequency of this signal is ω_2. So it is bandlimited, and according to Shannon's sampling theorem, one might consider a sampling frequency greater than $2\omega_2$; however, it is not necessary to choose a sampling frequency $\omega_s \geq 2\omega_2$ in order to ensure that we can reconstruct this signal from its sampled values. It has been shown [3] that when ω_2 is a multiple of B, we can recover the analog bandpass signal from its samples obtained with only a sampling frequency $\omega_s \geq 2B$. For example, when the bandpass signal has a Fourier transform between $\omega_1 = 4500$ and $\omega_2 = 5000$, we don't have to choose $\omega_s > 10{,}000$. We can choose $\omega_s > 1000$, since $\omega_2 = 10B$ in this example.

Example 3.1

Consider a continuous-time signal $x_a(t) = e^{-0.2t}u(t)$ that has the Fourier transform $X(j\omega) = 1/(j\omega + 0.2)$. The magnitude $|X(j\omega)| = |1/(j\omega + 0.2)| = \sqrt{1/(\omega^2 + 0.04)}$, and when we choose a frequency of 200π, we see that the magnitude is approximately $0.4(10^{-3})$. Although the function $x_a(t) = e^{-0.2t}u(t)$ is not bandlimited, we can assume that it is almost bandlimited with bandwidth of 200π and choose a sampling frequency of 400π rad/s or 200 Hz. So the sampling period $T = \frac{1}{200} = 0.005$ second and $\omega_s = 2\pi/T = 400\pi$ rad/s. To verify that (3.11) and (3.16) both give the same result, let us evaluate the DTFT at $\omega = 0.5$ rad/s. According to (3.11), the DTFT of $x(nT)$ is

$$\sum_{n=0}^{\infty} e^{-0.2(nT)} e^{-j\omega nT} = \sum_{n=0}^{\infty} e^{-0.001n} e^{-j\omega n(0.005)}$$

$$= X(e^{j\omega T}) = \frac{1}{1 - e^{-0.001} e^{-j(0.005\omega)}} \qquad (3.20)$$

and its magnitude at $\omega = 0.5$ is

$$\left| \frac{1}{1 - e^{-0.001}e^{-j(0.0025)}} \right| = 371.5765$$

According to (3.16), the DTFT for this example becomes

$$\frac{1}{0.005} \sum_{k=-\infty}^{\infty} \frac{1}{0.2 + j(\omega + k400\pi)} \tag{3.21}$$

and at $\omega = 0.5$, we can neglect the duplicates at $jk400\pi$ and give the magnitude of the frequency response as

$$\frac{1}{0.005} \left| \frac{1}{0.2 + j0.5} \right| = 371.3907$$

The two magnitudes at $\omega = 0.5$ are nearly equal; the small difference is attributable to the slight aliasing in the frequency response. See Figure 3.6, which illustrates the equivalence of the two equations. But (3.16) is not useful when a sequence of arbitrary values (finite or infinite in length) is given because it is difficult to guess the continuous-time signal of which they are the sampled values; even if we do know the continuous-time signal, the choice of a sampling frequency to avoid aliasing may not be practical, for example, when the signal is a highpass signal. Hence we refer to (3.11) whenever we use the acronym DTFT in our discussion.

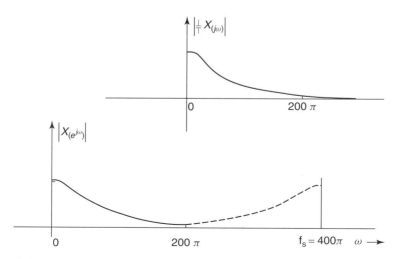

Figure 3.6 Equivalence of the two definitions for the Fourier transform of a discrete-time signal.

3.3 DTFT AND IDTFT

The expressions for the DTFT $X(e^{j\omega})$ and the IDTFT $x(n)$ are

$$X(e^{j\omega}) = \sum_{n=0}^{\infty} x(n)e^{-j\omega n} \qquad (3.22)$$

$$x(n) = \frac{1}{2\pi} \int_{-\pi}^{\pi} X(e^{j\omega})e^{j\omega n} d\omega \qquad (3.23)$$

The DTFT and its inverse (IDTFT) are extensively used for the analysis and design of discrete-time systems and in applications of digital signal processing such as speech processing, speech synthesis, and image processing. Remember that the terms *frequency response of a discrete-time signal* and the *discrete-time Fourier transform* (DTFT) are synonymous and will be used interchangeably. This is also known as the *frequency spectrum*; its magnitude response and phase response are generally known as the *magnitude spectrum* and *phase spectrum*, respectively. We will also use the terms *discrete-time signal*, *discrete-time sequence*, *discrete-time function*, and *discrete-time series synonymously*.

We will represent the frequency response of the digital filter either by $H(e^{j\omega T})$ or more often by $H(e^{j\omega})$ for convenience. Whenever it is expressed as $H(e^{j\omega})$—which is very common practice in the published literature—the frequency variable ω is to be understood as the normalized frequency $\omega T = \omega/f_s$. We may also represent the normalized frequency ωT by θ (radians). In Figure 3.7a, we have shown the magnitude response of an ideal lowpass filter, demonstrating that it transmits all frequencies from 0 to ω_c and rejects frequencies higher than ω_c. The frequency response $H(e^{j\omega})$ is periodic, and its magnitude is an even function. In Figure 3.7b suppose we have shown the magnitude response of the lowpass filter only over the frequency range [0 π]. We draw its magnitude for negative values of ω since it is an even function and extend it by repeated duplication with a period of 2π, thereby obtaining the magnitude response for all values of ω over the range $(-\infty, \infty)$. Therefore, if the frequency specifications are given over the range [0 π], we know the specifications for all values of the normalized frequency ω, and the specifications for digital filters are commonly given for only this range of frequencies. Note that we have plotted the magnitude response as a function of the normalized frequency ω. Therefore the range [0 π] corresponds to the actual frequency range [0 $\omega_s/2$] and the normalized frequency π corresponds to the Nyquist frequency (and 2π corresponds to the sampling frequency).

Sometimes the frequency ω is even normalized by πf_s so that the Nyquist frequency has a value of 1, for example, in MATLAB functions. In Figures 3.7c,d, we have shown the magnitude response of an ideal highpass filter. In Figure 3.8 we show the magnitude responses of an ideal bandpass and bandstop filter.

It is convenient to do the analysis and design of discrete-time systems on the basis of the normalized frequency. When the frequency response of a filter, for example, shows a magnitude of 0.5 (i.e., −6 dB) at the normalized

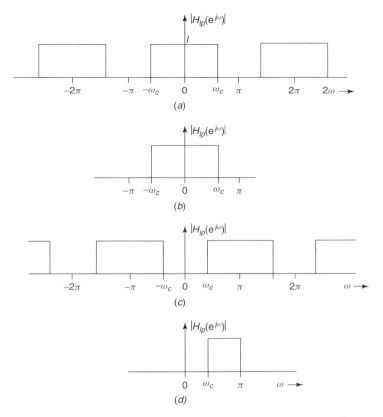

Figure 3.7   Magnitude responses of ideal lowpass and highpass filters.

frequency 0.3π, the actual frequency can be easily computed as 30% of the Nyquist frequency, and when the sampling period T or the sampling frequency ω_s (or $f_s = 1/T$) is given, we know that 0.3π represents $(0.3)(\omega_s/2)$ rad/s or $(0.3)(f_s/2)$ Hz. By looking at the plot, one should therefore be able to determine what frequency scaling has been chosen for the plot. And when the actual sampling period is known, we know how to restore the scaling and find the value of the actual frequency in radians per second or in hertz. So we will choose the normalized frequency in the following sections, without ambiguity.

The magnitude response of the ideal filters shown in Figures 3.7 and 3.8 cannot be realized by any transfer function of a digital filter. The term "designing a digital filter" has different meanings depending on the context. One meaning is to find a transfer function $H(z)$ such that its magnitude $\left|H(e^{j\omega})\right|$ approximates the ideal magnitude response as closely as possible. Different approximation criteria have been proposed to define how closely the magnitude $\left|H(e^{j\omega})\right|$ approximates the ideal magnitude. In Figure 3.9a, we show the approximation of the ideal lowpass filter meeting the elliptic function criteria. It shows an error in the passband as

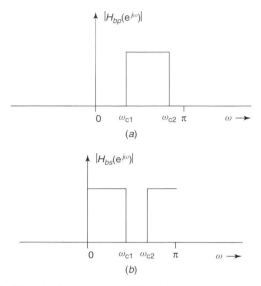

Figure 3.8 Magnitude responses of ideal bandpass and bandstop filters.

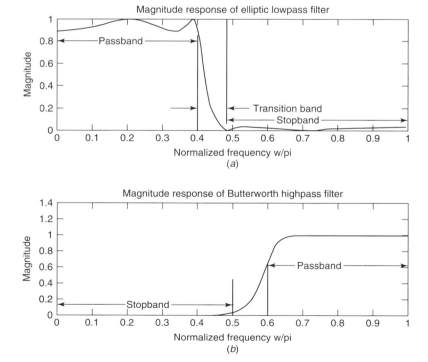

Figure 3.9 Approximation of ideal lowpass and highpass filter magnitude response.

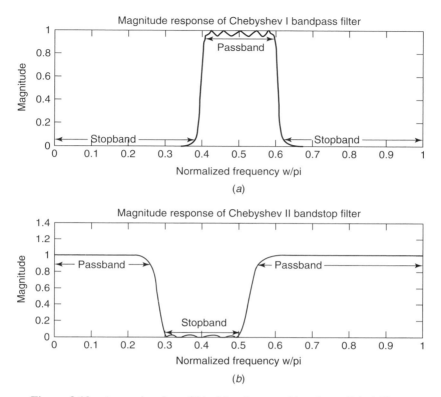

Figure 3.10   Approximation of ideal bandpass and bandstop digital filters.

well as in the stopband, which is equiripple in nature, whereas in Figure 3.9b, the magnitude of a highpass filter is approximated by a Butterworth type of approximation, which shows that the magnitude in the passband is "nearly flat" and decreases monotonically as the frequency decreases from the passband.

Figure 3.10a illustrates a Chebyshev type I approximation of an ideal band-pass filter, which has an equiripple error in the passband and a monotonically decreasing response in the stopband, whereas in Figure 3.10b, we have shown a Chebyshev type II approximation of an ideal bandstop filter; thus, the error in the stopband is equiripple in nature and is monotonic in the passband. The exact definition of these criteria and the design of filters meeting these criteria will be discussed in the next two chapters.

3.3.1   Time-Domain Analysis of Noncausal Inputs

Let the DTFT of the input signal $x(n)$ and the unit impulse response $h(n)$ of a discrete-time system be $X(e^{j\omega})$ and $H(e^{j\omega})$, respectively. The output $y(n)$ is obtained by the convolution sum $x(n) * h(n) = y(n) = \sum_{k=-\infty}^{\infty} h(k)x(n-k)$, which shows that the convolution sum is applicable even when the input signal is defined for $-\infty < n < 0$ or $-\infty < n < \infty$. In this case, the unilateral z transform of $x(n)$ cannot be used. Therefore we cannot find the output $y(n)$ as the inverse z transform of $X(z)H(z)$. However, we can find the DTFT of the input sequence even when it is defined for $-\infty < n < \infty$, and then multiply it by the DTFT of $h(n)$ to get the DTFT of the output as $Y(e^{j\omega}) = X(e^{j\omega})H(e^{j\omega})$. Its IDTFT yields the output $y(n)$. This is one advantage of using the discrete-time Fourier transform theory. So for time-domain analysis, we see that the DTFT-IDTFT pair offers an advantage over the z-transform method, when the input signal is defined for $-\infty < n < 0$ or $-\infty < n < \infty$. An example is given later to illustrate this advantage over the z-transform theory in such cases.

The relationship $Y(e^{j\omega}) = X(e^{j\omega})H(e^{j\omega})$ offers a greater advantage as it is the basis for the design of all digital filters. When we want to eliminate certain frequencies or a range of frequencies in the input signal, we design a filter such that the magnitude of $H(e^{j\omega})$ is very small at these frequencies or over the range of frequencies that would therefore form the stopband. The magnitude of the frequency response $H(e^{j\omega})$ at all other frequencies is maintained at a high level, and these frequencies constitute the passband. The magnitude and phase responses of the filter are chosen so that the magnitude and phase responses of the output of the filter will have an improved quality of information. We will discuss the design of digital filters in great detail in Chapters 4 and 5. We give only a simple example of its application in the next section.

Example 3.2

Suppose that the input signal has a lowpass magnitude response with a bandwidth of 0.7π as shown in Figure 3.11 and we want to filter out all frequencies outside the range between $\omega_1 = 0.3\pi$ and $\omega_2 = 0.4\pi$. Note that the sampling frequency of both signals is set at 2π. If we pass the input signal through a bandpass filter with a passband between $\omega_1 = 0.3\pi$ and $\omega_2 = 0.4\pi$, then the frequency response of the output is given by a bandpass response with a passband between $\omega_1 = 0.3\pi$ and $\omega_2 = 0.4\pi$, with all the other frequencies having been filtered out. It is interesting to observe that the maximum frequency in the output is 0.4π; therefore, we can reconstruct $y(t)$ from the samples $y(n)$ and then sample at a lower sampling frequency of 0.8π, instead of the original frequency of 2π.

If the sampling frequency in this example is 10,000 Hz, then the Nyquist frequency is 5000 Hz, and therefore the input signal has a bandwidth of 3500 Hz, corresponding to the normalized bandwidth of 0.7π, whereas the bandpass filter has a passband between 1500 and 2000 Hz. The output of the bandpass filter has a passband between 1500 and 2000 Hz. Since the maximum frequency in the output signal is 2000 Hz, one might think of reconstructing the continuous-time signal using a sampling frequency of 4000 Hz. But this is a bandpass signal with a bandwidth of 500 Hz, and 2000 Hz is 8 times the bandwidth; according to the sampling theorem for bandpass signals, we can reconstruct the output signal $y(t)$ using a sampling frequency of twice the bandwidth, namely, 1000 Hz instead of 4000 Hz. The theory and the procedure for reconstructing the analog

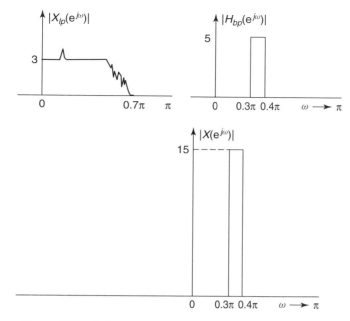

Figure 3.11 A lowpass signal processed by a bandpass filter.

bandpass signal from its samples is beyond the scope of this book and will not be treated further.

3.3.2 Time-Shifting Property

If $x(n)$ has a DTFT $X(e^{j\omega})$, then $x(n-k)$ has a DTFT equal to $e^{-j\omega k}X(e^{j\omega})$, where k is an integer. This is known as the *time-shifting property* and it is easily proved as follows: DTFT of $x(n-k) = \sum_{n=-\infty}^{\infty} x(n-k)e^{-j\omega n} = e^{-j\omega k}\sum_{n=-\infty}^{\infty} x(n)e^{-j\omega n} = e^{-j\omega k}X(e^{j\omega})$. So we denote this property by

$$x(n-k) \Leftrightarrow e^{-j\omega k}X(e^{j\omega})$$

3.3.3 Frequency-Shifting Property

If $x(n) \Leftrightarrow X(e^{j\omega})$, then

$$e^{j\omega_0 n}x(n) \Leftrightarrow X(e^{j(\omega-\omega_0)})$$

This is known as the *frequency-shifting property*, and it is easily proved as follows:

$$\sum_{n=-\infty}^{\infty} x(n)e^{j\omega_0 n}e^{-j\omega n} = \sum_{n=-\infty}^{\infty} x(n)e^{-j(\omega-\omega_0)n} = X(e^{j(\omega-\omega_0)})$$

3.3.4   Time Reversal Property

Let us consider $x(n) = a^n u(n)$. Its DTFT $X(e^{j\omega}) = \sum_{n=0}^{\infty} a^n e^{-j\omega n}$. Next, to find the DTFT of $x(-n)$, if we replace n by $-n$, we would write the DTFT of $x(-n)$ as $\sum_{n=0}^{-\infty} a^{-n} e^{j\omega n}$ (but that is wrong), as illustrated by the following example:

$$X(e^{j\omega}) = \sum_{n=0}^{\infty} a^n e^{-j\omega n} = 1 + a e^{-j\omega} + a^2 e^{-j2\omega} + a^3 e^{-j3\omega} + \cdots$$

But the correct expression for the DTFT of $x(-n)$ is of the form $1 + a e^{j\omega} + a^2 e^{j2\omega} + a^3 e^{j3\omega} + \cdots$.

So the compact form for this series is $\sum_{n=-\infty}^{0} a^{-n} e^{-j\omega n}$. With this clarification, we now prove the property that if $x(n) \Leftrightarrow X(e^{j\omega})$ then

$$x(-n) \Leftrightarrow X(e^{-j\omega}) \tag{3.24}$$

Proof: DTFT of $x(-n) = \sum_{n=-\infty}^{\infty} x(-n) e^{-j\omega n}$. We substitute $(-n) = m$, and we get $\sum_{n=-\infty}^{\infty} x(-n) e^{-j\omega n} = \sum_{m=-\infty}^{\infty} x(m) e^{j\omega m} = \sum_{m=-\infty}^{\infty} x(m) e^{-j(-\omega)m} = X(e^{-j\omega})$.

Example 3.3

Consider $x(n) = \delta(n)$. Then, from the definition for DTFT, we see that $\delta(n) \Leftrightarrow X(e^{j\omega}) = 1$ *for all* ω.

From the time-shifting property, we get

$$\delta(n - k) \Leftrightarrow e^{-j\omega k} \tag{3.25}$$

The Fourier transform $e^{-j\omega k}$ has a magnitude of one at all frequencies but a linear phase as a function of ω that yields a constant group delay of k samples. If we extend this result by considering an infinite sequence of unit impulses, which can be represented by $\sum_{k=-\infty}^{\infty} \delta(n - k)$, its DTFT would yield $\sum_{k=-\infty}^{\infty} e^{-j\omega k}$. But this does not converge to any form of expression. Hence we resort to a different approach, as described below, and derive the result (3.28).

Example 3.4

We consider $x(n) = \delta(n + k) + \delta(n - k)$. Its DTFT is given by $X(e^{j\omega}) = e^{j\omega k} + e^{-j\omega k} = 2\cos(\omega k)$. In this example, note that the DTFT is a function of the continuous variable ω whereas k is a fixed number. It is a periodic function of ω with a period of 2π, because $2\cos((\omega + 2r\pi)k) = 2\cos(\omega k)$, where r is an integer. In other words, the inverse DTFT of $X(e^{j\omega}) = 2\cos(\omega k)$ is a pair of impulse functions at $n = k$ and $n = -k$, and this is given by

$$\cos(\omega k) \Leftrightarrow \tfrac{1}{2}[\delta(n + k) + \delta(n - k)] \tag{3.26}$$

Example 3.5

Now we consider the infinite sequence of $x(n) = 1$ *for all n*. We represent it in the form $x(n) = \sum_{k=-\infty}^{\infty} \delta(n-k)$. We prove below that its DTFT is given as $2\pi \sum_{k=-\infty}^{\infty} \delta(\omega - 2\pi k)$, which is a periodic train of impulses in the frequency domain, with a strength equal to 2π and a period equal to 2π (which is the normalized sampling frequency). We prove this result given by (3.27), by showing that the inverse DTFT of $2\pi \sum_{k=-\infty}^{\infty} \delta(\omega - 2\pi k)$ is equal to one for all n.

$$2\pi \sum_{k=-\infty}^{\infty} \delta(\omega - 2\pi k) \Leftrightarrow 1 \text{ (for all } n) \tag{3.27}$$

Proof: The inverse DTFT of $2\pi \sum_{k=-\infty}^{\infty} \delta(\omega - 2\pi k)$ is evaluated as

$$\frac{1}{2\pi} \int_{-\pi}^{\pi} \left[2\pi \sum_{k=-\infty}^{\infty} \delta(\omega - 2\pi k) \right] e^{j\omega n}\, d\omega$$

$$= \int_{-\pi}^{\pi} \left[\sum_{k=-\infty}^{\infty} \delta(\omega - 2\pi k) \right] e^{j\omega n}\, d\omega$$

From the sifting property we get

$$\left[\sum_{k=-\infty}^{\infty} \delta(\omega - 2\pi k) \right] e^{j\omega n} = \left[\sum_{k=-\infty}^{\infty} \delta(\omega - 2\pi k) \right] e^{j2\pi kn}$$

$$= \left[\sum_{k=-\infty}^{\infty} \delta(\omega - 2\pi k) \right]$$

where we have used $e^{j2\pi kn} = 1$ for all n. When we integrate the sequence of impulses from $-\pi$ to π, we have only the impulse at $\omega = 0$.

Therefore

$$\int_{-\pi}^{\pi} \left[\sum_{k=-\infty}^{\infty} \delta(\omega - 2\pi k) \right] e^{j\omega n}\, d\omega$$

$$= \int_{-\pi}^{\pi} \sum_{k=-\infty}^{\infty} \delta(\omega) e^{j\omega n}\, d\omega = 1 \quad \text{(for all } n)$$

Thus we have derived the important result

$$\sum_{k=-\infty}^{\infty} \delta(n-k) \Leftrightarrow 2\pi \sum_{k=-\infty}^{\infty} \delta(\omega - 2\pi k) \tag{3.28}$$

To point out some duality in the results we have obtained above, let us repeat them:

When $x(n) = 1$ at $n = 0$ and 0 at $n \neq 0$, that is, when we have $\delta(n)$, its DTFT $X(e^{j\omega}) = 1$ for all ω.

When $x(n) = 1$ for all n, specifically, when we have $\sum_{k=-\infty}^{\infty} \delta(n-k)$, its DTFT $X(e^{j\omega}) = 2\pi \sum_{k=-\infty}^{\infty} \delta(\omega - 2\pi k)$.

Using the frequency-shifting property, we get the following results:

$$e^{j\omega_0 n} \Leftrightarrow 2\pi \sum_{k=-\infty}^{\infty} \delta(\omega - \omega_0 - 2\pi k) \tag{3.29}$$

From these results, we can obtain the DTFT for the following sinusoidal sequences:

$$\cos(\omega_0 n) = \frac{1}{2}[e^{j\omega_0 n} + e^{-j\omega_0 n}] \Leftrightarrow \pi \sum_{k=-\infty}^{\infty} \delta(\omega - \omega_0 - 2\pi k) + \delta(\omega + \omega_0 - 2\pi k)$$

$$\sin(\omega_0 n) = \frac{1}{2j}[e^{j\omega_0 n} - e^{-j\omega_0 n}] \Leftrightarrow \frac{\pi}{j} \sum_{k=-\infty}^{\infty} \delta(\omega - \omega_0 - 2\pi k) - \delta(\omega + \omega_0 - 2\pi k)$$

$$\tag{3.30}$$

Now compare the results in (3.28) and (3.30), which are put together in (3.31) and (3.32) in order to show the dualities in the properties of the two transform pairs. Note in particular that $\cos(\omega k)$ is a discrete-time Fourier transform and a function of ω, where k is a fixed integer, whereas $\cos(\omega_0 n)$ is a discrete-time sequence where ω_0 is fixed and is a function of n:

$$\tfrac{1}{2}[\delta(n+k) + \delta(n-k)] \Longleftrightarrow \cos(\omega k) \tag{3.31}$$

$$\cos(\omega_0 n) \Longleftrightarrow \pi \sum_{k=-\infty}^{\infty} \delta(\omega - \omega_0 - 2\pi k) + \delta(\omega + \omega_0 - 2\pi k)$$

$$\tag{3.32}$$

Let us show the duality of the other functions derived in (3.26) and (3.29)

$$\delta(n) \Longleftrightarrow 1 \quad \text{for all } \omega$$

whereas

$$x(n) = 1 \quad \text{for all } n \Longleftrightarrow 2\pi \sum_{k=-\infty}^{\infty} \delta(\omega - 2\pi k)$$

Using the time- and frequency-shifting properties on these functions, we derived the following Fourier transform pairs as well:

$$\delta(n-k) \Longleftrightarrow e^{-j\omega k}$$

$$e^{j\omega_0 n} \Longleftrightarrow 2\pi \sum_{k=-\infty}^{\infty} \delta(\omega - \omega_0 - 2\pi k)$$

Example 3.6

This is another example chosen to highlight the difference between the expressions for the discrete-time sequence $x(n)$ and its DTFT $X(e^{j\omega})$. So if we are given $F(e^{j\omega}) = 10\cos(5\omega) + 5\cos(2\omega) = 5e^{j5\omega} + 5e^{-j5\omega} + 2.5e^{j2\omega} + 2.5e^{-j2\omega}$, its IDTFT is obtained by using the result $\delta(n-k) \Leftrightarrow e^{-j\omega k}$, and we get $f(n) = 5\delta(n+5) + 2.5\delta(n+2) + 2.5\delta(n-2) + 5\delta(n-5)$, which is plotted in Figure 3.12a. Obviously it is a finite sequence with four impulse functions and therefore is not periodic.

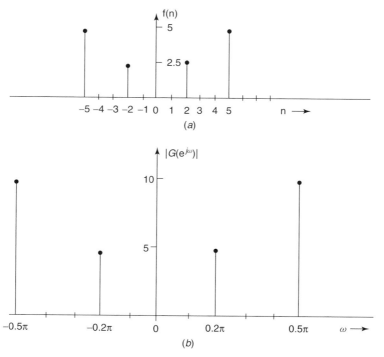

Figure 3.12 A sequence of impulses in the discrete-time domain and a sequence of impulses in the discrete-frequency domain.

If we are given a function $g(n) = 10\cos(0.5\pi n) + 5\cos(0.2\pi n)$, the first thing we have to recognize is that it is a discrete-time function and is a periodic function in its variable n. So we find its DTFT, using (3.30), as

$$G(e^{j\omega}) = 10\pi \sum_{k=-\infty}^{\infty} \delta(\omega - 0.5\pi - 2\pi k) + 10\pi \sum_{k=-\infty}^{\infty} \delta(\omega + 0.5\pi - 2\pi k)$$

$$+ 5\pi \sum_{k=-\infty}^{\infty} \delta(\omega - 0.2\pi - 2\pi k) + 5\pi \sum_{k=-\infty}^{\infty} \delta(\omega + 0.2\pi - 2\pi k)$$

This DTFT is shown in Figure 3.12b. We notice that it represents an infinite number of impulses in the frequency domain that form a periodic function in the frequency variable ω. Because it has discrete components, the impulse functions are also called the *spectral components* of $g(n)$.

We have chosen a DTFT $F(e^{j\omega})$ and derived its IDTFT $f(n)$, which is a sequence of impulse functions in the time domain as shown in Figure 3.12a; then we chose a discrete-time function $g(n)$ and derived its DTFT $G(e^{j\omega})$, which is a sequence of impulse functions in the frequency domain as shown in Figure 3.12b.

Example 3.7

Consider the simple example of a discrete-time sinsusoidal signal $x(n) = 4\cos(0.4\pi n)$. It is periodic when the frequency $(0.4N)$ is an integer or a ratio of integers. We choose $N = 5$ as the period of this function, so $x(n) = x(n + 5K) = 4\cos[0.4\pi(n + 5K)]$, where K is any integer.

We rewrite $x(n) = 2[e^{j0.4\pi n} + e^{-j0.4\pi n}]$, and therefore its DTFT $X(e^{j\omega}) = 2\pi \sum_{k=-\infty}^{\infty} \delta(\omega - 0.4\pi - 2\pi k) + 2\pi \sum_{k=-\infty}^{\infty} \delta(\omega + 0.4\pi - 2\pi k)$. It consists of impulse functions of magnitude equal to 2π, at $\omega = \pm(0.4\pi + 2\pi K)$ in the frequency domain and with a period of 2π.

Given $f(n) = 2\delta(n + 4) + 2\delta(n - 4)$, its DTFT is $F(e^{j\omega}) = 4\cos(4\omega)$, and if $x(n) = 4\cos(0.4\pi n)$, its DTFT is $X(e^{j\omega}) = 2\pi \sum_{k=-\infty}^{\infty} \delta(\omega - 0.4\pi - 2\pi k) + 2\pi \sum_{k=-\infty}^{\infty} \delta(\omega + 0.4\pi - 2\pi k)$.

Examples 3.6 and 3.7 have been chosen in particular to distinguish the differences between the two Fourier transform pairs.

Example 3.8

Let us consider the DTFT of some more sequences. For example, the DTFT of $x_1(n) = a^n u(n)$ is derived below:

$$X_1(e^{j\omega}) = \sum_{n=0}^{\infty} a^n e^{-j\omega n} = \sum_{n=-\infty}^{\infty} \left(ae^{-j\omega}\right)^n$$

This infinite series converges to $1/(1 - ae^{-j\omega}) = e^{j\omega}/(e^{j\omega} - a)$ when $|ae^{-j\omega}| < 1$, that is, when $|a| < 1$. So, the DTFT of $(0.4)^n u(n)$ is $1/(1 - 0.4e^{-j\omega})$ and the DTFT of $(-0.4)^n u(n)$ is $1/(1 + 0.4e^{-j\omega})$. Note that both of them are causal sequences.

If we are given a sequence $x_{13}(n) = a^{|n|}$, where $|a| < 1$, we split the sequence as a causal sequence $x_1(n)$ from 0 to ∞, and a noncausal sequence $x_3(n)$ from $-\infty$ to -1. In other words, we can express $x_1(n) = a^n u(n)$ and $x_3(n) = a^{-n} u(-n - 1)$. We derive the DTFT of $x_{13}(n)$ as

$$X_{13}(e^{j\omega}) = \sum_{n=0}^{\infty} a^n e^{-j\omega n} + \sum_{n=-\infty}^{-1} a^{-n} e^{-j\omega n} X_1(e^{j\omega}) + X_3(e^{j\omega})$$

Substituting $m = -n$ in the second summation for $X_3(e^{j\omega})$, we get

$$X_{13}(e^{j\omega}) = \sum_{n=0}^{\infty} \left(ae^{-j\omega}\right)^n + \sum_{m=1}^{\infty} \left(ae^{j\omega}\right)^m$$

$$= \sum_{n=0}^{\infty} \left(ae^{-j\omega}\right)^n - 1 + \sum_{m=0}^{\infty} \left(ae^{j\omega}\right)^m$$

$$= \frac{1}{1 - ae^{-j\omega}} - 1 + \frac{1}{1 - ae^{j\omega}} \qquad \text{for } |a| < 1$$

$$= \frac{1}{1 - ae^{-j\omega}} + \frac{ae^{j\omega}}{1 - ae^{j\omega}}$$

$$= \frac{1 - a^2}{1 - 2a \cos\omega + a^2} \qquad \text{for } |a| < 1$$

Hence we have shown that

$$a^{|n|} \Leftrightarrow \frac{1 - a^2}{1 - 2a \cos\omega + a^2} \qquad \text{for } |a| < 1$$

These results are valid when $|a| < 1$. From the result $a^n u(n) \Leftrightarrow 1/(1 - ae^{-j\omega})$, by application of the time-reversal property, we also find that $x_4(n) = x_1(-n) = a^{-n} u(-n) \Leftrightarrow 1/(1 - ae^{j\omega})$ for $|a| < 1$ whereas we have already determined that $x_3(n) = a^{-n} u(-n - 1) \Leftrightarrow ae^{j\omega}/(1 - ae^{j\omega})$. Note that $x_3(n)$ is obtained from $x_4(n)$ by deleting the sample of $x_4(n)$ at $n = 0$, specifically, $x_4(n) - 1 = x_3(n)$. We used this result in deriving $X_3(e^{j\omega})$ above. The sequence $x_{13}(n)$ is plotted in Figure 3.13, while the plots of $x_1(n), x_3(n)$ are shown in Figures 3.14 and 3.15, respectively.

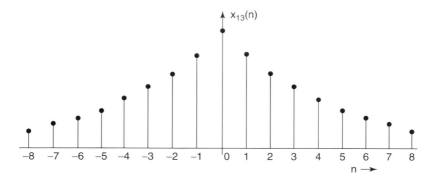

Figure 3.13   The discrete-time sequence $x_{13}(n)$.

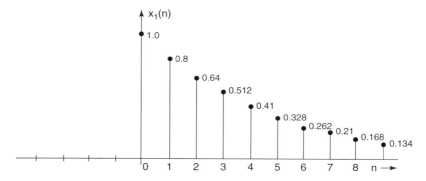

Figure 3.14   The discrete-time sequence $x_1(n)$.

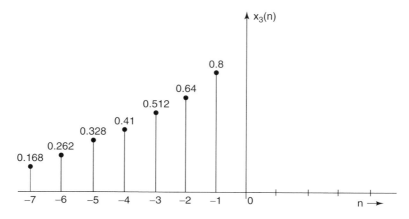

Figure 3.15   The discrete-time sequence $x_3(n)$.

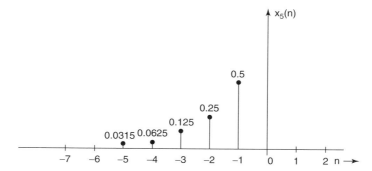

Figure 3.16 The discrete-time sequence $x_5(n)$.

Now let us consider the case of $x_5(n) = \alpha^n u[-(n+1)]$, where $|\alpha| > 1$. A plot of this sequence is shown in Figure 3.16 for $\alpha = 2$. Its DTFT is derived below:

$$X_5(e^{j\omega}) = \sum_{n=-\infty}^{\infty} \alpha^n u[-(n+1)]e^{-j\omega n}$$

$$= \sum_{n=-1}^{-\infty} \left(\alpha e^{-j\omega}\right)^n = \sum_{n=-1}^{-\infty} \left(\frac{1}{\alpha}e^{j\omega}\right)^{-n}$$

By a change of variable $n = -m$, we get

$$X_5(e^{j\omega}) = \sum_{m=1}^{\infty} \left(\frac{1}{\alpha}e^{j\omega}\right)^m = -1 + \sum_{m=0}^{\infty} \left(\frac{1}{\alpha}e^{j\omega}\right)^m$$

$$= -1 + \frac{1}{1 - \left(\frac{1}{\alpha}e^{j\omega}\right)}$$

$$= \frac{1}{\alpha e^{-j\omega} - 1}$$

So we have the transform pair

$$x_5(n) = \alpha^n u[-(n+1)] \Leftrightarrow \frac{1}{\alpha e^{-j\omega} - 1} = \frac{e^{j\omega}}{\alpha - e^{j\omega}} \quad \text{when } |\alpha| > 1 \quad (3.33)$$

It is important to exercise caution in determining the differences in this pair (3.33), which is valid for $|\alpha| > 1$, and the earlier pairs, which are valid for $|a| < 1$. All of them are given below (again, the differences between the different DTFT-IDTFT pairs and the corresponding plots should be studied carefully and clearly understood):

$$x_1(n) = a^n u(n) \Leftrightarrow \frac{1}{1 - ae^{-j\omega}} = \frac{e^{j\omega}}{e^{j\omega} - a} \quad \text{when } |a| < 1 \quad (3.34)$$

$$x_4(n) = a^{-n}u(-n) \Leftrightarrow \frac{1}{1 - ae^{j\omega}} = \frac{e^{-j\omega}}{e^{-j\omega} - a} \qquad \text{when } |a| < 1 \quad (3.35)$$

$$x_3(n) = a^{-n}u(-n - 1) \Leftrightarrow \frac{ae^{j\omega}}{1 - ae^{j\omega}} \qquad \text{when } |a| < 1 \quad (3.36)$$

$$x_{13}(n) = x_1(n) + x_3(n) \Leftrightarrow \frac{1 - a^2}{1 - 2a\cos\omega + a^2} \qquad \text{when } |a| < 1 \quad (3.37)$$

For the sequence $x_5(n) = \alpha^n u[-(n + 1)]$, note that the transform pair is given by (3.38), which is valid when $|\alpha| > 1$:

$$x_5(n) = \alpha^n u[-(n + 1)] \Leftrightarrow \frac{1}{\alpha e^{-j\omega} - 1} = \frac{e^{j\omega}}{\alpha - e^{j\omega}} \qquad \text{when } |\alpha| > 1 \quad (3.38)$$

Example 3.9

A few examples are given below to help explain these differences. From the results given above, we see that

1. If the DTFT $X_1(e^{j\omega}) = 1/(1 - 0.8e^{-j\omega})$, its IDTFT is $x_1(n) = (0.8)^n u(n)$.
2. The IDTFT of $X_3(e^{j\omega}) = 0.8e^{j\omega}/(1 - 0.8e^{j\omega})$ is given by $x_3(n) = (0.8)^{-n}[u(-n - 1)]$.
3. The IDTFT of $X_4(e^{j\omega}) = 1/(1 - 0.8e^{j\omega})$ is $x_4(n) = (0.8)^{-n}u(-n)$. But
4. The IDTFT of $X_5(e^{j\omega}) = e^{j\omega}/(2 - e^{j\omega})$ is $x_5(n) = (2)^n u(-n - 1)$.

Note the differences in the examples above, particularly the DTFT-IDTFT pair for $x_5(n)$.

The magnitude and phase responses of $X_1(e^{j\omega})$, $X_3(e^{j\omega})$, and $X_{13}(e^{j\omega})$ are shown in Figures 3.17, 3.18, and 3.19, respectively. The magnitude responses of $X_1(e^{j\omega})$, $X_4(e^{j\omega})$, and $X_3(e^{j\omega})$ given below appear the same except for a scale

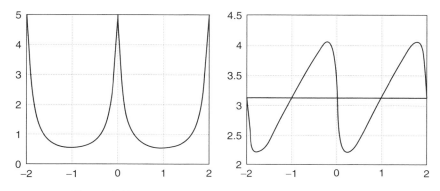

Figure 3.17   The magnitude and phase responses of $x_1(n)$.

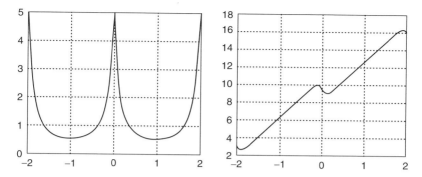

Figure 3.18   The magnitude and phase responses of $x_3(n)$.

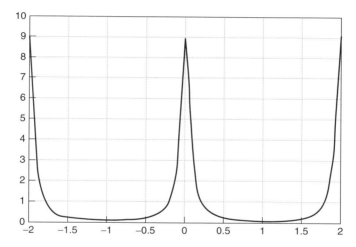

Figure 3.19   The magnitude response of $x_{13}(n)$.

factor in $X_3(e^{j\omega})$. The phase response of $X_3(e^{j\omega})$ exceeds that of $X_1(e^{j\omega})$ by ω radians as seen in Figures 3.17 and 3.18. The frequency response (DTFT) $X_{13}(e^{j\omega})$ shown in Figure 3.19 is a real function and therefore has zero phase. We obtain

$$\left|X_1(e^{j\omega})\right| = \frac{1.0}{\sqrt{[1-0.8\cos(\omega)]^2 + [0.8\sin(\omega)]^2}} \tag{3.39}$$

$$= \frac{1.0}{\sqrt{[1+0.64-1.6\cos(\omega)]}} \tag{3.40}$$

$$\mathrm{Ang}[X_1(e^{j\omega})] = \mathrm{Ang}[X_3(e^{j\omega})] = -\tan^{-1}\left[\frac{a\sin(\omega)}{1-a\cos(\omega)}\right] \tag{3.41}$$

$$\left|X_3(e^{j\omega})\right| = \frac{0.8}{\sqrt{[1 - 0.8\cos(\omega)]^2 + [0.8\sin(\omega)]^2}} \tag{3.42}$$

$$= \frac{0.8}{\sqrt{[1 + 0.64 - 1.6\cos(\omega)]}} \tag{3.43}$$

$$X_{13}(e^{j\omega}) = \frac{0.36}{1 - 1.6\cos\omega + 0.64} \tag{3.44}$$

3.4   DTFT OF UNIT STEP SEQUENCE

Note that $a^n u(n) \Leftrightarrow 1/(1 - ae^{-j\omega}) = e^{j\omega}/(e^{j\omega} - a)$ is valid only when $|a| < 1$. When $a = 1$, we get the unit step sequence $u(n)$, but the DTFT $1/(1 - e^{-j\omega})$ has an infinite number of poles at $\omega = 0, \pm k2\pi$, where k is an integer. In order to avoid these singularities in $1/(1 - e^{-j\omega}) = e^{j\omega}/(e^{j\omega} - 1)$, the DTFT of the unit step sequence $u(n)$ is derived in a different way as described below.

We express the unit step function as the sum of two functions

$$u(n) = u_1(n) + u_2(n)$$

where

$$u_1(n) = \tfrac{1}{2} \quad \text{for} \ -\infty < n < \infty$$

and

$$u_2(n) = \begin{cases} \tfrac{1}{2} & \text{for } n \geq 0 \\ -\tfrac{1}{2} & \text{for } n < 0 \end{cases}$$

Therefore we express $\delta(n) = u_2(n) - u_2(n-1)$. Using $\delta(n) \Leftrightarrow 1$ and $u_2(n) - u_2(n-1) \Leftrightarrow U_2(e^{j\omega}) - e^{-j\omega}U_2(e^{j\omega}) = U_2(e^{j\omega})[1 - e^{-j\omega}]$, and equating the two results, we get

$$1 = U_2(e^{j\omega})[1 - e^{-j\omega}]$$

Therefore

$$U_2(e^{j\omega}) = \frac{1}{[1 - e^{-j\omega}]}$$

We know that the DTFT of $u_1(n) = \pi \sum_{k=-\infty}^{\infty} \delta(\omega - 2\pi k) = U_1(e^{j\omega})$. Adding these two results, we have the final result

$$u(n) \Leftrightarrow \pi \sum_{k=-\infty}^{\infty} \delta(\omega - 2\pi k) + \frac{1}{(1 - e^{-j\omega})} \tag{3.45}$$

This gives us the DTFT of the unit step function $u(n)$, which is unique.

Applying the time-shifting property, frequency-shifting property, and time reversal property on $u(n)$, we can derive the DTFT of a few more discrete-time functions. For example

$$u(n - k) \Leftrightarrow e^{-j\omega k} \left[\pi \sum_{k=-\infty}^{\infty} \delta(\omega - 2\pi k) + \frac{1}{(1 - e^{-j\omega})} \right] \qquad (3.46)$$

$$e^{j\omega_0 n} u(n) \Leftrightarrow \pi \sum_{k=-\infty}^{\infty} \delta(\omega - \omega_0 - 2\pi k) + \frac{1}{(1 - e^{-j(\omega-\omega_0)})} \qquad (3.47)$$

$$\cos(\omega_0 n)u(n) \Leftrightarrow \frac{1}{2} \left[\pi \sum_{k=-\infty}^{\infty} \delta(\omega - \omega_0 - 2\pi k) + \frac{1}{(1 - e^{-j(\omega-\omega_0)})} \right.$$

$$\left. + \pi \sum_{k=-\infty}^{\infty} \delta(\omega + \omega_0 - 2\pi k) + \frac{1}{(1 - e^{-j(\omega+\omega_0)})} \right] \qquad (3.48)$$

It is worth comparing the DTFT of $e^{j\omega_0 n} u(n)$ given above with the DTFT of $e^{-an} u(n)$, where $|a| < 1$:

$$e^{-an} u(n) \Leftrightarrow \frac{1}{1 - e^{-a} e^{-j\omega}} \qquad (3.49)$$

3.4.1 Differentiation Property

To prove that $nx(n) \Leftrightarrow j[dX(e^{j\omega})]/d\omega$, we start with $X(e^{j\omega}) = \sum_{n=-\infty}^{\infty} x(n)e^{-j\omega n}$ and differentiate both sides to get $[dX(e^{j\omega})]/d\omega = \sum_{n=-\infty}^{\infty} x(n)(-jn)e^{-j\omega n}$ and multiplying both sides by j, we get $j[dX(e^{j\omega})]/d\omega = \sum_{n=-\infty}^{\infty} nx(n)e^{-j\omega n}$. The proof is similar to that used in Chapter 2 to prove that the z transform of $nx(n)u(n)$ is $-z[dX(z)]/dz$.

Given $x(n) = a^n u(n) \Leftrightarrow 1/(1 - ae^{-j\omega}) = X(e^{j\omega})$, we can derive the following, using the differentiation property:

$$j \frac{dX(e^{j\omega})}{d\omega} = j \left[\frac{-jae^{-j\omega}}{(1 - ae^{-j\omega})^2} \right] = \frac{ae^{-j\omega}}{(1 - ae^{-j\omega})^2}$$

$$na^n u(n) \Leftrightarrow \frac{ae^{-j\omega}}{(1 - ae^{-j\omega})^2} \qquad (3.50)$$

Since the DTFT of $a^n u(n)$ is $1/(1 - ae^{-j\omega})$, we add this DTFT to that of $na^n u(n)$ and get

$$(n + 1)a^n u(n) \Leftrightarrow \frac{1}{(1 - ae^{-j\omega})^2} \qquad (3.51)$$

Example 3.10

Consider a rectangular pulse

$$x_r(n) = \begin{cases} 1 & |n| \leq N \\ 0 & |n| > N \end{cases}$$

which is plotted in Figure 3.20. It is also known as a rectangular window (of length $2N + 1$) and will be used in Chapter 5 when we discuss the design of FIR filters. Its DTFT is derived as follows:

$$X_r(e^{j\omega}) = \sum_{n=-N}^{N} e^{-j\omega n}$$

To simplify this summation, we use the identity[5]

$$\sum_{n=-N}^{N} r^n = \frac{r^{N+1} - r^{-N}}{r - 1}; \quad r \neq 1 \tag{3.52}$$

$$= 2N + 1; \quad r = 1 \tag{3.53}$$

and get

$$X_r(e^{j\omega}) = \frac{e^{-j(N+1)\omega} - e^{jN\omega}}{e^{-j\omega} - 1}$$

$$= \frac{e^{-j0.5\omega} \left(e^{-j(N+0.5)\omega} - e^{j(N+0.5)\omega} \right)}{e^{-j0.5\omega}(e^{-j0.5\omega} - e^{j0.5\omega})}$$

$$= \begin{cases} \dfrac{\sin[(N + 0.5)\omega]}{\sin[0.5\omega]} & \omega \neq 0 \\ 2N + 1 & \omega = 0 \end{cases}$$

which is shown in Figure 3.21.

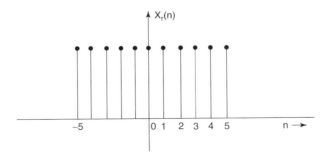

Figure 3.20   A rectangular pulse function.

---

[5]Proof:
$\sum_{n=-N}^{N} (r^{n+1} - r^n) = (r^{-N+1} + r^{-N+2} + \cdots + r^{-1} + 1 + r + r^2 + \cdots + r^N + r^{N+1}) - (r^{-N} + r^{-N+1} + r^{-N+2} + \cdots + 1 + r + r^2 + \cdots + r^N) = r^{N+1} - r^{-N}$. Therefore $\sum_{n=-N}^{N} (r^{n+1} - r^n) = (r - 1) \sum_{n=-N}^{N} r^n$ and $\sum_{n=-N}^{N} r^n = (r^{N+1} - r^{-N})/r - 1; r \neq 1 = 2N + 1; r = 1$.

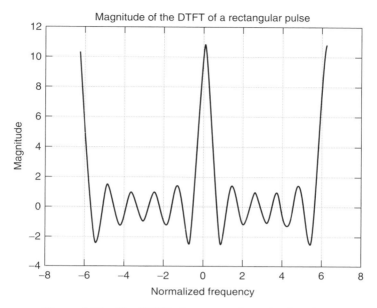

Figure 3.21   The DTFT of a rectangular pulse function.

Using the time-shifting property, we can find the DTFT of the sequence $x_{r2}(n) = x_1(n - N)$ as

$$X_{r2}(e^{j\omega}) = e^{-jN\omega}\frac{\sin[(N + 0.5)\omega]}{\sin[0.5\omega]} \tag{3.54}$$

where $x_{r2}(n) = \begin{cases} 1 & 0 \le n \le 2N \\ 0 & \text{otherwise} \end{cases}$

Example 3.11

Let us find the IDTFT of a rectangular spectrum $H(e^{j\omega})$ which is shown as the magnitude of an ideal lowpass filter in Figure 3.7a with a cutoff frequency of ω_c.

$$\begin{aligned} h(n) &= \frac{1}{2\pi} \int_{-\pi}^{\pi} H(e^{j\omega})e^{j\omega n} d\omega \\ &= \frac{1}{2\pi} \int_{-\omega_c}^{\omega_c} e^{j\omega n} d\omega \\ &= \frac{1}{2\pi} \left(\frac{e^{j\omega n}}{jn}\right)\Bigg|_{-\omega_c}^{\omega_c} \\ &= \frac{1}{\pi n} \sin(\omega_c n) = \frac{\omega_c}{\pi}\text{sinc}(\omega_c n) \end{aligned} \tag{3.55}$$

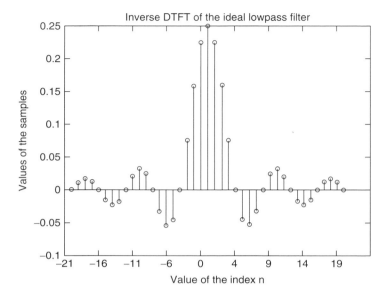

Figure 3.22   The inverse DTFT of an ideal lowpass filter.

This is a line spectrum which is shown in Figure 3.22. It is interesting to compare the general shape of the rectangular pulse function $x_r(n)$ and its frequency response $X_r(e^{j\omega})$ with the frequency response $H(e^{j\omega})$ of the lowpass filter and its inverse DTFT $h(n)$ which are derived above. However, it should be noted that they are not duals of each other, because $X_r(e^{j\omega})$ is not exactly a sinc function of ω.

3.4.2   Multiplication Property

When two discrete -time sequences are multiplied, for example, $x(n)h(n) = y(n)$, the DTFT of $y(n)$ is the convolution of $X(e^{j\omega})$ and $H(e^{j\omega})$ that is carried out in the frequency domain as an integral over one full period. Choosing the period $[-\pi \quad \pi]$ in the convolution integral, symbolically denoted by $X(e^{j\omega})*$ $H(e^{j\omega}) = Y(e^{j\omega})$, we have the property

$$x(n)h(n) \Leftrightarrow \frac{1}{2\pi} \int_{-\pi}^{\pi} X(e^{j\varsigma})H(e^{j(\omega-\varsigma)}) \, d\varsigma \tag{3.56}$$

Remember that we will use (3.55) and (3.56) in the design of FIR filters discussed in Chapter 5.

Example 3.12

The properties and the DTFT-IDTFT pairs discussed here are often used in frequency-domain analysis of discrete-time systems, including the design of filters. However, as mentioned earlier, they can also be used in time-domain analysis, particularly when the z-transform technique cannot be used. To illustrate this point, we provide the following examples.

Let the unit impulse response of a discrete-time system be given as $h(n) = (0.2)^n u(n)$ and the input sequence be given as $x(n) = (0.5)^{-n} u(-n)$. Therefore

$$H(e^{j\omega}) = \frac{1}{1 - 0.2e^{-j\omega}} = \frac{e^{j\omega}}{e^{j\omega} - 0.2}$$

$$X(e^{j\omega}) = \frac{1}{1 - 0.5e^{j\omega}} = \frac{e^{-j\omega}}{e^{-j\omega} - 0.5}$$

$$Y(e^{j\omega}) = H(e^{j\omega})X(e^{j\omega}) = \left(\frac{e^{j\omega}}{e^{j\omega} - 0.2}\right)\left(\frac{e^{-j\omega}}{e^{-j\omega} - 0.5}\right)$$

Now let

$$Y(e^{j\omega}) = \frac{k_1 e^{j\omega}}{e^{j\omega} - 0.2} + \frac{k_2 e^{-j\omega}}{e^{-j\omega} - 0.5}$$

so that we can easily obtain the inverse DTFT of each term. Note the difference in the two terms.

Then we compute k_1 from the following method, which is slightly different from the partial fraction method we have used earlier:

$$Y(e^{j\omega})e^{-j\omega}(e^{j\omega} - 0.2) = \left(\frac{e^{-j\omega}}{e^{-j\omega} - 0.5}\right) = k_1 + \frac{k_2(e^{j\omega} - 0.2)}{(e^{-j\omega} - 0.5)}e^{-j2\omega}$$

Evaluating both terms at $e^{j\omega} = 0.2$ yields

$$k_1 = \left(\frac{e^{-j\omega}}{e^{-j\omega} - 0.5}\right)\Bigg|_{e^{j\omega}=0.2} = \frac{5}{4.5} = 1.111$$

Similarly, the constant k_2 is evaluated as follows (again, this is slightly different from the partial fraction expansion method we have used earlier):

$$Y(e^{j\omega})e^{j\omega}(e^{-j\omega} - 0.5) = \frac{k_1 e^{j2\omega}(e^{-j\omega} - 0.5)}{e^{j\omega} - 0.2} + k_2 = \left(\frac{e^{j\omega}}{e^{j\omega} - 0.2}\right)$$

Evaluating the two terms at $e^{j\omega} = 2.0$ yields $k_2 = \frac{2}{1.8} = 1.111$. Therefore we have $Y(e^{j\omega}) = 1.111e^{j\omega}/(e^{j\omega} - 0.2) + 1.111e^{-j\omega}/(e^{-j\omega} - 0.5)$, and the output is $y(n) = 1.111(0.2)^n u(n) + 1.111(0.5)^{-n} u(-n)$.

Now we describe a preferred method of finding the inverse DTFT of

$$Y(e^{j\omega}) = H(e^{j\omega})X(e^{j\omega}) = \left(\frac{e^{j\omega}}{e^{j\omega} - 0.2}\right)\left(\frac{e^{-j\omega}}{e^{-j\omega} - 0.5}\right)$$

which we express in the form of

$$\frac{1}{(1 - 0.2e^{-j\omega})(1 - 0.5e^{j\omega})}$$

where each term in the denominator is of the general form $(1 - ae^{-j\omega})$ or $(1 - ae^{j\omega})$. The partial fraction expansion is now chosen to be in the form of

$$Y(e^{j\omega}) = \frac{K_1}{(1 - 0.2e^{-j\omega})} + \frac{K_2}{(1 - 0.5e^{j\omega})}$$

The residue K_1 is determined by evaluating

$$Y(e^{j\omega})(1 - 0.2e^{-j\omega})\big|_{e^{j\omega}=0.2} = \frac{1}{(1 - 0.5e^{j\omega})}\bigg|_{e^{j\omega}=0.2} = 1.1111$$

Similarly $K_2 = Y(e^{j\omega})(1 - 0.5e^{j\omega})\big|_{e^{j\omega}=2} = \frac{1}{(1 - 0.2e^{-j\omega})}\bigg|_{e^{j\omega}=2} = 1.111$

Example 3.13

Let $x(n) = e^{j(0.3\pi n)}$ and $h(n) = (0.2)^n u(n)$. As in Example 3.12, we can find the DTFT of $x(n) = e^{j(0.3\pi n)}$ as $X(e^{j\omega}) = 2\pi \sum \delta(\omega - 0.3\pi - 2\pi k)$ and the DTFT of $h(n)$ as

$$H(e^{j\omega}) = \left(\frac{1}{1 - 0.2e^{-j\omega}}\right) = \left(\frac{e^{j\omega}}{e^{j\omega} - 0.2}\right)$$

Thus

$$Y(e^{j\omega}) = X(e^{j\omega})H(e^{j\omega}) = 2\pi \sum \delta(\omega - 0.3\pi - 2\pi k)H(e^{j\omega})$$

$$= 2\pi \sum_{k=-\infty}^{\infty} \delta(\omega - 0.3\pi - 2\pi k)H(e^{j0.3\pi})$$

$$= \left[\frac{e^{j0.3\pi}}{(e^{j0.3\pi} - 0.2)}\right] 2\pi \sum \delta(\omega - 0.3\pi - 2\pi k)$$

$$= \left[1.1146e^{-j(0.1813)}\right] 2\pi \sum \delta(\omega - 0.3\pi - 2\pi k)$$

Therefore $y(n) = \left[1.1146e^{-j(0.1813)}\right] e^{j(0.3\pi n)} = 1.1146e^{j(0.3\pi n - 0.1813)}$.

As an alternative method, we recollect that from the convolution of $e^{j\omega n}$ and $h(n)$, we obtained $y(n) = e^{j\omega n}H(e^{j\omega})$. In this example $H(e^{j\omega}) = [e^{j\omega}/(e^{j\omega} - 0.2)]$ and $\omega = 0.3\pi$. Therefore $y(n) = e^{j0.3\pi n}H(e^{j0.3\pi})$:

$$y(n) = e^{j0.3\pi n}\left[\frac{e^{j0.3\pi}}{(e^{j0.3\pi} - 0.2)}\right] = 1.1146e^{j(0.3\pi n - 0.1813)}$$

By this method, we can also find that when the input is $\mathrm{Re}\{x(n)\} = \cos(0.3\pi n)$, the output is given by $y(n) = \mathrm{Re}\{1.1146e^{j(0.3\pi n - 0.1813)}\} = 1.1146\cos(0.3\pi n - 0.1813)$.

3.4.3 Conjugation Property

Here we assume the samples $x(n)$ to be complex-valued and in the general form $x(n) = (ae^{j\theta})^n$ and the complex conjugate to be $x^*(n) = (ae^{-j\theta})^n$.
   Let us find their DTFT:

$$x(n) \Leftrightarrow X_1(e^{j\omega}) = \sum_{n=-\infty}^{\infty} (ae^{j\theta})^n e^{-j\omega n}$$

$$= \sum_{n=-\infty}^{\infty} (a)^n e^{j\theta n} e^{-j\omega n}$$

$$x^*(n) \Leftrightarrow X_2(e^{j\omega}) = \sum_{n=-\infty}^{\infty} (ae^{-j\theta})^n e^{-j\omega n}$$

$$= \sum_{n=-\infty}^{\infty} (a)^n e^{-j\theta n} e^{-j\omega n}$$

Now we replace ω by $-\omega$ in $X_2(e^{j\omega})$ to get $X_2(e^{-j\omega}) = \sum_{n=-\infty}^{\infty}(a)^n e^{-j\theta n} e^{j\omega n}$, and its conjugate is obtained as $X_2^*(e^{-j\omega})$:

$$X_2^*(e^{-j\omega}) = \sum_{n=-\infty}^{\infty} (a)^n e^{j\theta n} e^{-j\omega n} = X_1(e^{j\omega})$$

In words, this result $X_2^*(e^{-j\omega}) = X_1(e^{j\omega})$ means that we find the DTFT of the complex conjugate sequence $(ae^{-j\theta})^n$ and replace ω by $-\omega$ and then find the complex conjugate of the result, which is the same as the DTFT of the sequence $(ae^{j\theta})^n$.
   However, when $x(n)$ is real, we know that $x(n) = x^*(n)$, in which case $X_1(e^{j\omega}) = X_2(e^{j\omega})$. So we have the following result:

$$X_1(e^{j\omega}) = X_1^*(e^{-j\omega}) \quad \text{when } x(n) \text{ is real} \tag{3.57}$$

3.4.4 Symmetry Property

From the result in (3.57), the following symmetry properties can be derived when sequence $x(n)$ is real:

$$\mathrm{Re}\{X(e^{j\omega})\} = \mathrm{Re}\{X(e^{-j\omega})\} \tag{3.58}$$

$$\mathrm{Im}\{X(e^{j\omega})\} = -\mathrm{Im}\{X(e^{-j\omega})\} \tag{3.59}$$

$$\left|X(e^{j\omega})\right| = \left|X(e^{-j\omega})\right| \qquad (3.60)$$

$$\text{Ang } X(e^{j\omega}) = -\text{Ang } X(e^{-j\omega}) \qquad (3.61)$$

The even and odd parts of the sequence $x(n)$ are defined by $x_e(n) = [x(n) + x(-n)]/2$ and $x_0(n) = [x(n) - x(-n)]/2$ respectively. When $x(n)$ is real, and we use the time reversal property, we get $x_e(n) \Leftrightarrow [\{X(e^{j\omega})\} + \{X(e^{-j\omega})\}]/2 = \text{Re}\{X(e^{j\omega})\}$:

$$x_e(n) \Leftrightarrow \text{Re}\{X(e^{j\omega})\} \qquad (3.62)$$

Similarly, $x_0(n) \Leftrightarrow [\{X(e^{j\omega})\} - \{X(e^{-j\omega})\}]/2 = j\text{Im}\{X(e^{j\omega})\}$:

$$x_0(n) \Leftrightarrow j\text{Im}\{X(e^{j\omega})\} \qquad (3.63)$$

From (3.60) and (3.61), we see that the magnitude response $\left|X(e^{j\omega})\right|$ is an even function of ω and the phase response is an odd function of ω.

The basic properties of the discrete-time Fourier transform and examples of some common DTFT-IDTFT pairs that have been described above are listed in Tables 3.1 and 3.2.

TABLE 3.1 Properties of Discrete-Time Fourier Transform

Property	Time Domain $x(n), x_1(n), x_2(n)$	Frequency Domain $X(e^{j\omega}), X_1(e^{j\omega}), X_2(e^{j\omega})$
Linearity	$ax_1(n) + bx_2(n)$	$aX_1(e^{j\omega}) + bX_2(e^{j\omega})$
Convolution	$x_1(n) * x_2(n)$	$X_1(e^{j\omega})X_2(e^{j\omega})$
Time shifting	$x(n - k)$	$e^{-j\omega k}X(e^{j\omega})$
Frequency shifting	$e^{j\omega_0 n}x(n)$	$X(e^{j(\omega-\omega_0)})$
Time reversal	$x(-n)$	$X(e^{-j\omega})$
Multiplication	$x_1(n)x_2(n)$	$(1/2\pi)\int_{-\pi}^{\pi} X_1(e^{j\zeta})X_2(e^{j(\omega-\zeta)})d\zeta$
Differentiation	$nx(n)$	$j[dX(e^{j\omega})]/d\omega$
Conjugation	$x^*(n)$	$X^*(e^{-j\omega})$
Even part of $x(n)$	$x_e(n) = \frac{1}{2}[x(n) + x(-n)]$	$\text{Re}\{X(e^{j\omega})\}$
Odd part of $x(n)$	$x_0(n) = \frac{1}{2}[x(n) - x(-n)]$	$j\text{Im}\{X(e^{j\omega})\}$
Symmetry		$\text{Re}\{X(e^{j\omega})\} = \text{Re}\{X(e^{-j\omega})\}$
		$\text{Im}\{X(e^{j\omega})\} = -\text{Im}\{X(e^{-j\omega})\}$
		$\left|X(e^{j\omega})\right| = \left|X(e^{-j\omega})\right|$
		$\text{Ang } X(e^{j\omega}) = -\text{Ang } X(e^{-j\omega})$

TABLE 3.2   Common IDTFT-DTFT Pairs

Signal (IDTFT):$x(n)$	Discrete-Time Fourier Transform (DTFT):$X(e^{j\omega})$
$\delta(n)$	1
$\delta(n-k)$	$e^{-j\omega k}$
1 (for all n)	$2\pi \sum_{k=-\infty}^{\infty} \delta(\omega - 2\pi k)$
$e^{j\omega_0 n}$	$2\pi \sum_{k=-\infty}^{\infty} \delta(\omega - \omega_0 - 2\pi k)$
$\cos(\omega_0 n)$	$\pi \sum_{k=-\infty}^{\infty} \delta(\omega - \omega_0 - 2\pi k) + \delta(\omega + \omega_0 - 2\pi k)$
$\sin(\omega_0 n)$	$\frac{\pi}{j} \sum_{k=-\infty}^{\infty} \delta(\omega - \omega_0 - 2\pi k) - \delta(\omega + \omega_0 - 2\pi k)$
$e^{-an}u(n); \quad |a| < 1$	$1/(1 - e^{-a}e^{-j\omega})$
$a^n u(n); \quad |a| < 1$	$1/(1 - ae^{-j\omega})$
$na^n u(n); |a| < 1$	$ae^{-j\omega}/(1 - ae^{-j\omega})^2$
$(n+1)a^n u(n); \quad |a| < 1$	$1/(1 - ae^{-j\omega})^2$
$x(n) = \begin{cases} 1 & |n| \le N \\ 0 & |n| > N \end{cases}$	$\sin(N+0.5)\omega / \sin(0.5\omega)$
$(1/\pi n)\sin(\omega_c n)$	$\begin{cases} 1 & |\omega| \le \omega_c \\ 0 & |\omega| > \omega_c \end{cases}$
$u(n)$	$1/(1 - e^{-j\omega}) + \pi \sum_{k=-\infty}^{\infty} \delta(\omega - 2\pi k)$

3.5   USE OF MATLAB TO COMPUTE DTFT

If a function is a finite sequence, such as the unit impulse response of an FIR filter $H(z^{-1}) = \sum_{k=0}^{N} b_k z^{-k}$, then the difference equation for that filter is given by

$$y(n) = \sum_{k=0}^{M} b_k x(n-k) \tag{3.64}$$

We find its frequency response or its Fourier transform (DTFT) to be

$$Y(e^{j\omega}) = H(e^{j\omega})X(e^{j\omega}) = \sum_{k=0}^{M} b_k X(e^{j\omega})e^{-j\omega k}$$

where the frequency response for this FIR filter is given by

$$H(e^{j\omega}) = \sum_{k=0}^{N} b_k e^{-j\omega k} \tag{3.65}$$

It is also the DTFT of the signal $h(k) = [b_0, b_1, b_2, \ldots, b_N]$.

Suppose that we are given the transfer function of an IIR filter:

$$H(z^{-1}) = \frac{\sum_{k=0}^{M} b_k z^{-k}}{1 + \sum_{k=1}^{N} a_k z^{-k}}$$

There are two equivalent approaches to find the frequency response of this filter as described below.

We find the inverse z transform $h(n)$ of $H(z^{-1})$, which gives an infinite number of samples of its unit impulse response, and now we can evaluate its frequency response or its DTFT as $H(e^{-j\omega}) = \sum_{r=0}^{\infty} h(n)e^{-j\omega r}$. The other approach uses the difference equation $y(n) + \sum_{k=1}^{N} a_k y(n-k) = \sum_{k=0}^{M} b_k x(n-k)$ and finds the DTFT of both sides as given by

$$Y(e^{j\omega}) \left[1 + \sum_{k=1}^{N} a_k e^{-j\omega k} \right] = X(e^{j\omega}) \sum_{k=0}^{M} b_k e^{-j\omega k}$$

so that

$$H(e^{-j\omega}) = \frac{\sum_{k=0}^{M} b_k e^{-j\omega k}}{1 + \sum_{k=1}^{N} a_k e^{-j\omega k}} \qquad (3.66)$$

In short, we can state that $H(e^{-j\omega}) = H(z^{-1})\big|_{z=e^{j\omega}}$, provided both exist.

To compute and plot the magnitude, phase, and/or the group delay of the FIR or IIR filter transfer functions $H(z^{-1})$, we use the MATLAB functions `freqz`, `abs`, `angle`, `unwrap`, `grpdelay` very extensively in signal processing and filter design. These functions are found in the Signal Processing Toolbox of MATLAB.

When the sequence of coefficients b_k and a_k are known, they are entered as the values in the vectors for the numerator and denominator. The function `freqz` is used with several variations for the input variables as described below:

```
[h,w] = freqz(num,den,w)
[h,w] = freqz(num, den, f, Fs)
[h,w] = freqz(num,den,K,Fs)
[h,w] = freqz(num,den,K,'whole')
[h,f] = freqz(num,den,K,'whole',Fs)}
```

The vectors `num` and `den` are the row vectors of the numerator and denominator coefficients a_k and b_k, respectively. The function `freqz` computes the values of the frequency response as a column vector `h` at the discrete values of the frequency `w`. The set of default frequencies `w` lie between 0 and π, and the set `f` is the vector of values for the frequencies we can arbitrarily distinguish between 0 and `Fs/2`, where `Fs` is the sampling frequency in hertz. We can choose a value for `K` as the number of frequency points within the default range; preferably `K` is chosen as a power of 2 such as 256, 512, or 1024 to get faster computation. When K is not specified, the default value of 512 is chosen by the program. When we include the argument 'whole' in the function freqz, the frequency range of w and f changes to [0 2π] and [0   F$_s$], respectively.

After we have computed the values of the frequency response at the discrete frequencies, we can compute their magnitude using H = abs(h) or the magnitude in decibels using HdB=20*log10(H). The phase response (in radians) of the filter is obtained from the function ph=angle(h), and then we can use Ph=unwrap(ph) to unwrap the phase response so that the phase angle lies between 0 and 2π. The group delay of the filter is computed by the MATLAB function grpdelay (and not from the function freqz) as follows:

```
[gd,w]=grpdelay(num,den,K,)
[gd,w]=grpdelay(num,den,K,'whole')
```

Note that we can change the name for the variables num,den,h,H, HdB,f,FT,K,ph,Ph,gd in the statements above to other variables as we like. After we have computed H,HdB, ph,Ph,gd, we plot them using the plotting function with different choices of variables, as illustrated in the examples given below. When we plot H, Hdb, ph, Ph, or grpdelay, we normally plot them as a function of the normalized frequency on a linear scale, between 0 and π. But the function semilog(.....) plots them as a function of log10(w) and therefore a plot of semilog(HdB) becomes the familiar Bode plot of the digital filter; alternatively, we define ww = log10(w) as the new frequency variable and plot the magnitudes using plot(ww, H) or plot(ww, HdB).

The MATLAB function freqz(num,den) without any other arguments computes and plots the magnitude in decibels as well as the phase response as a function of frequency in the current figure window.

Example 3.14

```
%Program to compute and plot the magnitude and phase responses
%  of a filter
b=[0.0532 0.3725 1.1176 1.8626 1.8626 1.1176 0.3725 0.0532];
a=[1.0000 1.5473 2.1992 1.2240 0.8269 0.0347 0.0587 -0.0790];
[h,w]=freqz(b,a,256);
H=abs(h);
HdB=20*log10(H);
ph=angle(h);
Ph=unwrap(ph);
[gd,w]=grpdelay(b,a,256);
subplot(1,2,1)
plot(w,H);grid
title('Magnitude of the frequency response')
ylabel('Magnitude')
```

```
xlabel('Normalized frequency')
subplot(1,2,2)
plot(w,HdB);grid
title('Magnitude in dB of the frequency response')
ylabel('Magnitude in dB')
xlabel('Normalized frequency')
figure(2)
subplot(1,2,1)
plot(w,ph);grid
title('Phase response of the filter')
ylabel('Phase angle in radians')
xlabel('Normalized frequency')
subplot(1,2,2)
plot(w,Ph);grid
title('Unwrapped phase response filter')
ylabel('Phase angle in radians')
xlabel('Normalized frequency')
%end
```

The magnitude response and phase response of this IIR filter are plotted in Figures 3.23 and 3.24, respectively.

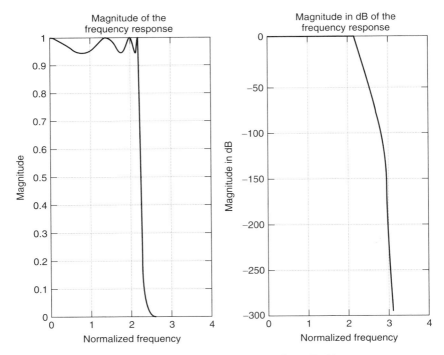

Figure 3.23   Magnitude response of an IIR filter.

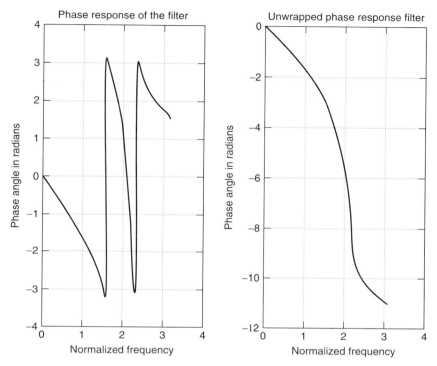

Figure 3.24   Phase response of an IIR filter.

Example 3.15

Now we consider an FIR filter with a finite number of coefficients as [1.0 0.8 0.6 0.4 0.6 0.8 1.0]. The MATLAB script used to compute its frequency response and plot the magnitude and phase for the whole range of 0 to 2π is shown below:

```
%Program to compute and plot the frequency response or DTFT
%  of an FIR filter
b=[1.0 0.8 0.6 0.4 0.6 0.8 1.0];
[h,w]=freqz(b,1,256,'whole');
H=abs(h);
ph=angle(h);
plot(w,H);grid
title('Magnitude of the FIR filter')
ylabel('Magnitude')
xlabel('Normalized frequency from 0 to 2*pi')
figure
plot(w,ph);grid
```

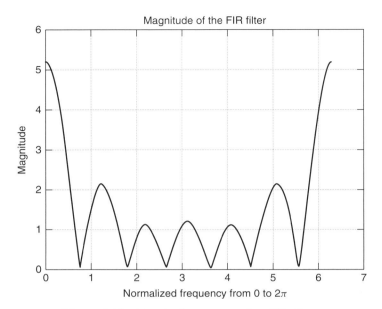

Figure 3.25   Magnitude response of an FIR filter.

```
title('Phase response of the FIR filter')
ylabel('Phase angle in radians')
xlabel('Normalized frequency')
%end
```

The magnitude and phase responses for the normalized frequency range from 0 to 2π are shown in Figures 3.25 and 3.26, respectively. The phase response is found to be linear as a function of the frequency in this example. We will work out many more examples of computing and plotting the DTFT or the frequency response of filters in Chapter 4, using the MATLAB functions listed above.

Example 3.16

In this example, we choose the sampling frequency $F_s = 200$ Hz, and the Nyquist interval is divided into 100 equal parts as seen in the statement f = [0:99] in the MATLAB program given below. The sample values of the signal are entered by us, when prompted by the program. In the example, we entered [0.4   0.6   0.8] as the input signal. The magnitude and phase are plotted in Figure 3.27 as a function of the frequency from 0 to 100 Hz. But the group delay is plotted as a function of the normalized frequency from 0 to π radians.

```
% Program to compute and plot the magnitude and phase and
%    group delay of an FIR filter
```

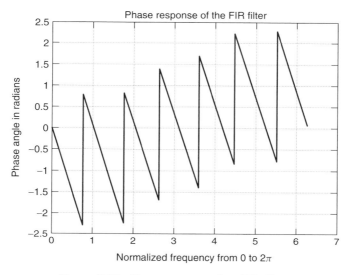

Figure 3.26   Phase response of an FIR filter.

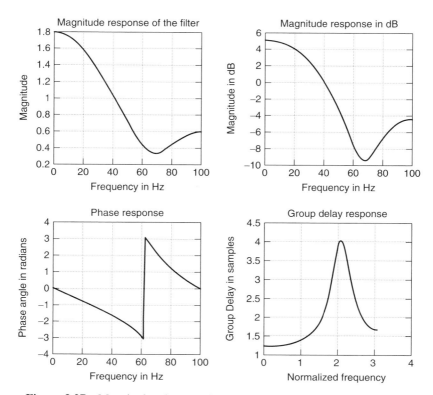

Figure 3.27   Magnitude, phase, and group delay responses of an FIR filter.

```
b=input('Type the values of the signal');
a=1;
f=0:99;
Fs=200;
[H,w]=freqz(b,a,f,Fs);
mag=abs(H);
DB=20*log10(mag);
phase=angle(H);
[grp,w]=grpdelay(b,a,256);
subplot(2,2,1)
plot(f,mag);grid
title('Magnitude response of the filter')
ylabel('Magnitude')
xlabel('Frequency in Hz')
subplot(2,2,2)
plot(f,DB);grid
title('Magnitude response in dB')
ylabel('Magnitude in dB')
xlabel('Frequency in Hz')
subplot(2,2,3)
plot(f,phase);grid
title('Phase response')
ylabel('Phase angle in radians')
xlabel('Frequency in Hz')
subplot(2,2,4)
plot(w,grp);grid
title('Group Delay response'))
ylabel('Group Delay in samples'))
xlabel('Normalized frequency')
%end
```

3.6 DTFS AND DFT

3.6.1 Introduction

We discussed the DTFT-IDTFT pair for a discrete-time function given by

$$X(e^{j\omega}) = \sum_{n=-\infty}^{\infty} x(n)e^{-j\omega n} \qquad (3.67)$$

and

$$x(n) = \frac{1}{2\pi} \int_{-\pi}^{\pi} X(e^{j\omega})e^{j\omega n} d\omega \qquad (3.68)$$

The theory for deriving the pair and their properties and applications are very elegant, but from practical point of view, we see some limitations in computing the DTFT and IDTFT. For example, the input signal is usually aperiodic and may be finite in length, but the unit impulse response of an IIR filter is also aperiodic but infinite in length; however, the values of its samples become almost negligible in many practical applications as n becomes large but finite. So in (3.67), it is reasonable to assume that the number of terms is finite, but $X(e^{j\omega})$ is a function of the continuous variable ω. We have given some examples of analytically deriving closed-form expressions for this function and plotting it as a function of the variable ω. We showed how we can do it by using MATLAB functions.

Let us consider one more example of a discrete-time function $x(n)$ and its DTFT $X(e^{j\omega})$. Figure 3.28a shows a nonperiodic discrete-time function $x(n)$

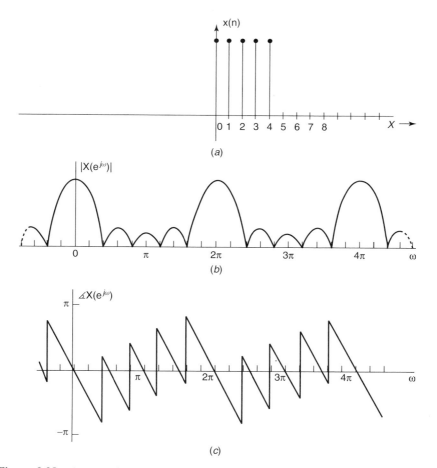

Figure 3.28   A nonperiodic signal; (b) its magnitude response; (c) its phase response.

that is of finite length. Figure 3.28b,c show the magnitude response $\left|X(e^{j\omega})\right|$ and phase response $\angle X(e^{j\omega})$ of the DTFT $X(e^{j\omega})$.

The function $X(e^{j\omega})$ in (3.68) is a function of the continuous variable ω, and the integration is not very suitable for computation by a digital computer. Of course, we can discretize the frequency variable and find discrete values for $X(e^{j\omega_k})$ where ω_k are discrete values of the frequency. In contrast to the case of a continuous-time signal with a frequency response $X(j\omega)$, we notice that we need to compute the DTFT at only a finite number of values since $X(e^{j\omega})$ is periodic, and therefore we need to compute it over one period only. In (3.68), $x(n)$ can be computed approximately, if the integration is substituted by a summation and such a summation will be finite because the values of $X(e^{j\omega_k})$ have to be chosen only over the interval $[-\pi, \quad \pi]$. [We may also note that the reconstruction formula used to obtain $x(t)$ from its samples $x(n)$ is not suitable for digital computer, either.] These limitations are mitigated by a theory based on the model for a discrete-time signal that is *periodic*, and in the next section, we describe the discrete-time Fourier series (DTFS) representation for such discrete-time periodic signals. This theory exploits the property of the DTFT that it is periodic, and hence we need to use only a finite frequency range of one period that is sufficient to find its inverse.

3.6.2 Discrete-Time Fourier Series

We consider a discrete-time aperiodic signal $x(n)$ that is finite in length equal to N samples and generate a periodic sequence with a period N so that it satisfies the condition $x_p(n + KN) = x_p(n)$, where K is any integer. The complex Fourier series representation of this periodic signal contains the sum of the discrete-time complex exponentials $e^{jk\omega_0 n}$, where $\omega_0 = 2\pi/N$ is its fundamental frequency and $\omega_0 k$ is its kth harmonic. The Fourier series is a weighted sum of the fundamental and higher harmonics in the form $x_p(n) = \sum_{k=0} X_p(k)e^{j\omega_0 kn}$, where $X_p(k)$ is the coefficient of the kth harmonic in the Fourier series. These coefficients are complex-valued in general and hence have a magnitude and a phase: $X_p(k) = \left|X_p(k)\right| \angle X_p(k)$

In Chapter 1, we pointed out an important property of the discrete-time exponentials (in contrast to the continuous-time exponentials $e^{j\omega_0 kt}$) that the exponentials with frequencies that are separated by integer multiples of 2π are the same

$$e^{j(\omega_0 \pm 2\pi)k} = e^{j\omega_0 k}e^{j\pm 2\pi k} = e^{j\omega_0 k} \tag{3.69}$$

and therefore the coefficient of the complex Fourier series $X_p(k) = X_p(k \pm N)$. Consequently there are only N independent harmonics (in contrast to the infinite number of harmonics in the case of the continuous-time periodic function), and we have used a subscript to denote that these coefficients $X_p(k)$ are periodic.

Therefore, in its complex Fourier series form, we have

$$x_p(n) = \sum_{k=0}^{N-1} X_p(k) e^{j(2\pi/N)kn} \tag{3.70}$$

To find these coefficients, let us multiply both sides by $e^{-jm\omega_0 k}$ and sum over n from $n = 0$ to $(N - 1)$:

$$\sum_{n=0}^{N-1} x_p(n) e^{-jm\omega_0 k} = \sum_{n=0}^{N-1}\sum_{k=0}^{N-1} X_p(k) e^{j(2\pi/N)kn} e^{-jm\omega_0 k} \tag{3.71}$$

By interchanging the order of summation on the right side, we get

$$\sum_{k=0}^{N-1} X_p(k) \left[\sum_{n=0}^{N-1} e^{j(2\pi/N)k(n-m)} \right] \tag{3.72}$$

It is next shown that $[\sum_{n=0}^{N-1} e^{j(2\pi/N)k(n-m)}]$ is equal to N when $n = m$ and zero for all values of $n \neq m$. When $n = m$, the summation reduces to $[\sum_{n=0}^{N-1} e^{j0}] = N$, and when $n \neq m$, we apply (3.52) and find that the summation yields zero. Hence there is only one nonzero term $X_p(k)N$ in (3.72). The final result is

$$X_p(k) = \frac{1}{N} \sum_{n=0}^{N-1} x_p(n) e^{-jn\omega_0 k} \tag{3.73}$$

Now we notice that

$$\frac{1}{N} \sum_{n=0}^{N-1} x_p(n) e^{-jn\omega_0 k} = \frac{1}{N} \sum_{n=0}^{N-1} x(n) e^{-j(2\pi/N)nk}$$

$$= \left(\frac{1}{N} \right) X_p(e^{j\omega}) \Big|_{\omega_k=(2\pi/N)k} = X_p(k) \tag{3.74}$$

In other words, when the DTFT of the finite length sequence $x(n)$ is evaluated at the discrete frequency $\omega_k = (2\pi/N)k$, (which is the kth sample when the frequency range $[0, \quad 2\pi]$ is divided into N equally spaced points) and dividing by N, we get the value of the Fourier series coefficient $X_p(k)$.

The expression in (3.70) is known as the *discrete-time Fourier series* (DTFS) representation for the discrete-time, periodic function $x_p(n)$ and (3.73), which gives the complex-valued coefficients of the DTFS is the inverse DTFS (IDTFS). Because both $x_p(n)$ and $X_p(k)$ are periodic, with period N, we observe that the two expressions above are valid for $-\infty < n < \infty$ and $-\infty < k < \infty$, respectively. Note that some authors abbreviate DTFS to DFS.

To simplify the notation, let us denote $e^{-j(2\pi/N)n}$ by W_N so that (3.70) and (3.73) are rewritten in compact form for the DTFS-IDTFS pair as

$$x_p(n) = \sum_{k=0}^{N-1} X_p(k) W^{-kn}, \qquad -\infty < n < \infty \qquad (3.75)$$

$$X_p(k) = \frac{1}{N} \sum_{n=0}^{N-1} x_p(n) W^{kn}, \qquad -\infty < k < \infty \qquad (3.76)$$

Figure 3.29a shows an example of the periodic discrete-time function $x_p(n)$ constructed from Figure 3.28a while Figures 3.29b,c show the samples of the magnitude $N \left| X_p(k) \right|$ and phase $\angle X_p(k)$ of the DTFT at the discrete frequencies $\omega_k = k(2\pi/N), k = 0, 1, 2, \ldots, (N-1)$.

By comparing (3.73) and (3.67), we notice the following. Remember that $X(e^{j\omega})$ given by (3.67) is the DTFT of a nonperiodic sequence that may be of finite or infinite length. But when we assume that the signal is of finite length N,

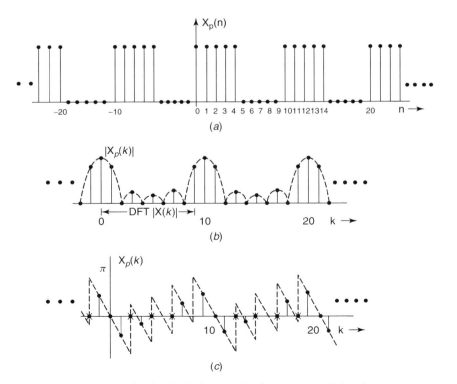

Figure 3.29 A periodic signal; (b) its magnitude response; (c) its phase response.

and have $x_p(n) = x(n)$ for $n = 0, 1, 2, \ldots, (N-1)$, we have its DTFT as

$$X(e^{j\omega}) = \frac{1}{N} \sum_{k=0}^{N-1} x(n) e^{-j\omega n}$$

In (3.73) we evaluate the DTFT at N discrete frequencies ω_k and divide these samples by N to get $X_p(k)$. From (3.70), we see that the coefficients $X_p(k)$ of the DTFS for $x_p(n)$ are also the coefficients of the Fourier series for the discrete-time periodic sequence $x_p(n)$, and they are also referred to as the *spectral components* of $x_p(n)$. In other words, the Fourier series coefficients of a periodic signal $x_p(n)$ is $1/N$ times the DTFT of $x(n)$ evaluated at the discrete frequencies ω_k. We repeat that $X_p(k) = (1/N)X(e^{j\omega_k})$, where $X(e^{j\omega})$ is the DTFT of a sequence $x(n)$. This result is based on the assumption that $x(n)$ is a sequence of finite length N.

3.6.3 Discrete Fourier Transform

We will discuss some properties of the DTFS-IDTFS pairs later in this section. Here we use the argument that if (3.75) is valid for all values of n (i.e., for $-\infty < n < \infty$), it is valid for $0 \le n \le N - 1$ or for any sequence of length N; similarly, (3.76) is valid for $0 \le k \le N - 1$. Thus we denote $X_p(k); 0 \le n \le N - 1$ by the notation $X(k)$, whereas we already have represented $x(n) = x_p(n); 0 \le n \le N - 1$:

$$x(n) = \sum_{k=0}^{N-1} X(k) e^{j(2\pi/N)kn} = \sum_{k=0}^{N-1} X(k) W^{-kn}, \qquad 0 \le n \le N - 1 \quad (3.77)$$

$$X(k) = \frac{1}{N} \sum_{n=0}^{N-1} x(n) e^{-j(2\pi/N)kn} = \frac{1}{N} \sum_{n=0}^{N-1} x(n) W^{kn}, \quad 0 \le k \le N - 1 \quad (3.78)$$

Note that we have not derived these properties from any new theory but only defined them as a part of the infinite sequences for the DTFS and IDTFS derived above.

Also note that whereas (3.75) is termed the *discrete-time Fourier series* (DTFS) representation of $x_p(n)$, in which $X_p(k)$ are the coefficients of the Fourier series [and (3.76) is the IDTFS], it is (3.78) that is known as the *discrete-time Fourier transform* (DFT) [and (3.77) is known as the *inverse DFT* (IDFT)]! In Sections 3.6.1 and 3.6.2, note that we have used different notations to distinguish the DTFT-IDTFT pair from the DFT-IDFT pair.

In most of the textbooks, and in MATLAB, the DFT-IDFT are simply defined as given below, without any reference to the theory for deriving the DTFS, from which the DFT are selected. Also note that the scale factor $(1/N)$ has been moved from (3.78) to (3.77) in defining the DFT-IDFT pair as shown in (3.79) and (3.80) *(we will use these two equations for the DFT-IDFT pair in the remaining pages)*:

$$x(n) = \frac{1}{N} \sum_{k=0}^{N-1} X(k) e^{j(2\pi/N)kn} = \frac{1}{N} \sum_{k=0}^{N-1} X(k) W^{-kn}, \quad 0 \le n \le N-1 \quad (3.79)$$

$$X(k) = \sum_{n=0}^{N-1} x(n) e^{-j(2\pi/N)kn} = \sum_{n=0}^{N-1} x(n) W^{kn}, \qquad 0 \le k \le N-1 \quad (3.80)$$

In Figure 3.29b, we have shown the DFT as a subset of the Fourier series coefficients $X_p(k)$, for $k = 0, 1, 2, \ldots, (N-1)$. But we can choose any other N consecutive samples as the DFT of $x(n)$ [e.g., $-[(N-1)/2] \le n \le [(N-1)/2]$], so we will use the notation $\langle N \rangle = n$ modulo N to denote that n ranges over one period of N samples.

Given a nonperiodic discrete-time function $x(n)$, we constructed a mathematical artifact $x_p(n)$ and derived the Fourier series representation for it and also derived its inverse to get $x_p(n)$. Then we defined the DFT and IDFT as argued above so that we could determine the frequency response of the non-periodic function as samples of the DTFT $X(e^{j\omega})$ at N equally spaced points $\omega_k = (2\pi/N)k$. We know $x(n)$ is nonperiodic, but since $X(e^{j\omega})$ is periodic with a period 2π, $X(e^{j\omega_k}) = X_p(k)$ is periodic with a period N, so one can choose the range $n = \langle N \rangle$ in Equations (3.79) and (3.80).

The two equations for the DFT and IDFT give us a numerical algorithm to obtain the frequency response at least at the N discrete frequencies, and by choosing a large value for N, we get a fairly good idea of the frequency response for $x(n)$.[6] Indeed, we show below that from the samples of $X(k)$, we can reconstruct the DTFT of $x(n) = X(e^{j\omega})$, which is a function of the continuous variable ω. This is the counterpart of Shannon's reconstruction formula to obtain $x(t)$ from its samples $x(n)$, provided $x(n)$ is bandlimited and the sampling period $T_s < (\pi/\omega_b)$. There are similar conditions to be satisfied in deriving the formula in the frequency domain, to reconstruct $X(e^{j\omega})$ from its samples $X(e^{j\omega_k}) = X(k)$.

3.6.4 Reconstruction of DTFT from DFT

First we consider the DTFT of $x(n)$ and substitute $x(n)$ by the formula (3.79) for finding the IDFT of $X(k)$ as explained below:

$$X(e^{j\omega}) = \sum_{n=0}^{N-1} x(n) e^{-j\omega n} = \sum_{n=0}^{N-1} \left[\frac{1}{N} \sum_{k=0}^{N-1} X(k) e^{j(2\pi kn/N)} \right] e^{-j\omega n}$$

$$= \frac{1}{N} \sum_{k=0}^{N-1} X(k) \sum_{n=0}^{N-1} e^{j(2\pi kn/N)} e^{-j\omega n} \qquad (3.81)$$

---

[6]Later we will discuss what is known as the "picket fence effect," because of which we may not get a fairly good idea of the frequency response.

Now we use (3.52) in the summation $\sum_{n=0}^{N-1} e^{j(2\pi kn/N)} e^{-j\omega n}$ and reduce it as follows:

$$\sum_{n=0}^{N-1} e^{j(2\pi kn/N)} e^{-j\omega n} = \frac{1 - e^{-j(\omega N - 2\pi k)}}{1 - e^{-j[\omega - (2\pi k/N)]}}$$

$$= \frac{e^{-j[(\omega N - 2\pi k)/2]}}{e^{-j[(\omega N - 2\pi k)/2N]}} \cdot \frac{\sin\left[\dfrac{\omega N - 2\pi k}{2}\right]}{\sin\left[\dfrac{\omega N - 2\pi k}{2N}\right]}$$

$$= \frac{\sin\left[\dfrac{\omega N - 2\pi k}{2}\right]}{\sin\left[\dfrac{\omega N - 2\pi k}{2N}\right]} e^{-j[\omega - (2\pi k/N)][(N-1)/2]} \qquad (3.82)$$

Substituting the last expression in (3.81), we obtain the final result to reconstruct the DTFT $X(e^{j\omega})$, from only the finite number of the DFT samples $X(k)$, as given below:

$$X(e^{j\omega}) = \frac{1}{N} \sum_{k=0}^{N-1} X(k) \frac{\sin\left[\dfrac{\omega N - 2\pi k}{2}\right]}{\sin\left[\dfrac{\omega N - 2\pi k}{2N}\right]} e^{-j[\omega - (2\pi k/N)][(N-1)/2]} \qquad (3.83)$$

If $x(n)$ has M samples and we sample $X(e^{j\omega})$ at N points in the range $[0, \quad 2\pi]$, where $N > M$, then the N-point IDFT will yield N samples in the discrete-time domain. It can be shown that this result will give rise to aliasing of the N-point sequences (in the time domain). So we pad the given function $x(n)$ with $(M - N)$ zeros to make it a discrete-time function of length N; otherwise, we have to choose $N \le M$. In that case the sampling interval satisfies the condition $(2\pi/N) \ge (2\pi/M)$, which is dual to the condition that the sampling period $T \le (1/2B)$ to be satisfied for Shannon's reconstruction formula in the time domain. To satisfy this condition for reconstruction in the frequency domain, we make $M = N$ by padding with zeros $x(n)$ to avoid aliasing in the discrete-time domain.

3.6.5 Properties of DTFS and DFT

We have already listed some of the properties of DTFT in Table 3.1. Since the samples $X(k)$ of DFT are a subset of the Fourier series coefficients $X_p(k)$, there is some similarity between the properties of $X_p(k)$ and $X(k)$ and also those of the DTFT $X(e^{j\omega})$ of $x(n)$. Tables 3.3 and 3.4 list the properties of $X_p(k)$ and $X(k)$, respectively, which also show some similarities.

Remember again that the DFT $X(k)$ is defined over one period usually for $k = 0, 1, 2, \ldots, (N - 1)$ and it is considered to be zero outside this range. So

TABLE 3.3   Properties of DTFs Coefficients

Property	Periodic Signal $x(n)$ and $y(n)$ with Period N	DTFS Coefficients $X_p(k)$ $X_p(k)$ and $Y_k(k)$
Linearity	$ax(n) + by(n)$	$aX_p(k) + bY_p(k)$
Periodic convolution	$x(n) \circledast y(n)$	$X_p(k)Y_p(k)$
Time shifting	$x(n - k)$	$e^{-j(2\pi/N)km}X_p(k) = W_N^{km}X_p(k)$
Frequency shifting	$e^{j(2\pi/N)mn}x(n) = W^{-mn}x(n)$	$X_p(k - m)$
Time reversal	$x(-n)$	$X_p(-k)$
Multiplication	$x(n)y(n)$	$\frac{1}{N}\sum_{m=0}^{N-1} X_p(m)Y_p(k - m)$
Conjugation	$x^*(n)$	$X_p^*(-k)$
Even part of $x(n)$	$x_e(n) = \frac{1}{2}\left[x(n) + x^*(-n)\right]$	$\mathrm{Re}\left[X_p(k)\right]$
Odd part of $x(n)$	$x_0(n) = \frac{1}{2}\left[x(n) - x^*(-n)\right]$	$j\,\mathrm{Im}\left[X_p(k)\right]$
Symmetry	$x(n)$ is a real sequence	$X_p(k) = X_p^*(-k)$ $X_p(k) = X_p^*(-k)$ $\mathrm{Re}X_p(k) = \mathrm{Re}X_p(-k)$ $\mathrm{Im}X_p(k) = -\mathrm{Im}X_p(-k)$ $\left|X_p(k)\right| = \left|X_p(-k)\right|$ $\angle X_p(k) = -\angle X_p(-k)$

TABLE 3.4   Properties of DFT Coefficients

Property	Signal $x(n)$ and $y(n)$ of Length N	DFT Coefficients $X(k)$ and $Y(k)$ of Length N
Linearity	$ax(n) + by(n)$	$aX(k) + bY(k)$
Convolution	$\sum_{m=0}^{N-1} x(m)y((n - m))_N$	$X(k)Y(k)$
Time shifting	$x(n - m)_N$	$e^{-j(2\pi/N)km}X(k) = W_N^{km}X(k)$
Frequency shifting	$e^{j(2\pi/N)mn}x(n) = W^{-mn}x(n)$	$X((k - m))_N$
Multiplication	$x(n)y(n)$	$\frac{1}{N}\sum_{m=0}^{N-1} X(m)Y((k - m))_N$
Conjugation	$x^*(n)$	$X^*((-k))_N$
Even part of $x(n)$	$x_e(n) = \frac{1}{2}\left[x(n) + x^*((-n))_N\right]$	$\mathrm{Re}X(k)$
Odd part of $x(n)$	$x_0(n) = \frac{1}{2}\left[x(n) - x^*((-n))_N\right]$	$j\,\mathrm{Im}X(k)$
		$X(k) = X^*((-k))_N$ $\mathrm{Re}X(k) = \mathrm{Re}X((-k))_N$ $\mathrm{Im}X(k) = -\mathrm{Im}X((-k))_N$ $|X(k)| = |X((-k))_N|$ $\angle X(k) = -\angle X_p((-k))_N$

in Table 3.4, we have used a notation such as $X((-k))_N$, which means that we choose DTFS coefficients $X_p(k)$, use time reversal to get $X_p(-k)$, and then select any N samples that form a period. The double bracket with a subscript N calls for three operations: choosing the DTFS coefficients $X_p(k)$, carrying out the operation indicated by the index within the brackets, and then selecting $n = 0, 1, 2, \ldots, (N-1)$ or n modulo N. This again confirms the statement that all operations are carried out by the DTFS and then one period of the result is chosen as the DFT of $x(n)$. This is very significant when we carry out the periodic convolution of the DTFS of $x(n)$ and $f(n)$ and select the values of this convolution for $n = 0, 1, 2, \ldots, (N-1)$. We illustrate this by Example 3.17.

Example 3.17

Let $x(n) = [1.0 \quad 1.0 \quad 0.6 \quad 0.6]$ and $f(n) = [1.0 \quad 0.6 \quad 0.4]$. We can easily find the output $y_1(n)$ by using either one of two methods: (1) the convolution sum $y_1(n) = x(n) * f(n) = \sum_{m=0}^{N-1} x(m) f(n-m)$ or (2) one of the two transforms, namely, the z transform or the discrete-time Fourier transform (DTFT) of $x(n)$ and $f(n)$, and find the inverse z transform of $[X(z)F(z)]$ or the inverse DTFT of $\left[X(e^{j\omega}) F(e^{j\omega}) \right]$. Indeed, we can give a proof to show that the z

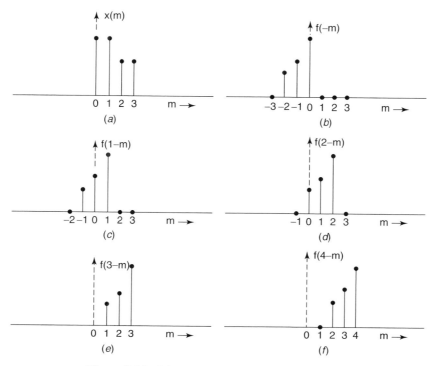

Figure 3.30   Linear convolution of $x(n)$ and $f(n)$.

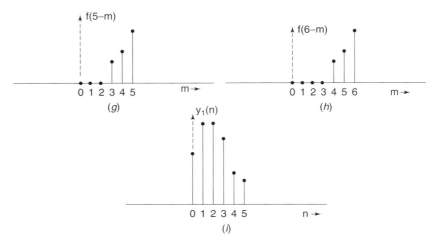

Figure 3.30   (*Continued*)

transform of the convolution sum $y_1(n) = x(n) * f(n)$ is $[X(z)F(z)]$. Therefore, the results from both these methods agree with each other and we get
the output $y_1(n) = [1.0 \quad 1.6 \quad 1.6 \quad 1.36 \quad 0.6 \quad 0.24]$, which is a sequence of
length 6. It is identified as the result of linear convolution. The three sequences
are shown in Figure 3.30, including the graphical procedure for carrying out the
linear convolution.

Now we ask the following question. What do we get if we compute the DTFS
of the periodic sequences $x_p(n)$ and $f_p(n)$ generated by extending $x(n)$ and
$f(n)$, multiply $X_p(k)$, and $F_p(k)$, and find the inverse DTFS of their product
$\left[X_p(k)F_p(k)\right]$ to get $y_p(n)$. From Table 3.3, we notice that $\left[X_p(k)F_p(k)\right]$ is
the DTFS of the periodic convolution $x(n) \circledast f(n) = \sum_{m=0}^{N-1} x(m)f(n-m)_N =$
$y_p(n)$—a result than can be proved analytically. We will provide a numerical
example below to verify this property. However, does this result of periodic
convolution match with the result of applying the familiar linear convolution?
We show in the example chosen below that $y_p(n)$ is not the periodic extension
of $y_1(n)$, that is, the result of the periodic convolution and the linear convolution
do not match in the example chosen.

Example 3.18

The DTFS coefficients of $x(n)$, when we choose $N = 4$, are computed from the
formula $X_p(k) = \sum_{n=0}^{N-1} x(n)e^{-j(2\pi/N)kn}$

$$X_p(0) = \sum_{n=0}^{3} x(n)e^{-j(2\pi/N)(0.n)} = x(0)e^{-j(2\pi/4)(0)} + x(1)e^{-j(2\pi/4)(0)}$$

$$+ x(2)e^{-j(2\pi/4)(0)} + x(3)e^{-j(2\pi/4)(0)} = 3.2$$

$$X_p(1) = \sum_{n=0}^{3} x(n)e^{-j(2\pi/N)(1.n)} = x(0)e^{-j(2\pi/4)(0)} + x(1)e^{-j(2\pi/4)(1)}$$

$$+ x(2)e^{-j(2\pi/4)(2)} + x(3)e^{-j(2\pi/4)(3)} = 0.4 - j0.4$$

$$X_p(2) = \sum_{n=0}^{3} x(n)e^{-j(2\pi/N)(2.n)} = x(0)e^{-j(2\pi/4)(0)} + x(1)e^{-j(2\pi/4)(2)}$$

$$+ x(2)e^{-j(2\pi/4)(4)} + x(3)e^{-j(2\pi/4)(6)} = 0.0 + j0.0$$

$$X_p(3) = \sum_{n=0}^{3} x(n)e^{-j(2\pi/N)(3.n)} = x(0)e^{-j(2\pi/4)(0)} + x(1)e^{-j(2\pi/4)(3)}$$

$$+ x(2)e^{-j(2\pi/4)(6)} + x(3)e^{-j(2\pi/4)(9)} = 0.4 + j0.4$$

Similarly, the DTFT of $f(n)$ are computed as

$$F_p(0) = \sum_{n=0}^{3} f(n)e^{-j(2\pi/N)(0.n)} = f(0)e^{-j(2\pi/4)(0)} + f(1)e^{-j(2\pi/4)(0)}$$

$$+ f(2)e^{-j(2\pi/4)(0)} + f(3)e^{-j(2\pi/4)(0)} = 2.0$$

$$F_p(1) = \sum_{n=0}^{3} f(n)e^{-j(2\pi/N)(1.n)} = f(0)e^{-j(2\pi/4)(0)} + f(1)e^{-j(2\pi/4)(1)}$$

$$+ f(2)e^{-j(2\pi/4)(2)} + f(3)e^{-j(2\pi/4)(3)} = 0.6 - j0.6$$

$$F_p(2) = \sum_{n=0}^{3} f(n)e^{-j(2\pi/N)(2.n)} = f(0)e^{-j(2\pi/4)(0)} + f(1)e^{-j(2\pi/4)(2)}$$

$$+ f(2)e^{-j(2\pi/4)(4)} + f(3)e^{-j(2\pi/4)(6)} = 0.8 + j0.0$$

$$F_p(3) = \sum_{n=0}^{3} f(n)e^{-j(2\pi/N)(3.n)} = f(0)e^{-j(2\pi/4)(0)} + f(1)e^{-j(2\pi/4)(3)}$$

$$+ f(2)e^{-j(2\pi/4)(6)} + f(3)e^{-j(2\pi/4)(9)} = 0.6 + j0.6$$

The term-by-term product of these vectors gives the DTFS of the output $Y_p(k) = X_p(k)F_p(k)$ as

$$Y_p(k) = [6.4 \quad 0 - j0.48 \quad 0 + j0 \quad 0.0 + j0.48]$$

and its inverse DTFS is computed from the formula

$$y_p(n) = \frac{1}{N} \sum_{k=0}^{3} Y_p(k)e^{j(2\pi/N)kn}$$

and we get $y_p(n) = [1.6 \quad 1.84 \quad 1.6 \quad 1.36]$.

Using the formula for the periodic convolution $x(n) \circledast f(n) = \sum_{m=0}^{N-1} x(m) f(n-m)_N$ directly, as illustrated in Figure 3.31, we get the same result for $y_p(n)$. This verifies the property that the DTFS of the periodic convolution $x(n) \circledast f(n)$ is $X_p(k) F_p(k)$.

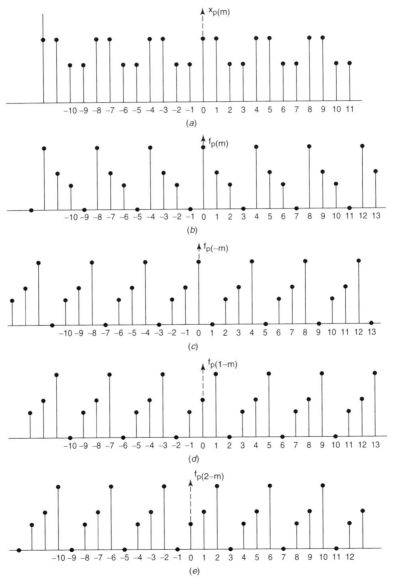

Figure 3.31   Circular (periodic) convolution of $x_p(n)$ and $f_p(n)$ with $N = 4$.

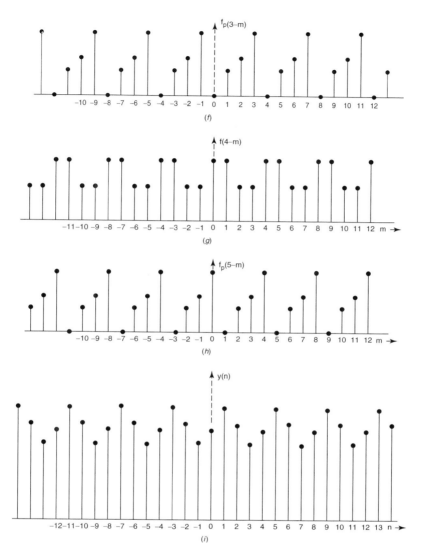

Figure 3.31   (*Continued*)

But we notice that this does not match the result of the linear convolution $y_1(n) = x(n) * f(n) = [1.0 \quad 1.6 \quad 1.6 \quad 1.36 \quad 0.6 \quad 0.24]$. It is obvious that the length of $y_1(n)$ is 6, whereas $x_p(n)$, $f_p(n)$, $X_p(k)$, $F_p(k)$, and $y_p(n)$ are all of length 4, and for that reason alone, we do not expect the two results to match. If we look carefully at Figure 3.31 and Figure 3.30, we see another reason why they do not match. In Figures 3.31, $f(4-m)$, $f(5-m)$, $f(6-m)$, $f(7-m)$ are found to be the same as the sequence $f(0)$, $f(1-m)$, $f(2-m)$, $f(3-m)$, respectively; therefore $y_p(n)$ is periodic with a period $N = 4$, whereas $y_1(n)$ is nonperiodic and is of length 6. When computing $y_p(n)$, we see that products of the additional terms from the adjacent period are added, whereas when computing $y_1(n)$, no such overlap takes place. So in order to avoid this overlap, we choose $N = 8$ and compute $X_p(k)$, $F_p(k)$ and $y_p(n)$ as follows.

Example 3.19

$$X_p(0) = \sum_{n=0}^{7} x(n)e^{-j(2\pi/N)(0 \cdot n)}$$

$$= x(0)e^{-j(2\pi/8)(0)} + x(1)e^{-j(2\pi/8)(0)} + x(2)e^{-j(2\pi/8)(0)}$$
$$+ x(3)e^{-j(2\pi/8)(0)} + \cdots + x(7)e^{-j(2\pi/8)(0)} = 3.2$$

$$X_p(1) = \sum_{n=0}^{7} x(n)e^{-j(2\pi/N)(1 \cdot n)}$$

$$= x(0)e^{-j(2\pi/4)(0)} + x(1)e^{-j(2\pi/8)(1)} + x(2)e^{-j(2\pi/8)(2)}$$
$$+ x(3)e^{-j(2\pi/8)(3)} + \cdots + x(7)e^{-j(2\pi/8)(7)} = 1.2828 - j1.7314$$

$$X_p(2) = \sum_{n=0}^{7} x(n)e^{-j(2\pi/N)(2 \cdot n)}$$

$$= x(0)e^{-j(2\pi/8)(0)} + x(1)e^{-j(2\pi/8)(2)} + x(2)e^{-j(2\pi/8)(4)}$$
$$+ x(3)e^{-j(2\pi/8)(6)} + \cdots + x(7)e^{-j(2\pi/8)(14)} = 0.4 - j0.4$$

$$X_p(3) = \sum_{n=0}^{7} x(n)e^{-j(2\pi/N)(3 \cdot n)}$$

$$= x(0)e^{-j(2\pi/8)(0)} + x(1)e^{-j(2\pi/8)(3)} + x(2)e^{-j(2\pi/8)(6)}$$
$$+ x(3)e^{-j(2\pi/4)(9)} + \cdots + x(7)e^{-j(2\pi/8)(21)} = 0.7172 - j0.5314$$

$$X_p(4) = \sum_{n=0}^{7} x(n)e^{-j(2\pi/N)(4 \cdot n)}$$

$$= x(0)e^{-j(2\pi/8)(0)} + x(1)e^{-j(2\pi/8)(4)} + x(2)e^{-j(2\pi/8)(8)}$$
$$+ x(3)e^{-j(2\pi/4)(12)} + \cdots + x(7)e^{-j(2\pi/8)(28)} = 0.0 + j0.0$$

$$X_p(5) = \sum_{n=0}^{7} x(n)e^{-j(2\pi/N)(5 \cdot n)}$$

$$= x(0)e^{-j(2\pi/8)(0)} + x(1)e^{-j(2\pi/8)(5)} + x(2)e^{-j(2\pi/8)(10)}$$
$$+ x(3)e^{-j(2\pi/4)(15)} + \cdots + x(7)e^{-j(2\pi/8)(35)} = 0.7172 + j0.5314$$

$$X_p(6) = \sum_{n=0}^{7} x(n)e^{-j(2\pi/N)(6 \cdot n)}$$

$$= x(0)e^{-j(2\pi/8)(0)} + x(1)e^{-j(2\pi/8)(6)} + x(2)e^{-j(2\pi/8)(12)}$$

$$+ x(3)e^{-j(2\pi/4)(18)} + \cdots + x(7)e^{-j(2\pi/8)(56)} = 0.4 + j0.4$$

$$X_p(7) = \sum_{n=0}^{7} x(n)e^{-j(2\pi/N)(7 \cdot n)}$$

$$= x(0)e^{-j(2\pi/8)(0)} + x(1)e^{-j(2\pi/8)(7)} + x(2)e^{-j(2\pi/8)(14)}$$

$$+ x(3)e^{-j(2\pi/4)(21)} + \cdots + x(7)e^{-j(2\pi/8)(49)} = 1.2828 + j1.7314.$$

Similarly, we compute $F_p(k)$ with $N = 8$ and get the vector

$$F_p(k) = [2.0 \quad 1.4243 - j0.8423 \quad 0.6 - j0.6 \quad 0.5757 - j0.0243$$

$$0.8 + j0.0 \quad 0.5757 + j0.0243 \quad 0.6 + j0.6 \quad 1.4243 + j0.8423].$$

The term-by-term multiplication of $X_p(k)$ and $F_p(k)$ yields

$$Y_p(k) = [6.4 \quad 0.4 - j3.5233 \quad 0.0 - j0.48 \quad 0.4 - j0.3233 \quad 0.0 + j0.0$$

$$0.4 + j0.3233 \quad 0.0 + j0.48 \quad 0.4 + j3.5233].$$

and the inverse DTFS of $Y_p(k)$ given by $y_p(n) = 1/N \sum_{k=0}^{7} Y_p(k)e^{j(2\pi/N)kn}$ is computed to obtain $y_p(n) = [1.0 \quad 1.6 \quad 1.6 \quad 1.36 \quad 0.6 \quad 0.24 \quad 0.0 \quad 0.0]$.

As shown in Figures 3.32 and 3.33, we get the same result from the periodic convolution. Moreover, we see that this result matches the result $y_1(n)$ obtained by linear convolution!

In general, if the length of $x(n)$ is l_1 and that of $f(n)$ is l_2, we know that the length of $y_1(n)$ from linear convolution will be $l_1 + l_2 - 1$. So what we need to do to match the result of linear convolution and periodic convolution of two signals is to choose N to be equal to or greater than $l_1 + l_2 - 1$. With such a choice, we can use the DTFS coefficients $X_p(k)$ and $F_p(k)$, each of length $N \geq l_1 + l_2 - 1$, and then compute the N inverse DTFS coefficients of $X_p(k)F_p(k)$. Because the formulas for computing the N coefficients of their DFT [i.e., $X(k)$ and $F(k)$] are the same as for computing their DTFS coefficients and consequently the DFT (and inverse DFT) coefficients are a subset of the coefficients of DTFS (and IDTFS), we conclude that if we are given, say, $x(n)$ of length l_1 as the input signal and $h(n)$ of length l_2 as the unit impulse response of a linear discrete-time system, then we can pad each of the signals with an appropriate number of zeros to make both of them to be of length $N \geq l_1 + l_2 - 1$, and find the inverse DFT of $X(k)H(k)$ to get the N samples of the output $y(n)$ of the linear discrete-time system. Conversely, if we are given any signal, we can easily obtain the N

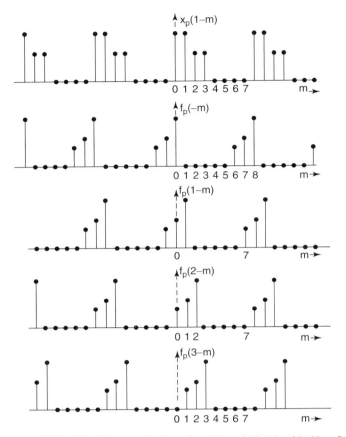

Figure 3.32   Circular convolution of $x_p(n)$ and $f_p(n)$ with $N = 8$.

coefficients of its DFT, which indicates the frequency response of the signal at N discrete frequencies equally spaced between 0 and 2π.

3.7   FAST FOURIER TRANSFORM

Note that when we computed each of the eight samples of the DFT in the previous example, there was multiplication of the complex number $e^{j(2\pi/N)kn} = W^{-kn}$, $k = 0, 1, 2, \ldots, (N - 1)$, with the eight real-valued samples of the signal and the product were added. So the total number of multiplications is $8^2 = 64$ and the number of additions are $7^2 = 49$ in computing the eight samples of the DFT. The same number of multiplications and additions are required to find the inverse DFT; in this case, samples of both $X(k)$ and W^{-kn} are complex-valued. In general, direct computation of the DFT and IDFT using (3.79) and (3.80) requires N^2 multiplications and $(N - 1)^2$ additions; so they become very large

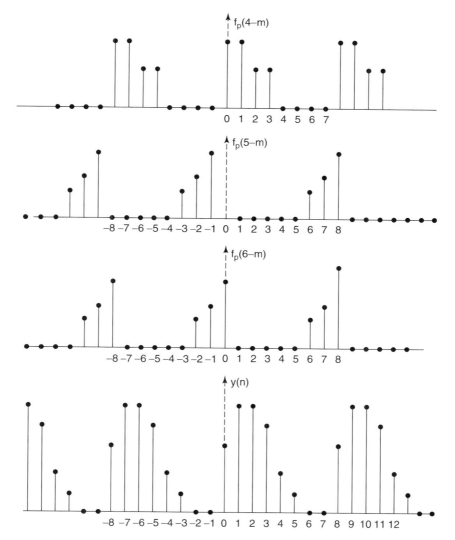

Figure 3.33   Circular convolution of $x_p(n)$ and $f_p(n)$ with $N = 8$ (continued from Fig. 3.34).

numbers when N is chosen very large, in order to increase the resolution of the frequency response $X(k)$ of a given signal or to find the unit impulse response of a filter as the IDFT of the given frequency response of a filter.

Fast Fourier transform (FFT) is a numerical algorithm that has been developed to improve the computational efficiency by an enormous amount and is the most popular method used in spectral analysis in digital signal processing, specifically, to find the DFT of the signal and also the inverse DFT of the frequency response to get the discrete-time signal. This is only a computational algorithm and not another transform. In this FFT algorithm, when the value for the radix N is chosen as 2^R, where R is an integer, the number of complex multiplications is of the order $(N/2)\log_2(N)$ and the number of complex additions is of the order $N\log_2 N$. As an illustration of this efficiency, let us choose $N = 256$; in this case the number of complex multiplications is 65,536 in the direct computation, whereas the number of complex multiplications is 1024 in the FFT algorithm, which is an improvement by a factor of 64. As N increases to higher values, the improvement factor increases very significantly, for example, when $N = 1024$, we realize an improvement by a factor of 204.

Algorithms based on a radix $N = 4$ have been developed to further improve the computational efficiency. Also when the length of a signals to be convolved is large (e.g., $N = 1024$), some novel modifications to the FFT algorithm have also been proposed. They are called the *overlap-add method* and the *overlap-save method*. Basically in these methods, the signals are decomposed as a sequence of contiguous segments of shorter length, their convolution is carried out in the basic form, and then the responses are carefully added to get the same result as that obtained by the direct FFT method applied on their original form. The MATLAB function `y = fftfilt(b,x)` and `y = fftfilt(b,x,N)` implements the convolution between the input signal `x` and the unit impulse response `b` of the FIR filter, using the overlap-add method, the default value for the radix, is `N` 512; but it can be changed to any other value by including it as an argument in the second command.

3.8 USE OF MATLAB TO COMPUTE DFT AND IDFT

Example 3.20

Let us consider the same example for the signal $x(n)$ that was chosen in the previous example; that is, let $x(n) = [1.0 \quad 1.0 \quad 0.6 \quad 0.6]$. First we compute its DTFT and plot it in Figure 3.34. Then we compute a 10-point DFT of the same signal using the function `fft` found in the Signal Processing Toolbox of MATLAB. The function is described by the following simple command:

```
[X,w] = fft(x,N)
```

In this function, `x` is the output vector of the complex-valued DFT of the given signal $x(n)$ and `N` is the value for the radix, which is chosen as 10 in this example. The absolute value of the DFT is computed, and the magnitude $|X(k)|$, $k = 0, 1, 2, \ldots, 9$ is superimposed on the same plot. It is seen that the values of DFT match the value of DTFT at the discrete frequencies $e^{j(2\pi/10)k}$, $k = 0, 1, 2, \ldots, 9$, as we expect. But we have chosen this example with $N = 10$ particularly to illustrate what is known as the "picket fence effect". Note that the frequency response in Figure 3.34 has a local minimum value at the normalized frequency of 2.5 and 7.5. But if we plot the DFT values alone, we will miss the fact that the frequency response of the signal has a minimum value at these frequencies. This

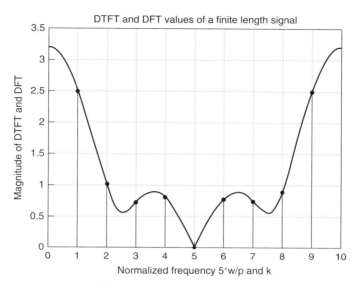

Figure 3.34 DTFT/DFT plot.

phenomenon becomes serious if the signal has a single sinusoidal frequency, in which case the frequency response will have an impulse function and will appear as a spike at the corresponding normalized frequency. Because we have chosen a low value for N, and therefore the fundamental frequency $2\pi/N$ is relatively large, it is likely that the presence of this single frequency will be completely missed. This is known as the "picket fence effect," as if we "see" the continuous frequency response through a picket fence and miss some part of the frequency response that lies behind the pickets. Hence it is important to select a fairly high value for the radix N so that we have less chance of missing the single frequencies but at the same time not too high a value, which would increase the computation time.

Students are strongly recommended to have a thorough understanding of the theory while they use MATLAB in signal processing. In this example, when we compute the DFT using the MATLAB function, its output is actually displayed for $k = 1, 2, 3, \ldots, N$, since the MATLAB function computes the `fft` of $x(n)$ according to the algorithm

$$X(k+1) = \sum_{n=0}^{N-1} x(n+1) W_N^{kn} \tag{3.84}$$

and the inverse DFT is computed for $n = 1, 2, 3, \ldots, N$ from

$$x(n+1) = \frac{1}{N} \sum_{k=0}^{N-1} X(k+1) W^{-kn} \tag{3.85}$$

whereas from theory we know that both indices run from 0 to $(N - 1)$ and the frequency response is normally displayed by MATLAB for the frequency range of $[0 \quad \pi]$.

In superimposing the values of DFT on the plot for the DTFT, this fact about the MATLAB function `fft` is important. It serves as an example where a thorough understanding of theory is necessary for using MATLAB in digital signal processing.

Example 3.21

We now consider another example showing the use of the MATLAB function `fft(x,N)` and comparing the values of its DFT with the frequency response (DTFT) of a discrete-time signal. We pick a signal $x(n) = \sin[0.1(\pi n)]$ for $0 \leq n \leq 10$, which is plotted in Figure 3.35. We find its frequency response using the function `[h,w]=freqz(x,1,'whole')` and plot it for the full period of 2π in Figure 3.36, in order to compare it with the values of its DFT $X(k)$, which always gives N samples for $0 \leq k \leq (N - 1)$, which corresponds to the full frequency range of $[0 \quad 2\pi]$. The DFT $X(k)$ are computed from the MATLAB function `X=fft(x,64)`. The absolute values of $X(k)$ are plotted in Figure 3.37 showing that they match $\left| X(e^{j\omega}) \right|$.

Example 3.22

In this example, we consider the same signal $x(n) = [1 \quad 1 \quad 0.6 \quad 0.6]$ and $h(n) = [1 \quad 0.6 \quad 0.4]$, which we considered in Example 3.17 and find the output

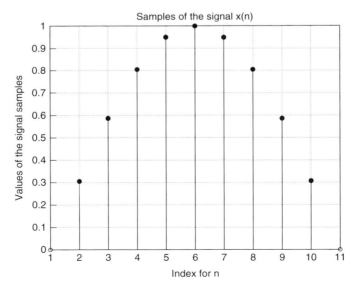

Figure 3.35 A discrete-time signal.

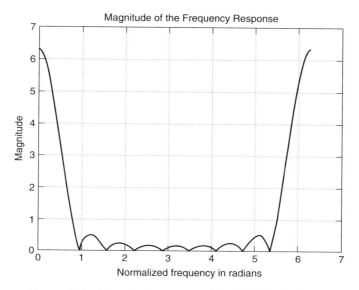

Figure 3.36   Magnitude response of the DTFT of a signal.

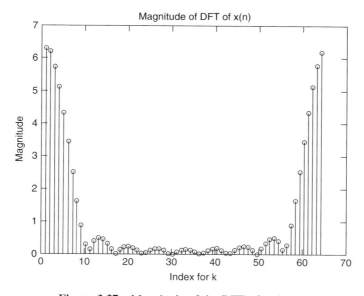

Figure 3.37   Magnitude of the DFT of a signal.

$y(n)$ of the discrete-time system using the FFT technique. The MATLAB program we use and the final output from the program are given below:

```
x = [ 1   1   0.6   0.6];
h = [ 1   0.6   0.4];
```

```
X=fft(x,8);
H=fft(h,8);
Y=X.*H;
y=ifft(Y,8)
```

The output is

$$y = 1.0000\ 1.6000\ 1.6000\ 1.3600\ 0.6000\ 0.2400\ 0\ 0$$

In this program, the MATLAB function y = $\texttt{ifft(Y,8)}$ computes the 8-point IFFT of the product $X(k)H(k)$ and the last line lists the output $y(n)$, which is, not surprisingly, the same as the result of linear convolution $x(n) * h(n)$.

Example 3.23

Let us consider the DFT samples of a lowpass filter response as given below and use the MATLAB function x = $\texttt{ifft(X,8)}$ and plot the output $x(n)$. The MATLAB program and the output $x(n)$ are given below and the plot of $x(n)$ is shown in Figure 3.38. Again note that the time index n in this figure runs from 1 to 8, instead of from 0 to 7 in this 8-point IDFT:

```
X=[1 exp(-j*7*pi/8) 0 0 0 0 exp(j*7*pi/8)];
x=ifft(X,8);
stem(x)
```

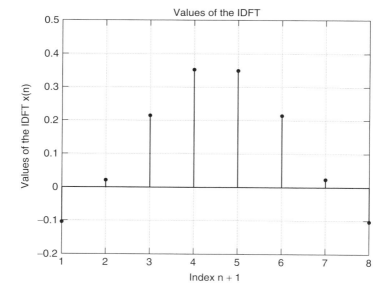

Figure 3.38   IDFT of a lowpass filter.

```
title('Values of the IDFT')
ylabel('Values of the IDFT')
xlabel('Index n')

x
```

The output is

$$-0.1060\ 0.0293\ 0.2207\ 0.3560\ 0.3560\ 0.2207\ 0.0293\ -0.1060$$

3.9 SUMMARY

We have discussed several topics in this chapter. First we showed that if a signal is bandlimited and we sample it at a frequency larger than twice the maximum frequency in the signal, we can use digital signal processing of the signal instead of analog signal processing, because the digital signal has all the information that is contained in the analog signal. Shannon's sampling theorem and the formula for reconstructing the analog signal from the samples was explained. When such an analog signal is sampled, the frequency response of the discrete-time signal is a continuous function of the digital frequency but is periodic with a period equal to the sampling frequency. Next we discussed several properties of the frequency response of the discrete-time signal (DTFT), illustrating them with numerical examples; they are summarized below:

DTFT of a nonperiodic signal $x(n)$:

$$X(e^{j\omega}) = \sum_{n=0}^{\infty} x(n)e^{-j\omega n} \tag{3.86}$$

IDTFT of $X(e^{j\omega})$:

$$x(n) = \frac{1}{2\pi} \int_{-\pi}^{\pi} X(e^{j\omega})e^{j\omega n}\, d\omega \tag{3.87}$$

Then we considered a discrete-time signal that is periodic with a period N. Its Fourier series representation was expressed in terms of its Fourier series coefficients, and the formula for finding the values of the periodic discrete-time signal from the Fourier series coefficients was presented. Properties of the discrete-time Fourier series (DTFS) and the inverse DTFS were discussed and illustrated with examples. They are summarized as follows:

DTFS of a periodic signal with period N:

$$x_p(n) = \sum_{k=0}^{N-1} X(k)e^{j(2\pi/N)kn} = \sum_{k=0}^{N-1} X(k)W^{-kn}, \quad -\infty \le n \le \infty \tag{3.88}$$

IDTFS of $X(k)$ with period N:

$$X_p(k) = \frac{1}{N}\sum_{n=0}^{N-1}x(n)e^{-j(2\pi/N)kn} = \frac{1}{N}\sum_{n=0}^{N-1}x(n)W^{kn}, \qquad -\infty \le k \le \infty$$

$$(3.89)$$

The discrete Fourier transform (DFT) and its inverse (IDFT) are a subset of the DTFS and IDTFS coefficients, derived from the periodic DTFS and IDTFS coefficients. They can be considered as nonperiodic sequences. A few examples were worked out to show that the values of the DTFT, when evaluated at the discrete frequencies, are the same as the DFT coefficients:

DFT of $x(n)$ with length N:

$$X(k) = \sum_{n=0}^{N-1}x(n)e^{-j(2\pi/N)kn} = \sum_{n=0}^{N-1}x(n)W^{kn}, \qquad 0 \le k \le (N-1)$$

$$(3.90)$$

IDFT of $X(k)$ with length N:

$$x(n) = \frac{1}{N}\sum_{k=0}^{N-1}X(k)e^{j(2\pi/N)kn} = \frac{1}{N}\sum_{k=0}^{N-1}X(k)W^{-kn}, \quad 0 \le n \le (N-1)$$

$$(3.91)$$

The FFT algorithm for computing the DFT-IDFT coefficients offers very significant computational efficiency and hence is used extensively in signal processing, filter analysis, and design. It provides a unified computational approach to find the frequency response from the time domain and vice versa. More examples are added to show that the use of FFT and IFFT functions from MATLAB provides a common framework for getting the frequency response of a discrete-time system from the discrete-time signal and finding the discrete-time signal from the frequency response. Remember that the terms *discrete-time* (digital) *signal, sequence*, or *function* have been used interchangeably in this book; we have also used the terms *discrete-time Fourier transform* (DTFT), *frequency response*, and *spectrum* synonymously in this chapter.

PROBLEMS

3.1 A signal $f(t) = e^{-0.1t}u(t)$ is sampled to generate a DT signal $f(n)$ at such a high sampling rate that we can assume that there is no aliasing. Find a closed-form expression for the frequency response of the sequence $f(n)$.

3.2 Find the Fourier transform $X(j\omega)$ of the signal $x(t) = te^{-0.1t}u(t)$ and choose a frequency at which the attenuation is more than 60 dB. Assuming

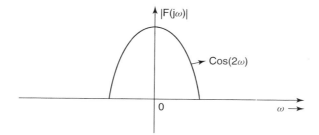

Figure 3.39   Problem 3.4

that the signal is bandlimited by that frequency, what is the minimum sampling frequency one can choose to sample $x(t)$ without losing too much information?

3.3   A continuous-time function $f(t)$ with a bandwidth of 200 Hz is sampled at 1000 Hz, and the sampled values are given by $f(nT) = \{1.0$
$0.4 \quad 0.1 \quad 0.001\}$. Find the value of $f(t)$ at $t = 0.005$.

3.4   A bandlimited analog signal $f(t)$ has a Fourier transform $F(j\omega)$ as shown in Figure 3.39. What is the maximum sampling period T that can be used to avoid aliasing in the frequency response $F(e^{j\omega})$ of the sampled sequence $f(n)$? Find the Fourier series coefficients for $F(e^{j\omega})$.

3.5   Find the DTFT of $x(n) = \{-1 \quad 1 \quad 0 \quad 1 \quad -1\}$ and compute its value
$\uparrow$
at $j\omega = j0.4\pi$. If the 10-point DFT $X_k(j\omega_k)$ of this $x(n)$ is computed, what is the value of the index k at which the DFT is equal to $X(e^{j0.4\pi})$?

3.6   Find the DTFT of a finite sequence $\{1.0 \quad 0.0 \quad -1.0\}$ and evaluate it at
$\uparrow$
$\omega = 0.5\pi$. Calculate the value of the DTFT at $\omega = 0.5\pi$, using the DFT for this sequence to verify this result.

3.7   Find the DTFT of the following two functions:
(a) $x_1(n) = 10(0.5)^n \cos(0.2\pi n + \frac{\pi}{3})u(n)$
(b) $x_2(n) = n(0.2)^n u(n)$

3.8   Find the DTFT of $x_1(n) = (0.5)^n u(n)$ and $x_2(n) = (0.5)^n; -5 \leq n \leq 5$.

3.9   Find the DTFT of the following sequences:

$x_1(n) = u(n) - u(n - 6)$

$x_2(n) = (0.5)^n u(n + 3)$

$x_3(n) = (0.5)^{n+3} u(n)$

$x_4(n) = (0.5)^{-n+2} u(-n + 2)$

$x_5(n) = (0.3)^{n-2} u(-n + 2)$

3.10 Find the DTFT of the following two functions:
(a) $x_1(n) = x(-n-2)$ where $x(n) = e^{-0.5n}u(n)$
(b) $x_2(n) = 5^{-n}u(n)$.

3.11 Given the DTFT of $x_1(n) = \{1 \quad 0 \quad -1 \quad 0\}x$ as $X_1(e^{j\omega})$, express the DTFT of $x_2(n) = \{1 \quad 0 \quad -1 \quad 0 \quad 1 \quad 0 \quad -1 \quad 0\}$ in terms of $X_1(e^{j\omega})$. Express the DTFT of $x_3(n) = \{1 \quad 0 \quad -1 \quad 1 \quad 0 \quad -1 \quad 0 \quad 0\}$ in terms of $X_1(e^{j\omega})$.

3.12 An LTI-DT system is described by the difference equation

$$y(n) - 0.5y(n-1) = x(n) - bx(n-1)$$

Determine the value of b (other than 0.5) such that the square of the magnitude of its transfer function $H(e^{j\omega})$ is a constant equal to b^2 for all frequencies.

3.13 A comb filter is defined by its transfer function $H(z) = (1 - z^{-N})/N$. Determine the frequency response of the filter in a closed-form expression for $N = 10$.

3.14 Show that the magnitude response of an IIR filter with

$$H(z) = \frac{2 + 0.2z^{-1} - 0.2z^{-3} - 2z^{-4}}{(1 - z^{-4})}$$

is a real function of ω and an even function of ω.

3.15 A discrete-time signal with a lowpass frequency response that is a constant equal to 5 and has a bandwidth equal to 0.4π is the input to an ideal bandpass filter with a passband between $\omega_{p1} = 0.3\pi$ and $\omega_{p2} = 0.6\pi$ and a magnitude of 4. What is the bandwidth of the output signal?

3.16 A DT signal $x(n) = 4\cos(0.4\pi n) + 6\cos(0.8\pi n) + 10\cos(0.9\pi n)$ is the input to an allpass filter with a constant magnitude of 5 for all frequencies. What is the output $y(n)$ of the filter?

3.17 Given $x_{(n)} = a^n u(n)$ and $h(n) = b^n u(n)$, where $0 < a < 1, 0 < b < 1$, $a \neq b$ show that $y(n) = x(n) * h(n) \equiv a^{n+1} - b^{n+1}/a - b$.

3.18 Find the DTFT of $x(n) = n^2(0.1)^n u(n)$.

3.19 Prove that

$$\sum_{n=0}^{N-1} e^{j(2\pi/N)kn} = \begin{cases} N & k = 0, \pm N, \pm 2N, \ldots \\ 0 & \text{otherwise} \end{cases}$$

3.20 Show that the frequency response of a sequence

$$x(n) = \begin{cases} 1 & -N \le n \le N \\ 0 & \text{otherwise} \end{cases}$$

is given by $X(e^{j\omega}) = 1 + 2\sum_{n=1}^{N} \cos(\omega n) = \sin(N+0.5)\omega / \sin(0.5\omega)$.

3.21 Show that $\int_{-\pi}^{\pi} X(e^{j\omega}) d\omega = 2\pi x(0)$ where $X(e^{j\omega}) = \sum_{n=0}^{\infty} x(n)e^{-jn\omega}$.

3.22 Given $H(e^{j\omega})$ and $X(e^{j\omega})$ as shown below, find the output $y(n)$ of the discrete-time system

$$H(e^{j\omega}) = \frac{e^{j\omega}}{(1 - 0.6e^{-j\omega})}$$

$$X(e^{j\omega}) = 2e^{-j\omega} - 5e^{-j5\omega} + e^{-j6\omega}$$

3.23 Given $H(e^{j\omega})$ and $X(e^{j\omega})$ as shown below, find the output $y(n)$

$$H(e^{j\omega}) = \frac{1}{e^{j\omega} + 0.3}$$

$$X(e^{j\omega}) = \frac{e^{j\omega}}{(1 + 0.5e^{-j\omega})(1 - 0.5e^{j\omega})}$$

3.24 Find the IDTFT of the function given below:

$$Y(e^{j\omega}) = \frac{1 - e^{-j2\omega}}{(1 + 0.2e^{j\omega})(1 - 0.4e^{-j\omega})(e^{j\omega} + 0.5)}$$

3.25 Find the IDTFT of the function given below:

$$Y(e^{j\omega}) = \frac{1}{(e^{j\omega} + 0.1)(1 - e^{-j\omega})(1 + e^{j\omega})}$$

3.26 If the input of an LTI-DT system is $x(n) = (0.2)^n u(-n)$ and its unit pulse response $h(n)$ is $(0.4)^n u(n)$, what is its output $y(n)$?

3.27 Given an input $x(n) = (0.2)^{-n} u(-n) + (0.5)^n u(n)$ and the unit impulse response of an LTI-DT system as $(0.4)^n u(n)$, find its output $y(n)$.

3.28 Given a sequence $x_1(n) = (0.3)^{-n} u(-n)$ and another sequence $x_2(n) = (0.6)^n u(-n)$, find their convolution sum $x_1(n) * x_2(n)$, using their DTFT.

3.29 Find the convolution $y(n) = x_1(n) * x_2(n)$ where $x_1(n) = 0.5^{-n} u(-n)$ and $x_2(n) = (0.2)^{-n} u(-n)$.

3.30 Find the DTFT of $x_e(n)$ and $x_0(n)$ where $x(n) = (0.4)^n u(n)$, and $x_e(n) = [x(n) + x(-n)]/2$ is the even part of $x(n)$ and $x_0(n) = [x(n) - x(-n)]/2$ is the odd part of $x(n)$.

3.31 Find the IDTFT of

$$F(e^{jw}) = e^{j\omega}/[(1 - 0.4e^{-j\omega})(1 + 0.4e^{-j\omega})(1 + 0.4e^{j\omega})].$$

3.32 Find the IDTFT of $X(e^{j\omega}) = 3e^{j3\omega}/(e^{j\omega} - 0.4)$.

3.33 Find the IDTFT of
(a) $X(e^{j\omega}) = \cos^2(4\omega)$
(b) $X(e^{j\omega}) = \begin{cases} 1 & \text{for } \omega_{c1} \le \omega \le \omega_{c2} \\ 0 & \text{otherwise} \end{cases}$

3.34 Find the IDTFT of $X(e^{j\omega}) = 1 + 4\cos(\omega) + 3\cos(5\omega)$.

3.35 Find the IDTFT of the two functions given below:
(a) $H_1(e^{j\omega}) = 1 + 2\cos(\omega) + 4\cos(2\omega)$
(b) $H_2(e^{j\omega}) = 1 + 2\cos(\omega) + 4\cos^2(2\omega)$

3.36 Find the IDTFT of $H_1(e^{j\omega}) = 1 + 4\cos(\omega) + 3\cos(5\omega)\cos(\omega)$.

3.37 Find the IDTFT of the following two functions:
(a) $Y_1(e^{j\omega}) = j\sin(\omega)[4 + 4\cos(\omega) + 2\cos^2(\omega)]$
(b) $Y_2(e^{j\omega}) = je^{-j(\omega/2)}[4 + 2\cos(\omega) + 4\cos^2(\omega)]\sin(\omega/2)$

3.38 Find the IDTFT of $H_2(e^{j\omega})$ shown in Figure 3.40. Find the Fourier series coefficients of the periodic function $H_2(e^{j\omega})$.

3.39 An FIR filter is defined by $H(z^{-1}) = 1 + 0.5z^{-1} + 0.4z^{-2} + 0.4z^{-3}$. Find the magnitude of its frequency response at $\omega = 0.8\pi$, using the DFT formula.

3.40 Compute the DFT $X_8(3)$ and $X_{16}(6)$ of the sequence $x(n) = \{1.0 \quad 0.3 \quad 0.2 \quad 0.5\}$.

3.41 A discrete-time sequence $x(n) = \{1 \quad 1 \quad 1 \quad 1 \quad 1 \quad 1\}$ is sampled at 2400 Hz, and the magnitude of its DTFT at 600 Hz is known to be $\sqrt{2}$.

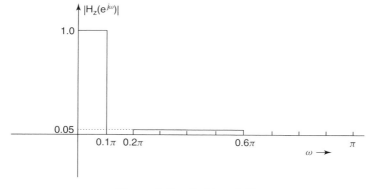

Figure 3.40 Problem 3.38.

What is the magnitude at 6600 Hz? Compute the sample $X_8(2)$ of its 8-point DFT.

3.42 Given the 6-point DFT of $f(n)$, as given below compute the value of $f(3)$:

$$F(0) = 10.0; \quad F(1) = -3.5 - j2.6; \quad F(2) = -2.5 - j0.866$$

$$F(3) = -2.0; \quad F(4) = -2.5 + j0.866; \quad F(5) = -3.5 + j2.6$$

3.43 Compute the 6-point IDFT of $X(k)$ given below:

$$X(k) = \{3 + j0 \quad -1 + j0 \quad -0 + j1.732 \quad 5 + j0 \quad 0 - j1.732$$
$$- 1 - j0\}$$

3.44 If the N-point DFT of a real sequence $x(n)$ is $X_N(k)$, prove that the DFT of $x((-n))_N$ is $X_N^*(k)$, using the property $x((-n))_N = X(N - n)$. Show that the DFT of the even part $x_e(n) = [x(n) + x(-n)]/2$ is given by $\mathrm{Re}X(k)$ and the DFT of the odd part $x_o(n) = [x(n) - x(-n)]/2$ is given by $j\mathrm{Im}X(k)$.

3.45 Find the even part and odd part of the following functions:

$x_1(n) = \{1 \quad -1 \quad 2 \quad 0 \quad 1 \quad 1\}$

$x_2(n) = \{1 \quad 2 \quad 1 \quad -1 \quad 0 \quad -2 \quad 0 \quad 1\}$

$x_3(n) = \{1 \quad 1 \quad -1 \quad 3\}$

$x_4(n) = \{0 \quad 1 \quad 2 \quad -1 \quad 1 \quad 0\}$

3.46 Determine which of the following functions have real-valued DFT and which have imaginary-valued DFT:

$x_1(n) = \{1 \quad 0.5 \quad 1 \quad 0 \quad 0 \quad 1 \quad 0.5\}$

$x_2(n) = \{1 \quad 0.5 \quad -1 \quad 1 \quad 0 \quad 1 \quad -1 \quad 0.5\}$

$x_3(n) = \{0 \quad 0.5 \quad -1 \quad 1 \quad 0 \quad -1 \quad 1 \quad - 0.5\}$

$x_4(n) = \{1 \quad 2 \quad 0 \quad 0 \quad 1 \quad 0 \quad 0 \quad -2\}$

3.47 Compute the 4-point DFT and 8-point DFT of $x(n) = \{1 \quad 0.5 \quad -1.5\}$. Plot their magnitudes and compare their values.

3.48 Calculate the 5-point DFT of the $x(n) = \{1 \quad 0.5 - 1.5\}$ above.

3.49 Calculate the 6-point DFT of $x(n) = \{1 \quad 1 \quad 0.5 \quad 0 \quad -0.5\}$.

3.50 Given the following samples of the 8-point DFT

$$X(1) = 1.7071 - j1.5858$$

$$X(3) = 0.2929 + j4.4142$$

$$X(6) = -0 + j2$$

find the values of $X(2)$, $X(5)$, and $X(7)$.

3.51 Given the values of $X(4)$, $X(13)$, $X(17)$, $X(65)$, $X(81)$, and $X(90)$ of an 128-point DFT function, what are the values of $X(124)$, $X(63)$, $X(115)$, $X(38)$, $X(111)$, and $X(47)$?

MATLAB Problems

3.52 Compute the 16-point and 32-point DFTs of the 4-point sequence $x(n) = \{1 \quad 0.5 \quad 0 \quad -0.5\}$. Plot their magnitudes and compare them.

3.53 Compute the 24-point DFT of the sequence in Problem 3.52, plot the magnitude of this DFT. Now compute 24-point IDFT of this DFT and compare it with $x(n)$ given above.

3.54 Plot the magnitude of the following transfer functions:

$$X_1(z) = \frac{0.5 + 1.2z^{-1}}{1 + 0.2z^{-1} + 0.4z^{-2} + z^{-3} - z^{-4} + 0.06z^{-5}}$$

$$X_2(z) = \frac{z^{-3} - 0.8z^{-5} + z^{-1} - 6}{1 + z^{-1} + 0.8z^{-2} - 0.4z^{-3} - 0.3z^{-4} + z^{-5} + 0.05z^{-6}}$$

$$X_3(z) = \frac{(1 - 0.3z)(1 + 0.2z + z^2)}{(z^2 + 0.2z + 1.0)(z^2 - 0.1z + 0.05)(z - 0.3)}$$

$$X_4(z) = \frac{z}{z + 0.4} - \frac{z + 0.5}{(z + 0.1)^2} + \frac{0.8}{z}$$

3.55 Plot the magnitude and phase responses of the following functions:

$$H_1(e^{j\omega}) = \frac{0.2e^{j\omega} + 0.9e^{j2\omega}}{1 - 0.6e^{j\omega} + 0.6e^{j2\omega} - 0.5e^{j3\omega} + e^{j4\omega}}$$

$$H_2(e^{j\omega}) = \frac{1 + 0.4e^{-j\omega}}{1 + 0.5e^{-j\omega} - 0.4e^{-j2\omega} + e^{-j3\omega} + 0.3e^{-j4\omega} + 0.1e^{-j5\omega}}$$

$$H_3(e^{j\omega}) = H_1(e^{j\omega})H_2(e^{j\omega})$$

3.56 Evaluate the magnitude response of the transfer function $H(z)$ at $\omega = 0.365\pi$ and at $\omega = 0.635\pi$:

$$H(z) = \frac{0.25 + z^{-1}}{1 - 0.8z^{-1} + 0.4z^{-2} - 0.05z^{-3}}$$

3.57 From the real sequence $x(n) = \{1 \quad -1 \quad 2 \quad 0.5 \quad 0 \quad -1 \quad 2 \quad 1\}$, show that the DFT of $[\, x_e(n)] = \text{Re}X(k)$ where the even part $x_e(n) = [x(n) + x((-n))_N]/2$.

3.58 From the real sequence in Problem 3.57, obtain its odd part and show that its DFT $= j\text{Im}X(k)$.

REFERENCES

1. B. A. Shenoi, *Magnitude and Delay Approximation of 1-D and 2-D Digital Filters*, Springer-Verlag, 1999.
2. C. E. Shannon, Communication in the presence of noise, *Proc. IRE* **37**, 10–12 (Jan. 1949).
3. J. G. Proakis and D. G. Manolakis, *Digital Signal Processing-Principles, Algorithms, and Applications*, Prentice-Hall, 1966.
4. B. P. Lathi, *Signal Processing and Linear Systems*, Berkeley Cambridge Press, 1998.
5. A. V. Oppenheim and R. W. Schafer, *Discrete-Time Signal Processing*, Prentice-Hall, 1989.
6. V. K. Ingle and J. G. Proakis, *Digital Signal Processing Using MATLAB* $^{(R)}$ *V.4*, PWS Publishing, 1997.
7. S. K. Mitra, *Digital Signal Processing—A Computer-Based Approach*, McGraw-Hill, 2001.
8. S. K. Mitra and J. F. Kaiser, eds., *Handbook for Digital Signal Processing*, Wiley-Interscience, 1993.
9. A. Antoniou, *Digital Filters, Analysis, Design and Applications*, McGraw-Hill, 1993.

CHAPTER 4

Infinite Impulse Response Filters

4.1 INTRODUCTION

In Chapter 2, we discussed the analysis of discrete-time systems to obtain their output due to a given input sequence in the time domain, using recursive algorithm, convolution, and the z-transform technique. In Chapter 3, we introduced the concept of their response in the frequency domain, by deriving the DTFT or the frequency response of the system. These two chapters and Chapter 1 were devoted to the analysis of DT systems. Now we discuss the synthesis of these systems, when their transfer functions or their equivalent models are given. If we are given the input–output sequence, it is easy to find the transfer function $H(z)$ as the ratio of the z transform of the output to the z transform of the input. If, however, the frequency response of the system is specified, in the form of a plot, such as when the passband and stopband frequencies along with the magnitude and phase over these bands, and the tolerances allowed for these specifications, are specified, finding the transfer function from such specifications is based on approximation theory. There are many well-known methods for finding the transfer functions that approximate the specifications given in the frequency domain. In this chapter, we will discuss a few methods for the design of IIR filters that approximate the magnitude response specifications for lowpass, highpass, bandpass, and bandstop filters. Usually the specifications for a digital filter are given in terms of normalized frequencies. Also, in many applications, the specifications for an analog filter are realized by a digital filter in the combination of an ADC in the front end with a DAC at the receiving end, and these specifications will be in the analog domain. The magnitude response of ideal, classical analog filters are shown in Figure 4.1. Several examples of IIR filter design are also included in this chapter, to illustrate the design of these filters and also filters with arbitrary magnitude response, by use of MATLAB functions. The design of FIR filters that approximate the specifications in the frequency domain is discussed in the next chapter.

Introduction to Digital Signal Processing and Filter Design, by B. A. Shenoi
Copyright © 2006 John Wiley & Sons, Inc.

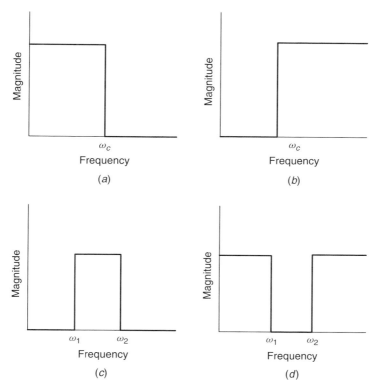

Figure 4.1 Magnitude responses of analog filters: (a) lowpass filter; (b) highpass filter; (c) bandpass filter; (d) bandstop filter.

Let us select any one of the following methods to specify the IIR filters. The recursive algorithm is given by

$$y(n) = -\sum_{k=1}^{N} a(k)y(n-k) + \sum_{k=0}^{M} b(k)x(n-k) \tag{4.1}$$

and its equivalent form is a linear difference equation:

$$\sum_{k=0}^{N} a(k)y(n-k) = \sum_{k=0}^{M} b(k)x(n-k); \qquad a(0) = 1 \tag{4.2}$$

The transfer function of the IIR filter is given by

$$H(z) = \frac{\sum_{k=0}^{M} b(k)z^{-k}}{\sum_{k=0}^{N} a(k)z^{-k}}; \qquad a(0) = 1 \tag{4.3}$$

Let us consider a few properties of the transfer function when it is evaluated on the unit circle $z = e^{j\omega}$, where ω is the normalized frequency in radians:

$$H(e^{j\omega}) = \frac{\sum_{k=0}^{M} b(k)\cos(k\omega) - j\sum_{k=0}^{M} b(k)\sin(k\omega)}{\sum_{k=0}^{N} a(k)\cos(k\omega) - j\sum_{k=0}^{M} a(k)\sin(k\omega)} \tag{4.4}$$

$$= \left| H(e^{j\omega}) \right| e^{j\theta(\omega)}$$

In this equation, $H(e^{j\omega})$ is the frequency response, or the discrete-time Fourier transform (DTFT) of the filter, $\left| H(e^{j\omega}) \right|$ is the magnitude response, and $\theta(e^{j\omega})$ is the phase response. If $X(e^{j\omega}) = \left| X(e^{j\omega}) \right| e^{j\alpha(\omega)}$ is the frequency response of the input signal, where $\left| X(e^{j\omega}) \right|$ is its magnitude and $\alpha(j\omega)$ is its phase response, then the frequency response $Y(e^{j\omega})$ is given by $Y(e^{j\omega}) = X(e^{j\omega})H(e^{j\omega}) = \left| X(e^{j\omega}) \right| \left| H(e^{j\omega}) \right| e^{j\{\alpha(\omega)+\theta(j\omega)\}}$. Therefore the magnitude of the output signal is multiplied by the magnitude $\left| H(e^{j\omega}) \right|$ and its phase is increased by the phase $\theta(e^{j\omega})$ of the filter:

$$\left| H(e^{j\omega}) \right| = \left\{ \frac{\left[\sum_{k=0}^{M} b(k)\cos(k\omega)\right]^2 + \left[\sum_{k=0}^{M} b(k)\sin(k\omega)\right]^2}{\left[\sum_{k=0}^{N} a(k)\cos(k\omega)\right]^2 + \left[\sum_{k=0}^{M} a(k)\sin(k\omega)\right]^2} \right\}^{1/2} \tag{4.5}$$

$$\theta(j\omega) = -\tan^{-1}\frac{\sum_{k=0}^{M} b(k)\sin(k\omega)}{\sum_{k=0}^{M} b(k)\cos(k\omega)} + \tan^{1}\frac{\sum_{k=0}^{M} a(k)\sin(k\omega)}{\sum_{k=0}^{N} a(k)\cos(k\omega)} \tag{4.6}$$

The magnitude squared function is

$$\left| H(e^{j\omega}) \right|^2 = \left| H(e^{j\omega})H(e^{-j\omega}) \right| = \left| H(e^{j\omega})H^*(e^{j\omega}) \right| \tag{4.7}$$

where $H^*(e^{j\omega}) = H(e^{-j\omega})$ is the complex conjugate of $H(e^{j\omega})$. It can be shown that the magnitude response is an even function of ω while the phase response is an odd function of ω.

Very often it is convenient to compute and plot the log magnitude of $\left| H(e^{j\omega}) \right|$ as $10\log\left| H(e^{j\omega}) \right|^2$ measured in decibels. Also we note that $H(e^{j\omega})/H(e^{-j\omega}) = e^{j2\theta(\omega)}$. The group delay $\tau(j\omega)$ is defined as $\tau(j\omega) = -[d\theta(j\omega)]/d\omega$ and is computed from

$$\tau(\omega) = \frac{1}{1+u^2}\frac{du}{d\omega} - \frac{1}{1+v^2}\frac{dv}{d\omega} \tag{4.8}$$

where

$$u = \frac{\sum_{k=0}^{M} b(k)\sin(k\omega)}{\sum_{k=0}^{M} b(k)\cos(k\omega)} \tag{4.9}$$

and

$$v = \frac{\sum_{k=0}^{N} a(k) \sin(k\omega)}{\sum_{k=0}^{N} a(k) \cos(k\omega)} \tag{4.10}$$

Designing an IIR filter usually means that we find a transfer function $H(z)$ in the form of (4.3) such that its magnitude response (or the phase response, the group delay, or both the magnitude and group delay) approximates the specified magnitude response in terms of a certain criterion. For example, we may want to amplify the input signal by a constant without any delay or with a constant amount of delay. But it is easy to see that the magnitude response of a filter or the delay is not a constant in general and that they can be approximated only by the transfer function of the filter. In the design of digital filters (and also in the design of analog filters), three approximation criteria are commonly used: (1) the Butterworth approximation, (2) the minimax (equiripple or Chebyshev) approximation, and (3) the least-pth approximation or the least-squares approximation. We will discuss them in this chapter in the same order as listed here. Designing a digital filter also means that we obtain a circuit realization or the algorithm that describes its performance in the time domain. This is discussed in Chapter 6. It also means the design of the filter is implemented by different types of hardware, and this is discussed in Chapters 7 and 8.

Two analytical methods are commonly used for the design of IIR digital filters, and they depend significantly on the approximation theory for the design of continuous-time filters, which are also called *analog filters*. Therefore, it is essential that we review the theory of magnitude approximation for analog filters before discussing the design of IIR digital filters.

4.2 MAGNITUDE APPROXIMATION OF ANALOG FILTERS

The transfer function of an analog filter $H(s)$ is a rational function of the complex frequency variable s, with real coefficients and is of the form[1]

$$H(s) = \frac{c_0 + c_1 s + c_2 s^2 + \cdots + c_m s^m}{d_0 + d_1 s + d_2 s^2 + \cdots + d_n s^n}, \qquad m \le n \tag{4.11}$$

The frequency response or the Fourier transform of the filter is obtained as a function of the frequency ω,[2] by evaluating $H(s)$ as a function of $j\omega$

$$H(j\omega) = \frac{c_0 + jc_1\omega - c_2\omega^2 - jc_3\omega^4 + c_4\omega^4 + \cdots + (j)^m c_m \omega^m}{d_0 + jd_1\omega - d_2\omega^2 - jd_3\omega^3 + d_4\omega^4 + \cdots + (j)^n c_n \omega^n} \tag{4.12}$$

$$= |H(j\omega)| \, e^{j\phi(\omega)} \tag{4.13}$$

---

[1] Much of the material contained in Sections 4.2–4.10 has been adapted from the author's book *Magnitude and Delay Approximation of 1-D and 2-D Digital Filters* and is included with permission from its publisher, Springer-Verlag.

[2] In Sections 4.2–4.8, discussing the theory of analog filters, we use ω and Ω to denote the angular frequency in radians per second. The notation ω should not be considered as the normalized digital frequency used in $H(e^{j\omega})$.

where $H(j\omega)$ is the frequency response, $|H(j\omega)|$ is the magnitude response, and $\theta(j\omega)$ is the phase response. We also find the magnitude squared and the phase response from the following:

$$|H(j\omega)|^2 = H(j\omega)H(-j\omega) = H(j\omega)H^*(j\omega) \qquad (4.14)$$

$$\frac{H(j\omega)}{H(-j\omega)} = e^{j2\theta(\omega)} \qquad (4.15)$$

The magnitude response of an analog filter is an even function of ω, whereas the phase response is an odd function. Although these properties of $H(j\omega)$ are similar to those of $H(e^{j\omega})$, there are some differences. For example, the frequency variable ω in $H(j\omega)$ is (are) in radians per second, whereas ω in $H(e^{j\omega})$ is the normalized frequency in radians. The magnitude response $|H(j\omega)|$ (and the phase response) is (are) aperiodic in ω over the doubly infinite interval $-\infty < \omega < \infty$, whereas the magnitude response $|H(e^{j\omega})|$ (and the phase response) is (are) periodic with a period of 2π on the normalized frequency scale.

Example 4.1

Let us take a simple example of a transfer function of an analog function as

$$H(s) = \frac{s+1}{s^2 + 2s + 2} \qquad (4.16)$$

The first step is to multiply $H(s)$ with $H(-s)$ and evaluate the product at $s = j\omega$:

$$\{H(s)H(-s)\}|_{s=j\omega} = |H(j\omega)|^2 \qquad (4.17)$$

$$|H(j\omega)|^2 = \{H(s)H(-s)\}|_{s=j\omega} = \left\{ \frac{(s+1)(-s+1)}{(s^2+s+2)(s^2-s+2)} \right\}\Bigg|_{s=j\omega} \qquad (4.18)$$

$$= \frac{\omega^2 + 1}{\omega^4 + 1} \qquad (4.19)$$

From this example, we see that to find the transfer function $H(s)$ in (4.16) from the magnitude squared function in (4.19), we reverse the steps followed above in deriving the function (4.19) from the $H(s)$. In other words, we substitute $j\omega = s$ (or $\omega^2 = -s^2$) in the given magnitude squared function to get $H(s)H(-s)$ and factorize its numerator and denominator. For every pole at s_k (and zero) in $H(s)$, there is a pole at $-s_k$ (and zero) in $H(-s)$. So for every pole in the left half of the s plane, there is a pole in the right half of the s plane, and it follows that a pair of complex conjugate poles in the left half of the s plane appear with a pair of complex conjugate poles in the right half-plane also, thereby displaying a quadrantal symmetry. Therefore, when we have factorized the product $H(s)H(-s)$, we pick all its poles that lie in the left half of the s-plane and identify them as the poles of $H(s)$, leaving their mirror images in the right half of the s-plane as the poles of $H(-s)$. This assures us that the transfer function is a stable function. Similarly, we choose the zeros in the left half-plane as the zeros of $H(s)$, but we are free to choose the zeros in the right half-plane as the zeros of $H(s)$ without affecting the magnitude. It does change the phase response of $H(s)$, giving a non−minimum phase response. Consider a simple example: $F_1(s) = (s + 1)$ and $F_2(s) = (s − 1)$. Then $F_{22}(s) = (s + 1)[(s − 1)/(s + 1)]$ has the same magnitude as the function $F_2(s)$ since the magnitude of $(s − 1)/(s + 1)$ is equal to $|(j\omega − 1)/(j\omega + 1)| = 1$ for all frequencies. But the phase of $F_{22}(j\omega)$ has increased by the phase response of the allpass function $(s − 1)/(s + 1)$. Hence $F_{22}(s)$ is a non−minimum phase function. In general any function that has all its zeros inside the unit circle in the z plane is defined as a minimum phase function. If it has atleast one zero outside the unit circle, it becomes a non−minimum phase function.

4.2.1 Maximally Flat and Butterworth Approximation

Let us choose the magnitude response of an ideal lowpass filter as shown in Figure 4.1a. This ideal lowpass filter passes all frequencies of the input continuous-time signal in the interval $|\omega| \le \omega_c$ with equal gain and completely filters out all the frequencies outside this interval. In the bandpass filter response shown in Figure 4.1c, the frequencies between ω_1 and ω_2 and between $-\omega_1$ and $-\omega_2$ only are transmitted and all other frequencies are completely filtered out.

In Figure 4.1, for the ideal lowpass filter, the magnitude response in the interval $0 \le \omega \le \omega_c$ is shown as a constant value normalized to one and is zero over the interval $\omega_c \le \omega < \infty$. Since the magnitude response is an even function, we know the magnitude response for the interval $-\infty < \omega < 0$. For

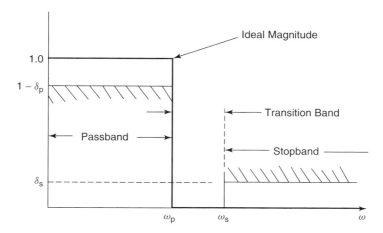

Figure 4.2   Magnitude response of an ideal lowpass analog filter showing the tolerances.

the lowpass filter, the frequency interval $0 \leq \omega \leq \omega_c$ is called the *passband*, and the interval $\omega_c \leq \omega < \infty$ is called the *stopband*. Since a transfer function $H(s)$ of the form (4.11) cannot provide such an ideal magnitude characteristic, it is common practice to prescribe tolerances within which these specifications have to be met by $|H(j\omega)|$. For example, the tolerance of δ_p on the ideal magnitude of one in the passband and a tolerance of δ_s on the magnitude of zero in the stopband are shown in Figure 4.2. A tolerance between the passband and the stopband is also provided by a transition band shown in this figure. This is typical of the magnitude response specifications for an ideal filter.

Since the magnitude squared function $|H(j\omega)| = H(j\omega)H(-j\omega)$ is an even function in ω, its numerator and denominator contain only even-degree terms; that is, it is of the form

$$|H(j\omega)|^2 = \frac{C_0 + C_2\omega^2 + C_4\omega^4 + \cdots + C_{2m}\omega^{2m}}{1 + D_2\omega^2 + D_4\omega^4 + \cdots + D_{2n}\omega^{2n}} \tag{4.20}$$

In order that it approximates the magnitude of the ideal lowpass filter, let us impose the following conditions

1. The magnitude at $\omega = 0$ is normalized to one.
2. The magnitude monotonically decreases from this value to zero as $\omega \to \infty$.
3. The maximum number of its derivatives evaluated at $\omega = 0$ are zero.

Condition 1 is satisfied when $C_0 = 1$, and condition 2 is satisfied when the coefficients $C_2 = C_4 = \cdots = C_{2m} = 0$. Condition 3 is satisfied when the denominator is $1 + D_{2n}\omega^{2n}$, in addition to condition 2 being satisfied. The magnitude response that satisfies conditions 2 and 3 is known as the *Butterworth response*, whereas the response that satisfies only condition 3 is known as the *maximally flat magnitude response*, which may not be monotonically decreasing. The magnitude squared function satisfying the three conditions is therefore of the form

$$|H(j\omega)|^2 = \frac{1}{1 + D_{2n}\omega^{2n}} \tag{4.21}$$

We scale the frequency ω by ω_p and define the normalized analog frequency $\Omega = \omega/\omega_p$ so that the passband of this filter is $\Omega_p = 1$. Now the magnitude of the lowpass filter satisfies the three conditions listed above and also the condition that its passband be normalized to $\Omega_p = 1$. Such a filter is called a *prototype* lowpass Butterworth filter having a transfer function $H(p) = H(s/p)$, which has its magnitude squared function given by

$$|H(j\Omega)|^2 = \frac{1}{1 + D_{2n}\Omega^{2n}} \tag{4.22}$$

The following specifications are normally given for a lowpass Butterworth filter: (1) a magnitude of H_0 at $\omega = 0$, (2) the bandwidth ω_p, (3) the magnitude at the bandwidth ω_p, (4) a stopband frequency ω_s, and (5) the magnitude of the filter at ω_s. The transfer function of the analog filter with practical specifications like these will be denoted by $H(p)$ in the following discussion, and the prototype lowpass filter will be denoted by $H(s)$.

Before we proceed with the analytical design procedure, we normalize the magnitude of the filter by H_0 for convenience and scale the frequencies ω_p and ω_s by ω_p so that the bandwidth of the prototype filter and its stopband frequency become $\Omega_p = 1$ and $\Omega_s = \omega_s/\omega_p$, respectively. The specifications about the magnitude at Ω_p and Ω_s are satisfied by the proper choice of D_{2n} and n in the function (4.22) as explained below. If, for example, the magnitude at the passband frequency is required to be $1/\sqrt{2}$, which means that the log magnitude required is -3 dB, then we choose $D_{2n} = 1$. If the magnitude at the passband frequency $\Omega = \Omega_p = 1$ is required to be $1 - \delta_p$, then we choose D_{2n}, normally denoted by ϵ^2, such that

$$|H(j1)|^2 = \frac{1}{1 + D_{2n}} = \frac{1}{1 + \epsilon^2} = (1 - \delta_p)^2 \qquad (4.23)$$

If the magnitude at the bandwidth $\Omega = \Omega_p = 1$ is given as $-A_p$ decibels, the value of ϵ^2 is computed by

$$10 \log \frac{1}{1 + \epsilon^2} = -A_p$$

$$10 \log(1 + \epsilon^2) = A_p$$

$$\log(1 + \epsilon^2) = 0.1 A_p$$

$$(1 + \epsilon^2) = 10^{0.1 A_p}$$

From the last equation, we get the formula $\epsilon^2 = 10^{0.1 A_p} - 1$ and $\epsilon = \sqrt{10^{0.1 A_p} - 1}$.

Let us consider the common case of a Butterworth filter with a log magnitude of -3 dB at the bandwidth of Ω_p to develop the design procedure for a Butterworth lowpass filter. In this case, we use the function for the prototype filter, in the form

$$|H(j\Omega)|^2 = \frac{1}{1 + \Omega^{2n}} \qquad (4.24)$$

This satisfies the following properties:

1. The magnitude squared of the filter response at $\Omega = 0$ is one.
2. The magnitude squared at $\Omega = 1$ is $\frac{1}{2}$ for all integer values of n; so the log magnitude is -3 dB.
3. The magnitude decreases monotonically to zero as $\Omega \to \infty$; the asymptotic rate is $-40n$ dB/decade.

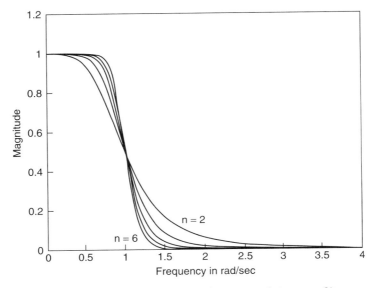

Figure 4.3 Magnitude responses of Butterworth lowpass filters.

The magnitude response of Butterworth lowpass filters is shown for $n = 2, 3, \ldots, 6$ in Figure 4.3. Instead of showing the log magnitude of these filters, we show their attenuation in decibels in Figure 4.4. Attenuation or loss measured in decibels is defined as

$$-10 \log |H(j\Omega)|^2 = 10 \log(1 + \Omega^{2n})$$

The attenuation over the passband only is shown in Figure 4.4a, and the maximum attenuation in the passband is 3 dB for all n; the attenuation characteristic of the filters over $1 \leq \Omega \leq 10$ for $n = 1, 2, \ldots, 10$ is shown in Figure 4.4b.

4.2.2 Design Theory of Butterworth Lowpass Filters

Let us consider the design of a Butterworth lowpass filter for which (1) the frequency ω_p at which the magnitude is 3 dB below the maximum value at $\omega = 0$, and (2) the magnitude at another frequency ω_s in the stopband are specified. When we normalize the gain constant to unity and normalize the frequency by the scale factor ω_p, we get the cutoff frequency of the normalized prototype filter $\Omega_p = 1$ and the stopband frequency $\Omega_s = \omega_s/\omega_p$. After we have found the transfer function $H(p)$ of this normalized prototype lowpass filter, we restore the frequency scale and the magnitude scale to get the transfer function $H(s)$ approximating the prescribed magnitude specification of the lowpass filter.

The analytical procedure used to derive $H(p)$ from the magnitude squared function of the prototype lowpass filter is carried out simply by reversing the

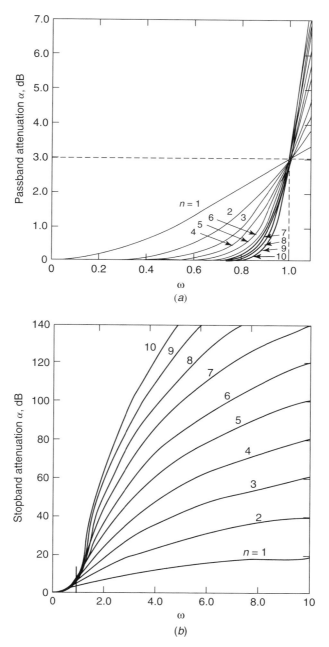

Figure 4.4 Attenuation characteristics of Butterworth lowpass filters in (a) passband; (b) stopband.

steps used to derive the magnitude squared function from $H(p)$ as illustrated by Example 4.1 earlier. First we substitute $\Omega = p/j$ or equivalently $\Omega^2 = -p^2$ in (4.24):

$$\left. \frac{1}{1+\Omega^{2n}} \right|_{\Omega^2=-p^2} = \frac{1}{1+(-1)^n p^{2n}} = H(p)H(-p) \tag{4.25}$$

The denominator has $2n$ zeros obtained by solving the equation

$$1 + (-)^n p^{2n} = 0 \tag{4.26}$$

or the equation

$$p^{2n} = \begin{cases} 1 = e^{j2k\pi} & n \text{ odd} \\ -1 = e^{j(2k+1)\pi} & n \text{ even} \end{cases} \tag{4.27}$$

This gives us the $2n$ poles of $H(p)H(-p)$, which are

$$p_k = e^{j(2k\pi/2n)\pi} \qquad k = 1, 2, \dots, (2n) \qquad \text{when } n \text{ is odd} \tag{4.28}$$

and

$$p_k = e^{j[(2k-1)/2n]\pi} \qquad k = 1, 2, \dots, (2n) \qquad \text{when } n \text{ is even} \tag{4.29}$$

or in general

$$p_k = e^{j[(2k+n-1)/2n]\pi} \qquad k = 1, 2, \dots, (2n) \tag{4.30}$$

We notice that in both cases, the poles have a magnitude of one and the angle between any two adjacent poles as we go around the unit circle is equal to π/n. There are n poles in the left half of the p plane and n poles in the right half of the p plane, as illustrated for the cases of $n = 2$ and $n = 3$ in Figure 4.5. For every pole of $H(p)$ at $p = p_a$ that lies in the left half-plane, there is a pole of $H(-p)$ at $p = -p_a$ that lies in the right half-plane. Because of this property, we identify n poles that are in the left half of the p plane as the poles of $H(p)$ so that it is a stable transfer function; the poles that are in the right half-plane are assigned as the poles of $H(-p)$. The n poles that are in the left half of the p plane are given by

$$p_k = \exp\left[j\left(\frac{2k+n-1}{2n}\right)\pi\right] \qquad k = 1, 2, 3, \dots, n \tag{4.31}$$

When we have found these n poles, we construct the denominator polynomial $D(p)$ of the prototype filter $H(p) = \frac{1}{D(p)}$ from

$$D(p) = \prod_{k=1}^{n}(p - p_k) \tag{4.32}$$

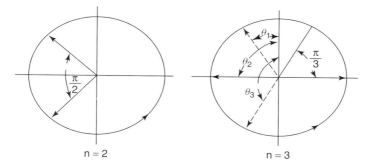

Figure 4.5 Pole locations of Butterworth lowpass filters of orders $n = 2$ and $n = 3$.

The only unknown parameter at this stage of design is the order n of the filter function $H(p)$, which is required in (4.31). This is calculated using the specification that at the stopband frequency Ω_s, the log magnitude is required to be no more than $-A_s$ dB or the minimum attenuation in the stopband to be A_s dB.

$$10 \log |H(j\Omega_s)|^2 = -10 \log(1 + \Omega_s^{2n}) \leq -A_s \qquad (4.33)$$

from which we derive the formula for calculating n as follows:

$$n \geq \frac{\log(10^{0.1 A_s} - 1)}{2 \log \Omega_s} \qquad (4.34)$$

Since we require that n be an integer, we choose the actual value of $n = \lceil n \rceil$ that is the next-higher integer value or the ceiling of n obtained from the right side of (4.34). When we choose $n = \lceil n \rceil$, the attenuation in the stopband is more than the specified value of A_s. We use this integer value for n in (4.31), to calculate the poles and then construct the denominator polynomial $D(p)$ of order n. By multiplying $(p - p_k)$ with $(p - p_k^*)$ where p_k and p_k^* are complex conjugate pairs, the polynomial is reduced to the normal form with real coefficients only. These polynomials, known as *Butterworth polynomials*, have many special properties. In the polynomial form, if we represent them as

$$D(p) = 1 + d_1 p + d_2 p^2 + \cdots + d_n p^n \qquad (4.35)$$

their coefficients can be computed recursively from ($d_0 = 1$)

$$d_k = \frac{\cos\left[(k-1)\frac{\pi}{2}\right]}{\sin\left[\frac{k\pi}{2n}\right]} d_{k-1} \qquad k = 1, 2, 3, \ldots, n \qquad (4.36)$$

But there is no need to do so, since they can be computed from (4.32). They are also listed in many books for n up to 10 in polynomial form and in some books in a factored form also [3,2]. We list a few of them in Table 4.1.

TABLE 4.1

n	Butterworth Polynomial $D(p)$ in Polynomial and Factored Form
1	$p + 1$
2	$p^2 + \sqrt{2}p + 1$
3	$p^3 + 2p^2 + 2p + 1 = (p + 1)(p^2 + p + 1)$
4	$p^4 + 2.61326p^3 + 3.41421p^2 + 2.61326p + 1$
	$= (p^2 + 0.76537p + 1)(p^2 + 1.84776p + 1)$
5	$p^5 + 3.23607p^4 + 5.23607p^3 + 5.23607p^2 + 3.23607p + 1$
	$= (p + 1)(p^2 + 0.618034p + 1)(p^2 + 1.931804p + 1)$
6	$p^6 + 3.8637p^5 + 7.4641p^4 + 9.1416p^3 + 7.4641p^2 + 3.8637p + 1$
	$= (p^2 + 0.5176p + 1)(p^2 + 1.4142p + 1)(p^2 + 1.9318p + 1)$

In the case of lowpass filters, usually the magnitude is specified at $\omega = 0$; hence it is also the magnitude at $\Omega = 0$. Therefore the specified magnitude is equated to the value of the transfer function $H(p)$ evaluated at $p = j0$. This is equal to $H(j0) = H_0/D(j0) = H_0$. So we restore the magnitude scale by multiplying the normalized prototype filter function by H_0. To restore the frequency scale by ω_p, we put $p = s/\omega_p$ in $H_0/D(p)$ and simplify the expression to get transfer function $H(s)$ for the specified lowpass filter. This completes the design procedure, which will be illustrated in Example 4.2.

Example 4.2

Design a lowpass Butterworth filter with a maximum gain of 5 dB and a cutoff frequency of 1000 rad/s at which the gain is at least 2 dB and a stopband frequency of 5000 rad/s at which the magnitude is required to be less than -25 dB.

The maximum gain of 5 dB is the magnitude of the filter function at $\omega = 0$. The edge of the passband is the cutoff frequency $\omega_p = 1000$, and the frequency range $0 \le \omega \le \omega_p$ is called the *bandwidth*. So we see that the magnitude of 2 dB at this frequency is 3 dB below the maximum value in the passband. We say that the filter has a 3 dB bandwidth equal to 1000 rad/s. The frequency scale factor is chosen as 1000 so that the passband of the prototype filter is $\Omega_p = 1$. The stopband frequency ω_s is specified as 5000 rad/s and is therefore scaled to $\Omega_s = 5$. The magnitude is normalized so that the normalized prototype lowpass filter function $H(p)^3$ has a magnitude of one (i.e., 0 dB) at $\Omega = 0$. It is this filter that has a magnitude squared function

$$|H(j\Omega)|^2 = \frac{1}{1 + \Omega^{2n}} \tag{4.37}$$

---

[3]Note that we have chosen $p = \Sigma + j\Omega$ as the notation for the complex frequency variable of the transfer function $H(p)$ for the lowpass prototype filter and the notation $s = \sigma + j\omega$ for the variable of the transfer function $H(s)$ for the specified filter.

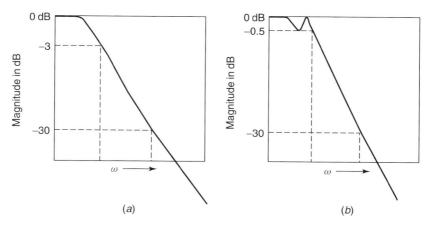

Figure 4.6   Magnitude response specifications of prototype filters: (a) Butterworth filter; (b) Chebyshev (equiripple) filter.

It is always necessary to reduce the given specifications to the specifications of this normalized prototype filter to which only the expressions derived above are applicable. The magnitude response of the normalized prototype filter (not to scale) for this example is shown in Figure 4.6a.

For this example, note that the maximum attenuation in the passband is $A_p = 3$ dB and the minimum attenuation in the stopband is $A_s = 30$ dB. From (4.34) we calculate the value of $n = 2.1457$ and choose $n = \lceil 2.1457 \rceil = 3$. From (4.31), we get the three poles as $p_1 = -0.5 + j\sqrt{0.75}$, $p_2 = -1.0$ and $p_3 = -0.5 - j\sqrt{0.75}$. Therefore the third-order denominator polynomial $D(p)$ is obtained from (4.32) or from Table 4.1:

$$D(p) = (p + 0.5 - j\sqrt{0.75})(p + 1)(p + 0.5 + \sqrt{0.75})$$
$$= (p^2 + p + 1)(p + 1) = p^3 + 2p^2 + 2p + 1 \qquad (4.38)$$

Hence the transfer function of the normalized prototype filter of third order is

$$H(p) = \frac{1}{p^3 + 2p^2 + 2p + 1} \qquad (4.39)$$

To restore the magnitude scale, we multiply this function by H_0. Now the filter function is

$$H(p) = \frac{H_0}{p^3 + 2p^2 + 2p + 1} \qquad (4.40)$$

which has a magnitude of H_0 at $p = j0$. From the requirement $20 \log(H_0) = 5$ dB, we calculate the value of $H_0 = 1.7783$. To restore the frequency scale, we substitute $p = s/1000$ in (4.40) and simplify to get $H(s)$ as shown below:

$$H(p)|_{p=s/1000} = \frac{1.7783}{\left(\dfrac{s}{1000}\right)^3 + 2\left(\dfrac{s}{1000}\right)^2 + 2\left(\dfrac{s}{1000}\right) + 1}$$

$$= \frac{(1.7783)10^9}{s^3 + (2 \times 10^3)s^2 + (2 \times 10^6)s + 10^9} \tag{4.41}$$

$$= H(s) \tag{4.42}$$

The magnitude of $H(p)$ plotted on the normalized frequency scale Ω shown in Figure 4.7 is marked as "Example (2)." It is found that the attenuation at the stopband edge $\Omega_s = 5$ is about 42 dB, which is more than the specified 30 dB.

It must be remembered that in (4.37) $\Omega_p = 1$ is the bandwidth of the prototype filter, and at this frequency, $|H(j\Omega)|^2$ has a value of $\frac{1}{2}$ or a magnitude of -3 dB. Hence formulas (4.31) and (4.34) cannot be used if the maximum attenuation A_p in the passband is different from 3 dB. In this case, we modify the function to the form (4.43), which is the general case:

$$|H(j\Omega)|^2 = \frac{1}{1 + \epsilon^2 \Omega^{2n}} \tag{4.43}$$

Now the attenuation at $\Omega = 1$ is given by $10\log(1 + \epsilon^2) = A_p$, from which we get $\epsilon^2 = (10^{0.1A_p} - 1)$. We may also note that $\epsilon^2 = 1$ in the previous case when $A_p = 3$. When A_p is other than 3 dB, the formulas for calculating n and p_k are

$$n \geq \frac{\log\left[(10^{0.1A_s} - 1)/(10^{0.1A_p} - 1)\right]}{2\log\Omega_s} \tag{4.44}$$

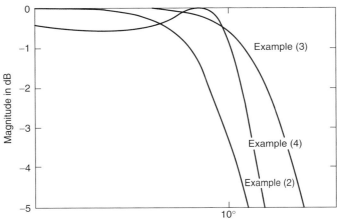

Figure 4.7 Magnitude responses of the prototype filters in Examples 4.1–4.3.

and

$$p_k = \epsilon^{-(1/n)} \exp\left[j \left(\frac{2k + n - 1}{2n} \right) \pi \right] \qquad k = 1, 2, 3, \dots, n \qquad (4.45)$$

Comparing (4.45) with (4.31), it is obvious that the poles have been scaled by a factor $\epsilon^{-(1/n)}$. So the maximum attenuation at $\Omega_p = 1$ is the specified value of A_p; also the frequency at which the attenuation is 3 dB is equal to $\epsilon^{-(1/n)}$.

Example 4.3

Design a lowpass Butterworth filter with a maximum magnitude of 5 dB, passband of 1000 rad/s, maximum attenuation in the passband $A_p = 0.5$ dB, and minimum attenuation $A_s = 30$ dB at the stopband frequency of 5000 rad/s.

First we scale the frequency by $\omega_p = 1000$ so that the normalized passband frequency $\Omega_p = 1$ and the stopband frequency ω_s is mapped to $\Omega_s = 5$. Also the magnitude is scaled by 5 dB. The magnitude response for the normalized prototype filter $H(p)$ is similar to that shown in Figure 4.6a, except that now $A_p = 0.5$ dB. Then we calculate $\epsilon^2 = (10^{0.1A_p} - 1) = 0.1220$ and therefore $\epsilon = 0.3493$. From (4.44), the value of $n = 2.7993$; it is rounded to $\lceil n \rceil = 3$. Next we compute the three poles from (4.45) as $p_1 = -0.71 + j1.2297$, $p_2 = -1.4199$, and $p_3 = -0.71 - j1.2297$. The transfer function of the filter with these poles is

$$H(p) = \frac{H_0}{(p + 1.4199)(p + 0.71 - j1.2297)(p + 0.71 + j1.2297)}$$

$$= \frac{H_0}{(p + 1.4199)(p^2 + 1.42p + 2.0163)} \qquad (4.46)$$

Since the maximum value has been normalized to 0 dB, which occurs at $\Omega = 0$, we equate the magnitude of $H(p)$ evaluated at $p = j0$ to one. Therefore $H_0 = (1.4199)(2.0163) = 2.8629$. To raise the magnitude level to 5 dB, we have to multiply this constant by $\sqrt{10^{0.5}} = 1.7783$. Of course, we can compute the same value for H_0 in one step, from the specification $20 \log |H(j0)| = 20 \log H(0) - 20 \log(1.4199)(2.0163) = 5$. The frequency scale is restored by putting $p = s/1000$ in (4.46) to get (4.47) as the transfer function of the filter that meets the given specifications:

$$H(s) = \frac{(2.8629)(1.7783)}{[s/1000 + 1.4199][(s/1000)^2 + 1.42(s/1000) + 2.0163]}$$

$$= \frac{5.09 \times 10^9}{[s + 1419.9][s^2 + 1420s + 2.0163 \times 10^6]} \qquad (4.47)$$

The plot is marked as "Example (3)" in Figure 4.7. It is the magnitude response of the prototype filter given by (4.46). It has a magnitude of -0.5 dB at $\Omega = 1$ and approximately -33 dB at $\Omega = 5$, which exceeds the specified value.

4.2.3   Chebyshev I Approximation

The Chebyshev I approximation for an ideal lowpass filter shows a magnitude that has the same values for the maxima and for the minima in the passband and decreases monotonically as the frequency increases above the cutoff frequency. It has equal-valued ripples in the passband between the maximum and minimum values as shown in Figure 4.6b. Hence it is known as the *minimax approximation* and also as the equiripple approximation. To approximate the ideal magnitude response of the lowpass filter in the equiripple sense, the magnitude squared function of its prototype is chosen to be

$$|H(j\Omega)|^2 = \frac{H_0^2}{1 + \epsilon^2 C_n^2(\Omega)} \tag{4.48}$$

where $C_n(\Omega)$ is the Chebyshev polynomial of degree n. It is defined by

$$C_n(\Omega) = \cos(n \cos^{-1} \Omega) \qquad |\Omega| \leq 1 \tag{4.49}$$

The polynomial $C_n(\Omega)$ approximates a value of zero over the closed interval $\Omega \in [-1, \quad 1]$ in the equiripple sense as shown by examples for $n = 2, 3, 4, 5$ in Figure 4.8a. These polynomials are

$$C_0(\Omega) = 1$$
$$C_1(\Omega) = \Omega$$
$$C_2(\Omega) = 2\Omega^2 - 1$$
$$C_3(\Omega) = 4\Omega^3 - 3\Omega$$
$$C_4(\Omega) = 8\Omega^4 - 8\Omega^2 + 1$$
$$C_5(\Omega) = 16\Omega^5 - 20\Omega^3 + 5\Omega \tag{4.50}$$

4.2.4   Properties of Chebyshev Polynomials

Some of the properties of Chebyshev polynomials that are useful for our discussion are described below. Let $\cos\phi = \Omega$. Then $C_n(n \cos^{-1} \Omega) = \cos(n\phi)$, and therefore we use the identity

$$\cos(k+1) = \cos(k\phi)\cos(\phi) - \sin(k\phi)\sin(\phi)$$
$$= 2\cos(k\phi)\cos(\phi) - \cos((k-1)\phi) \tag{4.51}$$

from which we obtain a recursive formula to generate Chebyshev polynomials of any order, as

$$C_0(\Omega) = 1$$
$$C_{k+1}(\Omega) = 2\Omega C_k(\Omega) - C_{k-1}(\Omega) \tag{4.52}$$

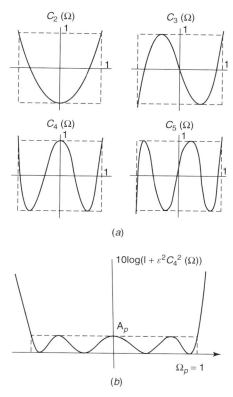

(a)

(b)

Figure 4.8   Chebyshev polynomials and Chebyshev filter: (a) magnitude of Chebyshev polynomials; (b) attenuation of a Chebyshev I filter.

To see that $C_n(\Omega) = \cos(n \cos^{-1} \Omega)$ is indeed a polynomial of order n, consider it in the following form:

$$\cos(n\phi) = \mathrm{Re}\left[e^{jn\phi}\right]$$

$$= \mathrm{Re}\left[\cos(\phi) + j \sin(\phi)\right]^n = \mathrm{Re}\left[\phi + j\sqrt{(1 - \phi^2)}\right]^n$$

$$= \mathrm{Re}\left[\phi + \sqrt{\phi^2 - 1}\right]^n \tag{4.53}$$

Expanding $\left[\phi + \sqrt{\phi^2 - 1}\right]^n$ by the binomial theorem and choosing the real part, we get the polynomial for

$$\cos(n\phi) = \phi^n + \frac{n(n-1)}{2!}\phi^{n-2}(\phi^2 - 1)$$

$$+ \frac{n(n-1)(n-2)(n-3)}{4!}\phi^{n-4}(\phi^2 - 1)^2 + \cdots \tag{4.54}$$

Recall that since n is a positive integer, the expansion expressed above has a finite number of terms, and hence we conclude that it is a polynomial (of degree n). We also note from (4.50) that

$$C_n^2(0) = \begin{cases} 0 & n \quad \text{odd} \\ 1 & n \quad \text{even} \end{cases} \tag{4.55}$$

But

$$C_n^2(1) = \begin{cases} 1 & n \quad \text{odd} \\ 1 & n \quad \text{even} \end{cases} \tag{4.56}$$

So we derive the following properties:

$$|H(0)|^2 = \begin{cases} 1 & n \quad \text{odd} \\ \frac{1}{1+\epsilon^2} & n \quad \text{even} \end{cases} \tag{4.57}$$

$$|H(1)|^2 = \frac{1}{1+\epsilon^2} \quad n \quad \text{odd or even} \tag{4.58}$$

The attenuation characteristics of the Chebyshev filter of order $n = 4$ is shown in Figure 4.8b as an example. The magnitude $|H(j\Omega)|$ plotted as "Example(4)" in Figure 4.7 has an equiripple response in the passband, with a maximum value of 0 dB and a minimum value of $10 \log[1/(1 + \epsilon^2)]$ decibels. However, the magnitude of Chebyshev I lowpass filters is $10 \log[1/(1 + \epsilon^2)]$ at $\Omega = 1$ for any order n. The magnitude of the ripple can be measured as either $|H(0)| - |H(1)|$ or $|H(0)|^2 - |H(1)|^2 = 1 - [1/(1 + \epsilon^2)] = [\epsilon^2/(1 + \epsilon^2)] \approx \epsilon^2$. We can always calculate $\epsilon^2 = (10^{0.1A_p} - 1)$.

Another property of Chebyshev I filters is that the total number of maxima and minima in the closed interval $[-1 \quad 1]$ is $n + 1$. The square of the magnitude response of Chebyshev lowpass filters is shown in Figure 4.9a to indicate some properties of the Chebyshev lowpass filters just described.

4.2.5 Design Theory of Chebyshev I Lowpass Filters

Typically the specifications for a lowpass Chebyshev filter specify the maximum and minimum values of the magnitude in the passband; the cutoff frequency ω_p, which is the highest frequency of the passband; a frequency ω_s in the stopband; and the magnitude at the frequency ω_s. As in the case of the Butterworth filter, we normalize the magnitude and the frequency and reduce the given specifications to those of the normalized prototype lowpass filter and follow similar steps to find the poles of $H(p)$.

Since Ω can take real values greater than one in general, let us assume ϕ to be a complex variable: $\phi = \varphi_1 + j\varphi_2$. From $1 + \epsilon^2 C_n^2(\Omega) = 0$, we get $\epsilon^2 C_n^2(\Omega) =$

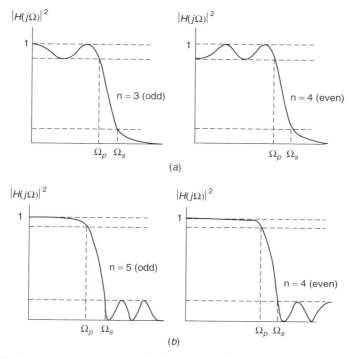

Figure 4.9 Magnitude response of Chebyshev filters: (a) Chebyshev I filters; (b) Chebyshev II filters.

$-1 = j^2$; we derive

$$C_n(\Omega) = \pm \frac{j}{\epsilon}$$
$$= \cos(n\phi) = \cos(n(\varphi_1 + j\varphi_2))$$
$$= \cos(n\varphi_1)\cosh(n\varphi_2) - j\sin(n\varphi_1)\sinh(n\varphi_2) \qquad (4.59)$$

Equating the real and imaginary parts, we get

$$\cos(n\varphi_1)\cosh(n\varphi_2) = 0 \qquad (4.60)$$

and

$$\sin(n\varphi_1)\sinh(n\varphi_2) = \mp\frac{1}{\epsilon} \qquad (4.61)$$

From (4.60) we get

$$\varphi_1 = \frac{(2k-1)\pi}{2n} \qquad (4.62)$$

Substituting this in (4.61), we obtain $\sinh(n\varphi_2) = \pm(1/\epsilon)$, from which we get

$$\varphi_2 = \frac{1}{n}\sinh^{-1}\left(\frac{1}{\epsilon}\right) \tag{4.63}$$

Now $\Omega = \cos(\phi) = \cos(\varphi_1 + j\varphi_2) = \cos(\varphi_1)\cosh(\varphi_2) - j\sin(\varphi_1)\sinh(\varphi_2)$.
Therefore

$$j\Omega = \sin(\varphi_1)\sinh(\varphi_2) + j\cos(\varphi_1)\cosh(\varphi_2) \tag{4.64}$$

These are the roots in the p plane that satisfy the condition $1 + \epsilon^2 C_n^2(\Omega) = 0$. Hence the $2n$ poles of $H(p)H(-p)$ are given by

$$p_k = \sinh(\varphi_2)\sin\left[\frac{(2k-1)\pi}{2n}\right] + j\cosh(\varphi_2)\cos\left[\frac{(2k-1)\pi}{2n}\right]$$

for

$$k = 1, 2, \ldots, (2n) \tag{4.65}$$

The $2n$ poles of $H(p)H(-p)$ given by (4.65) can be shown to lie on an elliptic contour in the p plane with a major semiaxis equal to $\cosh(\varphi_2)$ along the $j\Omega$ axis and a minor semiaxis equal to $\sinh(\varphi_2)$ along Σ axis, where $p = \Sigma + j\Omega$. We find that the frequency Ω_3 at which the attenuation of the prototype filter is 3 dB is given by

$$\Omega_3 = \cosh\left[\frac{1}{n}\cosh^{-1}\left(\frac{1}{\epsilon}\right)\right] \tag{4.66}$$

The poles in the left half of the p plane only are given by

$$p_k = -\sinh(\varphi_2)\sin\left[\frac{(2k-1)\pi}{2n}\right] + j\cosh(\varphi_2)\cos\left[\frac{(2k-1)\pi}{2n}\right]$$
$$= -\sinh(\varphi_2)\sin(\theta_k) + j\cosh(\varphi_2)\cos(\theta_k) \qquad k = 1, 2, 3, \ldots, n \quad (4.67)$$

where φ_2 is obtained from (4.63). In (4.67), note that θ_k are the angles measured from the imaginary axis of the p plane and the poles lie in the left half of the p plane.

The formula for finding the order n is derived from the requirement that $10\log[1 + \epsilon^2 C_n^2(\Omega_s)] \geq A_s$. It is

$$n \geq \frac{\cosh^{-1}\sqrt{[(10^{0.1A_s} - 1)/(10^{0.1A_p} - 1)]}}{\cosh^{-1}\Omega_s} \tag{4.68}$$

and the value of $\lceil n \rceil$ is chosen for calculating the poles using (4.67). Given ω_p, A_p, ω_s, and A_s as the specifications for a Chebyshev lowpass filter $H(s)$, its maximum value in the passband is normalized to one, and its frequencies are scaled by ω_p, to get the values of $\Omega_p = 1$ and $\Omega_s = \omega_s/\omega_p$ for the prototype filter at which the attenuations are A_p and A_s, respectively. The design procedure to find $H(s)$ starts with the magnitude squared function (4.48) and proceeds as follows:

1. Calculate $\epsilon = \sqrt{(10^{0.1A_p} - 1)}$.
2. Calculate n from (4.68) and choose $n = \lceil n \rceil$.
3. Calculate φ_2 from (4.63).
4. Calculate the poles p_k $(k = 1, 2, \ldots, n)$ from (4.67).
5. Compute $H(p) = H_0/[\prod_{k=1}^{n}(p - p_k)] = H_0/[\sum_{k=0}^{n} d_k p^k]$.
6. Find the value of H_0 by equating

$$H(0) = \frac{H_0}{d_0} = \begin{cases} 1 & n \quad \text{odd} \\ \sqrt{\dfrac{1}{1+\epsilon^2}} & n \quad \text{even} \end{cases}$$

7. Restore the magnitude scale.
8. Restore the frequency scale by substituting $p = s/\omega_p$ in $H(p)$ and simplify to get $H(s)$.

A simple example is worked out below to illustrate this design procedure.

Example 4.4

Let us choose the specifications of a lowpass Chebyshev filter with a maximum gain of 5 dB, a bandwidth of 2500 rad/s, and a stopband frequency of 12,500 rad/s; $A_p = 0.5$ dB, and $A_s = 30$ dB. For the prototype filter, the maximum value in the passband is one (0 dB), and we have $\Omega_p = 1$, $\Omega_s = 5$. So

1. $\epsilon = \sqrt{(10^{0.05} - 1} = 0.34931$.
2. $n \geq \{\cosh^{-1}\sqrt{[(10^3 - 1)/(10^{0.05} - 1)]}\}/[\cosh^{-1}(5)] = 2.2676$; choose $n = 3$.
3. $\varphi_2 = \frac{1}{3}\sinh^{-1}\left(\frac{1}{0.34931}\right) = 0.591378$.
4. $p_k = -0.313228 \pm j1.02192$ and -0.626456.
5. $H(p) = H_0/[(p + 0.31228 - j1.02192)(p + 0.31228 + j1.02192)(p + 0.626456)] = H_0/[(p^2 + 0.626456p + 1.142447)(p + 0.626456)]$.
6. $H(0) = H_0/[(1.142447)(0.626456)] = 1$ (since $n = 3$ is odd). Hence $H_0 = 0.715693$.
7. The transfer function with a direct-current (DC) gain of 0 dB is $H(p) = 0.715693/[(p^2 + 0.626456p + 1.142447)(p + 0.626456)]$. The magnitude scale is restored by multiplying $H(p)$ by 1.7783, so that the DC gain is raised to 5 dB.

8. The transfer function of the filter is

$$H(p) = \frac{(0.715693)(1.7783)}{(p^2 + 0.626456p + 1.142447)(p + 0.626456)} \tag{4.69}$$

When we substitute $p = s/2500$ in this $H(p)$ and simplify the expression, we get

$$H(s) = \frac{19.886 \times 10^{12}}{(s^2 + 1566s + 714 \times 10^6)(s + 1566)} \tag{4.70}$$

The magnitude response of the prototype filter in (4.70) is marked as "Example(4)" in Figure 4.7. The three magnitude responses are plotted in the same figure so that the response of the three filters can be compared. The attenuation of the Chebyshev filter at $\Omega_s = 5$ is found to be 47 dB. The abovementioned class of filters with equiripple passband response and monotonic response in the stopband are sometimes called *Chebyshev I filters*, to distinguish them from the following class of filters, known as *Chebyshev II filters*.

4.2.6 Chebyshev II Approximation

The Chebyshev II filters have a magnitude response that is maximally flat at $\omega = 0$; it decreases monotonically as the frequency increases and has an equiripple response in the stopband. Typical magnitudes of Chebyshev II filters are shown in Figure 4.9b. This class of filters are also called *Inverse Chebyshev filters*. The transfer function of Chebyshev II filters are derived by applying the following two transformations: (1) a frequency transformation $\Omega = 1/\omega$ in $|H(j\Omega)|^2$ of the lowpass normalized prototype filter gives the magnitude squared function of the highpass filter $|H(1/j\Omega)|^2$, with an equiripple passband in $|\Omega| > 1$ and a monotonically decreasing response in the stopband $0 < |\Omega| < 1$; (2) when it is subtracted from one, we get the magnitude squared function (4.72) of the inverse Chebyshev lowpass filter:

$$\left| H \frac{1}{j\Omega} \right|^2 = \frac{1}{1 + \epsilon^2 C_n^2(1/\Omega)} \tag{4.71}$$

$$1 - \frac{1}{1 + \epsilon^2 C_n^2(1/\Omega)} = \frac{\epsilon^2 C_n^2(1/\Omega)}{1 + \epsilon^2 C_n^2(1/\Omega)} = \frac{1}{\left[1 + \frac{1}{\epsilon^2 C_n^2(1/\Omega)}\right]} \tag{4.72}$$

The magnitude squared function $|H(j\Omega)|^2$ of a lowpass Chebyshev I filter and $|H(\frac{1}{j\Omega})|^2$ and $1 - |H(\frac{1}{j\Omega})|^2$ are shown in Figure 4.10.

We make two important observations in Figure 4.10. The normalized cutoff frequency $\Omega = 1$ becomes the lowest frequency in the stopband of the inverse Chebyshev filter at which the magnitude is $\epsilon^2/(1 + \epsilon^2)$. Hence the frequencies ω_p and ω_s specified for the inverse Chebyshev filter must be scaled by ω_s and not by ω_p to obtain the prototype of the inverse Chebyshev filter. We also observe that

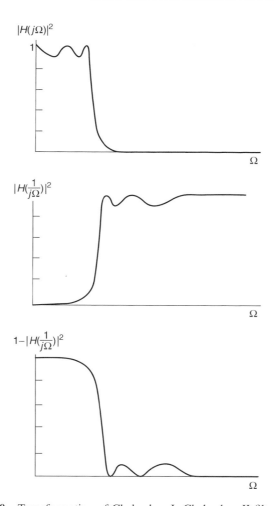

Figure 4.10   Transformation of Chebyshev I–Chebyshev II filter response.

when n is odd, the number of finite zeros in the stopband is $(n-1)/2 = m$. When n is an odd integer, the term $\sec\theta_k$, which is involved in the design procedure described below, attains a value of ∞ when $k = (n+1)/2$. So one of the zeros is shifted to $j\infty$; the remaining finite zeros appear in conjugate pairs on the imaginary axis, and hence the numerator of the Chebyshev II filter is expressed as shown in step 6 in Section 4.2.7. Note that the value of ϵ_i calculated in step 1 is different from the value calculated in the design of Chebyshev I filters and therefore the values of φ_i used in steps 3 and 4 are different from φ_2 used in the design of Chebyshev I filters. Hence it would be misleading to state that the poles of the Chebyshev II filters are obtained as "the reciprocals of the poles of the Chebyshev I filters."

4.2.7   Design of Chebyshev II Lowpass Filters

Given ω_p, A_p, ω_s, A_s and the maximum value in the passband, we scale the frequencies ω_p and ω_s by ω_s and deduce the specifications for the normalized prototype lowpass inverse Chebyshev filter. Equation (4.72) is the magnitude squared function of this inverse Chebyshev filter, and we follow the design procedure as outlined below:

1. Calculate $\epsilon_i = 1/\sqrt{(10^{0.1A_s} - 1)}$.
2. Calculate

$$n \geq \frac{\cosh^{-1}\sqrt{\left[(10^{0.1A_s} - 1)/(10^{0.1A_p} - 1)\right]}}{\cosh^{-1}\Omega_s}$$

   and choose $n = \lceil n \rceil$.
3. Calculate φ_i from $\varphi_i = (1/n)\sinh^{-1}(1/\epsilon_i)$.
4. Compute the poles in the left-half plane p_k:

$$p_k = \frac{1}{-\sinh(\varphi_i)\sin(\theta_k) + j\cosh(\varphi_i)\cos(\theta_k)} \qquad k = 1, 2, 3, \ldots, n$$

5. The zeros of the transfer function $H(p)$ are calculated as $z_k = \pm j\Omega_{0k} = j\sec\theta_k$ for $k = 1, 2, \ldots, m = \lfloor n/2 \rfloor$ and the numerator $N(p)$ of $H(p)$ as $\prod_{k=1}^{m}(p + \Omega_{ok}^2)$
6. Compute

$$H(p) = \frac{H_0 \prod_{k=1}^{m}(p + \Omega_{0k}^2)}{\prod_{k=1}^{n}(p - p_k)}$$

   and calculate $H_0 = \prod_{k=1}^{n}(p_k)/\prod_{k=1}^{m}(\Omega_{0k})^2$.
7. Restore the magnitude scale.
8. Restore the frequency scale by putting $p = s/\omega_s$ in $H(p)$ to get $H(s)$ for the inverse Chebyshev filter.

Example 4.5

Design the lowpass inverse Chebyshev filter with a maximum gain of 0 dB in the passband, $\omega_p = 1000$, $A_p = 0.5$ dB, $\omega_s = 2000$, and $A_s = 40$ dB. We normalize the frequencies by ω_s and get the lowest frequency of the stopband at $\Omega = 1$, while $\omega_p = 1000$ maps to $\Omega_p = 0.5$. We will have to denormalize the frequency by substituting $p = s/2000$ when the transfer function $H(p)$ of the inverse Chebyshev filter, obtained by the steps given above, is completed. The design procedure gives

1. $\epsilon_i = (\sqrt{10^4 - 1})^{-1} = \frac{1}{99.995}$.
2. $n = 5$.

3. $\varphi_i = \frac{1}{5} \sinh^{-1}(99.995) = 1.05965847$.

4. Poles in the left half-plane are $p_k = (-0.155955926 \pm j0.6108703175)$, $(-0.524799485 \pm j0.485389011)$, and (-0.7877702666).

5. Zeros are $z_1 = \pm j1.0515$ and $z_2 = \pm j1.7013$.

6. The transfer function of the inverse Chebyshev filter $H(p)$ is given by

$$\frac{H_0(p^2 + 1.0515^2)(p^2 + 1.7013^2)}{(p^2 + 0.3118311852p + 0.3974722176)} \tag{4.73}$$
$$(p^2 + 1.04959897p + 0.5110169847)(p + 0.787702666)$$

7. Calculate $H_0 = 0.049995$.

8. Hence we simplify $H(p)$ to the final form:

$$\frac{0.049995(p^4 + 4.04p^2 + 3.2002)}{p^5 + 2.1491328p^4 + 2.30818905p^3 + 1.54997p^2} \tag{4.74}$$
$$+ 0.65725515p + 0.15999426$$

The magnitude response of (4.73) is plotted in Figure 4.11. It is seen that the prototype filter meets the desired specifications. Now we only have to denormalize the frequency by 2000, so that the passband of the specified filter changes from 0.5 to 1000 rad/s, and it meets the specifications given in Example 4.5.

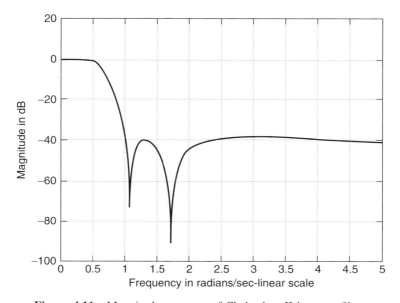

Figure 4.11 Magnitude response of Chebyshev II lowpass filter.

4.2.8 Elliptic Function Approximation

There is another type of filter known as the *elliptic function filter* or the *Cauer filter*. They exhibit an equiripple response in the passband and also in the stopband. The order of the elliptic filter that is required to achieve the given specifications is lower than the order of the Chebyshev filter, and the order of the Chebyshev filter is lower than that of the Butterworth filter. Therefore the elliptic filters form an important class, but the theory and design procedure are complex and beyond the scope of this book. However, in Section 4.11 we will describe the use of MATLAB functions to design these filters.

4.3 ANALOG FREQUENCY TRANSFORMATIONS

Once we have learned the methods of approximating the magnitude response of the ideal lowpass prototype filter, the design of filters that approximate the ideal magnitude response of highpass, bandpass, and bandstop filters is easily carried out. This is done by using well-known analog frequency transformations $p = g(s)$ that map the magnitude response of the lowpass filter $H(j\Omega)$ to that of the specified highpass, bandpass, or bandstop filters $H(j\omega)$. The parameters of the transformation are determined by the cutoff frequency (frequencies) and the stopband frequency (frequencies) specified for the highpass, bandpass, or bandstop filter so that frequencies in their passband(s) are mapped to the passband of the normalized, prototype filter, and the frequencies in the stopband(s) of the highpass, bandpass, or bandstop filters are mapped to the stopband frequency of the prototype filter. After the normalized prototype lowpass filter $H(p)$ is designed according to the methods discussed in the preceding sections, the frequency transformation $p = g(s)$ is applied to $H(p)$ to calculate the transfer function $H(s)$ of the specified filter. With this general outline, let us consider the design of each filter in some more detail.

4.3.1 Highpass Filter

It is easy to describe the design of a highpass filter by choosing an example. Suppose that a highpass filter with an equiripple passband $\omega_p \leq |\omega| < \infty$ is specified, along with a stopband frequency ω_s. The magnitude at ω_p, which is the cutoff frequency of the passband, and also the magnitude at ω_s (or A_p and A_s) are given. The lowpass–highpass (LP–HP) frequency transformation $p = g(s)$ to be used in designing the highpass (HP) filters is

$$p = \frac{\omega_p}{s} \tag{4.75}$$

It is seen that when $s = j\omega_p$, the value of $p = -j$ and when $s = -j\omega_p$, the value of $p = j$. It can also be shown that under this transformation, all frequencies in the passband of the highpass filter map into the passband frequencies

$-1 \leq \Omega \leq 1$ of the lowpass prototype filter. We calculate the frequency Ω_s to which the specified stopband frequency ω_s maps, by putting $s = j\omega_s$ in (4.75). The stopband frequency is found to be $\Omega_s = \omega_p/\omega_s$. So the specified magnitude response of the highpass filter is transformed into that of the lowpass prototype equiripple filter. We design the prototype lowpass filter to meet these specifications and then substitute $p = \omega_p/s$ in $H(p)$ to get the transfer function $H(s)$ of the specified highpass filter.

Example 4.6

The cutoff frequency of a Chebyshev highpass filter is $\omega_p = 2500$, which is the lowest frequency in the passband, and the maximum attenuation in the passband $A_p = 0.5$ dB. The maximum gain in the passband is 5 dB. At the stopband frequency $\omega_s = 500$, the minimum attenuation required is 30 dB. Design the highpass filter $H(s)$.

When we apply the LP–HP transformation $p = 2500/s$, the cutoff frequency $\omega_p = 2500$ maps to $\Omega_p = 1$ and the stopband frequency ω_s maps to $\Omega_s = 5$. In the lowpass prototype filter, we have $\Omega_p = 1$, $\Omega_s = 5$, $A_p = 0.5$ dB, $A_s = 30$ dB, and the maximum value of 5 dB in the passband. This filter has been designed in Example 4.3 and has a transfer function given by (4.70), which is repeated below:

$$H(p) = \frac{(0.715693)(1.7783)}{(p^2 + 0.626456p + 1.142447)(p + 0.626456)}$$

Next we substitute $p = 2500/s$ in this transfer function, and when simplified, the transfer function of the specified highpass Chebyshev filter becomes

$$H(s) = \left. \frac{(0.715693)(1.7783)}{(p^2 + 0.626456p + 1.142447)(p + 0.626456)} \right|_{p=2500/s}$$

$$= \frac{1.7783s^3}{[s^2 + 1370.9s + 5.4707 \times 10^6][s + 3990]} \tag{4.76}$$

The magnitude response of (4.76) is plotted in Figure 4.12 and is found to exceed the specifications of the given highpass filter. The design of a highpass filter with a maximally flat passband response or with an equiripple response in both the passband and the stopband is carried out in a similar manner.

4.3.2 Bandpass Filter

The normal specifications of a bandpass filter $H(s)$ as shown in Figure 4.13 are the cutoff frequencies ω_1 and ω_2, the maximum value of the magnitude in the passband between the cutoff frequencies, the maximum attenuation in this passband or the minimum magnitude at the cutoff frequencies ω_1 and ω_2, and a frequency ω_s ($= \omega_3$ or ω_4) in the stopband at which the minimum attenuation or

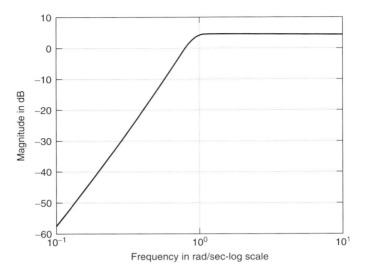

Figure 4.12   Magnitude response of a highpass filter.

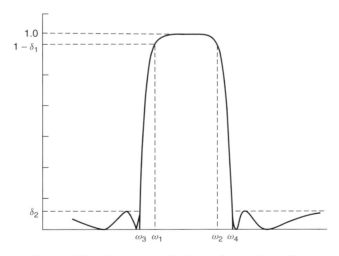

Figure 4.13   Typical specifications of a bandpass filter.

the maximum magnitude are specified. The type of passband response required may be a Butterworth or Chebyshev response.

The lowpass–bandpass (LP–BP) frequency transformation $p = g(s)$ that is used for the design of a specified bandpass filter is

$$p = \frac{1}{B} \left(\frac{s^2 + \omega_0^2}{s} \right) \tag{4.77}$$

where $B = \omega_2 - \omega_1$ is the bandwidth of the filter and $\omega_0 = \sqrt{\omega_1\omega_2}$ is the geometric mean frequency of the bandpass filter.

A frequency $s = j\omega_k$ in the bandpass filter is mapped to a frequency $p = j\Omega_k$ under this transformation, which is obtained by

$$j\Omega_k = \frac{j}{B}\left(\frac{\omega_0^2 - \omega_k^2}{\omega_k}\right) \tag{4.78}$$

$$= \frac{j\omega_0}{B}\left(\frac{\omega_k}{\omega_0} - \frac{\omega_0}{\omega_k}\right) \tag{4.79}$$

Therefore the frequencies ω_1 and ω_2 map to $\Omega = \mp 1$, and the frequencies $-\omega_1$ and $-\omega_2$ map to $\Omega = \pm 1$. Similarly, the positive value of the stopband frequency Ω_s to which the frequency ω_s maps is calculated from

$$\Omega_s = \left|\frac{1}{B}\left(\frac{\omega_0^2 - \omega_s^2}{\omega_s}\right)\right| \tag{4.80}$$

The magnitude or the attenuation at the frequencies $\Omega = 1$ and Ω_s for the prototype filter are the same as those at the corresponding frequencies of the bandpass filter. From the specification of the lowpass prototype filter, we obtain its transfer function $H(p)$, following the appropriate design procedure discussed earlier. Then we substitute (4.77) in $H(p)$ to get the transfer function $H(s)$ of the bandpass filter specified.

Example 4.7

The specifications of a Chebyshev I bandpass filter are $\omega_1 = 10^4$, $\omega_2 = 10^5$, $\omega_s = 2 \times 10^5$, $A_p = 0.8$ dB, and $A_s = 30$ dB, and the maximum magnitude in the passband $= 10$ dB. We use the following procedure to design the filter:

1. $B = \omega_2 - \omega_1 = 9 \times 10^4$ and $\omega_0 = \sqrt{\omega_2\omega_1} = \sqrt{10^9} = 31.62 \times 10^3$.
2. The LP–BP transformation is $p = 1/9 \times 10^4[(s^2 + 10^9)/s]$.
3. Let $s = j\omega_s = j2 \times 10^5$. From the preceding transformation, we get $\Omega_s = 2.1667$.
4. The lowpass Chebyshev prototype filter has a magnitude response as shown in Fig. 4.6b.
5. Calculate $\epsilon = \sqrt{10^{0.1A_p} - 1} = \sqrt{10^{0.08} - 1} = 0.4497$.
6. Calculate n from (4.68). Choose $n = \lceil 3.5 \rceil = 4$.
7. Calculate φ_2 from (4.63). We get $\varphi_2 = 0.3848$.
8. Calculate the poles from (4.67): $p_k = -0.15093 \pm j.9931$ and $-0.36438 \pm j.41137$.

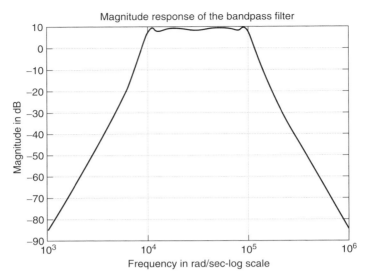

Figure 4.14   Magnitude response of the bandpass filter in Example 4.6.

9. The transfer function of the lowpass prototype Chebyshev filter is derived from $H(p) = H_0/[\prod_{k=1}^{4}(p - p_k)]$ where H_0 is fixed to match the gain of 10 dB at $\Omega = 0$:

$$H(p) = \frac{0.8788}{(p^2 + 0.3018p + 1.009)(p^2 + 0.7287p + 0.302)} \qquad (4.81)$$

10. Now substitute $p = (s^2 + 10^9)/(9 \times 10^4 s)$ in $H(p)$ and simplify to get $H(s)$

$$H(s) = \frac{5.7658 \times 10^{19} s^4}{D(s)}$$

where

$$D(s) = \left[\begin{array}{c} (s^4 + 2.7162 \times 10^4 s^3 + 101.729 \times 10^8 s^2 + 2.7162 \times 10^{13} s + 10^{18}) \\ \times (s^4 + 6.5583 \times 10^4 s^3 + 44.462 \times 10^8 s^2 + 6.5583 \times 10^{13} s + 10^{18}) \end{array} \right]$$

$$(4.82)$$

To verify the design, we have plotted the magnitude response of the bandpass filter in Figure 4.14.

4.3.3   Bandstop Filter

The normal specification of a bandstop (bandreject) filter is shown in Figure 4.15. The passband of this filter is given by $0 \leq \omega \leq \omega_1$ and $\omega_2 \leq \omega \leq \infty$, whereas

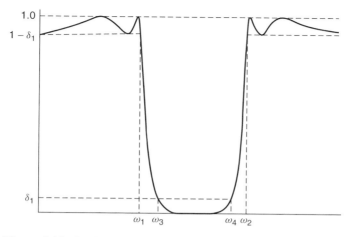

Figure 4.15   Typical magnitude specifications for a bandstop filter.

the frequencies ω_3 and ω_4 define frequencies in the stopband. Usually these frequencies and the corresponding magnitudes are given as the specifications. Note that in Figure 4.13, showing the magnitude response of a bandpass filter, the stopband is equiripple and the passband between ω_1 and ω_2 has a monotonic response; this it is a Chebyshev II type of filter. But in the bandstop filter response shown in Figure 4.15, the passband is equiripple and the stopband is maximally flat, so it is a Chebyshev I type of bandstop filter. It is important to remember that the parameter B in the LP-BS transformation is chosen as $\omega_2 - \omega_1$, and not the bandwidth $\omega_4 - \omega_3$ of the stopband! The mean frequency $\omega_0 = \sqrt{\omega_2\omega_1}$, and the LP–BS frequency transformation $p = g(s)$ is given by

$$p = B\left(\frac{s}{s^2 + \omega_0^2}\right) \tag{4.83}$$

This transformation transforms the entire passband of the bandstop filter to the passband $|\Omega| \leq 1$ of the prototype lowpass filter. So we have to find the frequency Ω_s to which the stopband frequency ω_s is transformed under the transformation. It is found from

$$\Omega_s = \left|\frac{B\omega_s}{\omega_s^2 - \omega_0^2}\right| \tag{4.84}$$

Thus we have reduced the specification of a bandstop filter to that of a prototype lowpass filter. It is designed by the procedures discussed earlier. When the transfer function $H(p)$ of the prototype filter is completed, the transformation $p = B[s/(s^2 + \omega_0^2)]$ is used to transform $H(p)$ into $H(s)$. The design of the bandstop filter is illustrated by the following example.

Example 4.8

Suppose that we are given the specification of a bandstop filter as shown in Figure 4.15. In this example, we are given $\omega_1 = 1500$, $\omega_2 = 2000$, $\omega_s = \omega_4 = 1800$, $A_p = 0.2$ dB, and $A_s = 55$ dB. The passband is required to have a maximally flat response. With these specifications, we design the bandstop filter following procedure given below:

1. $B = 2000 - 1500 = 500$ and $\omega_0 = \sqrt{(2000)(1500)} = 1732.1$.
2. The LP–BS frequency transformation is $p = 500[s/(s^2 + 3 \times 10^6)]$.
3. Let $s = j\omega_s = j1800$. Then we get $\Omega_s = 3.74$.
4. Following the design procedure used in Example 4.2, we get $\epsilon = \sqrt{10^{0.02} - 1} = 0.21709$, and from (4.44), we get $n = 5.946$ and choose $n = 6$.
5. The six poles are calculated from (4.45) as $p_k = -0.33385 \pm j1.2459$, $-0.9121 \pm j0.9121$, and $-1.246 \pm j0.3329$.
6. The transfer function of the lowpass prototype filter $H(p)$ is constructed from $H(p) = H_0/[\prod_{k=1}^{4}(p - p_k)]$ as

$$\frac{(1.664)^3}{(p^2 + 0.6677p + 1.664)(p^2 + 1.824p + 1.664)(p^2 + 2.492p + 1.664)}$$
(4.85)

7. Next we have to substitute $p = 500[s/(s^2 + 3 \times 10^6)]$ in this $H(p)$ and simplify the expression to get the transfer function $H(s)$ of the specified bandstop filter. This completes the design of the bandstop filter. The magnitude response is found to exceed the given specifications.

The sections above briefly summarize the theory of approximating the piecewise constant magnitude of analog filters. This theory will be required for approximating the magnitude of digital filters, which will be treated in the following sections. The analog frequency transformations $p = g(s)$ applied to the lowpass prototype to generate the other types of filters are listed in Table 4.2.

TABLE 4.2   Frequency Transformations to Design HP, BP, and BS Filters

Type of Transformation	Transformation $p = g(s)$	Parameters Used
LP–LP	$p = s/\omega_p$	ω_p = bandwidth-specified LP filter
LP–HP	$p = \omega_p/s$	ω_p = cutoff frequency of the specified HP filter
LP–BP	$p = (1/B)[(s^2 + \omega_0^2)/s]$	$B = \omega_2 - \omega_1$, where B is bandwidth of the specified BP filter: $\omega_0 = \sqrt{\omega_1\omega_2}$;
LP–BS	$p = B[s/(s^2 + \omega_0^2)]$	$B = \omega_2 - \omega_1$

4.4 DIGITAL FILTERS

In contrast to analog filters, digital filters are described by two types of transfer functions: transfer functions of finite impulse response filters and those of infinite impulse response filters. The methods for designing FIR filters will be treated in the next chapter. Now that we have reviewed the methods for approximating the magnitude of analog filters, it is necessary to understand the relationship between the frequency-domain description of analog and digital filters, in order to understand the frequency transformation that is used to transform the analog frequency response specifications to those of the digital filters.

4.5 IMPULSE-INVARIANT TRANSFORMATION

The procedures used for designing IIR filters employ different transformations of the form $s = f(z)$ to transform $H(s)$ into $H(z)$. The transformation $s = f(z)$ must satisfy the requirement that the digital filter transfer function $H(z)$ be stable, when it is obtained from the analog filter transfer functions $H(s)$. The transfer functions for the analog filters obtained by the methods described above are stable functions; that is, their poles are in the left half of the s plane. When $H(s)$ and $f(z)$ are stable in the s and z domains, respectively, the poles of $H(s)$ in the left half of the s plane map to the poles inside the unit circle in the z plane; therefore $H(z)$ also is a stable transfer function. We also would like to have frequencies from $-\infty$ to ∞ on the $j\omega$ axis of the s plane mapped into frequencies on the boundary of the unit circle—without encountering any discontinuities.

We have already introduced the transformation $z = e^{sT}$, in Chapter 2, when we derived the z transform of a discrete-time signal $x(nT)$ generated from the analog signal $x(t)$.

We plot the magnitude response of the analog filter as a function of ω. Under the impulse-invariant transformation, $s = j\omega$ maps to $z = e^{j\omega T}$. Although the magnitude of the digital filter $H(e^{j\omega T})$ is a function of the variable $e^{j\omega T}$, we cannot plot it as a function of $e^{j\omega T}$. We can plot the magnitude response of the digital filter only as a function of ωT. (Again, we point out that the normalized digital frequency ωT is commonly denoted in the DSP literature by the symbol ω.) When $s = j\omega$ increases values from $-j\infty$ along the imaginary axis to $+j\infty$, the variable $e^{j\omega T}$ increases counterclockwise from $e^{-j\pi}$ to $e^{j\pi}$ (passing through $z = 1$) along the boundary of the unit circle in the z plane and repeats itself since $e^{j\omega T} = e^{j(\omega T + 2r\pi)}$, where r is an integer. The strips in the left half of the s plane bounded by $\pm j[(2r-1)\pi/T]$ and $\pm j[(2r+1)\pi/T]$ on the $j\omega$ axis are mapped to the inside and the boundary of the unit circle in the z plane as shown in Figure 4.16. Therefore the frequency response $X^*(j\omega) = \sum_{n=0}^{\infty} x(nT)e^{-j\omega T}$ is periodic and will avoid aliasing only if the analog signal $x(t)$ is bandlimited.

Consider the transfer function $H(s)$ of an analog filter. Since the poles of an analog filter function such as the filters discussed in this chapter are simple, its

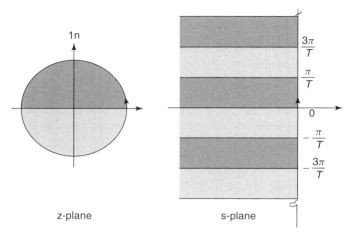

Figure 4.16   Mapping of s plane to z plane under the transformation $z = e^{sT}$.

partial fraction expansion is of the form

$$H(s) = \sum_{k=1}^{K} \frac{R_k}{s + s_k} \qquad (4.86)$$

The unit impulse response $h_k(t)$ of a typical term $R_k/(s + s_k)$ is $R_k e^{-s_k t}$. When it is sampled with a sampling period T, and the z transform is evaluated, it becomes

$$R_k \sum_{n=0}^{\infty} e^{-s_k nT} z^{-n} = R_k \frac{1}{1 - e^{-s_k T} z^{-1}} = R_k \frac{z}{z - e^{-s_k T}} \qquad (4.87)$$

Hence $H(z)$ derived from $H(s)$ under the transformation $z = e^{sT}$ is given by

$$H(z) = \sum_{k=1}^{K} \frac{R_k z}{z - e^{-s_k T}} \qquad (4.88)$$

Because the unit pulse response $h(nT)$ of the digital filter matches the unit impulse response $h(t)$ at the instants of sampling $t = nT$, the transformation $z = e^{sT}$ is called the *impulse-invariant transformation*. But the frequency response of $H(z)$ will not match the frequency response of $H(s)$ unless $h(t)$ is bandlimited. If the magnitude response of the analog filter $H(j\omega)$ is very small for frequencies larger than some frequency ω_b, and $h(t)$ is sampled at a frequency greater than $2\omega_b$, the frequency response of the digital filter $H(z)$ obtained from the impulse-invariant transformation may give rise to a small amount of aliasing that may or may not be acceptable in practical design applications. However, this method is not applicable for the design of highpass, bandstop, and allpass filters since their frequency responses are not bandlimited at all. If the impulse-invariant transformation is applied to a minimum phase analog filter $H(s)$, the resulting digital filter may or may not be a minimum phase filter. For these reasons, the impulse-invariant transformation is not used very often in practical applications.

4.6 BILINEAR TRANSFORMATION

The bilinear transformation is the one that is the most often used for designing IIR filters. It is defined as

$$s = \frac{2}{T}\left(\frac{z-1}{z+1}\right)$$ (4.89)

To find how frequencies on the unit circle in the z plane map to those in the s plane, let us substitute $z = e^{j\omega T}$ in (4.89). Note that ω is the angular frequency in radians per second and ωT is the normalized frequency in the z plane. Instead of using ω as the notation for the normalized frequency of the digital filter, we may denote θ as the normalized frequency to avoid any confusion in this section:

$$s = \frac{2}{T}\left(\frac{e^{j\omega T}-1}{e^{j\omega T}+1}\right) = \frac{2}{T}\left(\frac{e^{j(\omega T/2)}-e^{-j(\omega T/2)}}{e^{j(\omega T/2)}+e^{-j(\omega T/2)}}\right) = j\frac{2}{T}\tan\left(\frac{\omega T}{2}\right)$$

$$= j2f_s\tan\left(\frac{\omega T}{2}\right) = j\lambda$$

This transformation maps the poles inside the unit circle in the z plane to the inside of the left half of the s plane and vice versa. It also maps the frequencies on the unit circle in the z plane to frequencies on the entire imaginary axis of the s plane, where $s = \sigma + j\lambda$. So this transformation satisfies both conditions that we required for the mapping $s = f(z)$ mentioned in the previous section or its inverse relationship $z = b(s)$. This mapping is shown in Figure 4.17 and may be compared with the mapping shown in Figure 4.16.

To understand the mapping in some more detail, let us consider the frequency response of an IIR filter over the interval $(0, (\omega_s/2))$, where $\omega_s/2 = \pi/T$ is the Nyquist frequency. As an example, we choose a frequency response $|H(e^{\omega T})| = |H(e^{j\theta})|$ of a Butterworth bandpass digital filter as shown in Figure 4.18a.

In Figure 4.18, we have also shown the curve depicting the relationship between ωT and $\lambda = 2f_s\tan(\omega T/2)$. The value of λ corresponding to any value of $\omega T = \theta$ can be calculated from $\lambda = 2f_s\tan(\theta/2)$ as illustrated by mapping a few frequencies such as $\omega_1 T$, $\omega_2 T$ in Figure 4.18. The magnitude of the frequency response of the digital filter at any normalized frequency $\omega_k T$ is the magnitude of $H(s)$ at the corresponding frequency $s = j\lambda_k$, where $\lambda_k = 2f_s\tan(\omega_k T/2)$.

The plot in Figure 4.17 shows that the magnitude response of the digital filter over the Nyquist interval $(0, \pi)$ maps over the entire range $(0, \infty)$ of λ. So there is a nonlinear mapping whereby the frequencies in the ω domain are warped

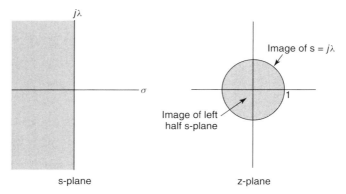

Figure 4.17 Mapping of s plane to z plane under bilinear transformation.

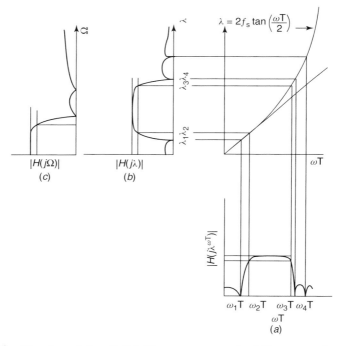

Figure 4.18 Mapping of the digital filter response under bilinear transformation and analog BP $\Rightarrow$ LP transformation.

when mapped to the λ domain. Similarly, the frequencies in the interval $(0, -\pi)$ are mapped to the entire interval $(0, -\infty)$ of λ. From the periodic nature of the function tan(.), we also see that the periodic replicates of the digital filter frequency response in the ω domain map to the same frequency response in the λ domain and the transfer function $H(s)$ obtained under the bilinear transform behaves like that of an analog filter. But it is to be pointed out that we use only the mathematical theory of analog filter approximation to solve the problem of finding such a function $H(s)$, and we are not designing an analog filter. In other words, the bilinear transformation helps us reduce the mathematical problem of approximating the frequency response of a digital filter in the variable ω, to the problem of approximating another function in the variable λ. Because of its similarity to the analog frequency, the approximation problem is solved by using the mathematical theory of approximation for the frequency response of analog filters. So, if the frequency response $|H(j\lambda)|$ is a lowpass frequency response, the frequency s is linearly scaled by λ_c to obtain the frequency response $|H(j\Omega)|$ of a lowpass prototype filter. If it is a highpass, bandpass, or bandstop response, then the appropriate analog frequency transformation $\mathbf{p} = g(s)$ listed in Table 4.2 is used to convert the specification $|H(j\lambda)|$ to that of an analog prototype lowpass filter. We obtain the transfer function $H(\mathbf{p})$ of the prototype filter, in which the complex frequency variable $\mathbf{p}$ is shown in bold in order to differentiate it from $H(p)$, and its magnitude is denoted by $|H(j\Omega)|$. The theory of analog filter approximation is used to find $H(\mathbf{p})$ such that its magnitude $|H(j\Omega)|$ approximates the magnitude response of the lowpass prototype filter. It is important to note that the unit impulse response of the filter $H(\mathbf{p})$ when sampled with a sampling period T does not match the unit pulse response of the digital filter $H(z)$, because the bilinear transformation is not impulse- invariant.

Once we have designed the lowpass prototype filter function $H(\mathbf{p})$, we apply the appropriate analog frequency transformation $\mathbf{p} = g(s)$ to $H(\mathbf{p})$ to get the function $H(s)$. Then we substitute $s = 2f_s[(z-1)/(z+1)]$ in $H(s)$ to get $H(z)$ as the transfer function of the digital filter.

Example 4.9

The specified magnitude response of a maximally flat bandpass digital filter has a maximum value of 1.0 in its passband, which lies between the cutoff frequencies $\theta_1 = 0.4\pi$ and $\theta_2 = 0.5\pi$. The magnitude at these cutoff frequencies is specified to be no less than 0.93, and at the frequency $\theta_3 = 0.7\pi$ in the stopband, the magnitude is specified to be no more than 0.004. Design the IIR digital filter that approximates these specifications, using the bilinear transformation.

It is obvious from these specifications that the frequencies are normalized frequencies. So $\theta_1 = 0.4\pi$ and $\theta_2 = 0.5\pi$ are the normalized cutoff frequencies and $\theta_3 = 0.7\pi$ is the frequency in the stopband. The specified magnitude response is plotted in Figure 4.19a. The two cutoff frequencies ω_1, ω_2 and the stopband frequency ω_3 map to and $\lambda_1, \lambda_2, \lambda_3$ as follows. In this example, we have chosen to scale the frequencies in the s plane by f_s; thus, the values for λ_1, λ_2, and λ_3 given below are obtained by the bilinear transform $s = 2[(z-1)/(z+1)]$:

$$\lambda_1 = 2\tan(0.2\pi) = 1.453 \text{ rad/s}$$
$$\lambda_2 = 2\tan(0.25\pi) = 2.00 \text{ rad/s}$$
$$\lambda_3 = 2\tan(0.35\pi) = 3.95 \text{ rad/s}$$

The frequency response of the "analog" filter $H(s)$ is plotted in Figure 4.19b.

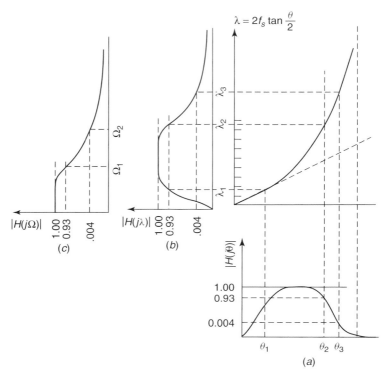

Figure 4.19   Mapping of filter responses under bilinear transformation.

Now we find the bandwidth $(BW) = \lambda_2 - \lambda_1 = 0.547$ and the center frequency $\lambda_0 = \sqrt{\lambda_2\lambda_1} = 1.705$ for the prewarped bandpass filter function $|H(j\lambda)|$. Next we define the lowpass–bandpass frequency transformation

$$\mathbf{p} = \frac{1}{(B)}\left(\frac{s^2 + \lambda_0^2}{s}\right) = \frac{1}{0.547}\left(\frac{s^2 + 1.705^2}{s}\right).$$

To find the frequency Ω_3, to which the frequency $\lambda_3 = 3.95$ maps, we substitute $s = j3.95$ in the preceding transformation and get $\mathbf{p} = j5.876 = j\Omega_2$, whereas the cutoff frequencies map to the normalized frequency $\Omega_p = 1$. Hence the magnitude response of the lowpass Butterworth prototype filter function is as shown in Figure 4.19c. Using the same notations as before, we get $A_p = 0.63$ dB, $A_s = 48$ dB, $\epsilon = 0.395$, and $n = 4$ for this prototype lowpass Butterworth filter.

The four poles in the left half of the $\mathbf{p}$ plane are calculated as the poles of the lowpass prototype Butterworth filters:

$$\mathbf{p}_1, \mathbf{p}_4 = -0.4827 \pm j1.1654$$

$$\mathbf{p}_2, \mathbf{p}_3 = -1.1654 \pm j0.4827$$

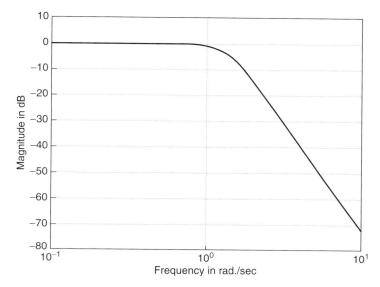

Figure 4.20 Magnitude response of the analog prototype lowpass filter in Example 4.8.

The transfer function of the prototype lowpass filter is therefore given by

$$H(\mathbf{p}) = \frac{2.5317}{\mathbf{p}^4 + 3.296\mathbf{p}^3 + 5.4325\mathbf{p}^2 + 5.24475\mathbf{p} + 2.5317} \qquad (4.90)$$

The magnitude response of this lowpass filter is plotted in Figure 4.20.

Next we substitute $\mathbf{p} = (1/0.547)[(s^2 + 1.705^2)/s]$, in (4.90) and after simplifying, the resulting transfer function is

$$H(s) = \frac{0.2267s^4}{D(s)}$$

where $D(s)$ is given by

$$\left[\begin{array}{l} (s^8 + 1.8030s^7 + 13.2535s^6 + 16.5824s^5 + 60.3813s^4 \\ \quad + 48.205s^3 + 112.0006s^2 + 44.2926s + 71.4135) \end{array} \right] \qquad (4.91)$$

Now we apply the bilinear transformation $s = 2[(z - 1)/(z + 1)]$ we chose in this example, on this $H(s)$, and simplify the transfer function $H(z)$ of the digital filter to

$$H(z) = \frac{3.6272z^8 - 14.5088z^6 + 21.7632z^4 - 14.5088z^2 + 3.6272}{\left[\begin{array}{l} (3825z^8 - 4221z^7 + 13127z^6 - 9857z^5 + 15753z^4 - 7615z^3 \\ \quad + 7849z^2 - 1934z + 1354) \end{array} \right]}$$

$$(4.92)$$

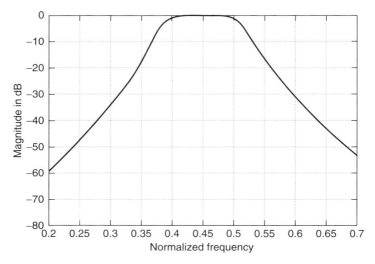

Figure 4.21   Magnitude response of a digital bandpass filter.

A plot of the magnitude response of this function is shown in Figure 4.21. It is found that the given specifications are met by this transfer function of the digital filter.

The design of lowpass, highpass, and bandstop filters use similar procedures. In contrast to the impulse-invariant transformation, we see that the bilinear transformation can be used for designing highpass and bandstop filters as well. Indeed, the use of bilinear transformation is the most popular method used for the design of IIR digital filter functions that approximate the magnitude-only specifications.

4.7   DIGITAL SPECTRAL TRANSFORMATION

In the design procedure described above, we used the bilinear transformation to convert the magnitude specification of an IIR digital filter to that of $H(j\lambda)$ by prewarping the frequencies on the λ axis. Then we either scaled the frequencies on the λ axis or applied the analog frequency transformations $\mathbf{p} = g(s)$ to reduce the frequency response to that of a lowpass, analog prototype filter function. There is an alternative method for designing IIR digital filters. It replaces the analog frequency transformation by a frequency transformation in the digital domain. Constantinides [1] derived a set of digital spectral transformations (DSTs) that convert the magnitude of a lowpass digital filter with an arbitrary bandwidth, say, θ_p, to that of digital highpass, bandpass, and bandstop filters or digital lowpass filters with a different passband. These transformations are similar to the analog frequency transformations, and the parameters of the transformation are determined by the cutoff frequencies of these filters just as in the case of the analog frequency transformations. Let us denote the cutoff frequency of the new digital lowpass filter or the highpass filter by θ'_p; and let us denote the upper and lower cutoff frequencies of the bandpass and bandstop filters by θ_u and θ_l, respectively—all of them are less than π radians on the normalized frequency basis. Whereas the lowpass, prototype analog filter always has a passband of 1 rad/s, the lowpass digital filter has a passband that is chosen arbitrarily as θ_p; yet, we will call it the lowpass digital, "prototype" filter, with a transfer function $H(\mathbf{z}^{-1})$. The digital spectral transformations applied on this digital filter are of the form $\mathbf{z}^{-1} = g(z^{-1})$. They map points inside the unit circle in the $\mathbf{z}$ plane to points inside the unit circle in the z plane, and map the boundary of the unit circle in the $\mathbf{z}$ plane to the boundary of the unit circle in the z plane. Using these necessary conditions, Constantinides derived the DSTs for the LP–LP, LP–HP, LP–BP, and LP–BS transformations and they are listed in Table 4.3, where $\theta = \omega T$ are normalized frequencies in radians.

Example 4.10

We choose the same specifications as in Example 4.9 and illustrate the procedure to design the IIR filter using the digital spectral transformation from Table 4.3. Let us choose the passband of the lowpass prototype digital filter to be $\theta_p = 0.5\pi$. The values for the cutoff frequencies specified for the bandpass filter are $\theta_l = 0.4\pi$, $\theta_u = 0.5\pi$. So we calculate

$$\alpha = \frac{\cos\left(\dfrac{0.5\pi + 0.4\pi}{2}\right)}{\cos\left(\dfrac{0.5\pi - 0.4\pi}{2}\right)} = 0.158$$

$$K = \cot\left(\frac{0.5\pi - 0.4\pi}{2}\right)\tan\left(\frac{0.5\pi}{2}\right) = 6.314$$

$$\mathbf{z}^{-1} = -\frac{z^{-2} - 0.273z^{-1} + 0.727}{0.727z^{-2} - 0.273z^{-1} + 1}$$

Now we have to find the frequency θ_s in the lowpass digital "prototype" filter to which the prescribed stopband frequency $\theta'_s = 0.7\pi$ of the bandpass filter maps, by substituting $z = e^{j0.7\pi}$ in the digital spectral transformation given above. The value is found to be $\theta_s = 2.8$ rad $= 0.8913\pi$ rad. Therefore the specification for the lowpass prototype digital filter to be designed is given as shown in Figure 4.22b.

Using the mapping of $\lambda = 2\tan(\frac{\theta}{2})$ versus θ, we map this lowpass frequency response to the lowpass filter response $|H(j\lambda)|$ as shown in Figure 4.22(c). We calculate $\lambda_p = 2\tan(\pi/4) = 1.998$ and $\lambda_s = 2\tan\left(\frac{2.8}{2}\right) = 11.6$ as the edge of the passband and the edge of the stopband of this filter, respectively. So we scale its frequency by 1.998 to get the frequency response of the lowpass prototype filter $H(j\Omega)$ in order to get a normalized bandwidth $\Omega_p = 1$. The stopband frequency Ω_s is scaled down to 5.8, which is slightly different from the value obtained in

TABLE 4.3 Digital Spectral Transformations

Type of Transformation	Transformation	Parameters Used
LP–LP	$z^{-1} = \dfrac{z^{-1} - a}{1 - az^{-1}}$	θ_p = passband of prototype filter θ'_p = passband of new LP filter $a = \dfrac{\sin\left(\dfrac{\theta_p - \theta'_p}{2}\right)}{\sin\left(\dfrac{\theta_p + \theta'_p}{2}\right)}$
LP–HP	$z^{-1} = -\left(\dfrac{z^{-1} + a}{1 + az^{-1}}\right)$	θ'_p = cutoff frequency of the HP filter $a = \dfrac{\cos\left(\dfrac{\theta_p + \theta'_p}{2}\right)}{\cos\left(\dfrac{\theta_p - \theta'_p}{2}\right)}$
LP–BP	$z^{-1} = -\left(\dfrac{z^{-2} - \dfrac{2\alpha K}{(K+1)} z^{-1} + \dfrac{(K-1)}{(K+1)}}{\dfrac{(K-1)}{(K+1)} z^{-2} - \dfrac{2\alpha K}{(K+1)} z^{-1} + 1}\right)$	θ_l = lower cutoff frequency of BP filter θ_u = upper cutoff frequency of BP filter $\alpha = \dfrac{\cos\left(\dfrac{\theta_u + \theta_l}{2}\right)}{\cos\left(\dfrac{\theta_u - \theta_l}{2}\right)}$ $K = \cot\left(\dfrac{\theta_u - \theta_l}{2}\right)\tan\left(\dfrac{\theta_p}{2}\right)$
LP–BS	$z^{-1} = \dfrac{z^{-2} - \dfrac{2\alpha}{(K+1)} z^{-1} + \dfrac{1-K}{1+K}}{\dfrac{1-K}{1+K} z^{-2} - \dfrac{2\alpha}{(K+1)} z^{-1} + 1}$	θ_l = lower cutoff frequency of BS filter θ_u = upper cutoff frequency of BS filter $\alpha = \dfrac{\cos\left(\dfrac{\theta_u + \theta_l}{2}\right)}{\cos\left(\dfrac{\theta_u - \theta_l}{2}\right)}$ $K = \tan\left(\dfrac{\theta_u - \theta_l}{2}\right)\tan\left(\dfrac{\theta_p}{2}\right)$

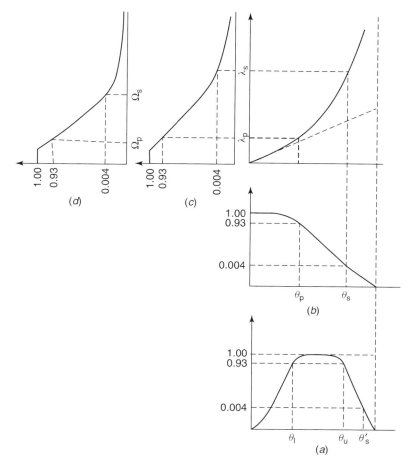

Figure 4.22   Mapping of magnitude responses under digital spectral transformation.

Example 4.8 because of numerical inaccuracies. But the order of the lowpass prototype analog filter is required to be the same, and hence the transfer function is the same as in Example 4.8. The transfer function is repeated below: Note, we use $H(\mathbf{p})$ to denote the lowpass filter in this example

$$H(\mathbf{p}) = \frac{2.5317}{\mathbf{p}^4 + 3.2962\mathbf{p}^3 + 5.4325\mathbf{p}^2 + 5.2447\mathbf{p} + 2.5317} \qquad (4.93)$$

Next we restore the frequency scale by substituting $\mathbf{p} = s/1.998$ in $H(\mathbf{p})$ to get the transfer function $H(s)$ as

$$H(s) = \frac{40.5072}{s^4 + 6.5924s^3 + 21.73s^2 + 41.9576s + 40.5072} \qquad (4.94)$$

and then apply the bilinear transformation $s = 2[(z-1)/(z+1)]$ on this $H(s)$ to get the transfer function of the lowpass prototype digital filter $H(\mathbf{z})$ as

$$H(\mathbf{z}) = \frac{(40.5072\mathbf{z}^4 + 162.0288\mathbf{z}^3 + 243.0432\mathbf{z}^2 + 162.0288\mathbf{z} + 40.5072)}{(280.0816\mathbf{z}^4 + 160.3808\mathbf{z}^3 + 165.2032\mathbf{z}^2 + 35.6768\mathbf{z} + 6.7728)}$$

(4.95)

The final step is to apply the digital spectral transformation (4.96) derived earlier, to $H(\mathbf{z})$ in (4.95):

$$\mathbf{z}^{-1} = -\frac{z^{-2} - 0.273z^{-1} + 0.727}{0.727z^{-2} - 0.273z^{-1} + 1}$$

(4.96)

The final result is the transfer function $H(z)$ of the required IIR filter, which is found to be the same as (4.92) obtained in Example 4.8. The magnitude is therefore found to be the same as in Figure 4.21 and is not plotted again. When compared with the method of Example 4.8, the method described above does not offer any advantages; indeed, it requires more computations, particularly in the final step. However, if we already have the transfer function of a lowpass IIR filter, we can use the digital spectral transformation to obtain the transfer function of a HP, BP, or BS filter if their magnitude responses are of the same type (i.e., Butterworth, Chebyshev, or elliptic type) and the tolerances in the passband as well as the stopband are the same as those for the lowpass filter.

4.8 ALLPASS FILTERS

Allpass filters have a magnitude response that is exactly equal to a constant at all frequencies, and hence there is no need for any approximation.

Such filters are of the form

$$H_{ap}(z^{-1}) = \pm\frac{a(N) + a(N-1)z^{-1} + \cdots + a(2)z^{-(N-2)} + a(1)z^{-(N-1)} + z^{-N}}{1 + a(1)z^{-1} + a(2)z^{-2} + \cdots + a(N-1)z^{-(N-1)} + a(N)z^{-N}}$$

(4.97)

This is the ratio of two polynomials expressed in descending powers of z. Note that the coefficients of the numerator polynomial are in an order reverse that of the coefficients of the denominator polynomial. We can express (4.97) in an alternate form:

$$H_{ap}(z^{-1}) = \pm z^{-N}\left[\frac{a(N)z^N + a(N-1)z^{N-1} + \cdots + a(2)z^2 + a(1)z + 1}{1 + a(1)z^{-1} + a(2)z^{-2} + \cdots + a(N-1)z^{-(N-1)} + a(N)z^{-N}}\right]$$

(4.98)

$$= \pm z^{-N}\left[\frac{1 + a(1)z + a(2)z^2 + \cdots + a(N-1)z^{(N-1)} + a(N)z^N}{1 + a(1)z^{-1} + a(2)z^{-2} + \cdots + a(N-1)z^{-(N-1)} + a(N)z^{-N}}\right]$$

(4.99)

If the denominator of (4.99) is denoted as $D(z^{-1})$, its numerator is $z^{-N}D(z)$, which is the mirror image polynomial of $D(z^{-1})$. Therefore, the allpass filter has a transfer function expressed in compact form as

$$H_{ap}(z^{-1}) = \frac{z^{-N}D(z)}{D(z^{-1})} \tag{4.100}$$

When the allpass filter has all its poles inside the unit circle in the z plane, it is a stable function and its zeros are outside the unit circle as a result of the mirror image symmetry. Therefore a stable, allpass filter function is non–minimum function.

From (4.99), it is easy to see that the magnitude response of $H_{ap}(e^{j\omega})$ is equal to one at all frequencies and is independent of all the coefficients:

$$\left| H_{ap}(e^{j\omega}) \right| = \left| \frac{1 + a(1)e^{j\omega} + a(2)e^{j2\omega} + \cdots + a(N)e^{jN\omega}}{1 + a(1)e^{-j\omega} + a(2)e^{-j2\omega} + \cdots + a(N)e^{-jN\omega}} \right| = 1 \tag{4.101}$$

But the phase response (and the group delay) is dependent on the coefficients of the allpass filter. We know that the phase response—as defined by (4.6)—of an IIR filter designed to approximate a specified magnitude response is a nonlinear function of ω and therefore its group delay defined by (4.8) is far from a constant value. When an allpass filter is cascaded with such a filter, the resulting filter has a frequency response $H_1(e^{j\omega})H_{ap}(e^{j\omega}) = \left| H_1(e^{j\omega})H_{ap}(e^{j\omega}) \right| e^{j[\theta(\omega)+\phi(\omega)]} = \left| H_1(e^{j\omega}) \right| e^{j[\theta(\omega)+\phi(\omega)]}$. So the magnitude response does not change when the IIR filter is cascaded with an allpass filter, but its phase response $\theta(\omega)$ changes by the addition of the phase response $\phi(\omega)$ contributed by the allpass filter. The allpass filters $H_{ap}(z)$ are therefore very useful for modifying the phase response (and the group delay) of filters without changing the magnitude of a given IIR filter $H_1(z)$, when they are cascaded with $H_1(z)$. However, the method used to find the coefficients of the allpass filter $H_{ap}(z)$ such that the group delay of $H_1(z)H_a(z)$ is a very close approximation to a constant in the passband of the filter $H_1(z)$ poses a highly nonlinear problem, and only computer-aided optimization has been utilized to solve this problem. When the allpass filters have been designed to compensate for the group delay of the IIR filters that have been designed to approximate a specified magnitude only, such that the cascade connection of the two filters has a group delay that approximates a constant value, the allpass filters are known as *delay equalizers*.

4.9 IIR FILTER DESIGN USING MATLAB

The design of IIR digital filters with Butterworth, Chebyshev I, Chebyshev II, and elliptic filter responses, using MATLAB functions, are based on the theories of bilinear transformation and analog filters. So they are commonly used to approximate the piecewise constant magnitude characteristic of ideal LP, HP, BP, and BS filters. The MATLAB function `yulewalk` is used to design IIR filters with arbitrary magnitude specifications. We will describe all of these functions in the following sections.

The design of IIR filters based on the bilinear transformation consists of two steps: (1) estimation of the filter order and (2) computation of the coefficients of the numerator and denominator of $H(z^{-1})$. The design of these filters starts with the following specifications:

1. The passband frequency Wp of the lowpass or highpass filter. It is a two-element vector [Wp1 Wp2] for the design of a bandpass or bandstop filter, where Wp2>Wp1.

2. The stopband frequency Ws of the lowpass or highpass filter, where Ws>Wp for the lowpass filter and Ws<Wp for the highpass filter. Ws is a two-element vector [Ws1 Ws2] for the bandpass or bandstop filter. We have Ws2>Wp2>Wp1>Ws1 for the bandpass filter and Wp2>Ws2>Ws1>Wp1 for the bandstop filter. All of these frequencies are specified within the interval [0   1], where 1 represents the Nyquist frequency.

3. The maximum attenuation Rp (in decibels) in the passband.

4. The minimum attenuation Rs (in decibels) in the stopband.

The four functions to estimate the order of the Butterworth, Chebyshev I, Chebyshev II, and elliptic filters are given respectively as

1. [N,Wn] = buttord(Wp,Ws,Rp,Rs)
2. [N,Wn] = cheb1ord(Wp,Ws,Rp,Rs)
3. [N,Wn] = cheb2ord(Wp,Ws,Rp,Rs)
4. [N,Wn] = ellipord(Wp,Ws,Rp,Rs)

where N is the order of the LP and HP filters (2N is the order of the BP and BS filters) and Wn is the frequency scaling factor. These two variables are then used in the four MATLAB functions to get the vectors b = [b(1) b(2) b(3) ... b(N+1)] and a = [a(1) a(2) a(3) ... a(N+1)], for the coefficients of the numerator and denominator of $H(z^{-1})$ in descending powers of z. The constant coefficient a(1) is equal to unity:

$$H(z^{-1}) = \frac{b(1) + b(2)z^{-1} + b(3)z^{-2} + \cdots + b(N+1)z^{-N}}{1 + a(2)z^{-1} + a(3)z^{-2} + \cdots + a(N+1)z^{-N}} \qquad (4.102)$$

Note that in the function [N,Wn] = buttord(Wp,Ws,Rp,Rs), the value of Rp is restricted to 3 dB because the analog prototype lowpass filter chosen to design the Butterworth filter obtained under the bilinear transformation uses a 3 dB bandwidth. There are several MATLAB functions available in the Signal Processing Toolbox for the design of analog filters—buttap, cheb1ap, cheb2ap, and ellipap—and the functions for implementing the analog frequency transformations discussed in this chapter are lp2bp, lp2hp, lp2bp and lp2bs. However, we focus on the four MATLAB functions that are available for designing IIR digital filters. They are described below, after we have obtained the order N of the IIR filter:

1. [b,a] = butter(N,Wn)
2. [b,a] = cheby1(N,Rp,Wn)
3. [b,a] = cheby2(N,Rs,Wn)
4. [b,a] = ellip(N,Rp,Rs,Wn)

After we have obtained the coefficients of the transfer function, we use the function freqz(b,a,N$_0$) to get the magnitude response, phase response, and group delay response, which can then be plotted. N$_0$ is the number of discrete frequencies in the interval [0 π] which is chosen by the user. For the design of a high pass filter and a bandstop filter, we have to include a string 'high' and 'stop' as the last argument in the filter functions, for example, [b,a] = butter(N,Wn,'high') for designing a Butterworth highpass filter and [b,a]=cheby2(N,Rs,Wn,'stop') for designing a Chebyshev II stopband filter. In these functions, the value of N and Wn are those obtained in the first step, as the output variables from the functions for estimating the order of the filter.

We illustrate the use of these MATLAB functions by a few examples.

Example 4.11

```
%MATLAB script to design a Elliptic Lowpass filter
 % with the specifications:.Wp = 0.4,Ws = 0.5, Rp = 0.5,
   % Rs = 60
 [N,Wn]=ellipord(0.4, 0.5, 0.5,60);
 [b,a]=ellip(N,0.5,60,Wn);
 [h,w]=freqz(b,a,256);
H=abs(h);
HdB=20*log10(H);
plot(w/pi,H);grid
title('Magnitude response of a Elliptic Lowpass filter')
ylabel('Magnitude')
xlabel('Normalized frequency')
figure
plot(w/pi,HdB);grid
title('Magnitude response of a Elliptic Lowpass filter')
ylabel('Magnitude in~dB')
xlabel('Normalized frequency')
%end
```

The order of this filter is found to be 7, and its magnitude is plotted in Figures 4.23 and 4.24. Figure 4.23 shows the equiripple in the passband; Figure 4.24 shows the equiripple magnitude (in decibels) in the stopband, and the minimum attenuation is seen to be 60 dB.

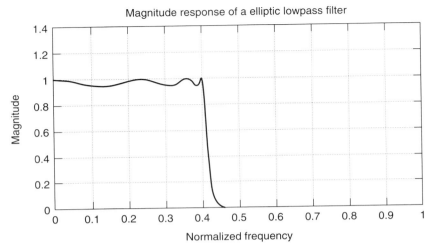

Figure 4.23   Magnitude response of an elliptic lowpass filter.

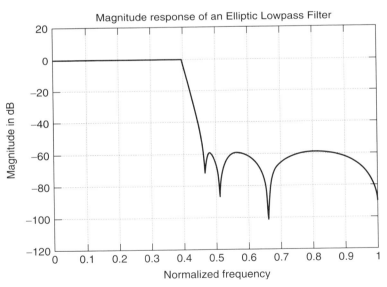

Figure 4.24   Magnitude response (in decibels) of an elliptic lowpass filter.

Example 4.12

```
%MATLAB Script to design a Chebyshev I (Equiripple) Bandpass
%  filter with Ws1 = 0.25, Wp1 = 0.3, Wp2 = 0.4 ,Ws2 = 0.45,
%  Rp = 0.5, Rs = 50
 [N,Wn]=chebyord([0.3 0.4],[0.25 0.45],0.5,50);
```

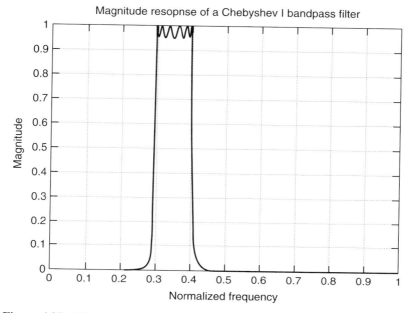

Figure 4.25 Magnitude response of a Chebyshev I (equiripple) bandpass filter.

```
[b,a]=cheby1(N,0.5,Wn)
[h,w]=freqz(b,a,256);
H=abs(h);
HdB=20*log10(H);
plot(w/pi,H);grid
title('Magnitude response of a Chebyshev I Bandpass filter')
ylabel('Magnitude')
xlabel('Normalized frequency')
%end
```

The order of this filter is found to be 12, and its magnitude response is shown in Figure 4.25.

Example 4.13

```
%MATLAB script to design a Butterworth Bandstop filter
%  with Wp1 = 0.18, Ws1 = 0.2, Ws2 = 0.205, Wp2 = 0.24,
%  Rp = 0.5 and Rs = 50
 Wp=[0.18 0.24];
 Ws=[0.2 0.205];
 [N,Wn]=buttord(Wp,Ws,0.5,50);
```

```
[b,a]=butter(N,Wn,'stop');
[h,w]=freqz(b,a,256);
H=abs(h);
plot(w/pi,H);grid
title('Magnitude response of a Butterworth Bandstop filter')
ylabel('Magnitude')
xlabel('Normalized frequency')
%end
```

The order of this filter is 8, and its magnitude response, shown in Figure 4.26, acts like a notch filter. It can be used to filter out a single frequency at which the attenuation is more than 65 dB. Since this frequency is $\omega = 0.2$, it is 20% of the Nyquist frequency or 10% of the sampling frequency. So if the sampling frequency is chosen as 600 Hz, we can use this filter to filter out the undesirable hum at 60 Hz due to power supply in an audio equipment.

The coefficients of the digital filter are copied below from the output of the MATLAB script shown above:

b = numerator coefficients (columns 1–9):

0.9168   −5.9000   17.9049   −32.9698   40.1175   −32.9698   17.9049

−5.9000   0.9168

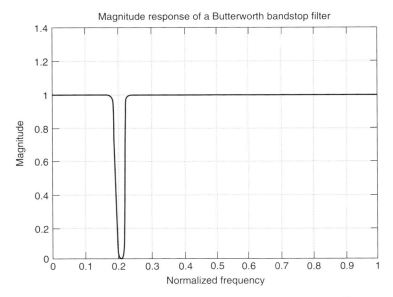

Figure 4.26 Magnitude response of a Butterworth bandstop filter.

a = denominator coefficients (columns 1–9):

  1.0000 −6.2955 18.6910 −33.6739 40.0927 −32.2433 17.1366
      −5.5267 0.8406

Example 4.14

```
%MATLAB script to design a Chebyshev II highpass filter
%with Wp=0.5,Ws=0.4,Rp=0.5 and Rs=60
[N,Wn]=cheb2ord(0.5,0.4,0.5,60)
[b,a]=cheby2(N,60,Wn,'high');
[h,w]=freqz(b,a,256);
H=abs(h);
HdB=20*log10(H);
plot(w/pi,H);grid
title('Magnitude response of a Chebyshev II Highpass Filter')
ylabel('Magnitude')
xlabel('Normalized frequency')
%end
```

The magnitude response of this filter is of order 11, is shown in Figures 4.27 and 4.28.

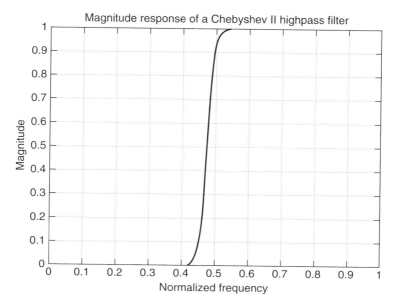

Figure 4.27   Magnitude response of a Chebyshev II highpass filter.

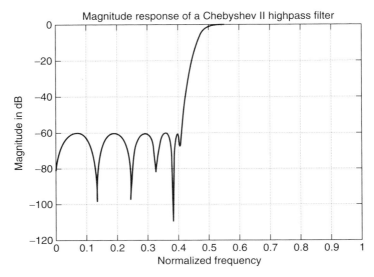

Figure 4.28   Magnitude response (in decibels) of a Chebyshev II highpass filter.

4.10 YULE–WALKER APPROXIMATION

Now we introduce another function called `yulewalk` to find an IIR filter that approximates an arbitrary magnitude response. The method minimizes the error between the desired magnitude represented by a vector `D` and the magnitude of the IIR filter $H(e^{j\omega})$ in the least-squares sense.

In addition to the maximally flat approximation and the minimax (Chebyshev or equiripple) approximation we have discussed so far, there is the least- squares approximation, which is used extensively in the design of filters as well as other systems. The error that is minimized in a more general case is known as the least-pth approximation. It is defined by

$$J_3(\omega) = \int_{\omega \in R} W(e^{j\omega}) \left| H(e^{j\omega}) - D(e^{j\omega}) \right|^P d\omega$$

and when $p = 2$, it is known as the *least-squares approximation*. In the error function shown above, $D(e^{j\omega})$ is the desired frequency response and $H(e^{j\omega})$ is the response of the filter designed, whereas $W(e^{j\omega})$ is a weighting function chosen by the designer. It has been found that as p approaches ∞, the error is minimized in the minimax sense, and in practice, choosing $p = 4, 5, 6$ gives a good approximation to $D(e^{j\omega})$ in the least-pth sense [14]. It is best to avoid sharp transitions in the specifications for the desired magnitude for the IIR filter when we use the MATLAB function `yulewalk`. The function has the form

```
[num,den] = yulewalk(N,F,D)
```

where F is a vector of discrete frequencies in the range between 0 and 1.0, where 1.0 represents the Nyquist frequency; the vector F must include 0 and 1.0. The vector D contains the desired magnitudes at the frequencies in the vector F; hence the two vectors have the same length. N is the order of the filter. The coefficients of the numerator and denominator are output data in the vectors num and den as shown in (4.102).

Example 4.15

```
%MATLAB script to design a IIR filter using the function
%  yulewalk.
 F=[0 0.3 0.7 0.8 1.0];
 D=[0 0.8 0.6 0.3 0.5];
 [num,den]=yulewalk(10,F,D);
 [h,w]=freqz(num,den,256);
 H=abs(h);
 plot(w/pi,H);grid
 title('Magnitude of an IIR filter by Yulewalker
    approximation')
 ylabel('Magnitude')
 xlabel('Normalized frequency')
```

The magnitude of the IIR filter of order 10 obtained in this example is shown in Figure 4.29. We can increase or decrease the order of the filter and choose the design that satisfies the requirements for the application under consideration.

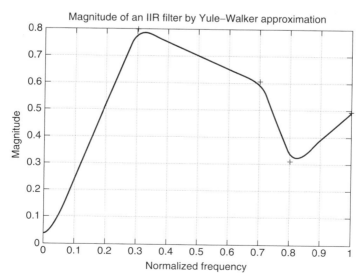

Figure 4.29   Magnitude response of an IIR filter, using Yule–Walker approximation.

4.11 SUMMARY

In this chapter, three major topics have been discussed. First, the theory and design procedure for approximating the piecewise constant magnitude of ideal analog filters was discussed, followed by the theory and design procedure for the design of the IIR filters. These are lowpass, highpass, bandpass, or bandstop filters that approximate the desired piecewise constant magnitudes in either the maximally flat sense or the equiripple sense. It is to be pointed out that the constant group delay of analog filters does not transform to a constant group delay of the IIR filter obtained by the bilinear transformation. Separate procedures for designing IIR filters that approximate a constant group delay have been described in [10].

Next we described the MATLAB functions that are used for designing these IIR filters as well elliptic function filters. Finally we described the use of the MATLAB function `yulewalk` that approximates an arbitrary magnitude response in the least-squares sense. Design of IIR filters that approximate given frequency specifications with additional approximation criteria are described in Chapter 7.

PROBLEMS

4.1 Find the function $|H(j\omega)|^2$ from the transfer functions given below:

$$H_1(s) = \frac{s+3}{s^2 + 2s + 2}$$

$$H_2(s) = \frac{s^2 + s + 1}{s(s^2 + 4s + 20)}$$

4.2 Find the transfer function $H(s)$ from the functions given below:

$$|H_1(j\omega)|^2 = \frac{(\omega^2 + 9)}{(\omega^2 + 4)(\omega^2 + 1)} \tag{4.103}$$

$$|H_2(j\omega)|^2 = \frac{(\omega^2 + 4)}{(\omega^2 + 16)(\omega^4 + 1)} \tag{4.104}$$

4.3 An analog signal $x(t) = e^{-2t}u(t)$ is sampled to generate the discrete-time sequence $x(nT) = e^{-2nT}u(n)$. Find the z transform $X(z)$ of the DT sequence for $T = 0.1, 0.05, 0.01$ s.

4.4 An analog signal $x(t) = 10\cos(2t)u(t)$ is sampled to generate the discrete-time sequence $x(nT) = 10\cos(2nT)u(n)$. Find the z transform $X(z)$ of the DT sequence for $T = 0.1, 0.01$ s.

4.5 Derive transfer function $H_1(z)$ obtained when the impulse-invariant transformation is applied and $H_2(z)$ when the bilinear transformation $s =$

$2[(z-1)/(z+1)]$ is applied to the transfer function $H(s) = 1/(s^2 + \sqrt{2}s + 1)$. Simplify the transfer functions as the ratio of polynomials in z.

4.6 Find the z transform obtained by the impulse-invariant transformation of $H(s)$ given below, assuming $T = 0.1$ s:

$$H_1(s) = \frac{1}{s(s+1)(s+3)}$$

$$H_2(s) = \frac{(s+1)}{(s+2)(s^2+2s+5)}$$

$$H_3(s) = \frac{s(s^2+4s+10)}{(s+5)(s^2+6s+15)}$$

4.7 By application of the impulse-invariant transformation of $H(s)$, the following transfer functions have been obtained. Find $H(s)$, assuming $T = 0.1$ s:

$$H_1(z) = \frac{2z}{(z-e^{-0.2})(z-e^{-0.1})}$$

$$H_2(z) = \frac{z-e^{-0.6}}{(z-e^{-0.5})(z-e^{-0.4})}$$

$$H_3(z) = \frac{z}{(z-0.9)(z-0.3)}$$

$$H_4(z) = \frac{z}{(z-0.4)(z-0.8)}$$

4.8 The following transfer functions of a digital filter are obtained by applying the bilinear transformation on analog transfer functions $H(s)$. Derive the transfer functions $H(s)$, assuming $T = 0.1$ s:

$$H_1(z) = \frac{z+1}{z^2+z+6}$$

$$H_2(z) = \frac{z+4}{z^2+6z+8}$$

$$H_3(z) = \frac{2z+5}{z^2+2z+2}$$

4.9 Find the magnitude (in decibels) at the frequency $\omega_s = 1000$ rad/s of a Fourth-order Chebyshev I highpass, analog filter with the magnitude response shown in Figure 4.30.

4.10 A Chebyshev I bandstop analog filter is to be designed to approximate the following specifications: $\omega_{p1} = 10^4$ and $\omega_{p2} = 7 \times 10^4$ are the cutoff frequencies of the passband. Passband ripple $= 0.5$ dB, $\omega_{s1} = 2 \times 10^4$ is a frequency in the stopband and the minimum attenuation in the stopband $= 30$ dB. What is the stopband frequency Ω_s and the order of the lowpass prototype filter $H(p)$?

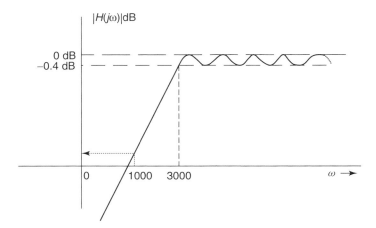

Figure 4.30   Problem 4.9.

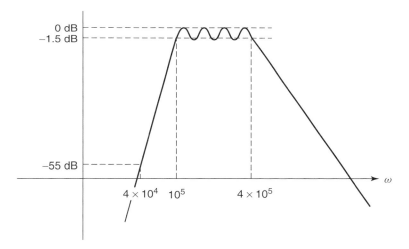

Figure 4.31   Problem 4.11.

4.11   What is the order of an analog bandpass Chebyshev I filter that has a magnitude response as shown in Figure 4.31?

4.12   Determine the sampling period T such that a frequency $s = j15$ of the analog filter maps to the normalized frequency $\omega = 0.3\pi$ of the digital filter.

4.13   A digital Butterworth lowpass filter is designed by applying the bilinear transformation on the transfer function of an analog Butterworth lowpass filter that has an attenuation of 45 dB at 1200 rad/s. What is the frequency in rad/s at which the digital filter has an attenuation of 45 dB, if its sampling frequency is 1000 Hz?

4.14 A digital Chebyshev bandpass filter is designed by applying the bilinear transformation on the transfer function of an analog Chebyshev bandpass filter that has a bandwidth of 200 rad/s between 1400 and 1600 rad/s. What is the bandwidth of the digital filter, if its sampling frequency is 1500 Hz?

4.15 A Butterworth bandpass IIR digital filter designed by using the bilinear transformation has a magnitude response as shown in Figure 4.32. Find the order of the filter.

4.16 An IIR lowpass Butterworth filter is to be designed, using the bilinear transformation, with a cutoff frequency $\omega_c = 0.3\pi$ at which the maximum attenuation is 0.5 dB. The minimum attenuation at the stopband cutoff frequency $\omega_s = 0.8\pi$ is 40 dB. Find the transfer function $H(p)$ of the lowpass prototype filter, when the bilinear transformation is used.

4.17 Find the magnitude of a lowpass Butterworth IIR filter at the frequency (0.8π). The order of the filter is 10, the sampling frequency is 10^3 Hz, and the 3 dB bandwidth of the filter is (0.2π).

4.18 What are the frequencies ω_{s2} and ω_{s1} at which the 10th-order Butterworth analog bandpass filter has a magnitude of 0.045? The filter has a magnitude response as shown in Figure 4.33.

4.19 What is the order of a Chebyshev bandpass IIR filter that has a magnitude response such as that shown in Figure 4.34.

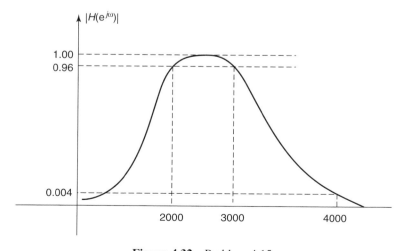

Figure 4.32 Problem 4.15.

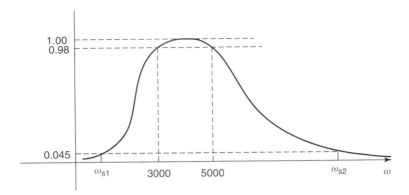

Figure 4.33 Problem 4.18.

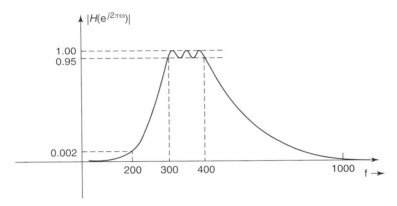

Figure 4.34 Problem 4.19.

4.20 Design a Chebyshev analog highpass filter that approximates the specifications as shown in Figure 4.35.

4.21 Design a Butterworth bandpass IIR filter that approximates the specifications given in Figure 4.36. Show all calculations step by step. Plot the magnitude using MATLAB.

4.22 A Butterworth bandpass IIR filter of order 10 meets the following specifications: $\omega_{p1} = 0.5\pi$, $\omega_{p2} = 0.65\pi$, $\omega_{s2} = 0.8\pi$, $A_p = 0.5$ dB. What is the attenuation at ω_{s2}?

4.23 A Chebyshev I bandstop digital filter meets the satisfy the following specifications: $\omega_{p1} = 0.1\pi$, $\omega_{p2} = 0.8\pi$, $\omega_{s2} = 0.4\pi$, $\alpha_p = 0.8$, $\alpha_s = 55$. Find the transfer function $H(p)$ of the lowpass analog prototype filter.

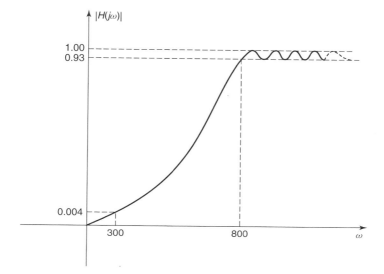

Figure 4.35   Problem 4.20.

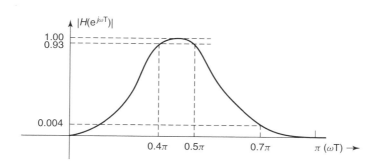

Figure 4.36   Problem 4.21.

4.24 A Butterworth highpass digital filter has a passband cutoff frequency of 1500 Hz, a stopband cutoff frequency of 650 Hz, a passband attenuation of 2.0 dB, and a stopband attenuation of 45 dB. The sampling period is 0.2×10^{-3} s. Find the transfer function $H(p)$ of the lowpass analog prototype filter.

4.25 Design a bandpass Chebyshev I IIR filter that approximates the specifications as shown in Figure 4.37. Show all calculations step by step, assuming a sampling frequency $f_s = 1000$ Hz. Plot the magnitude using MATLAB.

4.26 Obtain the transfer function of the Butterworth lowpass IIR filter with $\omega_p = 0.4\pi$, $\omega_s = 0.9\pi$, $R_p = 0.5$, $R_s = 20$. Using the digital spectral transformation LP–HP, find the transfer function of the highpass filter with a cutoff frequency of 0.75π.

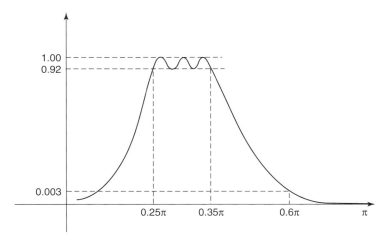

Figure 4.37 Problem 4.25.

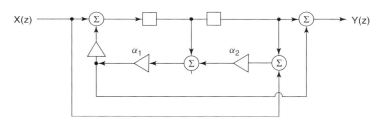

Figure 4.38 Problem 4.27a.

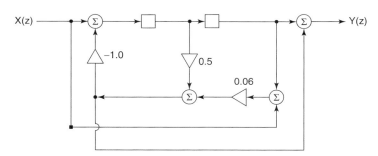

Figure 4.39 Problem 4.27b.

4.27 Derive the transfer function of the two circuits shown in Figures 4.38 and 4.39 and verify that they are allpass filters.

4.28 The transfer function of an analog allpass filter $H(s) = (s^2 - as + b)/(s^2 + as + b)$ has a magnitude response equal to one at all frequencies.

Show that the IIR filter obtained by the application of the bilinear transformation on $H(s)$ is also an allpass digital filter.

MATLAB Problems

4.29 Design a Butterworth bandstop filter with $W_{p1} = 0.2$, $W_{s1} = 0.35$, $W_{s2} = 0.55$, $W_{p2} = 0.7.0$, $R_p = 0.25$, and $R_s = 45$. Plot the magnitude and the group delay response.

4.30 Design a Chebyshev I bandpass filter to meet the following specifications: $W_{s1} = 0.4$, $W_{p1} = 0.45$, $W_{p2} = 0.55$, $W_{s2} = 0.6$, $R_p = 0.3$, $R_s = 50$. Plot the magnitude (in decibels) and the group delay to verify that the given specifications have been met.

4.31 Design a Chebyshev II highpass filter with $W_s = 0.1$, $W_p = 0.3$, $R_p = 0.8$, $R_s = 60$ dB. Plot the magnitude (in decibels) and the group delay of the filter to verify that the design meets the specifications.

4.32 Design an elliptic lowpass filter with $W_p = 0.2$, $W_s = 0.35$, $R_p = 0.8$, $R_s = 40$. Plot the magnitude (in decibels) and the group delay of the filter.

4.33 Design an elliptic lowpass filter with $W_{p1} = 0.3$, $W_s = 0.4$, $R_p = 0.5$, $R_s = 55$. Plot the magnitude (in decibels) and the group delay of the filter. Plot a magnified plot of the response in the stopband to verify that the specifications have been met.

4.34 Design a Butterworth bandpass filter with $W_{s1} = 0.3$, $W_{p1} = 0.5$, $W_{p2} = 0.55$, $W_{s2} = 0.8$, $R_p = 0.5$, and $R_s = 50$. Plot its magnitude and phase response.

4.35 Design an IIR filter with the following specifications: $F = [0 \quad 0.2 \quad 0.4 \quad 0.5 \quad 1.0]$, $D = [1.0 \quad 0.5 \quad 0.7 \quad 0.9 \quad 1.0]$, using `yulewalk` function. Plot the magnitude of the filter.

4.36 Design an IIR filter with the following specifications, using the MATLAB function `yulewalk`: $F = [0.0 \quad 0.3 \quad 0.5 \quad 0.7 \quad 0.9 \quad 1.0]$; $D = [0.2 \quad 0.4 \quad 0.5 \quad 0.3 \quad 0.6 \quad 1.0]$. Plot the magnitude of the filter.

4.37 Design an IIR filter that approximates the magnitude response with the specifications $F = [0.0 \quad 0.2 \quad 0.4 \quad 0.6 \quad 0.8 \quad 1.0]$; $D = [1.0 \quad 0.18 \quad 0.35 \quad 0.35 \quad 0.18 \quad 1.0]$ using the MATLAB function `yulewalk`. Plot the magnitude and group delay response of the filter.

REFERENCES

1. A. C. Constantinides, Spectral transformations for digital filters, *Proc. IEE* **117**, 1585–1590 (Aug. 1970).
2. A. I. Zverev, *Handbook of Filter Synthesis*, Wiley, 1967.

3. R. Schaumann and M. E. Van Valkenburg, *Design of Analog Filters*, Oxford Univ. Press, 2001.

4. S. K. Mitra, *Digital Signal Processing—A Computer-Based Approach*, McGraw-Hill, 2001.

5. J. G. Proakis and D. G. Manolakis, *Digital Signal Processing*, Prentice-Hall, 1996.

6. A. V. Oppenheim and R. W. Schafer, *Discrete-Time Signal Processing*, Prentice-Hall, 1989.

7. A. Antoniou, *Digital Filters, Analysis, Design and Applications*, McGraw-Hill, 1993.

8. E. C. Ifeachor and B. W. Jervis, *Digital Signal Processing, A Practical Approach*, Prentice-Hall, 2002.

9. L. R. Rabiner and B. Gold, *Theory and Application of Digital Signal Processing*, Prentice-Hall, 1975.

10. B. A. Shenoi, *Magnitude and Delay Approximation of 1-D and 2-D Digital Filters*, Springer-Verlag, 1999.

11. V. K. Ingle and J. G. Proakis, *Digital Signal Processing Using MATLAB$^{(R)}$ V.4*, PWS Publishing, 1997.

12. R. W. Hamming, *Digital Filters*, Prentice-Hall, 1989.

13. L. R. Rabiner and B. Gold, *Theory and Application of Digital Signal Processing*, Prentice-Hall, 1975.

14. G. C. Temes and D. Y. F. Zai, Least p^{th} approximation, *IEEE Trans. Circuit Theory* **CT-16**, 235–237 (1969).

15. MATLAB$^{(R)}$ and Signal Processing Tool Box, software from The MathWorks, Natick, MA.

CHAPTER 5

Finite Impulse Response Filters

5.1 INTRODUCTION

From the previous two chapters, we have become familiar with the magnitude response of ideal lowpass, highpass, bandpass, and bandstop filters, which was approximated by IIR filters. In the previous chapter, we also discussed the theory and a few prominent procedures for designing the IIR filters.

The general form of the difference equation for a linear, time-invariant, discrete-time system (LTIDT system) is

$$y(n) = -\sum_{k=1}^{N} a(k)y(n-k) + \sum_{k=0}^{M} b(k)x(n-k) \qquad (5.1)$$

The transfer function for such a system is given by

$$H(z^{-1}) = \frac{b_0 + b(1)z^{-1} + b(2)z^{-2} + \cdots + b(M)z^{-M}}{1 + a(1)z^{-1} + a(2)z^{-2} + a(3)z^{-3} + \cdots + a(N)z^{-N}} \qquad (5.2)$$

The transfer function of an FIR filter, in particular, is given by

$$H(z^{-1}) = b_0 + b(1)z^{-1} + b(2)z^{-2} + \cdots + b(M)z^{-M} \qquad (5.3)$$

and the difference equation describing this FIR filter is given by

$$y(n) = \sum_{k=0}^{M} b(k)x(n-k) \qquad (5.4)$$

$$= b(0)x(n) + b(1)x(n-1) + \cdots + b(M)x(n-M) \qquad (5.5)$$

In this chapter, the properties of the FIR filters and their design will be discussed. When the input function $x(n)$ is the unit sample function $\delta(n)$, the

Introduction to Digital Signal Processing and Filter Design, by B. A. Shenoi
Copyright © 2006 John Wiley & Sons, Inc.

output $y(n)$ can be obtained by applying the recursive algorithm on (5.4). We get the output $y(n)$ due to the unit sample input $\delta(n)$ to be exactly the values $b(0), b(1), b(2), b(3), \ldots, b(M)$. The output due to the unit sample function $\delta(n)$ is the unit sample response or the unit impulse response denoted by $h(n)$. So the samples of the unit impulse response $h(n) = b(n)$, which means that the unit impulse response $h(n)$ of the discrete-time system described by the difference equation (5.4) is finite in length. That is why the system is called the *finite impulse response filter* or the FIR filter. It has also been known by other names such as the transversal filter, nonrecursive filter, moving-average filter, and tapped delay filter. Since $h(n) = b(n)$ in the case of an FIR filter, we can represent (5.3) in the following form:

$$H(z^{-1}) = \sum_{k=0}^{M} h(k)z^{-k} = h(0) + h(1)z^{-1} + h(2)z^{-2} + \cdots + h(M)z^{-(M)} \quad (5.6)$$

The FIR filters have a few advantages over the IIR filters as defined by (5.1):

1. We can easily design the FIR filter to meet the required magnitude response in such a way that it achieves a constant group delay. *Group delay* is defined as $\tau = -(d\theta/d\omega)$, where θ is the phase response of the filter. The phase response of a filter with a constant group delay is therefore a linear function of frequency. It transmits all frequencies with the same amount of delay, which means that there will not be any phase distortion and the input signal will be delayed by a constant when it is transmitted to the output. A filter with a constant group delay is highly desirable in the transmission of digital signals.

2. The samples of its unit impulse response are the same as the coefficients of the transfer function as seen from (5.5) and (5.6). There is no need to calculate $h(n)$ from $H(z^{-1})$, such as during every stage of the iterative optimization procedure or for designing the structures (circuits) from $H(z^{-1})$.

3. The FIR filters are always stable and are free from limit cycles that arise as a result of finite wordlength representation of multiplier constants and signal values.

4. The effect of finite wordlength on the specified frequency response or the time-domain response or the output noise is smaller than that for IIR filters.

5. Although the unit impulse response $h(n)$ of an IIR filter is an infinitely long sequence, it is reasonable to assume in most practical cases that the value of the samples becomes almost negligible after a finite number; thus, choosing a sequence of finite length for the discrete-time signal allows us to use powerful numerical methods for processing signals of finite length.

5.1.1 Notations

It is to be remembered that in this chapter we choose the order of the FIR filter or degree of the polynomial $H(z^{-1}) = \sum_{n=0}^{N} h(n)z^{-n}$ as N, and the length of the filter equal to the number of coefficients in (5.6) is $N + 1$. If we are given $H(z^{-1}) = 0.3z^{-4} + 0.1z^{-5} + 0.5z^{-6}$, its order is 6, although only three terms are present and the correct number of coefficients equal to the length of the filter is 7, because $h(0) = h(1) = h(2) = h(3) = 0$. It becomes necessary to point out the notation used in this chapter, because in some textbooks, we may find $H(z^{-1}) = \sum_{n=0}^{N-1} h(n)z^{-n}$ representing the transfer function of an FIR filter, in which case the length of the filter is denoted by N and the degree or order of the polynomial is $(N - 1)$. (Therefore students have to be careful in using the formulas found in a chapter on FIR filters, in different books; but with some caution, they can replace N that appears in this chapter by $(N - 1)$ so that the formulas match those found in these books.)

The notation often used in MATLAB, is $H(z^{-1}) = h(1) + h(2)z^{-1} + h(3)z^{-2} + \cdots + h(N + 1)z^{-N}$, which is a polynomial of degree N, and has $(N + 1)$ coefficients. In more compact form, it is given by

$$H(z^{-1}) = \sum_{n=0}^{N} h(n + 1)z^{-n} \tag{5.7}$$

The notation and meaning of angular frequency used in the literature on discrete-time systems and digital signal processing also have to be clearly understood by the students. One is familiar with a sinusoidal signal $x(t) = A\sin(\mathbf{w}t)$ in which $\mathbf{w} = 2\pi f$ is the angular frequency in radians per second, f is the frequency in hertz, and its reciprocal is the period T_p in seconds. So we have $\mathbf{w} = 2\pi/T_p$ radians per second. Now if we sample this signal with a uniform sampling period, we need to differentiate the period T_p from the sampling period denoted by T_s. Therefore, the sampled sequence is given by $x(nT_s) = A\sin(\mathbf{w}nT_s) = A\sin(2\pi nT_s/T_p) = A\sin(2\pi f/f_s) = A\sin(\mathbf{w}/f_s)$. The frequency $\mathbf{w}$ (in radians per second) normalized by f_s is almost always denoted by ω and is called the normalized frequency (measured in radians). The frequency $\mathbf{w}$ is the *analog frequency* variable, and the frequency ω is the *normalized digital frequency*. On this basis, the sampling frequency $\omega_s = 2\pi$ radians. Sometimes, $\mathbf{w}$ is normalized by πf_s or $2\pi f_s$ so that the corresponding sampling frequency becomes 2 or 1 radian(s). Note that almost always, the sampling period is denoted simply by T in the literature on digital signal processing when there is no ambiguity and the normalized frequency is denoted by $\omega = \mathbf{w}T$. The difference between the angular frequency in radians per second and the normalized frequency usually used in DSP literature has been pointed out in several instances in this book.

5.2 LINEAR PHASE FIR FILTERS

Now we consider the special types of FIR filters in which the coefficients $h(n)$ of the transfer function $H(z^{-1}) = \sum_{n=0}^{N} h(n)z^{-n}$ are assumed to be symmetric or antisymmetric. Since the order of the polynomial in each of these two types can be either odd or even, we have four types of filters with different properties, which we describe below.

Type I. The coefficients are symmetric [i.e., $h(n) = h(N - n)$], and the order N is even.

Example 5.1

Let us consider a simple example:

$$H(z^{-1}) = h(0) + h(1)z^{-1} + h(2)z^{-2} + h(3)z^{-1} + h(4)z^{-4}$$
$$+ h(5)z^{-5} + h(6)z^{-6}.$$

As shown in Figure 5.1a, for this type I filter, with $N = 6$, we see that $h(0) = h(6)$, $h(1) = h(5)$, $h(2) = h(4)$. Using these equivalences in the above, we get

$$H(z^{-1}) = h(0)[1 + z^{-6}] + h(1)[z^{-1} + z^{-5}] + h(2)[z^{-2} + z^{-4}] + h(3)z^{-3}$$
$$(5.8)$$

This can also be represented in the form

$$H(z^{-1}) = z^{-3} \left\{ h(0)[z^3 + z^{-3}] + h(1)[z^2 + z^{-2}] + h(2)[z + z^{-1}] + h(3) \right\}$$
$$(5.9)$$

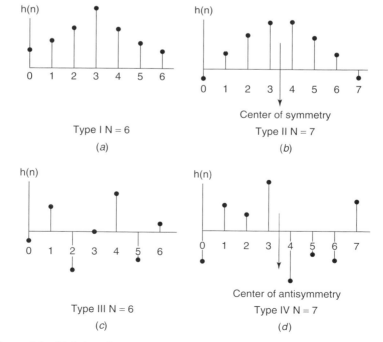

Type I N = 6

(a)

Center of symmetry
Type II N = 7

(b)

Type III N = 6

(c)

Center of antisymmetry
Type IV N = 7

(d)

Figure 5.1 Unit impulse responses of the four types of linear phase FIR filters.

Let us evaluate its frequency response (DTFT):

$$H(e^{-j\omega}) = e^{-j3\omega}\{2h(0)\cos(3\omega) + 2h(1)\cos(2\omega) + 2h(2)\cos(\omega) + h(3)\}$$
$$= e^{j\theta(\omega)}\{H_R(\omega)\}$$

The expression $H_R(\omega)$ in this equation is a real-valued function, but it can be positive or negative at any particular frequency, so when it changes from a positive value to a negative value, the phase angle changes by π radians (180°). The phase angle $\theta(\omega) = -3\omega$ is a linear function of ω, and the group delay τ is equal to three samples. Note that on the normalized frequency basis, the group delay is three samples but actual group delay is $3T$ seconds, where T is the sampling period.

In the general case, we can express $H(e^{j\omega})$ in a few other forms, for example

$$H(e^{j\omega}) = \sum_{n=0}^{N} h(n)e^{-jn\omega}$$

$$= h(0) + h(1)e^{-j\omega} + h(2)e^{-j2\omega} + \cdots + h(N-1)e^{-j(N\omega)}$$

$$= e^{-j[(N/2)\omega]}\left\{2h(0)\cos\left(\frac{N\omega}{2}\right) + 2h(1)\cos\left(\left(\frac{N}{2}-1\right)\omega\right)\right.$$

$$\left. + 2h(2)\cos\left(\left(\frac{N}{2}-2\right)\omega\right) + \cdots + h\left(\frac{N}{2}\right)\right\} \qquad (5.10)$$

We put it in a more compact form:

$$H(e^{j\omega}) = e^{-j[(N/2)\omega]}\left\{h\left(\frac{N}{2}\right) + 2\sum_{n=1}^{N/2} h\left[\frac{N}{2}-n\right]\cos(n\omega)\right\} = e^{j\theta(\omega)}\{H_R(\omega)\}$$

$$(5.11)$$

The total group delay is a constant $= N/2$ in the general case, for a type I FIR filter.

Type II. The coefficients are symmetric [i.e., $h(n) = h(N-n)$], and the order N is odd.

Example 5.2

Here we consider an example in which the coefficients are symmetric but $N = 7$, as shown in Figure 5.1b. For this example, we have

$$H(z^{-1}) = h(0) + h(1)z^{-1} + h(2)z^{-2} + h(3)z^{-1} + h(4)z^{-4} + h(5)z^{-5}$$
$$+ h(6)z^{-6} + h(7)z^{-7}$$

and because of symmetry

$$h(0) = h(7), \quad h(1) = h(6), \quad h(2) = h(5), \quad h(3) = h(4).$$

Therefore

$$H(z^{-1}) = h(0)[1 + z^{-7}] + h(1)[z^{-1} + z^{-6}] + h(2)[z^{-2} + z^{-5}]$$
$$+ h(3)[z^{-3} + z^{-4}]$$

The frequency response is given by

$$H(e^{-j\omega}) = e^{-j3.5\omega} \{2h(0)\cos(3.5\omega) + 2h(1)\cos(2.5\omega)$$
$$+ 2h(2)\cos(1.5\omega) + 2h(3)\cos(0.5\omega)\}$$
$$= e^{j\theta(\omega)} \{H_R(\omega)\}$$

The phase angle $\theta(\omega) = -3.5\omega$, and the group delay is $\tau = 3.5$ samples. In the general case of type II filter, we obtain

$$H(e^{-j\omega}) = \sum_{n=0}^{N} h(n)e^{-jn\omega} = e^{j\theta(\omega)} \{H_R(\omega)\}$$

$$= e^{-j(\frac{N}{2}\omega)} \left\{ \sum_{n=1}^{(N+1)/2} 2h\left[\frac{N+1}{2} - n\right]\cos\left(n - \frac{1}{2}\right)\omega\right\} \quad (5.12)$$

which shows a linear phase $\theta(\omega) = -[(N/2)\omega]$ and a constant group delay = $N/2$ samples.

Type III. The coefficients are antisymmetric [i.e., $h(n) = -h(N-n)$], and the order N is even.

Example 5.3

We consider an example of type III FIR filter of order $N = 6$ and as shown in Figure 5.1c, we have $h(0) = -h(6)$, $h(1) = -h(5)$, $h(2) = -h(4)$ and we must have $h(3) = 0$ to maintain antisymmetry for these samples:

$$H(z^{-1}) = h(0)[1 - z^{-6}] + h(1)[z^{-1} - z^{-5}] + h(2)[z^{-2} - z^{-4}] \quad (5.13)$$
$$= z^{-3} \left\{ h(0)[z^3 - z^{-3}] + h(1)[z^2 - z^{-2}] + h(2)[z - z^{-1}] \right\} \quad (5.14)$$

Now if we put $z = e^{j\omega}$, and $e^{j\omega} - e^{-j\omega} = 2j\sin(\omega) = 2e^{j(\pi/2)}\sin(\omega)$, we arrive at the frequency response for this filter as

$$H(e^{-j\omega}) = e^{-j3\omega}\{h(0)2j\sin(3\omega) + h(1)2j\sin(2\omega) + h(2)2j\sin(\omega)\} \quad (5.15)$$

$$= e^{-j3\omega}e^{j(\pi/2)}\{2h(0)\sin(3\omega) + 2h(1)\sin(2\omega) + 2h(2)\sin(\omega)\} \quad (5.16)$$

$$= e^{-j[3\omega-(\pi/2)]}H_R(\omega) \quad (5.17)$$

Note that the phase angle for this filter is $\theta(\omega) = -3\omega + \pi/2$, which is still a linear function of ω. The group delay is $\tau = 3$ samples for this filter.

In the general case, it can be shown that

$$H(e^{-j\omega}) = e^{-j[(N\omega-\pi)/2]}\left\{2\sum_{n=1}^{N/2}h\left[\frac{N}{2} - n\right]\sin(n\omega)\right\} \quad (5.18)$$

and it has a linear phase $\theta(\omega) = -[(N\omega - \pi)/2]$ and a group delay $\tau = N/2$ samples.

Type IV. The coefficients are antisymmetric [i.e., $h(n) = -h(N - n)$], and the order N is odd.

Example 5.4

We consider an example of type IV filter with $N = 7$ as shown in Figure 5.1d, in which $h(0) = -h(7)$, $h(1) = -h(6)$, $h(2) = -h(5)$, $h(3) = -h(4)$. Its transfer function is given by

$$H(z^{-1}) = h(0)[1 - z^{-7}] + h(1)[z^{-1} - z^{-6}] + h(2)[z^{-2} - z^{-5}]$$
$$+ h(3)[z^{-3} - z^{-4}] \quad (5.19)$$

The frequency response can be derived as

$$H(e^{-j\omega}) = e^{-j3.5\omega}\{h(0)[e^{j3.5\omega} - e^{-j3.5\omega}] + h(1)[e^{j2.5\omega} - e^{-j2.5\omega}]$$
$$+ h(2)[e^{j1.5\omega} - e^{-j1.5\omega}] + h(3)[e^{j0.5\omega} - e^{-j0.5\omega}]\}$$
$$= e^{-j3.5\omega}\{h(0)2j\sin(3.5\omega) + h(1)2j\sin(2.5\omega) + h(2)2j\sin(1.5\omega)$$
$$+ h(3)2j\sin(0.5\omega)\}$$
$$= e^{-j[3.5\omega-(\pi/2)]}\{2h(0)\sin(3.5\omega) + 2h(1)\sin(2.5\omega) + 2h(2)\sin(1.5\omega)$$
$$+ 2h(3)\sin(0.5\omega)\} \quad (5.20)$$

This type IV filter with $N = 7$ has a linear phase $\theta(\omega) = -3.5\omega + \pi/2$ and a constant group delay $\tau = 3.5$ samples.

The transfer function of the type IV linear phase filter in general is given by

$$H(e^{-j\omega}) = e^{-j[(N\omega - \pi)/2]} \left\{ 2 \sum_{n=1}^{(N+1)/2} h\left[\frac{N+1}{2} - n\right] \sin\left(\left(n - \frac{1}{2}\right)\omega\right) \right\}$$

$$(5.21)$$

The frequency responses of the four types of FIR filters are summarized below:

$$H(e^{j\omega}) = e^{-j[(N/2)\omega]} \left\{ h\left(\frac{N}{2}\right) + 2 \sum_{n=1}^{N/2} h\left[\frac{N}{2} - n\right] \cos(n\omega) \right\}$$

for type I

$$H(e^{-j\omega}) = e^{-j[(N/2)\omega]} \left\{ 2 \sum_{n=1}^{(N+1)/2} h\left[\frac{N+1}{2} - n\right] \cos\left(\left(n - \frac{1}{2}\right)\omega\right) \right\}$$

for type II

$$H(e^{-j\omega}) = e^{-j[(N\omega - \pi)/2]} \left\{ 2 \sum_{n=1}^{N/2} h\left[\frac{N}{2} - n\right] \sin(n\omega) \right\}$$

for type III

$$H(e^{-j\omega}) = e^{-j[(N\omega - \pi)/2]} \left\{ 2 \sum_{n=1}^{(N+1)/2} h\left[\frac{N+1}{2} - n\right] \sin\left(\left(n - \frac{1}{2}\right)\omega\right) \right\}$$

for type IV   (5.22)

5.2.1   Properties of Linear Phase FIR Filters

The four types of FIR filters discussed above have shown us that FIR filters with symmetric or antisymmetric coefficients provide linear phase (or equivalently constant group delay); these coefficients are samples of the unit impulse response. It has been shown above that an FIR filter with symmetric or antisymmetric coefficients has a linear phase and therefore a constant group delay. The reverse statement, that an FIR filter with a constant group delay must have symmetric or antisymmetric coefficients, has also been proved theoretically [4]. These properties are very useful in the design of FIR filters and their applications. To see some additional properties of these four types of filters, we have evaluated the magnitude response of typical FIR filters with linear phase. They are shown in Figure 5.2.

The following observations about these typical magnitude responses will be useful in making proper choices in the early stage of their design, as will be

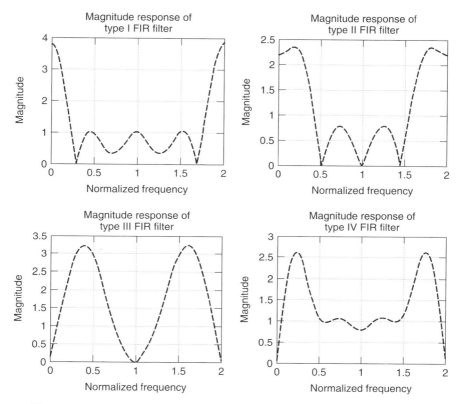

Figure 5.2   Magnitude responses of the four types of linear phase FIR filters.

explained later. For example, type I filters have a nonzero magnitude at $\omega = 0$ and also a nonzero value at the normalized frequency $\omega/\pi = 1$ (which corresponds to the Nyquist frequency), whereas type II filters have nonzero magnitude at $\omega = 0$ but a zero value at the Nyquist frequency. So it is obvious that these filters are not suitable for designing bandpass and highpass filters, whereas both of them are suitable for lowpass filters. The type III filters have zero magnitude at $\omega = 0$ and also at $\omega/\pi = 1$, so they are suitable for designing bandpass filters but not lowpass and bandstop filters. Type IV filters have zero magnitude at $\omega = 0$ and a nonzero magnitude at $\omega/\pi = 1$. They are not suitable for designing lowpass and bandstop filters but are candidates for bandpass and highpass filters.

In Figure 5.3a, the phase response of a type I filter is plotted showing the linear relationship. When the transfer function has a zero on the unit circle in the z plane, its phase response displays a jump discontinuity of π radians at the corresponding frequency, and the plot uses a jump discontinuity of 2π whenever the phase response exceeds $\pm\pi$ so that the total phase response remains within the principal range of $\pm\pi$. If there are no jump discontinuities of π radians, that is, if there are no zeros on the unit circle, the phase response becomes a

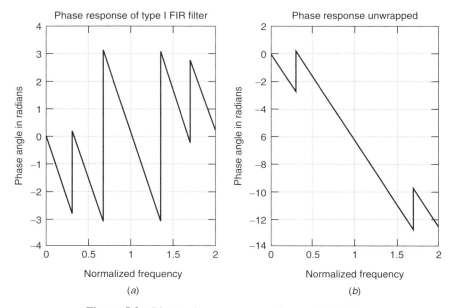

Figure 5.3   Linear phase responses of type I FIR filter.

continuous function of ω when it is unwrapped. The result of unwrapping the phase (Fig. 5.3a) is to remove the jump discontinuities in the phase response such that the phase response lies within $\pm\pi$ (Fig. 5.3b). If the order N of the FIR filter is even, its group delay is an integer multiple of samples equal to $N/2$ samples. If the order N is odd, then the group delay is equal to (an integer plus half) a sample. We will use all of these properties before we start the design of FIR filters with linear phase.

The linear phase FIR filters have some interesting properties in the z plane also. As seen in the examples, their transfer functions always contain pairs of terms such as $[z^n \pm z^{-n}]$. Denoting the transfer function of the FIR filters with symmetric coefficients by $H(z)$, we write

$$H(z) = \sum_{n=0}^{N} h(n)z^{-n} = \sum_{n=0}^{N} h(N-n)z^{-n} \qquad (5.23)$$

By making a change of variable $m = (N-n)$, we reduce the series $\sum_{n=0}^{N} h(N-n)z^{-n}$ to

$$\sum_{m=0}^{N} h(m)z^{-N+m} = z^{-N} \sum_{m=0}^{N} h(m)z^{m} = z^{-N} H(z^{-1}) \qquad (5.24)$$

so we have the following result:

$$H(z) = z^{-N} H(z^{-1}) \qquad (5.25)$$

Similarly, the FIR filters with antisymmetric coefficients satisfy the property

$$H(z) = -z^{-N} H(z^{-1}) \tag{5.26}$$

A polynomial $H(z)$ satisfying (5.25) is called a *mirror image polynomial*, and the polynomial that satisfies (5.26) is called an *anti–mirror image polynomial*. We see that a polynomial $H(z)$ that has symmetric coefficients is a mirror image polynomial and one with antisymmetric coefficients is an anti–mirror image polynomial. The reverse statement is also true and can be proved, namely, that a mirror image polynomial has symmetric coefficients and an anti–mirror image polynomial has antisymmetric coefficients.

From (5.25) and (5.26), it is easy to note that in a mirror image polynomial as well as an anti–mirror image polynomial, if $z = z_1$ is a zero of $H(z)$, then $1/z$ is also a zero of $H(z)$. If the zero z_1 is a complex number $r_1 e^{j\phi}$; $|r| < 1$, then $z_1^* = r_1 e^{-j\phi}$ is also a zero. Their reciprocals $(1/r_1)e^{-j\phi}$ and $(1/r_1)e^{j\phi}$ are also zeros of $H(z)$, which lie outside the unit circle $|z| = 1$. Therefore complex zeros of mirror image polynomials and anti–mirror image polynomials appear with quadrantal symmetry as shown in Figure 5.4. If there is a zero on the unit circle (e.g., at $z_0 = e^{j\phi}$), its reciprocal $z^{-1} = e^{-j\phi}$ is already located on the unit circle, as the complex conjugate of z_0, and therefore zeros on the unit circle do not have quadrantal symmetry. Obviously a zero on the real axis at $z_r = r$ inside the unit circle will be paired with one outside the unit circle on the real axis at $z_r^{-1} = 1/r$.

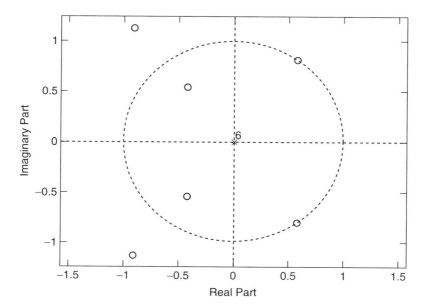

Figure 5.4   Zero and pole locations of a mirror image polynomial.

Example 5.5

We consider the example of a type I FIR filter with $H(z^{-1}) = 0.4 + 0.6z^{-1} + 0.8z^{-2} + 0.2z^{-3} + 0.8z^{-4} + 0.6z^{-5} + 0.4z^{-6}$, to illustrate these properties. When it is expressed in the form $H(z) = z^{-6}[0.4 + 0.6z + 0.8z^2 + 0.2z^3 + 0.8z^4 + 0.6z^5 + 0.4z^6]$ and factorized, we get

$$H(z) = \frac{(z - z_1)(z - z_1^*)(z - z^{-1})(z - z^{-1*})(z - z_2)(z - z_2^*)}{z^6} \tag{5.27}$$

where $z_1 = 0.69e^{j128.6^\circ}$, $z_1^* = 0.69e^{-j128.6^\circ}$, $z_1^{-1} = 1.45e^{-j128.6^\circ}$, $z_1^{-1*} = 1.45e^{j128.6^\circ}$, $z_2 = e^{j54.12^\circ}$, and $z_2^{-1*} = e^{-j54.12^\circ}$. They are plotted in Figure 5.4 along with the six poles of $H(z)$ at $z = 0$. The two zeros at z_2 and z_2^* are on the unit circle, and the other four zeros form a quadrantal symmetry in this plot. The magnitude of this type I filter is illustrated in Figure 5.2a, which shows that the magnitude has zero value at the two frequencies corresponding to the two zeros at z_2 and z_2^* that are on the unit circle. In Figure 5.3, the phase response also shows discontinuities at these two frequencies.

Some additional properties of the four types of FIR filters are listed below:

1. *Type I FIR filters* have either an even number of zeros or no zeros at $z = 1$ and $z = -1$.
2. *Type II FIR filters* have an even number of zeros or no zeros at $z = 1$ and an odd number of zeros at $z = -1$.
3. *Type III FIR filters* have an odd number of zeros at $z = 1$ and $z = -1$.
4. *Type IV FIR filters* have an odd number of zeros at $z = 1$ and either an even or odd number of zeros at $z = -1$.

These properties confirm the properties of the magnitude response of the filters as illustrated by Figure 5.2. A zero at $z = 1$ corresponds to $\omega = 0$, and a zero at $z = -1$ corresponds to $\omega = \pi$. As an example, we note that the type III FIR filter has zero magnitude at $\omega = 0$ and $\omega = 1$, whereas we stated above that the transfer function of the type III FIR filter has an odd number of zeros both at $z = 1$ and $z = -1$.

Another important result that will be used in the Fourier series method for designing FIR filters is given below. This is true of all FIR as well as IIR filters and not just linear phase FIR filters. The Fourier transform (DTFT) of any discrete-time sequence $x(n)$ is

$$X(e^{j\omega}) = \sum_{n=-\infty}^{n=\infty} x(n)e^{-jn\omega} \tag{5.28}$$

Since $H(e^{j\omega})$ is a periodic function with a period of 2π, it has a Fourier series representation in the form

$$X(e^{j\omega}) = \sum_{n=-\infty}^{n=\infty} c(n)e^{-jn\omega} \tag{5.29}$$

where

$$c(n) = \frac{1}{2\pi} \int_{-\pi}^{\pi} X(e^{j\omega})e^{jn\omega}\,d\omega \tag{5.30}$$

Comparing (5.28) and (5.29), we see that $x(n) = c(n)$ for $-\infty < n < \infty$. When we consider the frequency response of the LTI-DT system $H(e^{j\omega}) = \sum_{n=0}^{n=\infty} h(n)e^{-jn\omega}$, where $h(n) = 0$ for $n < 0$, we will find that $c(n) = 0$ for $n < 0$. So we note that the Fourier series coefficients $c(n)$ evaluated from (5.30) are the same as the coefficients $h(n)$ of the IIR or FIR filter. Evaluating the coefficients $c(n) = h(n)$ by the integral in the Equation (5.30) is easy when we choose $H(e^{j\omega})$ to be a constant in the subinterval within the interval of integration $[-\pi, \pi]$ with zero phase or when $H(e^{j\omega})$ is piecewise constant over different disjoint passbands and stopbands, within $[-\pi, \pi]$. This result facilitates the design of FIR filters that approximate the magnitude response of ideal lowpass, highpass, bandpass, and bandstop filters.[1] The Fourier series method based on the abovementioned properties of FIR filters for designing them is discussed next.

5.3 FOURIER SERIES METHOD MODIFIED BY WINDOWS

The magnitude responses of four ideal classical types of digital filters are shown in Figure 5.5. Let us consider the magnitude response of the ideal, desired, lowpass digital filter to be $H_{LP}(e^{j\omega})$, in which the cutoff frequency is given as ω_c. It has a constant magnitude of one and zero phase over the frequency $|\omega| < \omega_c$. From (5.30), we get

$$c_{LP}(n) = \frac{1}{2\pi} \int_{-\pi}^{\pi} H_{LP}(e^{j\omega})e^{jn\omega}\,d\omega = \frac{1}{2\pi} \int_{-\omega_c}^{\omega_c} e^{jn\omega}\,d\omega$$

$$= \frac{1}{2\pi} \left(\frac{e^{jn\omega}}{jn} \right)\bigg|_{-\omega_c}^{\omega_c} = \frac{e^{j\omega_c} - e^{-j\omega_c}}{2j(\pi n)}$$

$$= \frac{\sin(\omega_c n)}{\pi n} = -\infty < n < \infty \tag{5.31}$$

[1]Two other types of frequency response for which the Fourier series coefficients have been derived are those for the Hilbert transformer and the differentiator. Students interested in them may refer to other textbooks.

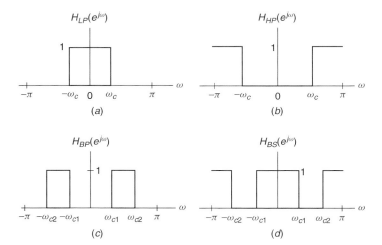

Figure 5.5 Magnitude responses of four ideal filters. (Reprinted from Ref. 9, with permission from John Wiley & Sons, Inc.)

Another form for the Fourier series coefficients is

$$c_{LP}(n) = \frac{\sin(\omega_c n)}{\pi n} = \left(\frac{\omega_c}{\pi}\right) \text{sinc}(\omega_c n); \qquad -\infty < n < \infty \qquad (5.32)$$

Note that $\text{sinc}(\omega_c n) = 1$ when $n = 0$, so we find another way of listing the coefficients as

$$c_{LP}(n) = \begin{cases} \dfrac{\omega_c}{\pi}; & n = 0 \\[2mm] \dfrac{\sin(\omega_c n)}{\pi n}; & |n| > 0 \end{cases} \qquad (5.33)$$

The Fourier series coefficients for the ideal HP, BP, and BS filter responses shown in Figures 5.5b–d can be similarly derived as follows:

$$c_{HP}(n) = \begin{cases} 1 - \dfrac{\omega_c}{\pi}; & n = 0 \\[2mm] -\dfrac{\sin(\omega_c n)}{\pi n}; & |n| > 0 \end{cases} \qquad (5.34)$$

$$c_{BP}(n) = \begin{cases} \dfrac{\omega_{c2} - \omega_{c1}}{\pi}; & n = 0 \\[2mm] \dfrac{1}{\pi n}[\sin(\omega_{c2}n) - \sin(\omega_{c1}n)]; & |n| > 0 \end{cases} \qquad (5.35)$$

$$c_{BS}(n) = \begin{cases} 1 - \dfrac{(\omega_{c2} - \omega_{c1})}{\pi}; & n = 0 \\[2mm] \dfrac{1}{\pi n}[\sin(\omega_{c1}n) - \sin(\omega_{c2}n)]; & |n| > 0 \end{cases} \qquad (5.36)$$

Continuing with the design of the lowpass filter, we choose the finite series $\sum_{n=-M}^{n=M} c_{LP}(n)e^{-jn\omega} = H_M(e^{j\omega})$, which contains $(2M+1)$ coefficients from $-M$ to M, as an approximation to the infinite series $\sum_{n=-\infty}^{n=\infty} c_{LP}(n)e^{-jn\omega}$. In other words, we approximate the ideal frequency response that exactly matches the given $H_{LP}(e^{j\omega})$ containing the infinite number of coefficients by $H_M(e^{j\omega})$, which contains a finite number of coefficients. As M increases, the finite series of $H_M(e^{j\omega})$ approximates the ideal response $H_{LP}(e^{j\omega})$ in the least mean-squares sense; that is, the error defined as

$$J(c, \omega) = \frac{1}{2\pi} \int_{-\pi}^{\pi} \left| H_M(e^{j\omega}) - H_{LP}(e^{j\omega}) \right|^2 d\omega \tag{5.37}$$

$$= \frac{1}{2\pi} \int_{-\pi}^{\pi} \left| \sum_{n=-M}^{n=M} \left(\frac{\sin(\omega_c n)}{\pi n} \right) e^{-jn\omega} - H_{LP}(e^{j\omega}) \right|^2 d\omega$$

attains a minimum at all frequencies, except at points of discontinuity.

We can make the error shown above as small as we like by choosing M as large as we wish. As M increases, the number of ripples in the passband (and the stopband) increases while the width between the frequencies at which the maximum error occurs in the passband ($0 \leq \omega \leq \omega_c$) and in the stopband ($\omega_c \leq \omega \leq \pi$) decreases. In other words, as M increases, the maximum deviation from the ideal value decreases except near the point of discontinuity, where the error remains the same, however large the value of M we choose! The maximum error or the overshoot from the ideal passband value or the stopband value is 11% of the difference between the ideal passband value that is normalized to 1 and the stopband value as shown in Figure 5.6. The magnitude response $\left| H_M(e^{j\omega}) \right|$ is plotted for two different values of M in Figure 5.6, where $H_{id}(\omega)$ is the ideal magnitude response of the lowpass filter as shown in Figure 5.5a.

5.3.1 Gibbs Phenomenon

These are some of the features of what is known as the "Gibbs phenomenon," which was mathematically derived by Gibbs. We explain it qualitatively as follows. The finite sequence $c(n)$; $-M \leq n \leq M$ can be considered as the result of multiplying the infinite sequence $c(n)$; $-\infty \leq n \leq \infty$ by a finite window function:

$$w_R(n) = \begin{cases} 1; & -M \leq n \leq M \\ 0; & |n| \geq M \end{cases} \tag{5.38}$$

$$\Psi(e^{j\omega}) = \sum_{n=-M}^{n=M} e^{-jn\omega} = \frac{\sin\{(2M+1)\omega/2\}}{\sin(\omega/2)} \tag{5.39}$$

So we have the product $h_w(n) = c(n) \cdot w_R(n)$, which is of finite length as shown in Figure 5.7(c). Therefore the frequency response of the product of these two

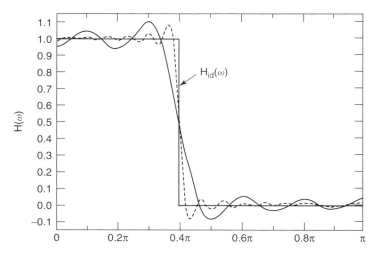

Figure 5.6   Frequency response of a lowpass filter, showing Gibbs overshoot. (Reprinted from Ref. 9, with permission from John Wiley & Sons, Inc.)

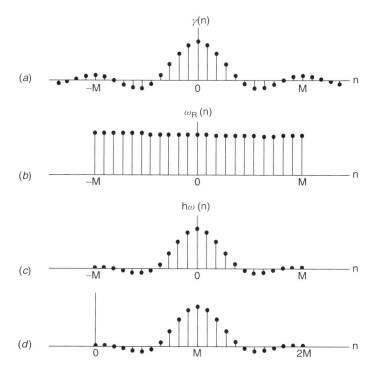

Figure 5.7   Coefficients of the FIR filter modified by a rectangular window function.

functions is obtained from the convolution of $\Psi(e^{j\omega})$ with the frequency response $H_{\mathrm{LP}}(e^{j\omega})$ of the ideal, desired, frequency response.

$$H_M(e^{j\omega}) = \frac{1}{2\pi} \int_{-\pi}^{\pi} H_{\mathrm{LP}}(e^{j\varphi})\Psi(e^{j(\omega-\varphi)})\, d\varphi \qquad (5.40)$$

The mainlobe of $\Psi(e^{j\omega})$, centered at $\omega = 0$, has a width defined by the first zero crossings on either sides of $\omega = 0$, which occur when $[(2M + 1)\frac{\omega}{2}] = \pm\pi$, that is, when $\omega = 2\pi(2M + 1)$ so that the width of the mainlobe is $4\pi/(2M + 1)$. As M increases, the width of the mainlobe and the sidelobes decreases, giving rise to more sidelobes or ripples in the same frequency band. At the same time, the peak amplitudes of the mainlobe and the sidelobes increase such that the area under each lobe remains constant. These features of $\Psi(e^{j\omega})$ directly reflect on the behavior of $H_M(e^{j\omega})$ when it is convolved with $H_{\mathrm{LP}}(e^{j\varphi})$. The effect of convolution between $H_{\mathrm{LP}}(e^{j\omega})$ and $\Psi(e^{j\omega})$ is illustrated by looking at the overlapping interval over which the product $H_{\mathrm{LP}}(e^{j\varphi})\Psi(e^{j(\omega-\varphi)})$ is integrated, for four different values of ω, in Figure 5.8. It is obvious that if the width of the mainlobe is extremely narrow, the resulting $H_M(e^{j\omega})$ will have a sharp drop at $\omega = \omega_c$. If the number of sidelobes or their peak values in $\Psi(e^{j\omega})$ increases, so also will the number of ripples and the maximum error in $H_M(e^{j\omega})$.

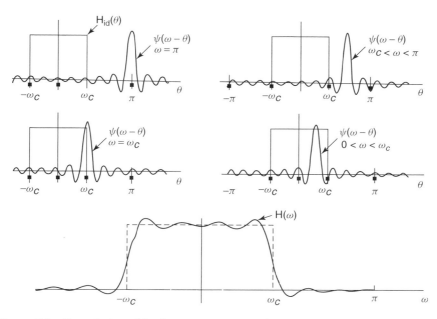

Figure 5.8 Convolution of the frequency response of a rectangular window with an ideal filter. (Reprinted from Ref. 9, with permission from John Wiley & Sons, Inc.)

5.3.2   Use of Window Functions

In order to reduce the effects of the Gibbs phenomenon, some researchers have proposed the use of tapered windows [11,12]; many others have proposed other types of window functions. Only a few of the more popular window functions are given below. Note that the number of coefficients generated by the window functions given below is $2M + 1 = N + 1$:

Bartlett window:[2]

$$w(n) = 1 - \frac{|n|}{M + 1}; \quad -M \leq n \leq M$$

Hann window:

$$w(n) = \frac{1}{2}\left[1 + \cos\left(\frac{2\pi n}{2M + 1}\right)\right]; \quad -M \leq n \leq M$$

Hamming window:

$$w(n) = 0.54 + 0.46\cos\left(\frac{2\pi n}{2M + 1}\right); \quad -M \leq n \leq M$$

Blackman window:

$$w(n) = 0.42 + 0.5\cos\left(\frac{2\pi n}{2M + 1}\right) + 0.08\cos\left(\frac{4\pi n}{2M + 1}\right); \quad -M \leq n \leq M$$

The frequency responses of the window functions listed above have different mainlobe widths $\Delta\omega_M$ and different peak magnitudes of their sidelobes. In the plot of $H_M(e^{j\omega})$ shown in Figure 5.9, it is seen that the difference between the two frequencies at which the peak error in $H_M(e^{j\omega})$ occurs is denoted as $\Delta\omega_M$. When the frequency response of the window functions is convolved with the frequency response of the desired lowpass filter, the transition bandwidth of the filter is determined by the width of the mainlobe of the window chosen and hence is different for filters modified by the different window functions. The relative sidelobe level A_{sl} is defined as the difference in decibels between the magnitudes of the mainlobe of the window function chosen and the largest sidelobe. It determines the maximum attenuation $A_s = -20\log_{10}(\delta)$ in the stopband of the filter.

In Figure 5.9 we have also shown the transition bandwidth $\Delta\omega$ and the center frequency $\omega_c = (\omega_p + \omega_c)/2$, where ω_p and ω_s are respectively the cutoff frequencies of the passband and the stopband. The value of the ripple δ does not depend on the length $(2M + 1)$ of the filter or the cutoff frequency ω_c of the

---

[2]In many textbooks, the Bartlett window is also called a *triangular window*, but in MATLAB, the Bartlett window is different from the triangular window.

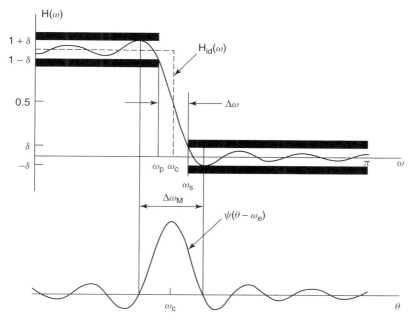

Figure 5.9   Frequency response of an ideal filter and final design. (Reprinted from Ref. 9, with permission from John Wiley & Sons, Inc.)

filter. The width of the mainlobe $\Delta\omega_M$, the transition bandwidth $\Delta\omega$, and the relative sidelobe attenuation A_{sl} for the few chosen window functions are listed in Table 5.1. The last column lists the minimum attenuation $A_s = -20\log_{10}\delta_s$ realized by the lowpass filters, using the corresponding window functions. It should be pointed out that the numbers in Table 5.1 have been obtained by simulating the performance of type I FIR filters with $\omega_c = 0.4\pi$ and $M = 128$ [1], and they would change if other types of filters and other values for ω_c and M are chosen. From Table 5.1, we see that as A_s increases, with fixed value for M, the transition bandwidth $\Delta\omega$ also increases. Since we like to have a large value for A_s and a small value for $\Delta\omega$, we have to make a tradeoff between them. The choice of the window function and the value for M are the only two freedoms that we have for controlling the transition bandwidth $\Delta\omega$, but the minimum stopband attenuation A_s depends only on the window function we choose, and not the value of M.

Two window functions that provide control over both δ_s (hence A_s) and the width of the transition bandwidth $\Delta\omega$ are the Dolph–Chebyshev window [6] and the Kaiser window functions [7], which have the additional parameters r and β, respectively. The Kaiser window is defined by

$$w(n) = \frac{I_0\left\{\beta\sqrt{1 - (n/M)^2}\right\}}{I_0\{\beta\}}; \quad -M \le n \le M \tag{5.41}$$

TABLE 5.1   Some Properties of Commonly Used Windows

Type of Window	$\Delta\omega_M$	$\Delta\omega$	A_{sl} (dB)	A_s (dB)
Rectangular	$4\pi/(2M+1)$	$0.92\pi/M$	13	20.9
Bartlett	$4\pi/(M+1)$	—[a]	26.5	—[a]
Hann	$8\pi/(2M+1)$	$3.11\pi/M$	31.5	43.9
Hamming	$8\pi/(2M+1)$	$3.32\pi/M$	42.7	54.5
Blackman	$12\pi/(2M+1)$	$5.56\pi/M$	58.1	75.3

[a]The frequency response of the Bartlett window decreases monotonically and therefore does not have sidelobes. So the transition bandwidth and sidelobe attenuation cannot be found for this window.

where $I_0\{\cdot\}$ is the modified zero-order Bessel function. It is a power series of the form

$$I_0\{x\} = 1 + \sum_{k=1}^{\infty} \left[\frac{(x/2)^k}{k!} \right]^2 \tag{5.42}$$

We compute the values of the Kaiser window function in three steps as follows:

- The parameter β required to achieve the desired attenuation $\alpha_s = -20\log_{10}(\delta_s)$ in the stopband is calculated from the following empirical formula derived by Kaiser (the ripple in the passband is nearly the same as δ_s):

$$\beta = \begin{cases} 0.1102(\alpha_s - 8.7) & \text{for } \alpha_s > 50 \\ 0.5842(\alpha_s - 21)^{0.4} + 0.07886(\alpha_s - 21) & \text{for } 21 \le \alpha_s \le 50 \\ 0 & \text{for } \alpha_s < 21 \end{cases} \tag{5.43}$$

- Next the order of the filter N (=2M) is estimated from another empirical formula derived by Kaiser:

$$N = \frac{(\alpha_s - 8)}{2.285(\Delta\omega)} \tag{5.44}$$

where $\Delta\omega = \omega_s - \omega_p$ is the transition bandwidth as shown in Figure 5.9.
- The third step is to compute $I_0\{x\}$. In practice, adding a finite number of terms, say, 20 terms of the infinite series, gives a sufficiently accurate value for $I_0\{x\}$. The parameter x in the numerator represents $\beta\sqrt{1 - (n/M)^2}$ in the numerator of (5.41), so the value of x takes different values as n changes.

5.3.3   FIR Filter Design Procedures

The steps discussed in the design procedure for linear phase FIR filters are summarized as follows:

1. Depending on the nature of the magnitude response, we choose a value for M and use (5.31), (5.34), (5.35), or (5.36) to compute the values of the coefficients $C_{LP}(n)$, $C_{HP}(n)$, $C_{BP}(n)$, or $C_{BS}(n)$ for $-M \le n \le M$. Then we choose a window function (Bartlett, Hamming, Hann, Kaiser, or other window) and compute its values $w(n)$ for $-M \le n \le M$. In the case of Kaiser's window, we find the value of $M = N/2$ from (5.44), whereas he has derived a few other empirical formulas to estimate the value of N, for designing FIR filters using other window functions.[3] Note that we have to choose the lowest even integer N greater than the value calculated from (5.44), since Kaiser's window is used for the design of type I filters only.

2. Then we multiply the coefficients $c(n)$ and $w(n)$ to get the values of $h_w(n)$. The filter with these finite numbers of coefficients has a frequency response given by $H_w(e^{j\omega}) = h_w(-M)e^{j\omega M} + h_w(-M+1)e^{j(-M+1)\omega} + \cdots + h_w(1)e^{j\omega} + h_w(0) + h_w(1)e^{-j\omega} + \cdots + h_w(M)e^{-jM\omega}$.

3. The next step is to multiply $H_w(e^{j\omega})$ by $e^{-jM\omega}$, which is equivalent to delaying the coefficients by M samples to get $h(n)$ [i.e., $h_w(n - M) = h(n)$]. By delaying the product of $c(n)$ and $w(n)$ by M samples, we have obtained a causal filter of finite length $(N + 1)$ with coefficients $h(n)$ for $0 \le n \le N$.

The procedure becomes a little better understood by considering Figure 5.7 (where a rectangular window has been used). Since $H_w(e^{j\omega})$ is a real function of ω, its magnitude does not change when we multiply it by $e^{-jM\omega}$. Now we have an FIR filter $H(z^{-1}) = \sum_{n=0}^{N} h(n)z^{-n}$, which is causal and is of length $(N + 1)$ and has the same magnitude as $|H_w(e^{j\omega})|$. Its phase response is $-M\omega$ with an additional angle of π radians when $H_w(e^{j\omega})$ attains a negative real value. Its group delay is a constant equal to M samples. This completes the general procedure for designing an FIR filter that approximates the ideal magnitude response of a lowpass FIR filter; similar procedures are used for designing highpass, bandpass, and bandstop filters. Let us illustrate this procedure by two simple examples.

---

[3]The formulas given by Kaiser may not give a robust estimate of the order for all cases of FIR filters. A more reliable estimate is given by an empirical formula [10] shown below, and that formula is used in the MATLAB function `remezord`:

$$N \cong \frac{D_\infty(\delta_p, \delta_s) - F(\delta_p, \delta_s)\left[\frac{(\omega_s - \omega_p)}{2\pi}\right]^2}{\left[\frac{(\omega_s - \omega_p)}{2\pi}\right]}$$

where $D_\infty(\delta_p, \delta_s)$ (when $\delta_p \ge \delta_s$) $= \left[a_1(\log_{10}\delta_p)^2 + a_2(\log_{10}\delta_p) + a_3\right]\log_{10}\delta_s - \left[a_4(\log_{10}\delta_p)^2 + a_5(\log_{10}\delta_p) + a_6\right]$, and $F(\delta_p, \delta_s) = b_1 + b_2\left[\log_{10}\delta_p - \log_{10}\delta_s\right]$, with $a_1 = 0.005309$, $a_2 = 0.07114$, $a_3 = -0.4761$, $a_4 = 0.00266$, $a_5 = 0.5941$, $a_6 = 0.4278$, $b_1 = 11.01217$, $b_2 = 0.51244$. When $\delta_p < \delta_s$, they are interchanged in the expression for $D_\infty(\delta_p, \delta_s)$ above.

Example 5.6

Design a bandpass filter that approximates the ideal magnitude response given in Figure 5.5(c), in which $\omega_{c2} = 0.6\pi$ and $\omega_{c1} = 0.2\pi$. Let us select a Hamming window of length $N = 11$ and plot the magnitude response of the filter.

The coefficients $c_{BP}(n)$ of the Fourier series for the magnitude response given are computed from formula (5.35) given below:

$$
c_{BP}(n) = \begin{cases} \dfrac{(\omega_{c2} - \omega_{c1})}{\pi}; & n = 0 \\[2ex] \dfrac{\sin(\omega_{c2}n)}{\pi n} - \dfrac{\sin(\omega_{c1}n)}{\pi n}; & |n| \geq 0 \end{cases}
$$

But since the Hamming window function has a length of 11, we need to compute the coefficients $c_{BP}(n)$ also, from $n = -5$ to $n = 5$ only. So also we calculate the 11 coefficients of the Hamming window, using the formula

$$
w_H(n) = 0.54 + 0.46 \cos\left(\frac{2\pi n}{N}\right); \quad -5 \leq n \leq 5
$$

Their products $h_w(n) = c_{BP}(n)w_H(n)$ are computed next. The 11 coefficients $c_{BP}(n)$, $w_H(n)$ and $h_w(n)$ for $-5 \leq n \leq 5$ are listed below. Next the coefficients $h_w(n)$ are delayed by five samples to get the coefficients of the FIR filter function [i.e., $h(n) = h_w(n-5)$], and these are also listed for $0 \leq n \leq 10$ below. The plot of the four sequences and the magnitude response of the FIR are shown in Figures 5.10 and 5.11, respectively.

$$
\begin{aligned}
c_{BP}(n) = 0.00 \quad & 0.0289 \quad -0.1633 \quad -0.2449 \quad 0.1156 \quad 0.400 \quad 0.1156 \\
& -0.2449 \quad -0.1633 \quad 0.0289 \quad 0.000
\end{aligned}
$$

$$
\begin{aligned}
w_H(n) = 0.08 \quad & 0.1679 \quad 0.0379 \quad 0.6821 \quad 0.9121 \quad 1.0 \quad 0.9121 \\
& 0.6821 \quad 0.0379 \quad 0.1679 \quad 0.0800
\end{aligned}
$$

$$
\begin{aligned}
h_w(n) = 0.00 \quad & 0.0049 \quad -0.0650 \quad -0.1671 \quad 0.1055 \quad 0.4000 \quad 0.1055 \\
& -0.1671 \quad -0.0650 \quad 0.0049 \quad 0.000
\end{aligned}
$$

$h(n)$	0.0000	0.0049	−0.0650	−0.1671	0.1055	0.4000
	0.1055	−0.1671	−0.0650	0.0049	0.0000	

Example 5.7

Design a lowpass FIR filter of length 11, with a cutoff frequency $\omega_c = 0.3\pi$. Using a Hamming window, find the value of the samples $h(3)$ and $h(9)$ of the FIR filter given by $H(z^{-1}) = \sum_{n=0}^{10} h(n)z^{-n}$.

Since the length of the FIR filter is given as 11, its order is $N = 10$. The coefficients $h_w(n)$ have to be known for $-5 \leq n \leq 5$ and delayed by five samples.

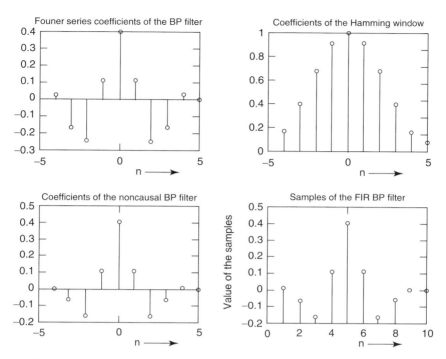

Figure 5.10 Coefficients of the filter obtained during the design procedure.

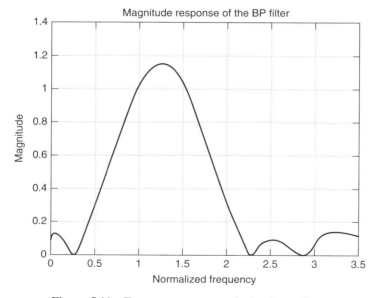

Figure 5.11 Frequency response of a bandpass filter.

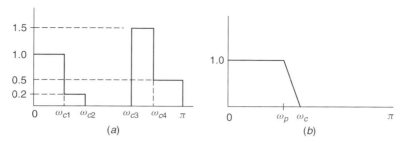

Figure 5.12 (a) Ideal magnitude response of a multilevel FIR filter; (b) Magnitude response of a lowpass filter with a spline function of zero order.

Since only $h(3)$ and $h(9)$ are asked for, by looking at Figure 5.10, we notice that these samples are the same as $h_w(-2)$ and $h_w(4)$ because when they are shifted by five samples, they become $h(3)$ and $h(9)$. So we have to calculate only $c_{LP}(-2)$, $c_{LP}(4)$ and the values $w(-2)$, $w(4)$ of the Hamming window. Then $h_w(-2) = c_{LP}(-2)w(-2)$ and $h_w(4) = c_{LP}(4)w(4)$.

If the frequency response of an FIR filter has multilevel magnitude levels, it is easy to extend the method as illustrated by Figure 5.12a. We design a lowpass filter with a cutoff frequency ω_{c1} and a maximum magnitude of 0.8, another lowpass filter with a cutoff frequency ω_{c2}, and a maximum magnitude of 0.2 in the passband; we design a highpass filter with a cutoff frequency ω_{c3} and a maximum value of 0.5 and another bandpass filter with cutoff frequencies ω_{c3} and ω_{c4} and a maximum magnitude of 1.0. If all of these filters are designed to have zero phase or the same phase response, then the sum of the four filters described above will approximate the magnitude levels over the different passbands. Each of the four filters should be designed to have very low sidelobes so that they don't spill over too much into the passbands of the adjacent filter.

Even when we design an FIR filter having a constant magnitude over one passband or one stopband, using the methods described above will produce a transition band between the ideal passband and the stopband. Instead of mitigating the Gibbs overshoot at points of discontinuity by using tapered windows, we can make a modification to the ideal piecewise, constant magnitude response to remove the discontinuities. We choose a spline function of order $p \geq 0$ between the passband and the stopband [5]. The spline function of zero order is a straight line joining the edge of the passband and the stopband as shown in Figure 5.12b The Fourier series coefficients for the lowpass frequency response in this are given by

$$h_{LP}(n) = \begin{cases} \dfrac{\omega_c}{\pi}; & n = 0 \\ \left(\dfrac{2\sin(\Delta\omega n/2)}{(\Delta\omega n)}\right)\left(\dfrac{\sin(\omega_c n)}{\pi n}\right); & |n| > 0 \end{cases} \qquad (5.45)$$

where $\Delta\omega = \omega_s - \omega_p$ and $\omega_c = [(\omega_s + \omega_p)/2]$.

A smoother transition is achieved when we choose a higher-order spline function (e.g., $p = 2,3,4$). In that case, the Fourier series coefficients are given by

$$h_{LP}(n) = \begin{cases} \dfrac{\omega_c}{\pi}; & n = 0 \\[2mm] \left(\dfrac{\sin(\Delta\omega)n/2p}{(\Delta\omega)n/2p}\right)^p \left(\dfrac{\sin(\omega_c n)}{\pi n}\right); & |n| > 0 \end{cases} \tag{5.46}$$

Design procedure using this formula seems easier than the Fourier series method using window functions—since we do not have to compute the coefficients of window functions and multiply these coefficients by those of the ideal frequency response. But it is applicable for the design of lowpass filters only. However, extensive simulation of this design procedure shows that as the bandwidth $\Delta\omega$ is decreased and as p is increased, the magnitude response of the filter exhibits ripples in the passband as well as the stopband, and it is not much better than the response we can obtain from the windowed FIR filters.

5.4 DESIGN OF WINDOWED FIR FILTERS USING MATLAB

5.4.1 Estimation of Filter Order

In the discussion of the Fourier series method, it was pointed out that we had a choice only between the windows (Bartlett, Hamming, Hann, etc.) and the order $N = 2M$ of the filter. There is no guideline for choosing the type of window or the value for N; in other words, they are chosen arbitrarily on a trial-and-error basis until the specifications are satisfied. But in the case of Kaiser and Dolph–Chebyshev windows, we have an empirical formula to estimate the order N that achieves a desired stopband attenuation α_s. However, it was pointed out earlier that some authors have derived empirical formulas for estimating the order N even when windows like those mentioned above are chosen. We use the MATLAB M-file `kaiserord` (available in the MATLAB Signal Processing Toolbox) to estimate the order N of the filter using the Kaiser window. We will, however, use the M-file `remezord` to estimate the order of the filter using the other windows. After the order of the filter has been obtained, the next step in the design procedure is to find the values of the unit impulse response $h(n)$ of the filter that are the same as the coefficients of the FIR filter transfer function. The MATLAB M-file `fir1` is used for designing filters with piecewise constant magnitudes discussed above, and `fir2` is the M-file used for arbitrary magnitude specifications. In the following examples, note that N is the order of the FIR filter that therefore has $N + 1$ coefficients but N is the number of coefficients in such MATLAB functions such as `hamming` used for computing the window functions!

Example 5.8

If the magnitude response specified in the passband of an FIR filter lies between $1 + \delta_p$ and $1 - \delta_p$, then the maximum attenuation α_p (in decibels) in the passband is $20 \log 10(1 + \delta_p) - 20 \log 10(1 - \delta_p) = 20 \log[(1 + \delta_p)/(1 - \delta_p)]$. Solving for δ_p in this case, we get

$$\delta_p = \frac{10^{0.05\alpha_p} - 1}{10^{0.05\alpha_p} + 1}$$

If the passband magnitude lies between 1 and $(1 - \delta_p)$, then the maximum attenuation in the passband $\alpha_p = -20 \log(1 - \delta_p)$, in which case δ_p is given by $(1 - 10^{-0.05\alpha_p})$. If the magnitude in the stopband lies below δ_s, the minimum attenuation in the stopband is given by $\alpha_s = -20 \log(\delta_s)$, from which we obtain $\delta_s = 10^{-0.05\alpha_s}$. These relations are used to find the value of δ_p and δ_s if the attenuations α_p and α_s in the passband and stopband are specified in decibels.

In the MATLAB function [N, fpoints, magpoints,wt] = remezord (edgepoints, bandmag, dev, Fs), the input vector edgepoints lists the edges of the disjoint bands between 0 and the Nyquist frequency but does not include the frequency at $\omega = 0$ and the Nyquist frequency, as the default value of the Nyquist frequency is 1.0 (and therefore the sampling frequency Fs=2). The vector bandmag lists the magnitudes over each of the passbands and stopbands. If there is transition band between the passband and stopband, it is considered as a "don't care" region. Since the first edge at 0 and the last one at the Nyquist frequency are not included in the vector edgepoints, the length of the vector edgepoints is two times that of bandmag minus 2. For example, let us choose a bandpass filter with a stopband [0   0.1], a transition band [0.1   0.12], a passband [0.12   0.3], a transition band [0.3   0.32], and a stopband [0.32   1.0]. The input vector edgepoints and the output vector fpoints are the same, when Fs=2, namely, [0.1   0.12   0.3   0.32]. The input vector bandmag is of length 3, and the values may be chosen, for example, as [0   1   0] for the bandpass filter. The vector dev lists the values for the maximum deviations δ_p and δ_s in the passbands and stopbands, calculated from the specifications for α_p and α_s as explained above. The output vector fpoints is the same as edgepoints when Fs has the default value of 2; if the edgepoints and the sampling frequency Fs are actual frequencies in hertz, then the output vector fpoints gives their values normalized by the actual Nyquist frequency Fs/2. But it must be pointed out that the output vector magpoints lists the magnitudes at *both* ends of the passbands and stopbands. In the above example, the vector magpoints is [0   0   1   1   0   0]. The output of this function is used as the input data to fir1 and (also the function remez, discussed later) to obtain the unit impulse response coefficients of the FIR filter.

Let us consider a lowpass filter with a passband over [0   0.3] and a magnitude 1.0 and a stopband over [0.4   1.0] with a magnitude 0.0. In this case, there is transition band between 0.3 and 0.4 over which the magnitude is not specified, and therefore it is a "don't care" region. The vector edgepoints is [0.3   0.4], and the vector bandmag is [1.0   0.0]. For the previous example of a bandpass filter, we have already mentioned that edgepoints is [0.1   0.12   0.3   0.32] and the vector bandmag is [0   1   0] . Let us select $\delta_p = \delta_s = 0.01$ for both filters, namely, a log magnitude of $\alpha_p = -20\log(1 - \delta_p) = 0.087$ dB for the ripple in the passband and a gain of -40 dB in the stopband.

The function `remezord` for estimating the order of the lowpass filter is as follows:

```
[N, fpoints, magpoints, wt] = remezord([0.3 0.4], [1.0 0.0],
   [0.01 0.01], 2)
```

and it yields a value $N = 39$, with the same vector `fpoints` as `bandmag` and the vector `wt=[1.0 1.0]`. If we choose a sampling frequency of 2000 Hz, we use `remezord([0.3 0.4], [1.0 0.0], [0.01 0.01], 2000)`, and the output would be $N = 39$, `fpoints=[0.3 0.4]`, `magpoints=[1 1 0 0]` and the vector `wt = [1.0 1.0]`. The elements in the vector `wt` will be unequal if $\delta_p \neq \delta_s$ [i.e., `wt = [(`δ_s/δ_p`) 1]]`. These output values are used as input in `fir1` (or `remez`) for the design of the lowpass filter.

The function for estimating the order of the bandpass filter is

```
[N, fpoints, magpoints, wt]=remezord([0.1 0.12 0.3 0.32],
   [0.0 1.0 0.0], [0.01 0.01 0.01], 2).
```

which gives $N = 195$, with the same vector `fpoints` as the input vector `edgepoints`, `magpoints= [0 0 1 1 0 0]`, and `wt = [1 1 1]` as in the input.

The MATLAB function `kaiserord` given below is used to estimate the order N of the FIR filter using the Kaiser window. The input parameters for this function are the same as for `remezord`, but the outputs are the approximate order N of the Kaiser window required to meet the input specifications, the normalized frequencies at the `bandedges`, the parameter `beta`, and the `filtertype`:

```
[N, Wc, Beta, ftype]=kaiserord(edgepoints, bandmag, dev, Fs)
```

For the lowpass filter specified above, we use

```
[N, Wc, Beta, ftype] =kaiserord([0.3 0.4], [1.0 0.0],
   [0.01 0.01], 2)
```

and we get `N=45`, `Wc=0.35`, `Beta=3.3953`.

For the bandpass filter, with the same input parameters as those used in `remezord`, we get the output parameters as `N=224`, `Wc=[0.11 0.31]`, `Beta=3.3953`, and `ftype=DC-0`. When `ftype=DC-0`, this means that the first band is a stopband and when it is `DC-1`, it indicates that the first band is a passband.

5.4.2 Design of the FIR Filter

After we have found the order of the filter and any other parameters as the output of the functions `remezord` and `kaiserord`, we use the function `fir1`, which takes various forms as described below:

```
b=fir1(N,Wc)
b=fir1(N,Wc,'ftype')
b=fir1(N,Wc,'ftype',window)
```

These forms give the $N + 1$ samples of the unit impulse response of the linear phase FIR filter or the coefficients of its transfer function. `Wc` is the cutoff frequency of the lowpass filter, and `ftype` is omitted; it is the cutoff of the highpass filter when `'ftype'` is typed as `'high'`. But `Wc` is a two-element vector `Wc=[W1 W2]`, which lists the two cutoff frequencies, ω_{c1} and ω_{c2} ($\omega_{c2} \geq \omega_{c1}$), of the bandpass filter. (Use `help fir1` to get details when there are multiple passbands.) The term `'ftype'` need not be typed. When `'ftype'` is typed as `'stop'`, the vector `Wc` represents the cutoff frequencies of the stopband filter.

If the filter is a lowpass, it becomes a type I filter when N as obtained from `remezord` is even and it is type II filter when N is odd. Note that the frequency response of type II filters has a zero magnitude at the Nyquist frequency, that is, their transfer function has a zero at $z = -1$ and therefore is a polynomial of odd order. The highpass and bandstop filters that do not have a zero magnitude at the Nyquist frequency cannot be realized as type II filters. When designing a highpass or bandstop filter, N must be an even integer, and the function `fir1` automatically increases the value of N by 1 to make it an even number if the output from `remezord` is an odd integer. Since the program assumes real values for the magnitude and zero value for the phase, we do not get types III and IV filters from this type of frequency specification. The window by default is the Hamming window in `fir1`, but we can choose the rectangular (boxcar), Bartlett, triangular, Hamming, Hanning, Kaiser, and Dolph–Chebyshev (`chebwin`) windows in the function `fir1`. After getting the coefficients of the FIR filter, we can find the magnitude (phase and group delay also) of the filter to verify that it meets the specifications; otherwise we may have to increase the value of N, or change the values in the vector `dev`.

Example 5.9

Now that we have obtained all the input data needed to design a LP filter with $N = 39$ and $\omega_c = 0.3$ and a BP filter with $N = 195$ and $\omega_c = [0.12 \quad 0.3]$, we design the FIR filters with the Hamming window and the Kaiser window. So we have four cases, discussed below.

The M-files for designing the four filters are given below, and the resulting magnitude responses are shown in Figures 5.13–5.17.

It must be noted from Figure 5.9 that the magnitude of the filter designed by the Fourier series method is 0.5 at ω_c, whatever the window function used to minimize the Gibbs overshoot. The order $N = 39$ for the lowpass filter, obtained from the function `remezord`, is only an estimate that is very conservative because it results in the magnitude response of the filter that does not meet the passband error $\delta_p = 0.01$ specified and used in that function. So we have to change the value for the cutoff frequency ω_c and the order N of the filter by trial and error

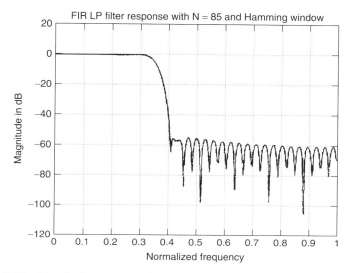

Figure 5.13 Magnitude response of a FIR lowpass filter using Hamming window.

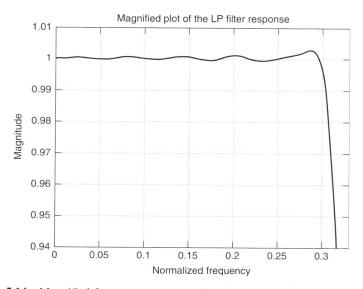

Figure 5.14 Magnified frequency response of a FIR lowpass filter in the passband.

until the specifications are met. For the lowpass FIR filter, we have had to choose $\omega_c = 0.35$ and $N = 65$ so that at the frequency $\omega = 0.3$, the error $\delta_p \leq 0.01$ and at $\omega = 0.4$, the error $\delta_s \leq 0.01$ (equal to 40 dB). The magnitude response of this final design is shown in Figures 5.13 and 5.14. Similar changes in the design of the other filters designed by the Fourier series method are necessary.

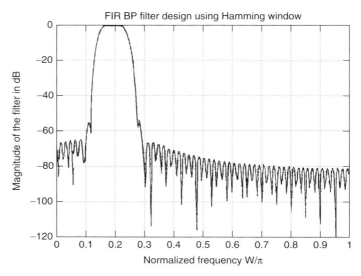

Figure 5.15 Magnitude response of a FIR bandpass filter using Hamming window.

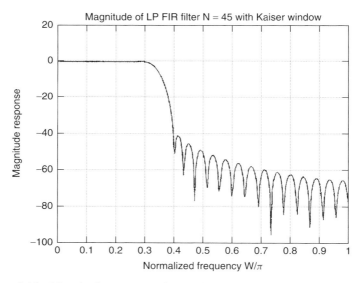

Figure 5.16 Magnitude response of a FIR lowpass filter using Kaiser window.

```
%Case 1:Design of the LP filter with N=39 and Hamming window
b1=fir1(39, 0.3);
[h1,w]=freqz(b1, 1, 256);
H1db=20*log10(abs(h));
plot(w/pi, H1db);grid
```

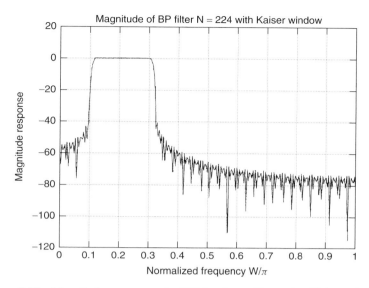

Figure 5.17 Magnitude response of a FIR bandpass filter using Kaiser window.

```
title('Magnitude response of FIR LP filter with N=39 and
  Hamming window');
ylabel('Magnitude in dB')
xlabel('Normalized frequency')

%Case 2:Design of the BP filter with N=195 and Haming window
b2=fir1(195, [0.12 0.31]);
[h2,w]=freqz(b2, 1, 256);
figure
H2db=20*log10(abs(h));
title('FIR BP filter with N=195 and Hamming window')
ylabel('Magnitude in dB')
xlabel('Normalized frequency')

%Case 3:Design of the LP Filter using the Kaiser window:
%The length of Kaiser window must be one higher than the
%  order(N=45) of the FIR filter
%obtained from the function Kaiserord
b3=fir1(45, 0.35, kaiser(46, 3.3953));
[h3,w]=freqz(b3,1,256);
H3db=20*log10(abs(h3));
plot(w/pi,H3db);
title('Magnitude of LP with N=45 and Kaiser window')
ylabel('Magnitude in dB')
xlabel('Normalized frequency').
```

```
%Case 4:Design of the BP Filter using the Kaiser window
b4=fir1(224, [0.11 0.31], kaiser(225, 3.3953));
[h4,w]=freqz(b4, 1, 256);
H4=abs(h4);
H4db=20*log10(H4);
figure
plot(w/pi,H4db);grid
title('Magnitude of BP filter N = 224 with Kaiser window')
ylabel('Magnitude in dB');
xlabel('Normalized frequency ')
```

5.5   EQUIRIPPLE LINEAR PHASE FIR FILTERS

The frequency response in the passband of FIR filters designed by using the modified Fourier series method as described above has a monotonically decreasing response and a maximum error from the desired ideal response in the passband, at the cutoff frequency ω_c. Now we discuss another important method that "spreads out" the error over the passband in an equiripple fashion, such that the maximum error is the same at several points and can be made very small. This method minimizes the maximum error in the passband and is called as the *minimax* design or the *equiripple design*. An example of the equiripple or Chebyshev response of a lowpass filter is shown in Figure 5.18.

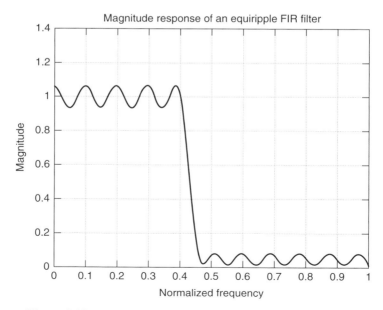

Figure 5.18   Magnitude response of an equiripple lowpass filter.

For types 1–4 FIR filters, the frequency response were shown in (5.22) to be of the following form:

$$H(e^{j\omega}) = e^{-j[(N/2)\omega]} \left\{ h\left(\frac{N}{2}\right) + 2 \sum_{n=1}^{N/2} h\left[\frac{N}{2} - n\right] \cos(n\omega) \right\}$$

$$\text{for type I} \quad (5.47)$$

$$H(e^{-j\omega}) = e^{-j[(N/2)\omega]} \left\{ 2 \sum_{n=1}^{(N+1)/2} h\left[\frac{N+1}{2} - n\right] \cos\left(\left(n - \frac{1}{2}\right)\omega\right) \right\}$$

$$\text{for type II} \quad (5.48)$$

$$H(e^{-j\omega}) = e^{-j[(N\omega-\pi)/2]} \left\{ 2 \sum_{n=1}^{N/2} h\left[\frac{N}{2} - n\right] \sin(n\omega) \right\}$$

$$\text{for type III} \quad (5.49)$$

$$H(e^{-j\omega}) = e^{-j[(N\omega-\pi)/2]} \left\{ 2 \sum_{n=1}^{(N+1)/2} h\left[\frac{N+1}{2} - n\right] \sin\left(\left(n - \frac{1}{2}\right)\omega\right) \right\}$$

$$\text{for type IV} \quad (5.50)$$

In general, Equations (5.47)–(5.50) are of the form $H(e^{j\omega}) = e^{-j(N\omega/2)} e^{j\beta} \times H_R(\omega)$, where[4] β is either 0 or $\pi/2$ depending on the type of filter, and $H_R(\omega)$ is a real function of ω, which can have positive or negative values. It is easy to see that $H_R(\omega)$ for type I filters can be reduced to the form ($2M = N$)

$$H_R(\omega) = \sum_{k=0}^{M} \tilde{a}[k] \cos(k\omega) \quad (5.51)$$

where

$$\tilde{a}[0] = h[M], \tilde{a}[k] = 2h[M - k], \quad 1 \le k \le M \quad (5.52)$$

Consider $H_R(\omega)$ for the type II filter shown in (5.48) and given below:

$$H_R(\omega) = 2 \sum_{n=1}^{(N+1)/2} h\left[\frac{N+1}{2} - n\right] \cos\left(\left(n - \frac{1}{2}\right)\omega\right)$$

This can be reduced to the form

$$H_R(\omega) = \sum_{k=1}^{(2M+1)/2} b[k] \cos\left(\left(k - \frac{1}{2}\right)\omega\right) \quad (5.53)$$

[4]This is not the same parameter β that is used in Kaiser's window.

where $b[k] = 2h\{[(2M + 1)/2] - k\}$, $1 \leq k \leq [(2M + 1)/2]$. This can be further reduced to the form

$$H_R(\omega) = \cos\left(\frac{\omega}{2}\right) \sum_{k=0}^{(2M-1)/2} \tilde{b}[k] \cos(k\omega) \qquad (5.54)$$

where

$$b[1] = \frac{1}{2}\left(\tilde{b}[1] + 2\tilde{b}[0]\right)$$

$$b[k] = \frac{1}{2}\left(\tilde{b}[k] + \tilde{b}(k - 1)\right), \qquad 2 \leq k \leq \frac{2M - 1}{2} \qquad (5.55)$$

$$b\left(\frac{2M + 1}{2}\right) = \frac{1}{2}\tilde{b}\left(\frac{2M - 1}{2}\right)$$

Let us consider the function $H_R(\omega)$ for a type III filter. Equation (5.49) can be reduced to the form

$$H_R(\omega) = \sum_{k=1}^{(2M+1)/2} c[k] \sin(k\omega) \qquad (5.56)$$

where $c[k] = 2h[M - k]$, $1 \leq k \leq M$. This can be reduced to the form

$$H_R(\omega) = \sin(\omega) \sum_{k=0}^{M-1} \tilde{c}[k] \cos(k\omega) \qquad (5.57)$$

where

$$c[1] = \left(\tilde{c}[0] - \tfrac{1}{2}\tilde{c}[1]\right)$$

$$c[k] = \tfrac{1}{2}\left(\tilde{c}[k - 1] - \tilde{c}[k]\right), \qquad 2 \leq k \leq M - 1 \qquad (5.58)$$

$$c[M] = \tfrac{1}{2}\tilde{c}[M - 1]$$

Finally we express $H_R(\omega)$ for a type IV filter as

$$H_R(\omega) = \sum_{k=1}^{(2M+1)/2} d[k] \sin\left(\left(k - \tfrac{1}{2}\right)\omega\right) \qquad (5.59)$$

where $d[k] = 2h\{[(2M + 1)/2] - k\}$, $1 \leq k \leq (2M + 1)/2$. Equation (5.59) can be reduced to the form

$$H_R(\omega) = \sin\left(\frac{\omega}{2}\right) \sum_{k=0}^{(2M-1)/2} \tilde{d}[k] \cos(k\omega) \qquad (5.60)$$

where

$$d[1] = \left(\tilde{d}[0] - \tfrac{1}{2}\tilde{d}[1]\right)$$

$$d[k] = \tfrac{1}{2}\left(\tilde{d}[k-1] - \tilde{d}[k]\right), \qquad 2 \le k \le \tfrac{2M-1}{2}$$

$$d\left[\frac{2M+1}{2}\right] = \tilde{d}\left[\frac{2M-1}{2}\right]$$

Note that we can express the coefficients $\tilde{a}[.]$, $\tilde{b}[.]$, $\tilde{c}[.]$, $\tilde{d}[.]$ in terms of $a[.]$, $b[.]$, $c[.]$, $d[.]$ since they are linearly related. We express Equations (5.51), (5.54), (5.57), and (5.60) in a common form, (5.61), in order to develop a common algorithm that obtains a minimax approximation for all four types of filters

$$H_R(\omega) = Q(\omega)P(\omega) \tag{5.61}$$

where

$$Q(\omega) = \begin{cases} 1 & \text{for type I} \\ \cos\left(\frac{\omega}{2}\right) & \text{for type II} \\ \sin(\omega) & \text{for type III} \\ \sin\left(\frac{\omega}{2}\right) & \text{for type IV} \end{cases} \tag{5.62}$$

and

$$P(\omega) = \sum_{k=0}^{K} \alpha[k]\cos(k\omega) \tag{5.63}$$

where

$$\alpha[k] = \begin{cases} \tilde{a}[k] & \text{for type I} \\ \tilde{b}[k] & \text{for type II} \\ \tilde{c}[k] & \text{for type III} \\ \tilde{d}[k] & \text{for type IV} \end{cases} \tag{5.64}$$

and

$$K = \begin{cases} M & \text{for type I} \\ \dfrac{2M-1}{2} & \text{for type II} \\ M-1 & \text{for type III} \\ \dfrac{2M-1}{2} & \text{for type IV} \end{cases} \tag{5.65}$$

We define a weighted error function

$$J(\omega) = W(e^{j\omega})\left[H_R(\omega) - H_d(e^{j\omega})\right] = W(e^{j\omega})\left[Q(\omega)P(\omega) - H_d(e^{j\omega})\right]$$

$$= W(e^{j\omega})Q(\omega)\left[P(\omega) - \frac{H_d(e^{j\omega})}{Q(e^{j\omega})}\right] \tag{5.66}$$

Using the notations $W(e^{j\omega})Q(\omega) = \tilde{W}(e^{j\omega})$ and $H_d(e^{j\omega})/Q(e^{j\omega}) = \tilde{H}_d(e^{j\omega})$, this equation is now rewritten in another form as

$$J(\omega) = \tilde{W}(e^{j\omega})\left[P(\omega) - \tilde{H}_d(e^{j\omega})\right] \tag{5.67}$$

In these equations, $H_d(e^{j\omega})$ is the desired frequency response normally specified over subintervals of $0 \leq \omega \leq \pi$ and $W(e^{j\omega})$ is a weighting function chosen by the designer to emphasize relative magnitude of the error over different subintervals. In usual filter design applications, the desired magnitude is given as

$$H_d(e^{j\omega}) = \begin{cases} 1 \pm \delta_p & \text{in the passband(s)} \\ 0 + \delta_s & \text{in the stopband(s)} \end{cases} \tag{5.68}$$

The weighting function $W(e^{j\omega})$ can be chosen as

$$W(e^{j\omega}) = \begin{cases} 1 & \text{in the passband(s)} \\ \dfrac{\delta_p}{\delta_s} & \text{in the stopband(s)} \end{cases}$$

or as

$$W(e^{j\omega}) = \begin{cases} \dfrac{\delta_s}{\delta_p} & \text{in the passband(s)} \\ 1 & \text{in the stopband(s)} \end{cases}$$

The coefficients $\alpha[k]$ in (5.67) are the unknown variables that have to be found such that the maximum absolute value of the error $|J(\omega)|$ over the subintervals of $0 \leq \omega \leq \pi$ is minimized. It has been shown [13] that when this minimum value is achieved, the frequency response exhibits an equiripple behavior:

$$\begin{array}{cc} \min & \max \\ \text{over } \{\alpha[k]\} & \text{over } \{S\} \end{array} \quad \left|\tilde{W}(e^{j\omega})\left[P(\omega) - \tilde{H}_d(e^{j\omega})\right]\right| \tag{5.69}$$

where $\{S\}$ is used to denote the union of the disjoint frequency bands in $0 \leq \omega \leq \pi$.

Once these coefficients are determined, the coefficients $h(n)$ can be obtained from the inverse relationships between $\alpha[k]$ and $a[k]$, $b[k]$, $c[k]$, and $d[k]$ depending on the type of filter and then using the relationship between $h[n]$ and these coefficients.

Parks and McClellan [2] were the original authors who solved the preceding problem of minimizing the maximum absolute value of the error function $J(\omega)$, using the theory of Chebyshev approximation, and developed an algorithm to implement it by using a scheme called the *Remez exchange* algorithm. They also published a computer program (in FORTRAN) for designing equiripple, linear phase FIR filters. Although major improvements have been made by others to this algorithm and to the software [13], it is still referred to as the *Parks–McClellan* algorithm or the *Remez exchange algorithm*. We will work out a few examples of designing such filters using the MATLAB function `remez` in the following section.

5.6   DESIGN OF EQUIRIPPLE FIR FILTERS USING MATLAB

The first step is to estimate the order of the FIR filter, using the function `reme-zord` which was explained earlier. The next step is to find the coefficients of the FIR filter using the function `remez`, which has several options:

```
b=remez(N, fpoints, magpoints)
b=remez(N, fpoints, magpoints, wt)
b=remez(N, fpoints, magpoints, 'ftype')
b=remez(N, fpoints, magpoints, wt, 'ftype')
```

The vector `fpoints` lists the edges of the passbands and stopbands, starting from $\omega = 0$ and ending with $\omega = 1$ (which is the normalized Nyquist frequency). In contrast to the function `remezord`, this vector `fpoints` includes 0 and 1.0 as the first and last entries. The edges between the passbands and the adjacent stopband must have a separation of at least 0.1; otherwise the program automatically creates a transition band of 0.1 between them, and these transition bands are considered as "don't care" regions. The vector `magpoints` lists the magnitudes in the frequency response at each edge of the passband and stopband. The weighting function can be prescribed for each frequency band as explained above. The function `remez` chooses type I filters for even-order N and type II filters for odd order as the default choice. The flags `'hilbert'` and `'differentiator'` are used for the option `ftype` for designing the Hilbert transformer and the differentiator, respectively. The other input variables are the same as the outputs obtained from `remezord`, and hence we can use the two functions `remezord` and `remez` together in one M-file to design an equiripple FIR filter with linear phase as listed and described below.

5.6.1   Use of MATLAB Program to Design Equiripple FIR Filters

Example 5.10

```
%Program to obtain the unit impulse response coefficients
%  of an equiripple, FIR filter with a linear phase
edgepoints= input('Type in the edge frequencies of
  each band =');
%Type in normalized edge frequencies between 0 and 1,
%  excluding 0 and 1, when Fs=2
%or actual frequencies in Hz and choose FT also in Hz
Fs= input('Sampling frequency in Hz =')
%The bandmag is the magnitude in each band from 0 to 1
bandmag =input('Type in the magnitude values for each
  passband and stopband =');
% There must be one value in dev and in wt for each band
dev=input('Desired ripple in each band =');
wt=input('Type in values for the relative weights in each
```

```
  band=');
[N, fpoints, magpoints, wt]=remezord(edgepoints, bandmag,
  dev, Fs);
disp('Order of the FIR filter is');disp(N);
b=remez(N, fpoints, magpoints, wt);
[h, w]=freqz(b, 1, 256);
H=abs(h);
Hdb=20*log10(H);
plot(w/pi,Hdb);grid
title('Magnitude response of the equiripple, linear phase
  FIR filter')
ylabel('Magnitude in dB')
xlabel('Normalized frequency')
```

This program can be used to design lowpass, highpass, bandpass, and bandstop filters. If the filter does not meet the given specification, one should increase the order of the filter by 1, 2, or 3 until the specifications in the passbands and stopbands are met. But when the cutoff frequencies are very close to 0 or 1, and when we are designing highpass and stopband filters, the value of N estimated by remezord may not be acceptable, and we may have to choose it arbitrarily to meet the given specifications. If one is interested in getting an enlarged view of the magnitude response over a frequency range such as the passband, then the following lines may be added to the program listed above. In the function axis, choose wc1 = 0 and wc2 = passband edge frequency for the lowpass filter and wc1 and wc2 as the lower and upper cutoff frequencies of the passband of a bandpass filter or the stopband of a bandstop filter:

```
%Add the following lines to get an enlarged view of the
%   magnitude response
figure
wc1=input('Type in the lower cutoff frequency =')
wc2=input('Type in the upper cutoff frequency=')
plot(w/pi,Hdb);Grid
axis([wc1 wc2 -0.5 0.5]);
title('Enlarged plot of the magnitude response')
ylabel('Magnitude in dB')
xlabel('Normalized frequency')
```

Example 5.11

Let us work a few examples using the program displayed above for designing lowpass and bandpass equiripple filters with the same specifications as the earlier ones. We type in the following input data for designing an equiripple lowpass filter:

```
edgepoints:[0.3 0.4]
```

```
bandmag    : [1 0]
dev        : [0.01 0.01]
wt         : [1 1]
```

The frequency response of the lowpass filter is shown in Figure 5.19, and a magnified view of the response in the passband is shown in Figure 5.20. It is seen that the deviation in the passband is within 0.087 dB, which is equivalent to $\delta_p = 0.01$ in the passband, but the magnitude in the stopband is not equal to or less than -40 dB, corresponding to $\delta_s = 0.01$.

Therefore we increase the value of N from 39 to 41 and show the resulting filter response displayed in Figure 5.21, which does meet the stopband magnitude required.

Next we design an equiripple bandpass filter meeting the same specifications as those that used the Hamming window and the Kaiser window. The input parameter values are the following:

```
edgepoints    : [0.1 0.12 0.3 0.32]
bandmag       : [0 1 0]
dev           : [0.01 0.01 0.01]
wt            : [1 1 1]
```

The magnitude response of the equiripple filter is shown in Figure 5.22.

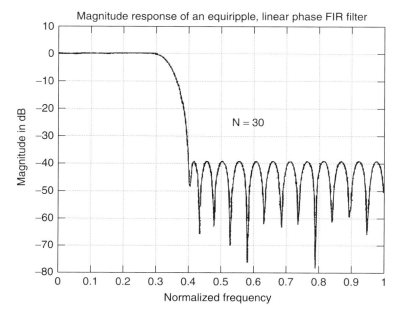

Figure 5.19   Magnitude response of an equiripple FIR lowpass filter with $N = 39$.

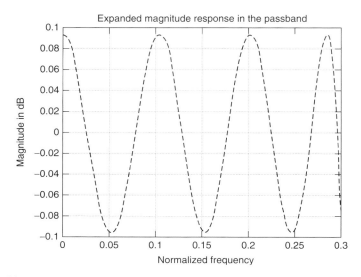

Figure 5.20   Magnified plot of the passband response of an equiripple FIR lowpass filter.

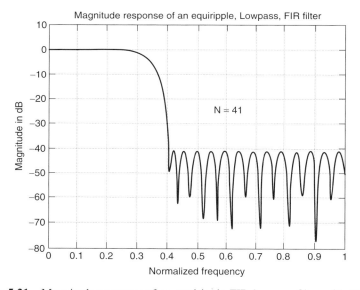

Figure 5.21   Magnitude response of an equiripple FIR lowpass filter with $N = 41$.

When we design an equiripple bandstop filter with the same vector edgepoints as in the preceding bandstop filter, we get a response that does not meet the desired specifications even after the order of the FIR filter is increased from 195 to 205. Also, the design of a highpass filter using the Remez algorithm is not always successful. In Section 5.7, an alternative approach to solve such problems is suggested.

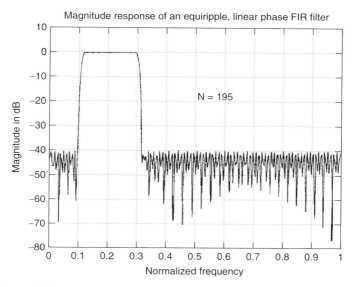

Figure 5.22 Magnitude response of an equiripple FIR bandpass filter.

It should also be remembered that the Remez algorithm is restricted to filters of order greater than 3. It is interesting to note that the bandpass filter of order 195, using the Fourier series and the Hamming window achieves a higher stopband attenuation than does a bandpass filter of the same length, using the Remez algorithm.

5.7 FREQUENCY SAMPLING METHOD

In the methods considered above for the design of linear phase FIR filters, the magnitude response was specified as constant over disjoint bands, and the transition bands were "don't care" regions. In this section, we discuss briefly the MATLAB function `fir2` that designs a linear phase filter with multistage magnitudes

```
b=fir2(N, F, M)
b=fir2(N, F, M, window)
b=fir2(N, F, M, window, npt)
```

and so on. As input parameters for this function, `N` is the order of the filter and `F` is the vector of frequencies between 0 and 1 at which the magnitudes are specified. In the vector `F`, we include the end frequencies 0 and 1 and list the magnitudes at these frequencies in the vector `M`, so the lengths of `F` and `M` are the same. The argument `npt` is the number of gridpoints equally spaced between 0 and 1; the default value is 512. Frequencies at the edge of adjacent bands can be included and will appear twice in the vector `F` indicating a jump discontinuity.

The output of this function is the $N + 1$ coefficients of the unit impulse response of the FIR filter with linear phase.

Example 5.12

```
%Program to design an FIR fiter using fir2
F =[0 0.25 0.25 0.5 0.65 0.75 0.9 1.0];
M = [0 1 0.5 0.5 0 0 0.3 0.3];
b=fir2(128, F, M);
[h,w]=freqz(b, 1, 256);
H=abs(h);
plot(w/pi,H);Grid;
title(''Multistage Magnitude Response of an FIR linear
  phase filter')
ylabel('Magnitude')
xlabel('Normalized frequency')
%end
```

The magnitude response of this filter is shown in Figure 5.23.

The function `fir2` utilizes the relationship between the DFT and IDFT of an FIR filter. Note that we prescribed the magnitude of the filter response over the frequency range $0-1.0$ and the function assumes that the samples of the DFT are symmetric about the Nyquist frequency and extrapolates the samples up to the sampling frequency before finding the inverse DFT. We also prescribe zero value for the phase, and therefore the function is restricted to types I and II FIR

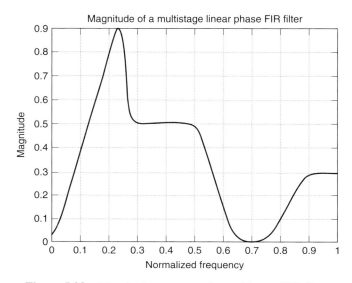

Figure 5.23 Magnitude response of a multistage FIR filter.

filters only. To design FIR filters with linear phase in general, let us first review the following results for the DTFT of a digital filter

$$H(e^{j\omega}) = H^*(e^{-j\omega}) = \left|H(e^{j\omega})\right| e^{-j(M\omega - \beta)} \; \lfloor\rfloor$$

where $M = (N-1)/2$ and $\beta = 0$ for types I and II filters and $M = (N-1)/2$ and $\beta = \pm(\pi/2)$ for types III and IV filters.

Next, be aware that in the notation commonly used for the DFT-IDFT pair, N is the length of the FIR filter or the number of unit impulse response coefficients $h(n)$ and is also equal to the number of DFT samples $H(k)$ as shown in the following relationships:

$$H(k) = H(e^{j(2\pi/N)k}) = \sum_{n=0}^{N-1} h(n)e^{-j(2\pi/N)kn} \tag{5.70}$$

$$= \left|H(e^{j(2\pi/N)k})\right| e^{-j[M(2\pi/N)k - \beta]} \qquad \text{for } k = 0, 1, 2, \ldots, (N-1)$$

$$h(n) = \frac{1}{N} \sum_{k=0}^{N-1} H(k)e^{j(2\pi/N)nk} \qquad \text{for } n = 0 \ldots (N-1) \tag{5.71}$$

For an FIR filters with linear phase, $h(n) = \pm h(N-1-n)$, $n = 0, 1, 2, \ldots, (N-1)$, where the plus sign is used for types I and II linear phase filters and the minus sign is used for types III and IV linear phase filters.

The DFT $H(k)$ must satisfy the following conditions:

$$H(k) = \begin{cases} H(0) & \text{for } k = 0 \\ H(N-k) & \text{for } k = 1, 2, \ldots, (N-1) \end{cases}$$

$$\angle H(k) = \begin{cases} -\left(\dfrac{N-1}{2}\right)\left(\dfrac{2\pi k}{N}\right) & \text{for } k = 0, 1, \ldots, \left\lfloor \dfrac{N-1}{2} \right\rfloor \\ & \text{and types I and II filters} \\[2ex] +\left(\dfrac{N-1}{2}\right)\left(\dfrac{2\pi(N-k)}{N}\right) & \text{for } k = \left\lfloor \dfrac{N-1}{2} \right\rfloor \\ & +1, \ldots (N-1) \\ & \text{and types I and II filters} \end{cases}$$

$$= \begin{cases} \left(\pm\dfrac{\pi}{2}\right) - \left(\dfrac{N-1}{2}\right)\left(\dfrac{2\pi k}{N}\right) & \text{for } k = 0, 1, \ldots, \\ & \left\lfloor \dfrac{N-1}{2} \right\rfloor \\ & \text{and types III and IV filters} \\[2ex] -\left(\pm\dfrac{\pi}{2}\right) + \left(\dfrac{N-1}{2}\right)\left(\dfrac{2\pi(N-k)}{N}\right) & \text{for } k = \left\lfloor \dfrac{N-1}{2} \right\rfloor \\ & +1, \ldots, (N-1) \text{ and} \\ & \text{types III and IV filters} \end{cases}$$

These relationships provide us with a general method for finding the unit sample response of an FIR filter with linear phase, from the values of the DFT samples that are the values of $\left|H(e^{j\omega})\right|e^{-j(M\omega-\beta)}$ at the discrete frequencies $\omega_k = (2\pi/N)k$. Therefore we can prescribe both magnitude and phase over the entire frequency range, including the transition bands of the filter. The method followed to find the unit sample response coefficients $h(n)$ is completely numerical, and we know that the efficient FFT techniques are used to compute the DFT and IDFT samples. We have already used the MATLAB functions `fft` and `ifft` that compute the DFT and IDFT, respectively, in Chapter 3, and the function `fir2` simply implements IDFT of $H(k)$ specified by the input vectors `F` and `M` in the function `fir2`.

5.8 SUMMARY

In this chapter, we discussed the design theory of FIR filters with linear phase and a magnitude response that approximate the magnitudes of ideal LP, HP, BP, and BS filters as well as some filters that have magnitude specifications that are smooth but not necessarily piecewise constant. We also described a few very efficient and well-known MATLAB functions that obtain very good results in designing these filters. But there are cases when these functions (and a few others not included in this chapter) may not work satisfactorily. Students are encouraged to work extensively these MATLAB functions with a variety of specifications and input arguments and build their experience and insight about the relative merits and advantages of the various methods and the MATLAB functions. It was pointed out that the function `remez` does not work very efficiently in designing highpass and bandstop filters. We suggest below an alternative approach to solve this problem. However, the three transformations given below [1] are more general and useful in transforming the magnitude response of a type I filter into that of a wide variety of other magnitude response characteristics.

Consider a type I filter $H(z) = \sum_{n=0}^{2M} h(n)z^{-n}$, $h(2M - n) = h(n)$ that has a passband frequency ω_p and stopband frequency ω_s. Its zero phase frequency response is $H_R(\omega) = h(M) + \sum_{n=1}^{M} 2h(M - n)\cos(n\omega)$. We can obtain three new classes of type I filters that have the following transfer functions:

$$G(z) = \begin{cases} z^{-M} - H(z) & \text{transformation A} \\ (-1)^M H(-z) & \text{transformation B} \\ z^{-M} - (-1)^M H(-z) & \text{transformation C} \end{cases}$$

The corresponding frequency response of these filters is given by

$$G(\omega) = \begin{cases} 1 - H(\omega) & \text{transformation A} \\ H(\pi - \omega) & \text{transformation B} \\ 1 - H(\pi - \omega) & \text{transformation C} \end{cases}$$

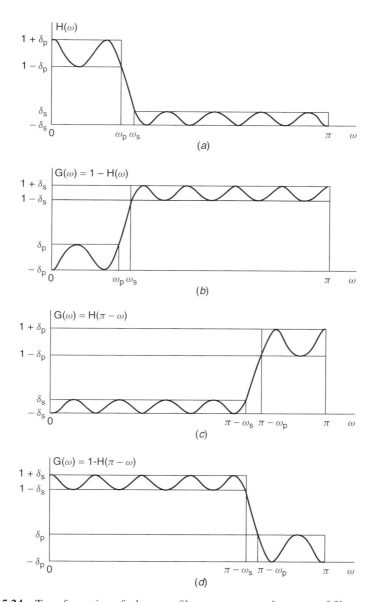

Figure 5.24   Transformation of a lowpass filter response to other types of filter responses.

The responses of these filters are plotted in Figure 5.24. We notice that transformation A transforms a type I, lowpass filter with a passband (cutoff) frequency ω_p and a stopband frequency ω_s, into a highpass filter with the cutoff frequency of ω_s and a stopband frequency ω_p, whereas transformation B transforms the lowpass filter response into a highpass filter with a cutoff frequency $(\pi - \omega_p)$ and a stopband frequency $(\pi - \omega_s)$.

To design an equiripple highpass FIR filter, with passband and stopband cutoff frequencies $\overline{\omega}_p$ and $\overline{\omega}_s$, respectively, we first design a lowpass type I equiripple FIR filter with a passband frequency $\omega_p = \pi - \overline{\omega}_p$ and a stopband frequency $\omega_s = \pi - \overline{\omega}_s$. Let its transfer function be $H(z) = \sum_{n=0}^{2M} h(n)z^{-n}$. Then, using the transformation $G(z) = (-1)^M H(-z)$, we get the transfer function of the highpass filter as $G(z) = \sum_{n=0}^{2M} \left[(-1)^{M+n}h(n)\right] z^{-n}$. Transformation C transforms the type I lowpass filter into another lowpass filter with a cutoff frequency $(\pi - \omega_s)$ and a stopband frequency $(\pi - \omega_p)$. These transformations provide us with additional tools to design filters in the event that any one method fails to give the right results.

PROBLEMS

5.1   Derive the function for the frequency response in the form $e^{j\theta}\{H_R(\omega)\}$ for the FIR filters $H(z^{-1})$ given below. Identify the type of filters also:

$$H_1(z^{-1}) = 1 + 0.6z^{-1} + 0.2z^{-2} + 0.4z^{-3} + 0.2z^{-4} + 0.6z^{-5} + z^{-6}$$

$$H_2(z^{-1}) = 1.2 + 0.1z^{-1} + 0.9z^{-2} + z^{-3} - z^{-4} - 0.9z^{-5}$$
$$- 0.1z^{-6} - 1.2z^{-7}$$

$$H_3(z^{-1}) = 1 + z^{-1} + z^{-2} - z^{-3} - z^{-4} - z^{-5}$$

$$H_4(z^{-1}) = 1 + z^{-3} + z^{-6}$$

$$H_5(z^{-1}) = 0.4z^{-1} - 0.6z^{-2} + 1.4z^{-3} + 0.6z^{-4} - 0.4z^{-5}$$

5.2   Given that a polynomial $P_1(z^{-1}) = 1 - 2.5z^{-1} + 5.25z^{-2} - 2.5z^{-3} + z^{-4}$ has a zero at $z = 1 + j\sqrt{3}$, find the other zeros of $P_1(z^{-1})$.

5.3   The polynomial $P_2(z^{-1}) = 1.0 - 1.5z^{-1} + 2.75z^{-2} + 2.75z^{-3} - 1.5z^{-4} + z^{-5}$ has zero at $z = 0.25 - j0.433$. Find the other zeros of $P_2(z^{-1})$.

5.4   The polynomial $P_3(z^{-1}) = 1 + 3.25z^{-2} - 3.25z^{-4} - z^{-6}$ has zero at $z = 0.5e^{j1.5\pi}$. Find the other zeros of $P_3(z^{-1})$.

5.5   Find the polynomial $N(z^{-1})$ that is the mirror image of the polynomial $D(z^{-1}) = 1 + 0.2z^{-1} - 0.5z^{-2} + 0.04z^{-3}$. Show that the magnitude of $H(e^{-j\omega}) = N(e^{-j\omega})/D(e^{-j\omega})$ is a constant for all frequencies.

5.6   Find the polynomial $N(z^{-1})$ that is the anti-mirror image of the polynomial $D(z^{-1}) = 1 + 0.32z^{-1} + 0.6z^{-2} - 0.4z^{-3} + 0.1z^{-4}$. Show that the magnitude of $H(e^{-j\omega}) = N(e^{-j\omega})/D(e^{-j\omega})$ is a constant for all frequencies.

5.7 The passband of a lowpass FIR filter lies between 1.04 and 0.96, and its stopband lies below 0.0016. Find the value of the passband attenuation α_p and the stopband attenuation α_s.

5.8 The passband of a lowpass FIR filter lies between 1.15 and 0.9, and its stopband lies below 0.0025. Find the value of the passband attenuation α_p and the stopband attenuation α_s.

5.9 The passband of a lowpass FIR filter lies between $1 + \delta_p$ and $1 - \delta_p$, and its stopband lies below δ_s. If the passband attenuation is 0.15 dB and the stopband attenuation is 45 dB, what are the values of δ_p and δ_s?

5.10 The passband of a lowpass FIR filter lies between $1 + \delta_p$ and $1 - \delta_p$, and its stopband lies below δ_s. If the passband attenuation is 0.85 dB and the stopband attenuation is 85 dB, what are the values of δ_p and δ_s?

5.11 Design a lowpass FIR filter of length of 15, with $\omega_c = 0.6\pi$, using the Fourier series method; truncate it with a Hann window, and delay the samples by seven samples to get the transfer function of the causal filter.

5.12 In designing an FIR BP filter with $\omega_{c2} = 0.5\pi$ and $\omega_{c1} = 0.1\pi$, using the Fourier series method and a rectangular window of length 9, what are the values of $h(3)$ and $h(9)$ in the transfer function of the causal FIR filter?

5.13 In designing a bandpass FIR filter $H(z^{-1}) = \sum_{n=0}^{10} h(n)z^{-n}$, using the Fourier series method and a Bartlett window in order to approximate the magnitude response of the filter with $\omega_{c2} = 5\pi/6$ and $\omega_{c1} = \pi/2$, what are the values of the samples $h(3)$ and $h(7)$?

5.14 An FIR bandpass filter has cutoff frequencies at 0.25π and 0.5π. Find the coefficients $h(3)$ and $h(6)$ of its transfer function $H(z^{-1}) = \sum_{n=0}^{10} h(n)z^{-n}$, assuming that it is designed using the Fourier series method and a Blackman window.

5.15 Design an FIR filter of length 9, to get a highpass response, with $\omega_c = 0.4\pi$, using a Hamming window.

5.16 The coefficients of the Fourier series for the frequency response of the differentiator are given by

$$c(n) = \begin{cases} 0 & \text{for } n = 0 \\ \dfrac{\cos(\pi n)}{n} & \text{for } |n| > 0 \end{cases}$$

Using a Hann window of length 9, find the value of the coefficient $h(6)$ of the causal FIR filter that approximates the magnitude response of the differentiator.

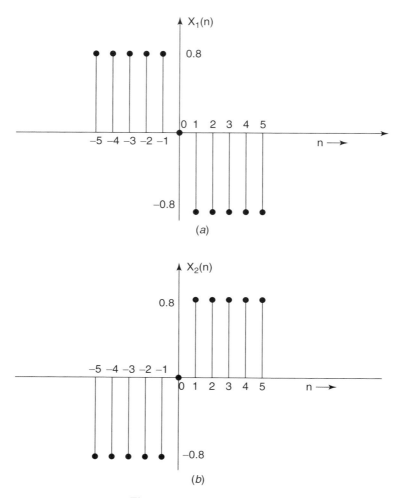

Figure 5.25   Problem 5.18.

5.17   The coefficients of the Fourier series for the frequency response of a digital filter are $c(n) = (0.5)^{|n|}$; $-\infty < n < \infty$. A window function $w(n) = (-1)^n$, for $-7 \le n \le 7$, is applied to this sequence, and the product is delayed by seven samples to get a causal sequence $h(n)$. What is the value of the fourth and eighth samples of $h(n)$?

5.18   Let $x_1(n)$ be a window of length 11 shown in Figure 5.25a and $y_1(n) = x_1(n) * x_1(n)$. Plot the function $y_1(n)$ and derive its frequency response $Y_1(e^{j\omega})$.

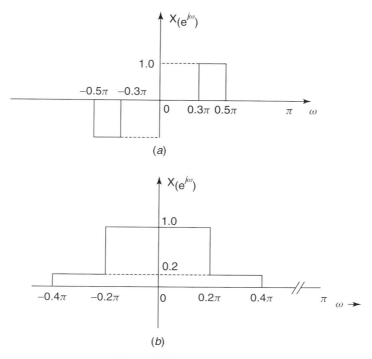

Figure 5.26   Problem 5.23.

5.19   Find the convolution sum $y_2(n) = x_2(n) * x_2(n)$ where $x_2(n)$ is as shown in Figure 5.25b. Plot $y_2(n)$ and derive its frequency response (DTFT) $Y_2(e^{j\omega})$.

5.20   What is the frequency response of the filter attained by cascading the two filters described by Figure 5.27a,b?

5.21   Plot the spectrum of the product $y(n) = x_1(n)x_2(n)$ where $x_1(n) = 10\cos(0.5\pi n)$ and $x_2(n) = \cos(0.25\pi n)$.

5.22   If the signal $y(n)$ given in Problem 5.21 is the input to the filter shown in Figure 5.27b what is the output signal?

5.23   Derive the expressions for the Fourier series coefficients (for $-\infty < n < \infty$) for the DTFT of an LTI DT system as shown in Figure 5.26a,b.

5.24   Derive the expressions for the Fourier series coefficients for $-\infty < n < \infty$ for the frequency response of the LTI-DT system as shown in Figure 5.27a,b, respectively.

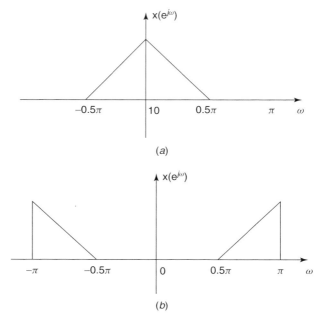

Figure 5.27 Problem 5.25.

5.25 Design an HP, FIR filter of length 21 and $\omega_c = 0.4\pi$, using a Hann window. Plot its magnitude response using the MATLAB function `fft`.

5.26 Derive the expressions for the Fourier series coefficients (for $-\infty < n < \infty$) for the DTFT of an LTI-DT system as shown in Figure 5.28a,b.

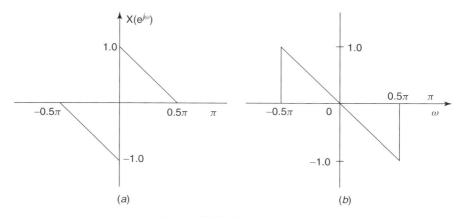

Figure 5.28 Problem 5.26.

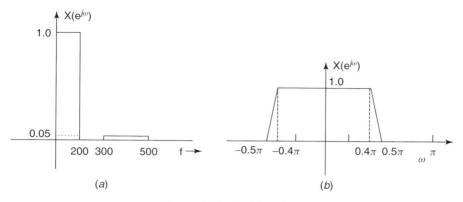

Figure 5.29   Problem 5.27.

5.27   Find the Fourier series coefficients for the frequency response of the low-pass digital filter as shown in Figure 5.29a, in which the Nyquist frequency is 500 Hz.

5.28   Find the Fourier series coefficients for $-5 < n < 5$ for the frequency response of the lowpass filter shown in Figure 5.29b.

5.29   Find the coefficients of the unit impulse response for $0 \leq n \leq 64$, using the MATLAB function `fir2` after sampling the frequency response of the lowpass filter shown in Figure 5.29b. Compare the result with that obtained in Problem 5.28.

MATLAB Problems

5.30   Design a lowpass FIR filter of length 21, with $\omega_p = 0.2\pi$ and $\omega_s = 0.5\pi$, using the spline function of order $p = 2, 4$ for the transition band. Plot the magnitude response of these filters on the same plot. Compare their characteristics.

5.31   Design a lowpass FIR filter of length 41 with $\omega_p = 0.3\pi$ and $\omega_s = 0.5\pi$, using the spline function of order $p = 2, 4$ for the transition band. Show the magnitude responses of these filters on the same plot. Compare their characteristics.

5.32   Design a lowpass FIR filter of length 41 with $\omega_p = 0.4\pi$ and $\omega_s = 0.5\pi$, using the spline function of order $p = 2, 4$ for the transition band. Give the magnitude responses of these filters on the same plot. Compare their characteristics.

5.33   Design a lowpass FIR filter with a passband cutoff frequency $\omega_c = 0.25\pi$ and a magnitude of 2 dB, a stopband frequency $\omega_s = 0.4\pi$, and a magnitude of 0.02. Use a Hamming window and a Hann window. Plot the magnitude response to verify that the specifications are met.

5.34   Design a highpass FIR filter with a passband cutoff frequency $\omega_c = 0.45\pi$ and a magnitude of 2 dB, a stopband frequency $\omega_s = 0.2\pi$, and a magnitude of 0.02. Use a Hamming window and a Kaiser window of length 50. Plot the magnitude response to verify that the specifications are met.

5.35   Design a bandpass FIR filter with the passband between $\omega_{c1} = 0.4\pi$ and $\omega_{c2} = 0.6\pi$ with a magnitude of 2.5. Use a Kaiser window. Plot the magnitude response of the filter.

5.36   Design a bandpass FIR filter with a passband between $f_{c1} = 5$ kHz and $f_{c2} = 6.5$ kHz with a magnitude of 2.5, and two stopbands with frequencies at $f_{s1} = 4.5$ kHz and $f_{s2} = 7$ kHz with a magnitude below 0.025. The sampling frequency is 20 kHz. Use a Kaiser window. Plot the magnitude response of the filter to verify that the specifications are met.

5.37   Design a bandstop FIR filter with a stopband between $\omega_{s1} = 0.35\pi$ and $\omega_{s2} = 0.65\pi$ with a magnitude of 0.05, and two passband frequencies at $\omega_{p1} = 0.2\pi$ and $\omega_{p2} = 0.8\pi$ with magnitudes above 0.95. Use a Kaiser window. Plot the magnitude response of the filter.

5.38   Design an equiripple, lowpass FIR filter with a passband cutoff frequency $\omega_c = 0.25\pi$ and $\delta_p = 0.05$, a stopband frequency $\omega_s = 0.4\pi$, and a magnitude below 0.01. Plot the magnitude and verify that the specifications are met.

5.39   Using the results obtained in Problem 5.38 and the frequency transformation B described in the main text at the end of this chapter, design an equiripple highpass FIR filter. Plot its magnitude response.

5.40   Using the results for the lowpass FIR filter obtained above, and the frequency transformation C described at the end of this chapter, design an equiripple lowpass FIR filter. Plot its magnitude response.

5.41   Design an equiripple highpass FIR filter with a passband cut-off frequency $\omega_c = 0.45\pi$ and a $\alpha_p = 0.15$ dB, a stopband frequency $\omega_s = 0.2\pi$, and a magnitude below 0.025.

5.42   Design an equiripple bandpass FIR filter with the passband between $\omega_{c1} = 0.4\pi$ and $\omega_{c2} = 0.6\pi$ with a magnitude between 1.02 and 0.8. Its stopbands have stopband frequencies at $\omega_{s1} = 0.2\pi$ and $\omega_{s2} = 0.8\pi$ with a magnitude below 0.005. Plot its magnitude to verify that the specifications are met.

5.43 Design a bandpass FIR filter with a passband between $f_{c1} = 6$ kHz and $f_{c2} = 7$ kHz with $\alpha_p = 0.2$ dB, and two stopbands with stopband frequencies at $f_{s1} = 4$ kHz and $f_{s2} = 9$ kHz with $\alpha_s = 35$ dB. The sampling frequency is 20 kHz. Plot the magnitude response to verify that the specifications are met.

REFERENCES

1. T. Saramaki, Finite impulse response filter design, in *Handbook for Digital Signal Processing*, S. K. Mitra and J. F. Kaiser, eds., Wiley-Interscience, New York, 1993, Chapter 4, pp. 155–278.
2. T. W. Parks and J. H. McClellan, Chebyshev approximation of nonrecursive digital filters with linear phase, *IEEE Trans. Circuit Theory* **CT-19**, 189–194 (1972).
3. G. C. Temes and D. Y. F. Zai, Least p^{th} approximation, *IEEE Trans. Circuit Theory* **CT-16**, 235–237 (1969).
4. L. R. Rabiner and B. Gold, *Theory and Application of Digital Signal Processing*, Prentice-Hall, 1975.
5. T. W. Parks and C. S. Burrus, *Digital Filter Design*, Wiley-Interscience, New York, 1987.
6. H. D. Helms, Nonrecursive digital filters: Design method for achieving specifications on frequency response, *IEEE Trans. Audio Electroacoust.* **AU-16**, 336–342 (Sept. 1968).
7. J. F. Kaiser, Nonrecursive digital filter design using the I_0-sinh window function, *Proc. 1974 IEEE Int. Symp. Circuits and Systems*, April 1974, pp. 20–23.
8. S. K. Mitra, *Digital Signal Processing—A Computer-Based Approach*, McGraw-Hill, New York, 2001.
9. S. K. Mitra and J. F. Kaiser, eds., *Handbook for Digital Signal Processing*, Wiley-Interscience, 1993.
10. O. Herrmann, L. R. Rabiner and D. S. K. Chan, "Practical design rules for optimum finite impulse response lowpass digital filters", *Bell System Tech. Journal*, vol. 52, pp. 769–799, 1973.
11. F. J. Harris, "On the use of windows for harmonic analysis with discrete Fourier transform", *Proc. IEEE*, 66, pp. 51–83, 1978.
12. J. K. Gautam, A. Kumar, and R. Saxena, "Windows: A tool in signal processing", *IETE Technical Review*, vol. 12, pp. 217–226, 1995.
13. Andreas Antoniou, *Digital Filters: Analysis, Design and Applications*, McGraw Hill, 1993.
14. Andreas Antoniou, "New improved method for the design of weighted-Chebyshev, non-recursive, digital filters", *IEEE Trans. on Circuits and Systems*, CAS-30, pp. 740–750, 1983.
15. R. W. Hamming, *Digital Filters*, Prentice-Hall, 1977.

16. J. H. McClellan and T. W. Parks, "A unified approach to the design of optimum FIR linear phase digital filters" *IEEE Trans. on Circuit Theory*, CT-20, pp. 697–701, 1973.

17. A. V. Oppenheim and R. W. Schafer, *Discrete-Time Signal Processing*, Prentice-Hall, 1989.

18. P. P. Vaidyanathan, "On maximally-flat linear phase FIR filters" *IEEE Trans. on Circuits and Systems*, CAS-31, pp. 830–832, 1989.

CHAPTER 6

Filter Realizations

6.1 INTRODUCTION

Once we have obtained the transfer function of an FIR or IIR filter that approximates the desired specifications in the frequency domain or the time domain, our next step is to investigate as many filter structures as possible, before we decide on the optimal or suboptimal algorithm for actual implementation or application. A given transfer function can be realized by several structures or what we will call "circuits," and they are all equivalent in the sense that they realize the same transfer function under the assumption that the coefficients of the transfer function have infinite precision. But in reality, the algorithms for implementing the transfer function in hardware depend on the filter structure chosen to realize the transfer function. We must also remember that the real hardware has a finite number of bits representing the coefficients of the filter as well as the values of the input signal at the input. The internal signals at the input of multipliers and the signals at the output of the multipliers and adders also are represented by a finite number of bits. The effect of rounding or truncation in the addition and multiplications of signal values depends on, for example, the type of representation of binary numbers, whether they are in fixed form or floating form, or whether they are in sign magnitude or two-complementary form. The effects of all these finite values for the number of bits used in hardware implementation is commonly called "finite wordlength effects," which we will study in Chapter 7.

In this chapter we develop several methods for realizing the FIR and IIR filters by different structures. The analysis or simulation of any transfer function can be easily done on a general-purpose computer, personal computer, or workstation with a high number of bits for the wordlength. We can also investigate the performance of noncausal systems or unstable systems on personal computers. Simulation of the performance of an actual microprocessor or a digital signal processor (DSP chip) by connecting it to the PC, a development kit that contains the microprocessor or the DSP chip, is far preferable to designing and building

Introduction to Digital Signal Processing and Filter Design, by B. A. Shenoi
Copyright © 2006 John Wiley & Sons, Inc.

the digital filter hardware with different finite wordlength and testing its performance. Of course, extensive analysis (simulation) of a given filter function under other design criteria such as stability, modularity, pipeline architecture, and noise immunity is also carried out on a personal computer or workstation using very powerful software that is available today.

It is true that a real hardware can be programmed to implement a large number of algorithms, by storing the data that represent the input signals and coefficients of the filter in a memory. But remember that it can implement an algorithm only in the time domain, whereas programming it to find the frequency response is only a simulation. Three algorithms in the time domain that we have discussed in earlier chapters are the recursive algorithm, convolution sum, and the FFT algorithm. It is the difference equations describing these algorithms that have to be implemented by real digital hardware.

Consider the general example of an IIR filter function:

$$H(z) = \frac{\sum_{n=0}^{M} b(n)z^{-n}}{1 + \sum_{n=1}^{N} a(n)z^{-n}} \tag{6.1}$$

The corresponding linear difference equation that implements it directly is

$$\sum_{k=0}^{N} a(k)y(n-k) = \sum_{k=0}^{M} b(k)x(n-k); \qquad a(0) = 1 \tag{6.2}$$

It can then be rewritten in the form of a recursive algorithm as follows:

$$y(n) = -a(1)y(n-1) + a(2)y(n-2) + a(3)y(n-3) + \cdots + a(N)y(n-N)$$
$$+ b(0)x(n) + b(1)x(n-1) + \cdots + b(M)y(n-M) \tag{6.3}$$

This recursive algorithm can be easily programmed on a general-purpose microprocessor, a computer, or a full-function DSP chip. The filter function we have obtained can be configured on these devices and convolution between its unit impulse response $h(n)$ and the input signal is the actual process used by the hardware to produce the output. The convolution sum is given by

$$y(n) = \sum_{k=0}^{\infty} h(k)x(n-k) \tag{6.4}$$

In the following pages, it will be shown that this transfer function (6.1) can be realized by several structures. We must remember that the algorithms used to implement them in the time domain will vary for the different structures. All the equivalent structures realize the same transfer function only under infinite precision of the coefficients; otherwise their performance depends on the number of bits used to represent the coefficients, as well as the input signal and the form for representing the binary numbers. The same statement can be made for the realization of an FIR filter function treated in the next section. The purpose of realizing different structures and studying the effects of quantization is to find the best possible structure that has the minimum quantization effect on the output of the system.

6.2 FIR FILTER REALIZATIONS

Example 6.1: Direct Form

Given the transfer function of an FIR filter as $H(z) = \sum_{n=0}^{M} h(n)z^{-n}$, let us consider its equivalent algorithm for the output, for example, when $M = 4$:

$$y(n) = h(0)x(n) + h(1)x(n-1) + h(2)x(n-2)$$
$$+ h(3)x(n-3) + h(4)x(n-4) \tag{6.5}$$

We have already discussed one structure employed to implement this algorithm in Chapter 5, and because the coefficients of the multipliers in it are directly available as the coefficients $h(n)$ in $H(z)$, it is called the *direct form I structure* and is shown in Figure 6.1.

Whenever we have a structure to implement an FIR or an IIR filter, an equivalent structure can be obtained as its transpose by the following operations:

1. Interchanging the input and the output nodes
2. Replacing adders by pickoff nodes and vice versa
3. Reversing all paths

Using these operations, we get the transpose of the structure of Figure 6.1 as Figure 6.2. This is known as *direct form II structure*; remember that this (direct form II) structure will be called *direct form I transposed structure* in the next chapter.

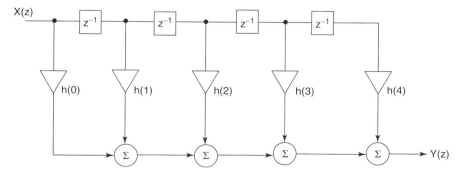

Figure 6.1   Direct form I of an FIR filter.

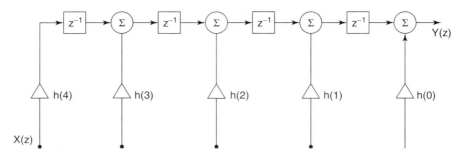

Figure 6.2   Direct form II of an FIR filter.

Example 6.2: Cascade Form

If we have an FIR filter of high order, it may be realized as a cascade of FIR filters of lower order, preferably as second-order filters when the order is even or the cascade of second-order filters and one first-order filter when the order is odd. We factorize the given FIR filter function $H(z) = \sum_{n=0}^{M} h(n)z^{-n}$ in the form

$$H(z) = \begin{cases} h(0)\left[\prod_{m=1}^{M/2} \left(1 + h(1m)z^{-1} + h(2m)z^{-2}\right)\right] \\ \qquad\qquad\qquad\qquad\qquad \text{when } M \text{ is even} \\ h(0)\left[(1 + h(10)z^{-1}) \prod_{m=1}^{(M-1)/2} \left(1 + h(1m)z^{-1} + h(2m)z^{-2}\right)\right] \\ \qquad\qquad\qquad\qquad\qquad \text{when } M \text{ is odd} \end{cases} \quad (6.6)$$

A cascade realization of this equation when $M = 5$ is shown in Figure 6.3, and its transpose is shown in Figure 6.4.

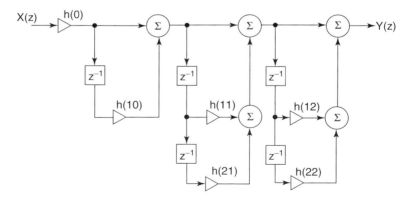

Figure 6.3   Cascade connection of an FIR filter.

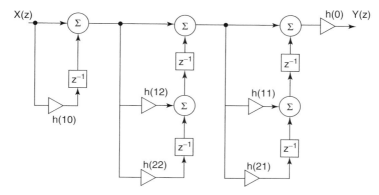

Figure 6.4   Transpose of the cascade connection shown in Figure 6.3.

Example 6.3: Polyphase Form

This realization is based on the polyphase decomposition of the FIR transfer function and is illustrated by choosing the following example:

$$H_1(z) = h(0) + h(1)z^{-1} + h(2)z^{-2} + h(3)z^{-3} + h(4)z^{-4}$$
$$+ h(5)z^{-5} + h(6)z^{-6} + h(7)z^{-7} + h(8)z^{-8} \qquad (6.7)$$

This can be expressed as the sum of two subfunctions, shown below:

$$H_1(z) = \left[h(0) + h(2)z^{-2} + h(4)z^{-4} + h(8)z^{-8}\right]$$
$$+ \left[h(1)z^{-1} + h(3)z^{-3} + h(5)z^{-5} + h(7)z^{-7}\right]$$
$$= \left[h(0) + h(2)z^{-2} + h(4)z^{-4} + h(8)z^{-8}\right]$$
$$+ z^{-1}\left[h(1) + h(3)z^{-2} + h(5)z^{-4} + h(7)z^{-6}\right] \qquad (6.8)$$

Let us denote $A_0(z) = \left[h(0) + h(2)z^{-2} + h(4)z^{-4} + h(8)z^{-8}\right]$ and

$$A_1(z) = \left[h(1)z^{-1} + h(3)z^{-3} + h(5)z^{-5} + h(7)z^{-7}\right]$$
$$= z^{-1}\left[h(1) + h(3)z^{-2} + h(5)z^{-4} + h(7)z^{-6}\right]$$

Since the polynomials in the square brackets contain only even-degree terms, we denote $A_0(z) = A_0(z^2)$ and $A_1(z) = z^{-1}A_1(z^2)$. Hence we express $H_1(z) = A_0(z^2) + z^{-1}A_1(z^2)$. A block diagram showing this realization is presented in Figure 6.5(a), where the two functions $A_0(z^2)$ and $A_1(z^2)$ are subfilters connected in parallel.

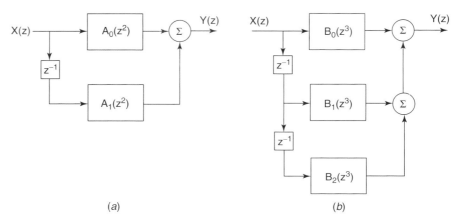

Figure 6.5   Polyphase structures of FIR filters.

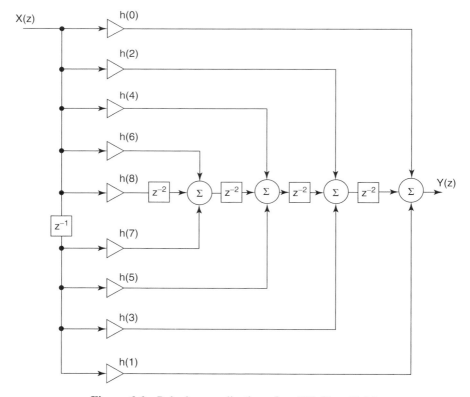

Figure 6.6   Polyphase realization of an FIR filter $H_1(z)$.

These filters can be realized in either the direct form I or direct form II as described earlier and illustrated in Figures 6.1 and 6.2, respectively. But there would be 8 unit delays in building $A_0(z)$ and 7 unit delays in $z^{-1}A_1(z)$, which adds up to 15 unit delay elements. We prefer to realize a circuit that would require a minimum number of unit delays that is equal to the order of the filter. A realization that contains the minimum number of delays is defined as a *canonic realization*. To reduce the total number of delays to 8, we cause the two subfilters to share the unit delays in order to get a canonic realization. Such a circuit realization is shown in Figure 6.6.

Example 6.4

Consider the same example and decompose (6.7) as the sum of three terms:

$$H(z) = \left[h(0) + h(3)z^{-3} + h(6)z^{-6} \right] + z^{-1} \left[h(1) + h(4)z^{-3} + h(7)z^{-6} \right]$$
$$+ z^{-2} \left[h(2) + h(5)z^{-3} + h(8)z^{-6} \right]$$
$$= B_0(z^3) + z^{-1}B_1(z^3) + z^{-2}B_2(z^3) \tag{6.9}$$

A block diagram for implementing this decomposition is shown in Figure 6.5b. A canonic realization of (6.9) is shown in Figure 6.7 and its transpose in Figure 6.8, each of which uses 8 unit delay elements. The FIR filter of order 8 chosen in (6.7) can be decomposed as the sum of four subfilters in the form $H(z) = C_0(z^4) + C_1(z^4) + C_2(z^4) + C_3(z^4)$ and can be realized by a canonic circuit.

In general, an FIR function of order N (i.e. $h(n) = 0$ for $n > N$) can be decomposed in the polyphase form with M subfilters connected in parallel as follows

$$H(z) = \sum_{m=0}^{M-1} z^{-m} E_m(z^M) \tag{6.10}$$

where

$$E_m(z) = \sum_{n=0}^{(N+1)/M} h(Mn + m)z^{-n} \tag{6.11}$$

6.2.1 Lattice Structure for FIR Filters

FIR filters can be realized in structures called *lattice structures* shown later in the chapter in Figure 6.17a and its transpose, in Figure 6.17b—for an example of a third-order filter. We will describe the design of these structures using a MATLAB function in Section 6.5.

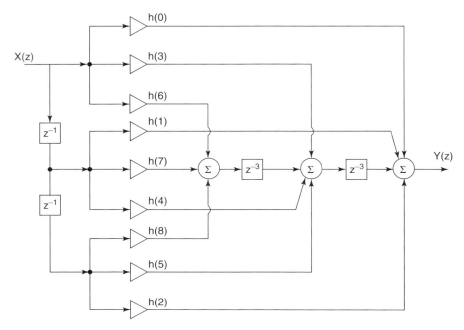

Figure 6.7   Polyphase structure of an FIR filter function $H_2(z)$.

6.2.2   Linear Phase FIR Filter Realizations

When the FIR filter has a linear phase, its coefficients are symmetric or antisymmetric, and hence the number of multipliers is reduced by almost half. For the symmetric FIR filter of order N, the samples of the unit impulse response that are the same as the multiplier coefficients satisfy the condition $h(n) = h(N - n)$ and it known as a *type I FIR filter*. The FIR filter with antisymmetric coefficients satisfies the condition $h(n) = -h(N - n)$ and is known as the *type II FIR filter*.

Example 6.5

Let us consider the example of a type I FIR filter, of order $N = 6$:

$$H_3(z) = h(0) + h(1)z^{-1} + h(2)z^{-2} + h(3)z^{-3} + h(4)z^{-4} + h(5)z^{-5} + h(6)z^{-6}$$

$$(6.12)$$

$$= h(0) + h(1)z^{-1} + h(2)z^{-2} + h(3)z^{-3} + h(2)z^{-4} + h(1)z^{-5} + h(0)z^{-6}$$

$$= h(0)(1 + z^{-6}) + h(1)(z^{-1} + z^{-5}) + h(2)(z^{-2} + z^{-4}) + h(3)z^{-3} \quad (6.13)$$

By sharing the multipliers, we get the realization shown in Figure 6.9, which uses only four multipliers. It is still a canonic realization that uses six delay elements.

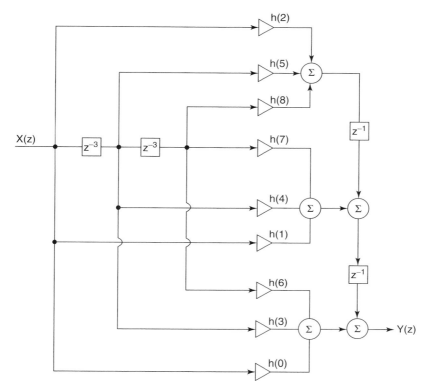

Figure 6.8   Transpose of the polyphase structure shown in Figure 6.7.

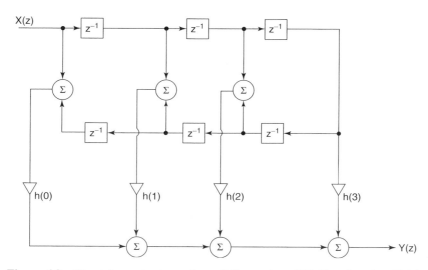

Figure 6.9   Direct-form structure of type I linear phase FIR filter function $H_3(z)$.

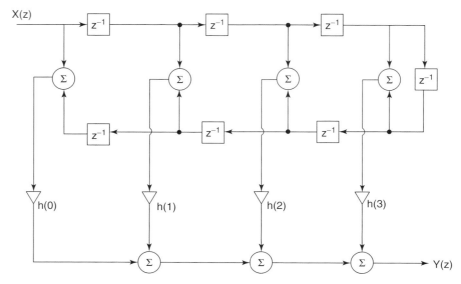

Figure 6.10   Direct-form structure of type II linear phase FIR filter function $H_4(z)$.

Example 6.6

If we consider a type II FIR filter of order 7, its transfer function is given by

$$H_4(z) = h(0) + h(1)z^{-1} + h(2)z^{-2} + h(3)z^{-3} + h(3)z^{-4} + h(2)z^{-5}$$
$$+ h(1)z^{-6} + h(0)z^{-7} \tag{6.14}$$
$$= h(0)(1 + z^{-7}) + h(1)(z^{-1} + z^{-6}) + h(2)(z^{-2} + z^{-5})$$
$$+ h(3)(z^{-3} + z^{-4}) \tag{6.15}$$

This is realized by the canonic circuit shown in Figure 6.10, thereby reducing the total number of multipliers from 7 to 4. Similar cost saving is achieved in the realization of FIR filters with antisymmetric coefficients.

6.3   IIR FILTER REALIZATIONS

In constructing several equivalent structures of an FIR filter, we used the direct-form decomposition of the filter transfer function as the product of second-order sections connected in cascade, polyphase decomposition, and transpose for each structure obtained by them. We used the symmetry of the coefficients of linear phase FIR filters to reduce the number of delay elements. We can also generate their transpose forms. Using similar strategies, in this section we present several structures for the IIR filters.

Example 6.7: Direct Forms

The transfer function (6.1) of an IIR filter is the ratio of a numerator polynomial to a denominator polynomial. First we decompose it as the product of an all-pole function $H_1(z)$ and a polynomial $H_2(z)$

$$H(z) = \frac{\sum_{n=0}^{M} b(n)z^{-n}}{1 + \sum_{n=1}^{N} a(n)z^{-n}} \tag{6.16}$$

$$= H_1(z)H_2(z) = \left[\frac{1}{1 + \sum_{n=1}^{N} a(n)z^{-n}} \right] \left[\sum_{n=0}^{M} b(n)z^{-n} \right] \tag{6.17}$$

and construct a cascade connection of an FIR filter $H_2(z)$ and the all-pole IIR filter $H_1(z)$. Again we select an example to illustrate the method. Let $H_2(z) = b_0 + b(1)z^{-1} + b(2)z^{-2} + b(3)z^{-3}$ and

$$H_1(z) = \frac{1}{1 + a(1)z^{-1} + a(2)z^{-2} + a(3)z^{-3}}$$

The realization of $H_1(z)$ in direct form I is shown in Figure 6.11 as the filter connected in cascade with the realization of the FIR filter $H_2(z)$ also in direct form I structure. The structure for the IIR filter is also called a *direct form I* because the gain constants of the multipliers are directly available from the coefficients of the transfer function.

We note that $H_1(z) = V(z)/X(z)$ and $H_2(z) = Y(z)/V(z)$. We also note that the signals at the output of the three delay elements of the filter for $H_1(z)$ are

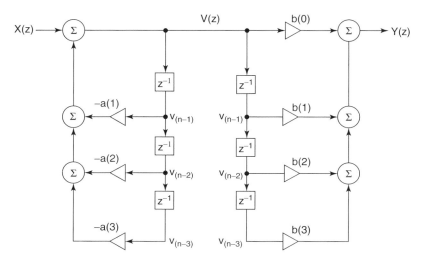

Figure 6.11   Direct form I of an IIR filter.

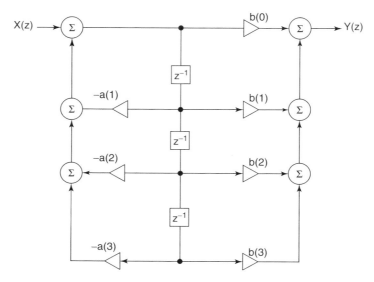

Figure 6.12   Direct form II structure of an IIR filter.

the same as those at the output of the three delay elements of filter $H_2(z)$. Hence we let the two circuits share one set of three delay elements, thereby reducing the number of delay elements. The result of merging the two circuits is shown in Figure 6.12 and is identified as the direct form II realization of the IIR filter. Its transpose is shown in Figure 6.13. Both of them use the minimum number of delay elements equal to the order of the IIR filter and hence are canonic realizations.

The two filters realizing $H_1(z)$ and $H_2(z)$ can be cascaded in the reverse order [i.e., $H(z) = H_2(z)H_1(z)$], and when their transpose is obtained, we see that the three delay elements of $H_2(z)$ can be shared with $H_1(z)$, and thus another realization identified as direct form I as well as its transpose can be obtained.

Example 6.8: Cascade Form

The filter function (6.16) can be decomposed as the product of transfer functions in the form

$$H(z) = \frac{N_1(z)N_2(z)\cdots N_K(z)}{D_1(z)D_2(z)D_3(z)\cdots D_K(z)} \tag{6.18}$$

$$= \left[\frac{N_1(z)}{D_1(z)}\right]\left[\frac{N_2(z)}{D_2(z)}\right]\left[\frac{N_3(z)}{D_3(z)}\right]\cdots\left[\frac{N_K(z)}{D_K(z)}\right] \tag{6.19}$$

$$= H_1(z)H_2(z)H_3(z)\cdots H_K(z) \tag{6.20}$$

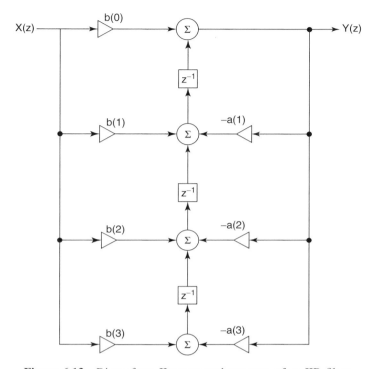

Figure 6.13 Direct form II transposed structure of an IIR filter.

where $K = N/2$ when N is even and the polynomials $D_1(z)$, $D_2(z)$, $D_3(z)$, and so on are second-order polynomials, with complex zeros appearing in conjugate pairs in any such polynomial. When N is odd, $K = (N - 1)/2$, and one of the denominator polynomials is a first-order polynomial. The numerator polynomials $N_1(z)$, $N_2(z)$, ... may be first-order or second-order polynomials or a constant:

$$H(z) = H_0 \left[\frac{1 + \beta_{11}z^{-1}}{1 + \alpha_{11}z^{-1}} \right] \prod_k \left[\frac{1 + \beta_{1k}z^{-1} + \beta_{2k}z^{-2}}{1 + \alpha_{1k}z^{-1} + \alpha_{2k}z^{-2}} \right] \qquad (6.21)$$

Each of the transfer functions $H_1(z)$, $H_2(z)$, ..., $H_K(z)$ is realized by the direct form I or direct form II or their transpose structures and then connected in cascade. They can also be cascaded in many other sequential order, for example, $H(z) = H_1(z)H_3(z)H_5(z) \dots$ or $H(z) = H_2(z)H_1(z)H_4(z)H_3(z) \dots$.

There are more choices in the realization of $H(z)$ in the cascade connection in addition to those indicated above. We can pair the numerators $N_1(z)$, $N_2(z)$, ... and denominators $D_1(z)$, $D_2(z)$, $D_3(z)$, ... in many different combinations; in other words, we can pair the poles and zeros of the polynomials in different ways. For example, we can define

$$H(z) = \left[\frac{N_1(z)}{D_2(z)}\right]\left[\frac{N_2(z)}{D_3(z)}\right]\left[\frac{N_3(z)}{D_4(z)}\right]\cdots\left[\frac{N_K(z)}{D_1(z)}\right]$$

$$= \left[\frac{N_2(z)}{D_1(z)}\right]\left[\frac{N_3(z)}{D_4(z)}\right]\left[\frac{N_4(z)}{D_3(z)}\right]\cdots\left[\frac{N_k(z)}{D_2(z)}\right]$$

$$= \left[\frac{N_K(z)}{D_1(z)}\right]\left[\frac{N_2(z)}{D_3(z)}\right]\left[\frac{N_4(z)}{D_2(z)}\right]\cdots$$

and cascade them in many different orders.

So the number of realizations that can be obtained from a nominal IIR transfer function is very large, in general. Besides the difference in the algorithms for each of these realizations and the consequent effects of finite wordlength when the coefficients of the filter and the signal samples are quantized to a finite number, we have to consider the effect on the overall magnitude of the output sequence and the need for scaling the magnitude of the output sequence at each stage of the cascade connection and so on.

Example 6.9

Consider a simple example of an IIR filter as follows:

$$H(z) = \frac{z(0.16z - 0.18)}{(z - 0.2)(z + 0.1)(z + 0.4)(z^2 + z + 0.5)} \tag{6.22}$$

A few alternate forms of expressing this are given below:

$$H(z) = \left[\frac{1}{(z^2 - 0.1z - 0.02)}\right]\left[\frac{(0.16z - 0.18)}{(z^2 + z + 0.5)}\right]\left[\frac{z}{(z + 0.4)}\right] \tag{6.23}$$

$$= \left[\frac{z}{(z + 0.4)}\right]\left[\frac{1}{(z^2 - 0.1z - 0.02)}\right]\left[\frac{(0.16z - 0.18)}{(z^2 + z + 0.5)}\right]$$

$$= \left[\frac{(0.16z - 0.18)}{(z^2 - 0.1z - 0.02)}\right]\left[\frac{z}{(z^2 + z + 0.5)}\right]\left[\frac{1}{(z + 0.4)}\right]$$

$$= \left[\frac{z}{(z^2 + z + 0.5)}\right]\left[\frac{1}{(z + 0.4)}\right]\left[\frac{(0.16z - 0.18)}{(z^2 - 0.1z - 0.02)}\right] \tag{6.24}$$

Let us choose the last expression, (6.24), and rewrite it in inverse powers of z, as given by

$$H(z^{-1}) = \left[\frac{z^{-1}}{1 + z^{-1} + 0.5z^{-2}}\right]\left[\frac{z^{-1}}{(1 + 0.4z^{-1})}\right]\left[\frac{(0.16z^{-1} - 0.18z^{-2})}{(1 - 0.1z^{-1} - 0.02z^{-2})}\right] \tag{6.25}$$

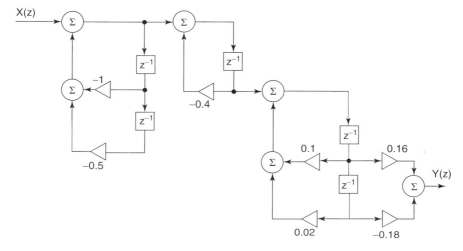

Figure 6.14   Cascade connection of an IIR filter.

One of the realizations used to implement this transfer function is shown in Figure 6.14.

Instead of combining the factors $(z - 0.2)$ and $(z + 0.1)$ and getting $(z^2 - 0.1z - 0.02)$, in the denominator of (6.22), we can combine $(z - 0.2)$ and $(z + 0.4)$ or $(z + 0.1)$ and $(z + 0.4)$ to generate new second-order polynomials and select many pole–zero pairs and order of second-order sections connected in cascade, adding to the many possible realizations of (6.22) in the cascade form. The cascade connection of second-order sections, each realized in direct form II, has been a popular choice for a long time and was investigated in great detail, until other structures became known for their better performance with respect to finite wordlength effects and practical applications.

Example 6.10: Parallel Form

The IIR transfer function can also be expanded as the sum of second-order structures. It is decomposed into its partial fraction form, combining the terms with complex conjugate poles together such that we have an expansion with real coefficients only. We will choose the same example as (6.22) to illustrate this form of realization.

One form of the partial fraction expansion of (6.22) is

$$H(z) = \frac{5.31165z}{z + 0.1} - \frac{1.111z}{z - 0.2} - \frac{5.21368z}{z + 0.4} + \frac{1.1314z^2 - 0.15947z}{z^2 + z + 0.5} \quad (6.26)$$

By combining $(z + 0.1)$, $(z - 0.2)$, $(z + 0.4)$ in different pairs to get the corresponding denominator polynomials, we get the following expressions for the transfer function given above:

$$H(z) = \frac{0.9797z^2 + 1.6033z}{z^2 + 0.5z + 0.04} - \frac{1.111z}{z - 0.2} + \frac{1.1314z^2 - 0.15947z}{z^2 + z + 0.5} \tag{6.27}$$

$$= \frac{-6.3248z^2 + 0.5983z}{z^2 + 0.2z - 0.08} + \frac{5.31165}{z + 0.1} + \frac{1.1314z^2 - 0.15947z}{z^2 + z + 0.5} \tag{6.28}$$

$$= \frac{4.200z^2 - 1.1173z}{z^2 - 0.1z - 0.02} - \frac{5.2134z}{z + 0.4} + \frac{1.1314z^2 - 0.15947z}{z^2 + z + 0.5} \tag{6.29}$$

The three terms in these expressions are rewritten in inverse powers of z, and any one of the IIR realizations (direct form or their transpose) is used to obtain the circuit for each of them, and they are connected in parallel. Let us select the last expression:

$$H(z) = \frac{4.200z^2 - 1.1173z}{z^2 - 0.1z - 0.02} - \frac{5.2134z}{z + 0.4} + \frac{1.1314z^2 - 0.15947z}{z^2 + z + 0.5}$$

$$= \frac{4.200 - 1.117z^{-1}}{1 - 0.1z^{-1} - 0.02z^{-2}} - \frac{5.2134}{1 + 0.4z^{-1}} + \frac{1.1314 - 0.1594z^{-1}}{1 + z^{-1} + 0.5z^{-2}} \tag{6.30}$$

Figure 6.15 shows a realization of the filter given by (6.30) in the parallel form of connection, and by using the transpose of each sections, a new circuit can be derived.

Another form of expanding the transfer function is the normal form of partial fraction expansion, indicated by

$$H(z) = \frac{R_1}{z + 0.1} + \frac{R_2}{z - 0.2} + \frac{R_3}{z + 0.4} + \frac{R_4z + R_5}{z^2 + z + 0.5}$$

$$= \frac{R_1z^{-1}}{1 + 0.1z^{-1}} + \frac{R_2z^{-1}}{1 - 0.2z^{-1}} + \frac{R_3z^{-1}}{1 + 0.4z^{-1}} + \frac{R_4z^{-1} + R_5z^{-2}}{1 + z^{-1} + 0.5z^{-2}} \tag{6.31}$$

which gives rise to additional structures.

So, the transfer function given by (6.22) was decomposed in the form of (6.25) and realized by the cascade structure shown in Figure 6.14; it was decomposed in the form of (6.30) and realized by the parallel connection in the structure shown in Figure 6.15.

The algorithm used to implement the structure in Figure 6.14 is of the form

$$y_1(n) = x(n) - y_1(n - 1) - 0.5y_1(n - 2)$$

$$y_2(n) = y_1(n) - 0.4y_2(n - 1)$$

$$y_3(n) = y_2(n) + 0.1y_3(n - 1) + 0.02y_3(n - 2)$$

$$y(n) = 0.16y_3(n - 1) - 0.18y_3(n - 2)$$

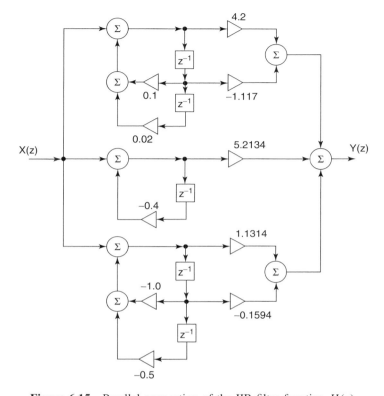

Figure 6.15   Parallel connection of the IIR filter function $H(z)$.

whereas the algorithm employed to implement the structure shown in Figure 6.15 has the form

$$\widetilde{y}_1(n) = x(n) + 0.1\widetilde{y}_1(n-1) + 0.02\widetilde{y}_1(n-2)$$
$$\widetilde{y}_2(n) = 4.2\widetilde{y}_1(n) - 1.117\widetilde{y}_1(n-1)$$
$$\widetilde{y}_3(n) = x(n) - 0.4\widetilde{y}_3(n-1)$$
$$\widetilde{y}_4(n) = x(n) - \widetilde{y}_4(n-1) - 0.5\widetilde{y}_4(n-2)$$
$$\widetilde{y}_5(n) = 1.1314\widetilde{y}_4(n) - 0.1594\widetilde{y}_4(n-1)$$
$$y(n) = \widetilde{y}_2(n) + 5.2134\widetilde{y}_3(n) + \widetilde{y}_5(n)$$

Remember that under ideal conditions both algorithms give the same output for a given input signal and the two structures realize the same transfer function (6.22). But when the two algorithms have to be programmed and implemented by hardware devices, the results would be very different and the accuracy of the resulting output, the speed of the execution, and the throughput, and other factors would depend not only on the finite wordlength but also on so many other factors, including the architecture of the DSP chip, program instructions per cycle, and dynamic range of the input signal. We will discuss these factors in a later chapter.

6.4   ALLPASS FILTERS IN PARALLEL

Next in importance is the structure shown in Figure 6.16. The transfer function $G(z) = Y(z)/X(z)$ is given by $\frac{1}{2}[A_1(z) + A_2(z)]$, where $A_1(z)$ and $A_2(z)$ are the allpass filters connected in parallel. But in this figure, there is another transfer function, $H(z) = V(z)/X(z)$, which is given by $H(z) = \frac{1}{2}[A_1(z) - A_2(z)]$. The structure shown in Figure 6.16 is also called the *lattice structure* or *lattice-coupled allpass structure* by some authors. A typical allpass filter function is of the form

$$A(z) = \frac{N(z)}{D(z)} = \pm \frac{a_n + a_{n-1}z^{-1} + a_{n-2}z^{-1} + \cdots + a_1 z^{-n+1} + a_0 z^{-n}}{a_0 + a_1 z^{-1} + a_2 z^{-2} + \cdots + a_{n-1}z^{-n+1} + a_n z^{-n}} \quad (6.32)$$

which shows that the order of the coefficients in the numerator is the reverse of that in the denominator, when both the numerator and denominator polynomial are expressed in descending powers of z. Equation (6.32) can be expressed in another form as

$$\begin{aligned} A(z) &= \frac{z^{-n}(a_0 + a_1 z + a_2 z^2 + \cdots + a_{n-1}z^{n-1} + a_n z^n)}{a_0 + a_1 z^{-1} + a_2 z^{-2} + \cdots + a_{n-1}z^{-n+1} + a_n z^{-n}} \\ &= \frac{z^{-n}D(z^{-1})}{D(z)} \quad (6.33) \end{aligned}$$

The zeros of the numerator polynomial $D(z^{-1})$ are the reciprocals of the zeros of the denominator $D(z)$, and therefore the numerator polynomial $D(z^{-1})$ is the mirror image polynomial of $D(z)$.

When the allpass filter has all its poles inside the unit circle in the z plane, it is a stable function and its zeros are outside the unit circle as a result of the mirror

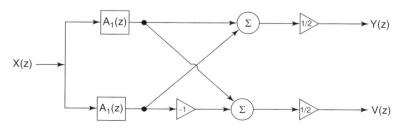

Figure 6.16   Two allpass filters in parallel (lattice-coupled allpass structure).

image symmetry. Therefore a stable, allpass filter function is a non–minimum phase function.

Letting $a_0 = 1$, we get the magnitude response of this filter to be a constant at all frequencies, because the numerator is the complex conjugate of the denominator. Since this filter transmits all frequencies with the same gain, it is called an *allpass filter*:

$$\left|A(e^{j\omega})\right| = \left|\frac{1 + a_1 e^{j\omega} + a_2 e^{j2\omega} + \cdots + a_n e^{jn\omega}}{1 + a_1 e^{-j\omega} + a_2 e^{-j2\omega} + \cdots + a_n e^{-jn\omega}}\right| = 1 \qquad (6.34)$$

But the phase response (and the group delay) is dependent on the coefficients of the allpass filter. We know that the phase response filter designed to approximate a specified magnitude response is a nonlinear function of ω, and therefore its group delay is far from a constant value. When an allpass filter is cascaded with such a filter, the resulting filter has a frequency response $H_1(e^{j\omega}) A(e^{j\omega}) = \left|H_1(e^{j\omega}) A(e^{j\omega})\right| e^{j[\theta(\omega)+\phi(\omega)]} = \left|H_1(e^{j\omega})\right| e^{j[\theta(\omega)+\phi(\omega)]}$. So the magnitude response does not change when the IIR filter is cascaded with an allpass filter, but its phase response $\theta(\omega)$ changes by the addition of the phase response $\phi(\omega)$ contributed by the allpass filter. The allpass filters $A(z)$ are therefore very useful for modifying the phase response (and the group delay) of filters without changing the magnitude of a given IIR filter $H_1(z)$, when they are cascaded with $H_1(z)$. However, the method used to find the coefficients of the allpass filter $A(z)$ such that the group delay of $H_1(z)A(z)$ is a very close approximation to a constant in the passband of the filter $H_1(z)$ poses a highly nonlinear problem, and only computer-aided optimization has been utilized to solve this problem. Normally IIR filters are designed from specifications for its magnitude only, and its group delay is far from a linear function of frequency. There are many applications that call for a constant group delay or a linear phase response, and in such cases, the filters are cascaded with an allpass filter that does not affect its magnitude—except by a constant—but is designed such that it compensates for the phase distortion of the IIR filter. Allpass filters designed for this purpose are cascaded with the IIR filters and are known as *delay equalizers*.

An important property of allpass filters is that if the coefficients change in wordlength, the magnitude response of an allpass filter at all frequencies does not change. Recall that a second-order allpass filter was analyzed in Chapter 2, and that if the transfer function of an allpass filter is of a higher order, it can be realized by cascading second-order filters and possibly one first-order allpass filter. We illustrate a few more structures that realize first-order allpass transfer functions as well as second-order allpass functions later in the chapter, in Figures 6.23 and 6.24.

Let us assume that the two allpass filters shown in Figure 6.16 are of order $(N - r)$ and r, respectively, and are given by

$$A_1(z) = \frac{z^{-(N-r)} D_1(z^{-1})}{D_1(z)} \qquad (6.35)$$

and

$$A_2(z) = \frac{z^{-r} D_2(z^{-1})}{D_2(z)} \tag{6.36}$$

Substituting them in $G(z) = \frac{1}{2}[A_1(z) + A_2(z)]$ and $H(z) = \frac{1}{2}[A_1(z) - A_2(z)]$, we get

$$G(z) = \frac{1}{2} \left[\frac{z^{-(N-r)} D_1(z^{-1}) D_2(z) + z^{-r} D_2(z^{-1}) D_1(z)}{D_1(z) D_2(z)} \right] \tag{6.37}$$

and

$$H(z) = \frac{1}{2} \left[\frac{z^{-(N-r)} D_1(z^{-1}) D_2(z) - z^{-r} D_2(z^{-1}) D_1(z)}{D_1(z) D_2(z)} \right] \tag{6.38}$$

If we express them in the form as

$$G(z) = \frac{P(z)}{D(z)} = \frac{\sum_{n=0}^{N} p_n z^{-n}}{D(z)} \tag{6.39}$$

and

$$H(z) = \frac{Q(z)}{D(z)} = \frac{\sum_{n=0}^{N} q_n z^{-n}}{D(z)} \tag{6.40}$$

then it can be shown that the following conditions are satisfied by (6.37) and (6.38).

Property 6.1 $P(z^{-1}) = z^N P(z)$. Hence $p_n = p_{N-n}$, that is, the coefficients of $P(z)$ are symmetric.

Property 6.2 $Q(z^{-1}) = -z^N Q(z)$. Hence $q_n = -q_{N-n}$, that is, the coefficients of $Q(z)$ are antisymmetric.

Property 6.3 $P(z)P(z^{-1}) + Q(z)Q(z^{-1}) = D(z)D(z^{-1})$. Hence

$$\left| G(e^{j\omega}) \right|^2 + \left| H(e^{j\omega}) \right|^2 = 1 \tag{6.41}$$

in other words, $G(z)$ and $H(z)$ are said to form a power complementary pair. In the next chapter the structure for realizing $G(e^{j\omega})$ will be termed a *lattice-coupled allpass filter* and because of the property stated here, the structure for realizing $H(e^{j\omega})$ will be called a *lattice-coupled allpass power complementary filter*.

Property 6.4

$$\left|G(e^{j\omega})\right| = \tfrac{1}{2}\left|e^{j\theta_1(\omega)} + e^{j\theta_2(\omega)}\right| = \tfrac{1}{2}\left|1 + e^{j(\theta_1(\omega)-\theta_2(\omega))}\right| \le 1 \qquad (6.42)$$

where $A_1(e^{j\omega}) = e^{j\theta_1(\omega)}$ and $A_2(e^{j\omega}) = e^{j\theta_2(\omega)}$.

In the following analysis, we will assume that the four conditions described above are satisfied by $G(z)$ and $H(z)$ and derive the results that they can be obtained in the form $G(z) = \tfrac{1}{2}[A_1(z) + A_2(z)]$ and $H(z) = \tfrac{1}{2}[A_1(z) - A_2(z)]$.

Consider Property 6.3: $P(z)P(z^{-1}) + Q(z)Q(z^{-1}) = D(z)D(z^{-1})$. Using Properties 6.1 and 6.2, we get

$$P(z)z^N P(z) - z^N Q(z)Q(z) = D(z)D(z^{-1}) \qquad (6.43)$$

$$P^2(z) - Q^2(z) = D(z)z^{-N}D(z^{-1}) \qquad (6.44)$$

$$[P(z) + Q(z)][P(z) - Q(z)] = z^{-N}D(z)D(z^{-1}) \qquad (6.45)$$

From Properties 6.1 and 6.2, we have $\left[P(z^{-1}) + Q(z^{-1})\right] = z^N[P(z) - Q(z)]$ and therefore $z^{-N}\left[P(z^{-1}) + Q(z^{-1})\right] = [P(z) - Q(z)]$, and we get

$$[P(z) + Q(z)][P(z) - Q(z)] = P^2(z) - Q^2(z) \qquad (6.46)$$

From (6.44), we have

$$P^2(z) - Q^2(z) = D(z)z^{-N}D(z^{-1}) \qquad (6.47)$$

$$[P(z) + Q(z)]z^{-N}\left[P(z^{-1}) + Q(z^{-1})\right] = D(z)z^{-N}D(z^{-1}) \qquad (6.48)$$

Therefore

$$[P(z) + Q(z)][P(z) - Q(z)] = z^{-N}D(z)D(z^{-1}) \qquad (6.49)$$

This shows that the zeros of $[P(z) - Q(z)]$ are reciprocals of the zeros of $[P(z) + Q(z)]$.

It has been found that the Butterworth, Chebyshev, and elliptic lowpass filters of odd order satisfy the four properties described above. We know from Chapter 4 that their transfer function $G(z)$ obtained from the bilinear transformation of the analog lowpass prototype filters has no poles on the unit circle. In other words, the zeros of $D(z)$ are within the unit circle, and therefore the zeros of $D(z^{-1})$ are outside the unit circle, because they are the reciprocals of the zeros of $D(z)$. From (6.49) we see that the zeros of $[P(z) + Q(z)]$ and $[P(z) - Q(z)]$ cannot lie on the unit circle. Let us assume that $[P(z) + Q(z)]$ has r zeros

$z_k (k = 1, 2, 3, \ldots, r)$ that are inside the unit circle and $(N - r)$ zeros $z_j (j = r + 1, r + 2, \ldots, N)$ that are outside the unit circle. Therefore $[P(z) - Q(z)]$ has r zeros $z_k^{-1} (k = 1, 2, 3, \ldots, r)$ outside the unit circle and $(N - r)$ zeros z_j^{-1} $(j = r + 1, r + 2, \ldots, N)$ inside the unit circle. From (6.49), we can therefore assume that $D(z)$ that has all its zeros inside the unit circle is of the form

$$D(z) = \left[\prod_{k=1}^{r} (1 - z^{-1} z_k) \prod_{j=r+1}^{N} (1 - z^{-1} z_j^{-1}) \right] \tag{6.50}$$

and

$$[P(z) + Q(z)][P(z) - Q(z)] = z^{-N} D(z) D(z^{-1})$$

$$= \left[\prod_{k=1}^{r} (1 - z^{-1} z_k) \prod_{j=r+1}^{N} (1 - z^{-1} z_j^{-1}) \right]$$

$$\times \left[\prod_{k=1}^{r} (z^{-1} - z_k) \prod_{j=r+1}^{N} (z^{-1} - z_j^{-1}) \right] \tag{6.51}$$

Thus we identify

$$P(z) + Q(z) = \alpha \prod_{k=1}^{r} (1 - z^{-1} z_k) \prod_{j=r+1}^{N} (z^{-1} - z_j^{-1}) \tag{6.52}$$

$$P(z) - Q(z) = \frac{1}{\alpha} \prod_{k=1}^{r} (z^{-1} - z_k) \prod_{j=r+1}^{N} (1 - z^{-1} z_j^{-1}) \tag{6.53}$$

Then

$$G(z) + H(z) = \frac{P(z) + Q(z)}{D(z)} = \alpha \prod_{j=r+1}^{N} \left(\frac{z^{-1} - z_j^{-1}}{1 - z^{-1} z_j^{-1}} \right) = \alpha A_1(z) \tag{6.54}$$

$$G(z) - H(z) = \frac{P(z) - Q(z)}{D(z)} = \frac{1}{\alpha} \prod_{k=1}^{r} \left(\frac{z^{-1} - z_k}{1 - z^{-1} z_k} \right) = \frac{1}{\alpha} A_2(z) \tag{6.55}$$

But from the power complementary property, we must have $\alpha^2 = 1$. Therefore, $\alpha = 1$, so that

$$G(z) = \tfrac{1}{2} [A_1(z) + A_2(z)] \tag{6.56}$$

$$H(z) = \tfrac{1}{2} [A_1(z) - A_2(z)] \tag{6.57}$$

So we have proved that when $G(z)$ is a Butterworth, Chebyshev, or elliptic lowpass filter of odd order (which satisfy the four properties listed above), we can decompose $G(z)$ as the sum of two allpass functions, $A_1(z)/2$ and $A_2(z)/2$. Once we have derived the two allpass functions, we easily obtain $H(z)$ as the difference of $A_1(z)/2$ and $A_2(z)/2$ and realize it by the structure of Figure 6.16. Because of the complementary power property, we see that $H(z)$ realizes a highpass filter.

6.4.1 Design Procedure

The procedure to find the poles and zeros of the two allpass filters from the given Butterworth, Chebyshev, or elliptic lowpass filters of odd order is described below. We have already pointed out that the transfer function $G(z) = P(z)/D(z)$ for these filters obtained from the corresponding analog prototype via the bilinear transformation have all their poles inside the unit circle of the z plane. Their magnitude response $\left|G(e^{j\omega})\right|$ has a maximum value at $\omega = 0$, which can be easily obtained as the value of $G(z)$ at $z = 1$. In order to satisfy Property 6.4, we have to divide $G(z)$ by $G(e^j)$ or multiply $G(z)$ by a scaling factor $k = D(1)/P(1)$ so that $\left|kG(e^{j\omega})\right| \leq 1$ as the first step in the design procedure. Let us assume that $G(z)$ has already been scaled by k in our further discussion.

From (6.47), we write

$$Q^2(z) = P^2(z) - D(z)z^{-N}D(z^{-1}) \tag{6.58}$$

We know the numerator polynomial $P(z)$ and the denominator polynomial $D(z)$ of the filter function $G(z)$, and hence we can compute the right side of the Equation 6.58. Let us denote $Q^2(z) = Q(z)Q(z)$ as $R(z) = \sum_{n=0}^{2N} r_n z^{-n}$. The coefficients of $R(z) = Q(z)Q(z)$ are computed by convolution of the coefficients of $Q(z)$ with the coefficients of $Q(z)$:

$$r_n = q_n * q_n = \sum_{k=0}^{n} q_k q_{n-k} \tag{6.59}$$

These coefficients can be computed recursively by the following algorithm:

$$q_0 = \sqrt{r_0} \tag{6.60}$$

$$q_1 = \frac{r_1}{2q_0} \tag{6.61}$$

$$q_n = \frac{r_n - \sum_{k=1}^{n-1} q_k q_{n-k}}{2q_0}, \qquad 2 \leq n \leq N \tag{6.62}$$

But we need to compute q_n for only $n = 0, 1, 2, \ldots, (N-1)/2$, since these coefficients are antisymmetric and $q_n = 0$ when $n = (N+1)/2$.

When we have computed the coefficients q_n and constructed the polynomial $Q(z) = \sum_{n=0}^{N} q_n z^{-n}$, we get $P(z) + Q(z)$, and now we factorize it to find its N zeros. We identify the zeros inside the unit circle as the r poles z_k ($k = 1, 2, 3, \ldots, r$) of $A_2(z)$. By reversing the coefficients of the polynomial having these zeros, we get the numerator of $A_2(z)$, which has the zeros at z_k^{-1}. We identify the zeros of $P(z) + Q(z)$ that are outside the unit circle as the $(N - r)$ zeros $z_j (j = r + 1, r + 2, \ldots, N)$ of $A_1(z)$. By reversing the order of the coefficients of the numerator polynomial having these zeros, we obtain the denominator polynomial of $A_1(z)$. It has $(N - r)$ zeros at z_j^{-1} as shown in (6.54). This completes the design procedure used to obtain $A_1(z)$ and $A_2(z)$ from $G(z)$. An example is worked out in Section 6.5.

6.4.2 Lattice–Ladder Realization

Another well-known realization of an IIR transfer function of the form (6.1) is shown in Figure 6.19a, and is known as the *lattice–ladder realization*. It is also called the *autoregressive moving-average* (ARMA) model in the literature on speech processing, adaptive filters, and signal processing in general. When the numerator of (6.1) is a constant, we have an all-pole model also known as the *autoregressive* (AR) *model*, and the structure to realize a third-order AR model is shown in Figure 6.19b, whereas when the denominator is a constant, we get an FIR model called the *moving-average* (MA) model. The structure shown in Figure 6.17a is the model for a third-order FIR filter function or the MA model, and the structure in Figure 6.17b is its transpose. We do not present the theoretical analysis of lattice structures for these models as it is beyond the scope of this book but explain the use of a MATLAB function `tf2latc` in the next section to derive the structures. This function implements the theoretical procedure, and for the ARMA model, it gives the N lattice parameters k_i, $i = 1, 2, \ldots, N$ and also the values of the $N + 1$ ladder coefficients v_i, $i = 0, 1, \ldots, N$. But

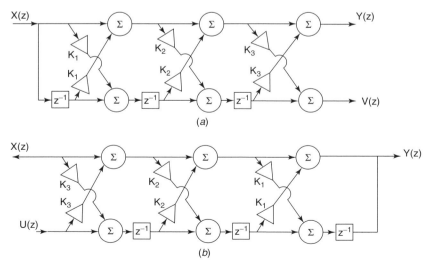

Figure 6.17 (a) Lattice structure for an FIR filter; (b) transpose of the lattice structure for the FIR filter in (a).

in Figure 6.19a, the value of the ladder coefficient v_5 happens to be zero for the numerical example, and therefore the multiplier v_5 is zero. The lattice parameters are also known as the *reflection coefficients*, and it has been shown that the poles of the IIR filter function are inside the unit circle of the z plane if $|k_i| \leq 1$. So this method is used to test whether an IIR filter is stable.

6.5   REALIZATION OF FIR AND IIR FILTERS USING MATLAB

Many of the computations involved in the realization of FIR and IIR filters as presented in this chapter can be carried out by MATLAB functions. For example, an FIR filter realization in the cascaded structure can be obtained by finding the roots of the transfer function and then finding the second-order polynomials with complex conjugate pair of the roots or a pair of two real zeros.

To find the roots of a polynomial $H(z) = \sum_{n=0}^{N} b(n)z^{-n}$, we use the MATLAB function `R = roots(b)` where the vector `b = [b(0), b(1), b(2), ⋯ b(N)]` and `R` is the vector of the `N` roots. Choosing a pair of complex conjugate roots or a pair of real roots, we construct the second-order polynomials using the MATLAB function `P_k=poly(R_k)`, where R_k is the list of two roots and P_k is the vector of the coefficients of the second-order polynomial. Of course, if $H(z)$ is an odd-order polynomial, one first-order polynomial with a single real root will be left as a term in the decomposition of $H(z)$.

Example 6.11

Using the MATLAB commands

```
b = [1.965 -3.202 4.435 -3.14 1.591 -0.3667];
R= roots(b)
```

we get the roots

```
0.2682 + 0.8986i
0.2682 - 0.8986i
0.3383 + 0.6284i
0.3383 - 0.6284i
0.4166
```

Then we continue

```
R1=[0.2682+0.8986*i 0.2682-0.8986*i];
P1=poly(R1)
P1=
1.0000 -0.5364 0.8794
R2=[0.3383+0.6284*i 0.3383-0.6284*i];
P2=poly(R2)
```

```
P2 =
1.0000 -0.6766 0.5093
```

Hence,   if $H(z) = 1.965 - 3.202z^{-1} + 4.435z^{-2} - 3.14z^{-3} + 1.591z^{-4} - 0.3667z^{-5}$, we construct a polynomial in positive powers of z and the coefficient of the highest-degree term normalized to unity:

$$N(z) = [1.965z^5 - 3.202z^4 + 4.435z^3 - 3.14z^2 + 1.591z - 0.3667]$$
$$= 1.965[z^5 - 1.6295z^4 + 2.257z^3 - 1.598z^2 + 0.8096z - 0.1866]$$

From the output data for the coefficients of P_1 and P_2 displayed above, we construct the polynomial

$$N(z) = 1.965(z^2 - 0.5364z + 0.8794)(z^2 - 0.6766z + 0.5093)(z - 0.4166)$$

Then we get $H(z)$ in the form

$$H(z) = 1.965(1 - 0.5364z^{-1} + 0.8794z^{-2})(1 - 0.6766z^{-1} + 0.5093z^{-2})$$
$$\times (1 - 0.4166z^{-1})$$

Example 6.12

Consider the same FIR filter as given in Example 6.11. We use the simple MATLAB function k = tf2latc(b) to get the vector output k listing the reflection coefficients k_i, $i = 1, 2, 3, 4, 5$, where b is the vector of the coefficients given in Example 6.11.

The vector output k for the lattice coefficients is

```
-0.3597
0.9325
-0.5745
0.5238
-0.1866
```

and the structure of the lattice realization for the FIR filter or the MA model is shown in Figure 6.18, where the lattice coefficients are as listed above.

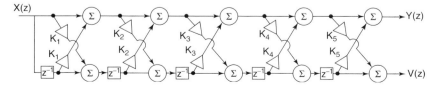

Figure 6.18   Lattice structure for a fifth-order FIR filter.

Example 6.13

To get a cascade realization of an IIR filter, one could factorize both the numerator and the denominator as the product of second-order polynomials (and possibly one first-order polynomial) as illustrated in Example 6.9. Another approach is to use the MATLAB functions tf2zp and zp2sos as explained below.

First we use the function [z,p,k] = tf2zp(num,den) to get the output vector [z,p,k], which lists the zeros, poles, and the gain constant for the IIR filter. Then the function sos = zp2sos(z,p,k) gives the coefficients of the second-order polynomials of each section in a matrix of order $L \times 6$ in the following format:

$$
\begin{bmatrix}
n_{01} & n_{11} & n_{21} & d_{01} & d_{11} & d_{21} \\
n_{02} & n_{12} & n_{22} & d_{02} & d_{12} & d_{22} \\
\cdot & \cdot & \cdot & \cdot & \cdot & \cdot \\
\cdot & \cdot & \cdot & \cdot & \cdot & \cdot \\
n_{0L} & n_{1L} & n_{2L} & d_{0L} & d_{1L} & d_{2L}
\end{bmatrix}
$$

The six elements in each row define the transfer function of each second-order section $H_i(z)$ used in the product form as indicated below:

$$
H(z) = \prod_{i=1}^{L} H_i(z) = \prod_{i=1}^{L} \left(\frac{n_{0i} + n_{1i}z^{-1} + n_{2i}z^{-2}}{d_{0i} + d_{1i}z^{-1} + d_{2i}z^{-2}} \right)
$$

These two MATLAB functions can be used to factorize an FIR function also. Instead of the algorithm described above, we let the polynomial $H(z)$ of the FIR filter, as the denominator polynomial of an IIR filter and the numerator, be unity. To illustrate this, let us consider the previous example and run the two functions in the following MATLAB script:

```
num=1;
den=b
[z,p,k] = tf2zp(num,den);
sos = zp2sos(z,p,k)
sos =
0    0.5089   0         1.0000   -0.4166   0
0    0        1.0000    1.0000   -0.6766   0.5094
0    0        1.0000    1.0000   -0.5363   0.8794
```

Therefore the product form is given by

$$
\left(\frac{0.5089z^{-1}}{1 - 0.4166z^{-1}} \right) \left(\frac{z^{-2}}{1 - 0.6766z^{-1} + 0.5094z^{-2}} \right)
$$
$$
\times \left(\frac{z^{-2}}{1 - 0.5363z^{-1} + 0.8794z^{-2}} \right)
$$

The terms in the denominator agree with those obtained in Example 6.11, which used the functions roots and poly.

Let us illustrate the decomposition of an IIR filter as the product of second-order functions; consider the transfer function

$$H(z) = \frac{0.5 + 0.2z^{-1} + 0.3z^{-2} + 0.1z^{-4}}{1.965 - 3.202z^{-1} + 4.435z^{-2} - 3.14z^{-3} + 1.591z^{-4} - 0.3667z^{-5}} \tag{6.63}$$

The MATLAB program used to obtain the factorized form to realize the cascade structure for an IIR filter is

```
num=[0.5 0.2 0.3 0.0 0.1]
den=[1.965 -3.202 4.435 -3.14 1.591 -0.3667];
[z,p,k]=tf2zp(num,den);
sos=zp2sos(z,p,k)
sos =
0          0.2545   0        1.0000   -0.4166   0
1.0000     0.8204   0.6247   1.0000   -0.6766   0.5094
1.0000    -0.4204   0.3201   1.0000   -0.5363   0.8794
```

Using the entries in this `sos` matrix, we write the factorized form of $H(z)$ as follows:

$$\left(\frac{0.2545z^{-1}}{1 - 0.4166z^{-1}}\right)\left(\frac{1 + 0.8204z^{-1} + 0.6247z^{-2}}{1 - 0.6766z^{-1} + 0.5094z^{-2}}\right)$$
$$\times \left(\frac{1 - 0.4204z^{-1} + 0.3201z^{-2}}{1 - 0.5363z^{-1} + 0.8794z^{-2}}\right) \tag{6.64}$$

Note that the numerator in this expression seems to be a fifth-order polynomial in inverse powers of z whereas the numerator of the transfer function (6.63) is a fourth-order polynomial. But the factorization of a polynomial is carried out when it is expressed in positive powers of z since the polynomials are of the form $\prod(z - z_i)$, where z_i are the zeros. So when the preceding factorized form is converted to the ratio of polynomials in positive powers of z, we get a fourth-order numerator polynomial and the fifth-order denominator:

$$\left(\frac{0.2545}{z - 0.4166}\right)\left(\frac{z^2 + 0.8204z + 0.6247}{z^2 - 0.6766z + 0.5094}\right)\left(\frac{z^2 - 0.4204z + 0.3201}{z^2 - 0.5363z + 0.8794}\right)$$
$$= \frac{0.5z^4 + 0.2z^3 + 0.3z^2 + 0.1}{1.965z^5 - 3.202z^4 + 4.435z^3 - 3.14z^2 + 1.591z - 0.3667}$$

This agrees with the result of expressing $H(z)$ as the ratio of a fourth-order numerator polynomial and a fifth-order denominator polynomial in positive powers of z. So care is to be taken to express the transfer function in positive powers of z and then check the results after constructing the factorized form, because the function `zp2sos` works only if the zeros are inside the unit circle of the z plane.

But the factorized form of $H(z)$ constructed from the `sos` matrix leads us correctly to the next step of drawing the realization structures for each section, for example, by the direct form, and connecting them in cascade. Such a realization is similar to that shown in Figure 6.14.

Example 6.14

In the previous chapter, we used the function `[r,p,k] = residuez(num,den)` to find the zeros, poles, and the gain constant of an IIR filter function $H(z)$. Now we can select the two residues in a vector `[rk(1) rk(2)]` and the corresponding poles `[pk(1) pk(2)]` in a complex conjugate pair or two real poles at a time to construct the numerator and denominator of each section in the vector form `[bk,ak]`. Then we express the IIR function $H(z)$ as the sum of such second-order functions—with one first-order section if $H(z)$ has an odd number of poles. We consider the same function $H(z)$ given by (6.63) to realize the parallel structure.

```
b =
0.5000 0.2000 0.3000 0 0.1000
a =
1.9650 -3.2020 4.4350 -3.1400 1.5910 -0.3667
[r,p,k]=residuez(b,a)
r =
-0.1632 - 0.1760i
-0.1632 + 0.1760i
0.1516 - 0.0551i
0.1516 + 0.0551i
0.2777
p =
0.2682 + 0.8986i
0.2682 - 0.8986i
0.3383 + 0.6284i
0.3383 - 0.6284i
0.4166
k =
[]
r1 =
[-0.1632 + 0.1760i -0.1632-0.1760i]
p1 =
0.2682 - 0.8986i 0.2682+0.8986i
r2 =
[0.1516 - 0.0551i 0.1516 + 0.0551i]
p2 =
0.3383 + 0.6284i  0.3383 - 0.6284i
[b1,a1]=residuez(r1,p1,0)
b1 =
-0.3264 0.4038 0
```

```
a1 =
1.0000 -0.5364 0.8794
[b2,a2]=residuez(r2,p2,0)
b2 =
0.3032 -0.0333 0
a2 =
1.0000 -0.6766 0.5093
```

The residue and the third pole are 0.2777 and 0.4166. So we construct the transfer function $H(z)$ as the sum of three terms

$$H(z) = \frac{-0.3264 + 0.4038z^{-1}}{1 - 0.5364z^{-1} + 0.8794z^{-2}} + \frac{0.3032 - 0.0333z^{-1}}{1 - 0.6766z^{-1} + 0.5093z^{-2}}$$
$$+ \frac{0.2777}{1 - 0.4166z^{-1}}. \tag{6.65}$$

The structure found in realizing the parallel connection is similar to that shown in Figure 6.15.

Example 6.15

We used the MATLAB function k = tf2latc(num) to obtain the lattice realization of an (MA) FIR filter in Example 6.12. It is a special case of the more general function [k,v] = tf2latc(num,den) used to obtain the lattice–ladder (ARMA) realization of an IIR filter, where k is the vector of the lattice coefficients (reflection coefficients) and the vector v gives the ladder coefficients—an example of which is shown in Figure 6.19a. Note that the lattice coefficients are in reverse order (i.e., they are shown from right to left) of that shown in Figure 6.17a; also note that the number of lattice coefficients in Figure 6.18(a) is N but the number of the ladder coefficients is $N + 1$. Another special case is the function k = tf2latc(1,den), which gives the lattice coefficients of an all-pole (AR) IIR filter. A structure for a third-order AR model is given in Figure 6.19b. Note the difference in the structure for this AR model and the structures for the FIR filter that is defined as the MA model shown in Figure 6.17.

Let us consider the transfer function $H(z)$ given in (6.63) to obtain its lattice–ladder realization. We use the following MATLAB function [k,v] = tf2latc(num,den) and get the vector outputs k and v immediately. The structure for this realization is shown in Figure 6.19a, where the values of the lattice and ladder coefficients are as follows:

```
b = [ 0.5000 0.2000 0.3000 0 0.1000];
a=[ 1.9650  -3.2020 4.4350 -3.1400 1.5910 -0.3667];
[k,v] = tf2latc(b,a)
k =
-0.3597
0.9325
```

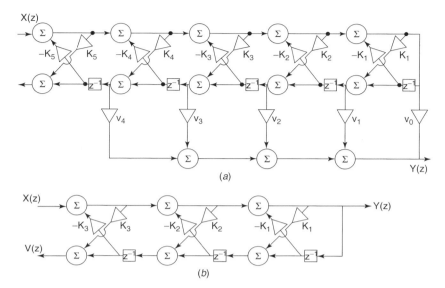

Figure 6.19 (a) Lattice–ladder structure for an IIR filter (ARMA model); (b) lattice structure for an all-pole IIR filter $Y(z)/X(z)$ (AR model) and an allpass filter $V(z)/X(z)$.

```
-0.5745
0.5238
-0.1866
v =
0.3831
0.3164
0.2856
0.1532
0.1000
0
```

Example 6.16

In order to illustrate the derivation of a lattice structure for an all-pole (AR model) filter, we select a transfer function

$$H(z^{-1}) = \frac{1}{1 - 0.2051z^{-1} - 0.0504z^{-2} + 0.0154z^{-3}} \qquad (6.66)$$

and use the MATLAB function [k] = tf2latc(1,den) to get the vector output for the lattice coefficients as shown below:

$$k = -0.2145$$
$$-0.0473$$
$$0.0154$$

The lattice structure for this filter is shown in Figure 6.19b, where $H(z^{-1}) = Y(z)/X(z)$.

Suppose that we select an allpass transfer function $H_{ap}(z^{-1})$

$$H_{ap}(z^{-1}) = \frac{0.0154 - 0.0504z^{-1} - 0.0205z^{-2} + z^{-3}}{1 - 0.2051z^{-1} - 0.0504z^{-2} + 0.0154z^{-3}} \quad (6.67)$$

and use the function [k,v] = tf2latc(num,den) we get the following outputs for the vectors k and v:

$$k = -0.2145$$
$$-0.0473$$
$$0.0154$$
$$v = 0.0000$$
$$0.0000$$
$$0.0000$$
$$1.0000$$

Although this allpass transfer function has a numerator and a denominator and hence is not an AR model, the lattice structure for realizing it is the same as the lattice structure for an AR model in Figure 6.19b, but the output is $V(z)$ and not $Y(z)$. Hence the allpass transfer function realized is $H_{ap}(z^{-1}) = V(z)/X(z)$.

When we compare Figure 6.17 for the lattice structure for the third-order FIR (MA) filter and Figure 6.19b for the lattice structure for the third-order IIR all-pole (AR) or the allpass (AP) filter, carefully note the direction of the multipliers and their signs, which are different. Also note that the output terminals are different for the all-pole filter and allpass filters in Figure 6.19b.

6.5.1   MATLAB Program Used to Find Allpass Filters in Parallel

A MATLAB program lp2apx.m, developed by the author, to obtain the decomposition of a lowpass filter as the sum of two allpass filters is given below. The input data consist of the cutoff frequency W_p of the passband, the stopband frequency W_s, the maximum attenuation A_p in the passband, and the minimum attenuation A_s in the stopband, which are entered according to the choice of the Butterworth, Chebyshev I, Chebyshev II, and elliptic lowpass filters. If the order of the filter derived from the functions buttord, cheb1ord, cheb2ord or ellipord is found to be an even integer, it is automatically increased by one to make it an odd-order integer. The program immediately makes available the magnitude response of the specified lowpass filter $G(z)$, the response of the lowpass filter computed from the two allpass filters $A_1(z)$ and $A_2(z)$, and also the highpass filter $H(z)$. The coefficients of the numerator and denominator polynomials of $A_1(z)$ and $A_2(z)$ are obtained by typing A1N, A1D, A2N, and

A2D, respectively. So also the coefficients of the numerator and denominator of $G(z)$ can be obtained by typing b and a, respectively. If we type A1, A2, G, or H, the program displays the transfer function as the ratio of two polynomials. The program may not work successfully if the specifications call for a very narrow transition band or a very high order for the filter, because of numerical inaccuracy.

```
%This Matlab Program lp2apx.m obtains the allpass filters
%   A₁(z) and A₂(z) from the lowpass (Butterworth, Chebyshev I
%   and Elliptic) filters of odd order.
clear all
Wp=input('Enter the passband cutoff frequency between 0
  and 1');
Ws=input('Enter the stopband cutoff frequency Wp<Ws<1');
Ap=input('Enter the max.attenuation in the passband');
As=input('Enter the min.attenuation in the stopband');
disp('As ftype,type in (1) for Butterworth, (2) for
  Chebyshev I, (3) Chebyshev II and (4) for Elliptic
  filters');
ftype=input('');
if ftype==1
disp('Butterworth Lowpass Filter');

[N,Wn]=buttord(Wp,Ws,Ap,As);
M=mod(N,2);
if M==0
N=N+1
end
[b,a]=butter(N,Wn);
end
if ftype==2
disp('Chebyshev I Lowpass Filter')
[N,Wn]=cheb1ord(Wp,Ws,Ap,As);
M=mod(N,2);
if M==0
N=N+1
end
[b,a]=cheby1(N,Ap,Wn);
end
if ftype==3
disp('Chebyshev II Lowpass filter')
[N,Wn]=cheb2ord(Wp,Ws,Ap,As);
M=mod(N,2);
if M==0
N=N+1
end
```

```
[b,a]=cheby2(N,As,Wn);
end
if ftype==4
disp('Elliptic Lowpass Filter')
[N,Wn]=ellipord(Wp,Ws,Ap,As);
M=mod(N,2);
if M==0
N=N+1
end
[b,a]=ellip(N,Ap,As,Wn);
end
[h0,w]=freqz(b,a,256);
H0=abs(h0);
plot(w/pi,H0);grid
axis([0.0 1.0 0.0 1.0])
title('MAGNITUDE OF SPECIFIED LP FILTER')
ylabel('Magnitude')
xlabel('Normalized frequency')
% TO FIND Q(z)
k=sum(a)/sum(b);
b=b*k;
fliped_a= fliplr(a);
%R(z)= Q2(z)=P2(z)-z^-N D(z^-1)D(z)
R=conv(b,b)-conv(a,fliped_a);
% Calculate Q
Q(1)=R(1)^(0.5);
Q(2)=R(2)/(2*Q(1));
for n=2:N
term=0;
for k=1:n-1
term=Q(k+1)*Q(n-k+1)+term;
end
Q(n+1)=(R(n+1)-term)/(2*Q(1));
end
%Zeros of P+Q is calculated
j=1;
k=0;
P_plus_Q=b+Q;
zeros=roots(P_plus_Q);
for i=1:N
if abs(zeros(i))<1
zero_in(j)=zeros(i);
j=j+1;
else
k=k+1;
```

```
zero_out(k)=zeros(i);
end
end
A1N=poly(zero_out);%Numerator of A_1(z)
A1D=fliplr(A1N); %Denominator of A_1(z)
A1=tf(A1N,A1D,1);
A2D=poly(zero_in);%Denominator of A_2(z)
A2N=fliplr(A2D);%Numerator of A_2(z)
A2=tf(A2N,A2D,1);
G=0.5*(A1+A2); % LOWPASS FILTER FROM THE TWO ALLPASS FILTERS
[numlp,denlp]=tfdata(G,'v');
[h1,w]=freqz(numlp,denlp,256);
H1=abs(h1);
figure
plot(w/pi,H1);grid
axis([0.0 1.0 0.0 1.0])
title('MAGNITUDE OF LP FILTER FROM THE TWO ALLPASS FILTERS')
ylabel('Magnitude')
xlabel('Normalized frequency')
H=0.5*(A1-A2); % HIGHPASS FILTER FROM THE TWO ALLPASS FILTERS
[numhp,denhp]=tfdata(H,'v');
[h2,w]=freqz(numhp,denhp,256);
H2=abs(h2);
figure
plot(w/pi,H2);grid
axis([0.0 1.0 0.0 1.0])
title('MAGNITUDE OF HP FILTER FROM THE TWO ALL PASS FILTERS')
ylabel('Magnitude')
xlabel('Normalized frequency')
%END
```

Example 6.17

We illustrate the use of this program by taking the example of an elliptic lowpass filter with the specifications $W_p = 0.4$, $W_s = 0.6$, $A_p = 0.3$, and $A_s = 35$, which have been chosen only to highlight the passband and stopband responses. A complete session for running this example is given below, including the three magnitude response plots mentioned above:

```
Enter the passband cutoff frequency between 0 and 1   0.4
Enter the stopband cutoff frequency Wp<Ws<1   0.6
Enter the max.attenuation in the passband   0.3
Enter the min.attenuation in the stopband   35
As ftype, type in (1) for Butterworth, (2) for Chebyshev I,
  (3) for Chebyshev II (4) for Elliptic filters
```

```
4
Elliptic Lowpass Filter
N =
5
A1N
A1N =
1.0000 -1.3289 1.9650
A1D
A1D =
1.9650 -1.3289 1.0000
A2N
A2N =
-0.3667 1.1036 -0.9532 1.0000
A2D
A2D =
1.0000 -0.9532 1.1036 -0.3667
A1

Transfer function:
z^2 - 1.329 z + 1.965
-----------------------
1.965 z^2 - 1.329 z + 1

Sampling time: 1

A2

Transfer function:
-0.3667 z^3 + 1.104 z^2 - 0.9532 z + 1
--------------------------------------
z^3 - 0.9532 z^2 + 1.104 z - 0.3667

Sampling time: 1

G

Transfer function:
0.1397 z^5 + 0.1869 z^4 + 0.3145 z^3 + 0.3145 z^2 + 0.1869 z
   + 0.1397
-------------------------------------------------------------
1.965 z^5 - 3.202 z^4 + 4.435 z^3 - 3.14 z^2 + 1.591 z
   - 0.3667

Sampling time: 1
```

H

```
Transfer function:
0.8603 z^5 - 2.469 z^4 + 4.021 z^3 - 4.021 z^2 + 2.469 z
  - 0.8603
----------------------------------------------------------------
1.965 z^5 - 3.202 z^4 + 4.435 z^3 - 3.14 z^2 + 1.591 z
  - 0.3667

Sampling time: 1
```

We rewrite the transfer function $G(z^{-1})$ in the following form for reference in the next chapter:

$$\left(\frac{0.1397}{1.965}\right) \frac{(1 + 1.337z^{-1} + 2.251z^{-2} + 2.251z^{-3} + 1.337z^{-4} + z^{-5})}{(1 - 1.629z^{-1} + 2.256z^{-2} - 1.597z^{-3} + 0.8096z^{-4} - 0.1866z^{-5})}$$
$$(6.68)$$

The magnitude response of the lowpass elliptic filter $G(z)$, the magnitude response of the parallel connection $G(z) = \frac{1}{2}[A_1(z) + A_2(z)]$, and that of the highpass filter $H(z) = \frac{1}{2}[A_1(z) - A_2(z)]$ are shown in Figures 6.20, 6.21, and 6.22, respectively.

The two allpass filter functions (6.69) and (6.71) obtained in the example above are expressed in the form of (6.70) and 6.72, respectively. The function $A_1(z)$ can be realized in the direct form, and $A_2(z)$ can be realized in many of the structures that we have already discussed, for example, the direct form,

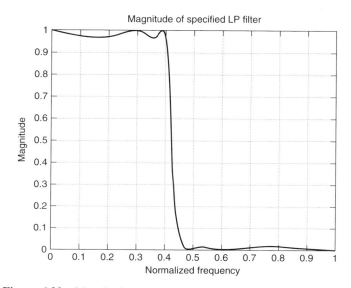

Figure 6.20   Magnitude response of the elliptic lowpass filter $G(z)$.

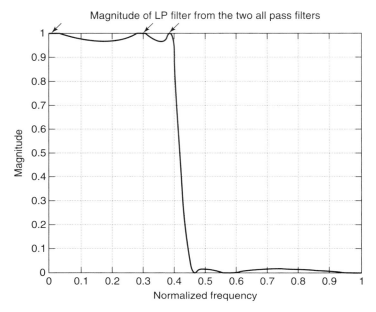

Figure 6.21   Magnitude response of two allpass filters in parallel.

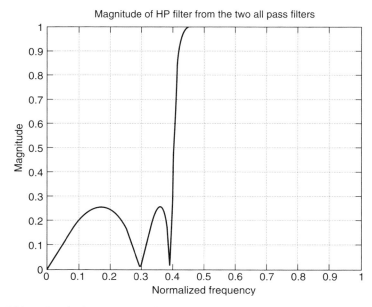

Figure 6.22   Magnitude response of a highpass filter from the two allpass filters in parallel.

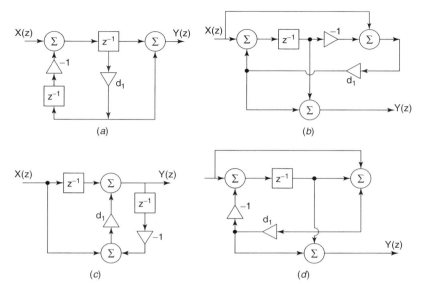

Figure 6.23   First-order allpass structures.

parallel form, or lattice–ladder form. But the class of allpass functions of first and second orders can be realized by many structures that employ the fewest multipliers [1]. A few examples of first-order and second-order allpass filters are shown in Figures 6.23 and 6.24, respectively. Their transfer functions are respectively given by

$$A_\mathrm{I}(z) = \frac{d_1 + z^{-1}}{1 + d_1 z^{-1}}$$

$$A_\mathrm{II}(z) = \frac{d_1 d_2 + d_1 z^{-1} + z^{-2}}{1 + d_1 z^{-1} + d_1 d_2 z^{-2}}$$

We choose the simpler structure of second-order allpass filter from Figure 6.24a for A_1 and $A_2(z)$, which requires fewer delay elements than do the remaining four second-order structures. When these two allpass filters are connected in parallel (as shown in Fig. 6.16), we get the structure shown in Figure 6.25 for the transfer function $G(z)$ of the fifth-order elliptic lowpass filter chosen in this example:

$$A_1(z) = \frac{z^2 - 1.329z + 1.965}{1.965z^2 - 1.329z + 1} \tag{6.69}$$

$$= \frac{1 - 1.329z^{-1} + 1.965z^{-2}}{1.965 - 1.329z^{-1} + z^{-2}}$$

$$= \frac{0.5089 - 0.6763z^{-1} + z^{-2}}{1 - 0.6763z^{-1} + 0.5089z^{-2}} \tag{6.70}$$

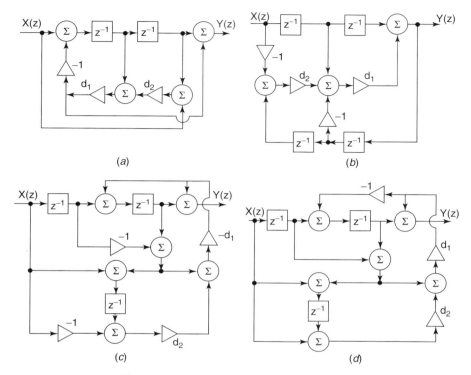

Figure 6.24 Second-order allpass structures.

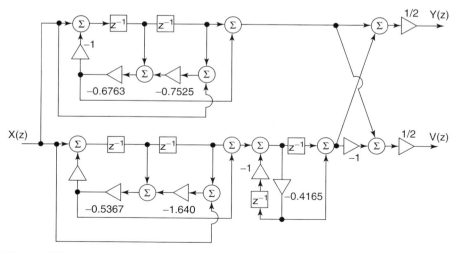

Figure 6.25 A fifth-order elliptic lowpass IIR filter realized as the parallel connection of two allpass structures.

$$A_2(z) = \frac{-0.3667z^3 + 1.104z^2 - 0.9532z + 1}{z^3 - 0.9532z^2 + 1.104z - 0.3667} \tag{6.71}$$

$$= \frac{-0.3667 + 1.104z^{-1} - 0.9532z^{-2} + z^{-3}}{1 - 0.9532z^{-1} + 1.104z^{-2} - 0.3667z^{-3}} \tag{6.72}$$

We express the third-order allpass function $A_2(z)$ in product form as shown in (6.73), using a second-order allpass structure from Figure 6.24a connected in cascade with a first-order allpass structure from Figure 6.23a to realize the third-order allpass filter $A_2(z)$. It is then connected in parallel with the second-order allpass filter $A_1(z)$. The structure for the lowpass elliptic filter $G(z) = \frac{1}{2}[A_1(z) + A_2(z)]$ is shown in Figure 6.25. We obtain

$$A_2(z) = \left(\frac{0.8805 - 0.5368z^{-1} + z^{-2}}{1 - 0.5367z^{-1} + 0.8805z^{-2}} \right) \left(\frac{-0.4165 + z^{-1}}{1 - 0.4165z^{-1}} \right) \tag{6.73}$$

Instead of designing the allpass functions found in Figures 6.24 and 6.25, we can design them in the form of lattice allpass structures as described earlier. The lattice coefficients for the second-order filter $A_1(z)$ and the third-order filter $A_2(z)$ are found by using the MATLAB function `[k,v]` = `tf2latc(num,den)`, and after obtaining the lattice structures for them, they are connected in parallel as shown in Figure 6.27.

```
%Design of the second order filter A₁(z)
A1num=[0.5089 -0.6763 1];
A1den=[1 -0.6763 0.5089];
[K1,V1]=tf2latc(A1num,A1den)

%Lattice and ladder coefficients for A₁(z)
K1 =
-0.4482
0.5089
V1 =
0
0
1


%Design of third order filter A₂(z)
A2num=[-0.3667 1.104 -0.9532 1];
A2den=fliplr(A2num)
[K2,V2]=tf2latc(A2num,A2den)
%Lattice and ladder coefficients for A₂(z)


K2 =
-0.3385
```

```
0.8717
-0.3667

V2 =
0
0
0
1
```

The circuit realizing the third-order transfer function $A_2(z)$ in the form of a lattice–ladder structure is shown in Figure 6.26, where the values of $V_0 = V_1 = V_2 = 0$ as shown by the vector V2 above.

The circuit realizing the fifth-order lowpass elliptic filter as the parallel connection of two allpass filters $A_1(z)$ and $A_2(z)$, each realized by the lattice structures, is shown in Figure 6.27.

Now let us compare the different circuits that we have designed to realize a lowpass fifth-order, IIR filter. All of these circuits have been designed to meet the following same specifications—$W_p = 0.4$, $W_s = 0.6$, $A_p = 0.3$, and $A_s = 35$—and have been realized by a cascade connection, a parallel connection, and a lattice–ladder connection as shown in Figures 6.14, 6.15, and 6.19, respectively. They use more than the minimum number of five multipliers, whereas the lattice-coupled allpass filter shown in Figure 6.25 uses five multipliers—disregarding the multipliers with a gain of -1 or $\frac{1}{2}$ because they represent

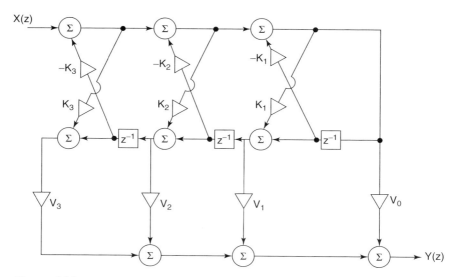

Figure 6.26 A third-order allpass filter $A_2(z)$ realized as a lattice–ladder structure.

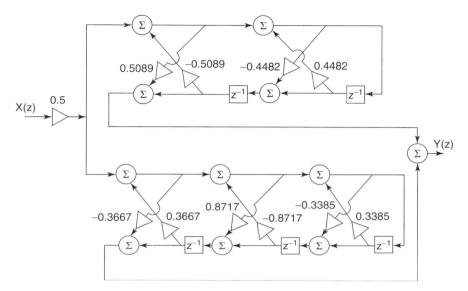

Figure 6.27   Two lattice–ladder allpass structures connected in parallel to realize a fifth-order lowpass elliptic filter.

minor operations on binary numbers. The direct-form IIR filter for a fifth-order filter would also require more than five multipliers, whereas the filter shown in Figure 6.27, which has lattice–ladder, coupled allpass filters, requires 10 multipliers. Therefore we conclude that the parallel connection of allpass filters as shown in Figure 6.25 requires a minimum number of delay elements and thus offers an advantage over the other structures.

The realization of IIR filters as a parallel connection of allpass filters has another advantage, as explained below. It was pointed out that the magnitude response of allpass filters does not change when the multiplier constants are quantized to finite wordlength. The other advantage is that there are many structures for realizing allpass filters that contain a minimum number of multipliers (and delay elements). In the method of realizing the lowpass filter by a connection of two allpass filters in parallel, we used Property (6.4) in Equation (6.42) which is reproduced below:

$$\left| G(e^{j\omega}) \right| = \tfrac{1}{2} \left| e^{j\theta_1(\omega)} + e^{j\theta_2(\omega)} \right| = \tfrac{1}{2} \left| 1 + e^{j(\theta_1(\omega) - \theta_2(\omega))} \right| \leq 1$$

This shows that the lowpass filter containing the two allpass structures in parallel has a magnitude response equal to or less than unity. The magnitude response in Figure 6.28 illustrates this property in the passband and attains the maximum value at three frequencies in the passband, which are marked by arrows. As

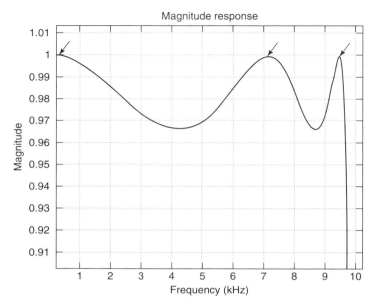

Figure 6.28   Magnified magnitude response of an elliptic lowpass filter.

long as the allpass filters maintain a constant magnitude at all frequencies and remain stable, as their multiplier constants change in wordlength, the magnitude response of the lowpass filter cannot exceed this constant at these three frequencies, where the derivative of the magnitude response is zero. Hence for small changes in wordlength (e.g., by 1 or 2 bits), the change in magnitude response at these frequencies is almost zero. At other frequencies in the passband, the change in magnitude is also expected to be small, if not zero. Simulation of their performance with small changes in wordlength has verified that the change in their magnitude response is significantly smaller than that displayed by the other structures. This shows that the structure of allpass filters in parallel has many advantages compared to the other structures that have been proposed for realizing IIR filters. In the next chapter, where the effect of finite wordlength is studied in greater detail, the structure for allpass filters in parallel will be called *lattice-coupled allpass structure*. But these structures can be used to design only lowpass filters (of odd order) whereas the lattice and lattice–ladder structures can realize any transfer function in general.

6.6   SUMMARY

When we have obtained the transfer functions of FIR and IIR filters that approximate a given set of specifications—as explained in the previous two chapters—our next step is to choose the best structures that would meet some important criteria before the algorithm in the time domain can be programmed or a filter can be designed and built in hardware. It is obvious that the algorithm for implementing a filter will depend on the particular structure being considered to realize it. Under ideal assumptions that the magnitude of the input signals and the values of the multiplier constants are available with infinite precision, any one of the several alternative structures will realize the transfer function. But when they are expressed with a finite number of bits, their actual performance may be quite different, particularly when they are represented by a fixed-point binary representation. So it is necessary to investigate in great detail their performance in the time domain and the frequency domain and compare them. Some of the performance criteria used for comparison are the effective degradation in the frequency response, the stability and potential limit cycles, complexity of the algorithm flow control, number of multiplications, and additions per sample output. Extensive simulation on a computer is essential to address these issues, before we chose a few structures for further investigation.

In this chapter, we discussed several structures to realize the FIR and IIR filters and commented on the effects of finite wordlength. More detailed discussion of this criterion and other issues will be included in the next chapter.

PROBLEMS

6.1 Draw the direct form and the cascade form of the FIR filter with the following transfer function:

$$H(z^{-1}) = 4(1 + 0.6z^{-1} - 0.5z^{-2})(1 - 0.25z^{-1} + 0.9z^{-2})$$

6.2 Find the polyphase structure for the FIR filter in Problem 6.1 and its transpose.

6.3 Determine the transpose of the direct-form structure realizing the FIR filter

$$H(z^{-1}) = 1 + z^{-1} - 0.5z^{-2} + 0.02z^{-3} + 0.003z^{-5}$$

6.4 Determine the polyphase structure for the FIR filter given in Problem 6.3.

6.5 Find the polyphase structure for the FIR filter

$$H(z^{-1}) = 1 + 0.5z^{-1} + 0.4z^{-2} - 0.6z^{-3} + z^{-4} + 1.2z^{-5} + 0.2z^{-6}$$

6.6 Obtain the transfer functions $H_1(z) = Y(z)/X(z)$ and $H_2(z) = G(z)/X(z)$ of the lattice circuit shown in Figure 6.29.

6.7 Draw the direct form and transpose of the circuit shown in Figure 6.29.

6.8 (a) Derive the transfer function $H_1(z) = Y(z)/X(z)$ of the lattice structure shown in Figure 6.30.

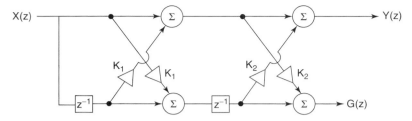

Figure 6.29   Problem 6.6.

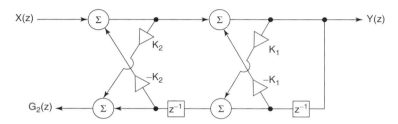

Figure 6.30   Problem 6.8.

(b) Derive the transfer function $G(z) = G_2(z)/Y(z)$ and show that the transfer function $H_2(z) = G_2(z)/X(z)$ is an allpass function.

(c) If the transfer function for the lattice structure shown in Figure 6.30 is $H_1(z) = 1/(1 + 1.38z^{-1} + 1.3z^{-2})$, what are the values of K_1 and K_2?

6.9   Draw the transpose of the lattice structure shown in Figure 6.29.

6.10   Plot the unit pulse response of the filter shown in Figure 6.31a,b.

6.11   Derive the transfer function $H(z) = Y(z)/X(z)$ for the structure shown in Figure 6.32.

6.12   Draw the transpose of the structure shown in Figure 6.32.

6.13   **(a)** Draw the circuit in a parallel structure, to realize the following transfer function $H(z^{-1})$ and find its inverse z transform $h(n)$:

$$H(z^{-1}) = \frac{(1 + 0.2z^{-1})z^{-2}}{(1 - 0.6z^{-1} + 0.25z^{-2})(1 + 0.4z^{-1})}$$

(b) Derive the inverse z transform of

$$H(z) = \frac{(1 + 0.2z)z^2}{(1 - 0.6z + 0.25z^2)(1 + 0.4z)}$$

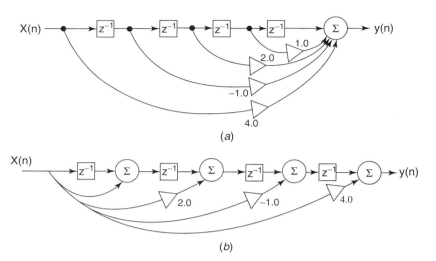

(a)

(b)

Figure 6.31 Problem 6.10.

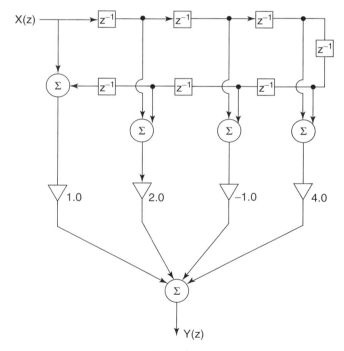

Figure 6.32 Problem 6.12.

6.14 Find the z transform $X(z)$ of $[(0.8)^n - (0.4)^n] u(n)$. What is the inverse z transform of $X(-z)$?

6.15 Draw the digital filter circuit in both cascade and parallel forms to realize the following transfer function:

$$H(z) = \frac{0.44z^2 + 0.36z + 0.02}{(z^2 + 0.8z + 0.5)(z - 0.4)}$$

6.16 Draw the direct form I, direct form II, cascade and parallel structures for the transfer function

$$H(z^{-1}) = \frac{z^{-1}}{(1 + 0.2z^{-1})(1 + 0.6z^{-1} + 0.2z^{-2})}$$

6.17 Draw the transpose of the structures obtained in Problem 6.16.

6.18 Given a transfer function

$$H(z^{-1}) = \frac{1 + 0.1z^{-1}}{(1 + 0.3z^{-1})(1 + 0.5z^{-1})}$$

obtain the cascade and parallel structures to realize it. Draw their transpose structures also.

6.19 Draw the direct form II structure for the structure shown in Figure 6.33. Find the unit pulse response of this structure for $r = 0.6$ and $\theta = \pi/5$.

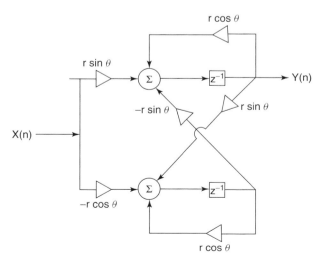

Figure 6.33 Problem 6.19.

6.20 Obtain as many structures as you can to realize the following transfer function:

$$H(z) = \frac{(z + 0.2)}{(z + 0.1)(z + 0.4)(z^2 + 0.5z + 0.06)}$$

6.21 Determine the cascade and parallel structures for the transfer function

$$H(z) = \frac{(1 + 0.3z^{-1})}{(1 - 0.3z^{-1})(1 - 0.5e^{j\frac{\pi}{3}}z^{-1})(1 - 0.5e^{-j\frac{\pi}{3}}z^{-1})}$$

MATLAB Problems

6.22 Find the direct-form and cascade structures realizing the FIR filter function $H(z^{-1})$

$$H(z^{-1}) = 1 + 0.2z^{-1} + 0.3z^{-2} - 0.4z^{-3} - 0.5z^{-5} + 0.6z^{-6} + z^{-7}$$

6.23 Find the direct-form and cascade structures realizing the FIR filters

$$H_1(z^{-1}) = 1 - 0.5z^{-1} + 0.3z^{-2} + 0.1z^{-3} + 0.02z^{-4} - 0.05z^{-5}$$

and

$$H_2(z^{-1}) = 1.0 + 0.8z^{-1} + 0.8z^{-2} + 0.08z^{-3} + 0.01z^{-4}$$

6.24 Determine the lattice structures to realize the FIR filters in Problem 6.23.

6.25 Find the direct form I and the cascade structures to realize the following IIR filters:

$$H_1(z) = \frac{1 - 0.25z^{-1}}{1 + 0.9z^{-1}} + \frac{z^{-1}}{1 + 0.5z^{-1}} + \frac{1 + 0.4z^{-1}}{1 + 0.2z^{-1} + 0.08z^{-2}}$$

$$H_2(z^{-1}) = \frac{1 + 0.1z^{-1} + z^{-2} - 0.2z^{-3}}{1 + z^{-1} + 0.24z^{-2}} + \frac{4z^{-1}}{(1 - 0.8z^{-1})(1 - 0.4z^{-1})}$$

6.26 Find the structure in the parallel and cascade connections to realize the following filters:

$$H_1(z^{-1}) = \left(\frac{z^{-1}}{1 - 0.5z^{-1}} + \frac{z^{-1}}{1 + 0.5z^{-1}} \right) \left(\frac{z^{-1}}{1 - 0.2z^{-1}} + \frac{z^{-1}}{1 + 0.2z^{-1}} \right)$$

$$H_2(z^{-1}) = \left(\frac{1 - 0.25z^{-1}}{1 + 0.9z^{-1}} + \frac{z^{-1}}{1 + 0.5z^{-1}} \right)$$

$$\times \left(\frac{1 + z^{-1}}{1 + 0.4z^{-1}} + \frac{2z^{-2}}{1 + 0.6z^{-1} + 0.6z^{-2}} \right)$$

6.27 Draw the structures in a cascade connection and in a parallel connection to realize the following IIR filter:

$$H(z^{-1}) = \frac{1.0 + 0.0141z^{-1} + 0.0284z^{-2}}{1 - 2.9061z^{-1} + 4.2077z^{-2} - 3.45412z^{-3} + 1.6046z^{-4} - 0.3365z^{-5}}$$

6.28 Draw the lattice structures to realize the following all-pole IIR filters. Are they stable?

$$H_1(z^{-1}) = \frac{1}{1.0 + 0.3z^{-1} - 0.04z^{-2} - 0.13z^{-3} - 0.02z^{-4}}$$

$$H_2(z^{-1}) = \frac{1}{1.0 + 2.3z^{-1} + 0.16z^{-2} - 0.25z^{-3} - 0.26z^{-4}}$$

$$H_3(z^{-1}) = \frac{1}{1.0 + 0.6z^{-1} - 6.01z^{-2} - 3.75z^{-3} - 1.5z^{-4}}$$

6.29 Draw the lattice structure for the following allpass filters:

$$A_1(z^{-1}) = \frac{0.01 - 0.75z^{-1} + z^{-2}}{1 - 0.75z^{-1} + 0.01z^{-2}}$$

$$A_2(z^{-1}) = \frac{-0.12 - 0.06z^{-1} + 0.1z^{-2} + z^{-3}}{1 + 0.1z^{-1} - 0.06z^{-2} - 0.12z^{-3}}$$

6.30 Find the lattice–ladder structure for the following IIR filter:

$$H(z^{-1}) = \frac{1.2 + z^{-1}}{1.0 + 1.1z^{-1} + 0.5z^{-2} + 0.1z^{-3}}$$

6.31 Find the lattice–ladder structure for the following IIR filter:

$$H(z^{-1}) = \frac{0.01 - 0.75z^{-1}}{1 - 0.75z^{-1} + 0.01z^{-2}}$$

6.32 Determine the lattice–ladder structure for the following IIR filter:

$$H(z^{-1}) = \frac{-0.12 - 0.06z^{-1} + 0.1z^{-2} + z^{-3}}{1 + 0.1z^{-1} - 0.06z^{-2} - 0.12z^{-3}}$$

6.33 Find the lattice–ladder structure for the following IIR filters:

$$H_1(z^{-1}) = \frac{0.9 + 0.7z^{-1} - 0.6z^{-2}}{1.0 + z^{-1} + 0.47z^{-2} + 0.098z^{-3} + 0.006z^{-4}}$$

$$H_2(z^{-1}) = \frac{1.0 + 0.5z^{-1} + 0.5z^{-2}}{1.0 + z^{-1} + 0.47z^{-2} + 0.098z^{-3} + 0.006z^{-4}}$$

$$H_3(z^{-1}) = \frac{1.0 + z^{-1} + z^{-2}}{1.0 + z^{-1} + 0.52z^{-2} + 0.12z^{-3} + 0.016z^{-4}}$$

6.34 Design a lowpass Butterworth filter with $W_p = 0.3$, $W_s = 0.6$, $A_p = 0.25$, $A_s = 55$ in an lattice-coupled allpass structure. Give the magnitude response of the Butterworth filter and the lattice-coupled allpass filter on the same plot.

6.35 Design a Chebyshev lowpass IIR filter with the specifications from Problem 6.34 in a lattice-coupled allpass structure. Give the magnitude response of the Chebyshev filter and the lattice-coupled allpass filter structure for the same filter on the same plot.

6.36 Design an elliptic lowpass IIR filter $W_p = 0.25$, $W_s = 0.5$, $A_p = 0.20$, $A_s = 60$, in a lattice-coupled allpass structure. Give the magnitude response of the elliptic filter and the lattice-coupled allpass filter for the same filter on the same plot.

REFERENCES

1. S. K. Mitra and K. Hirano, Digital allpass networks, *IEEE Trans. Circuits Syst.* **CAS-21**, 688–700 (1974).

2. J. G. Proakis and D. G. Manolakis, *Digital Signal Processing*, Prentice-Hall, 1996.

3. S. K. Mitra, *Digital Signal Processing—A Computer Based Approach*. McGraw-Hill, 2001.

4. S. K. Mitra and J. F. Kaiser, eds., *Handbook for Digital Signal Processing*, Wiley-Interscience, 1993.

5. B. A. Shenoi, *Magnitude and Delay Approximation of 1-D and 2-D Digital Filters*, Springer-Verlag, 1999.

CHAPTER 7

Quantized Filter Analysis

7.1 INTRODUCTION

The analysis and design of discrete-time systems, digital filters, and their realizations, computation of DFT-IDFT, and so on discussed in the previous chapters of this book were carried out by using mostly the functions in the Signal Processing Toolbox working in the MATLAB environment, and the computations were carried out with double precision. This means that all the data representing the values of the input signal, coefficients of the filters, or the values of the unit impulse response, and so forth were represented with 64 bits; therefore, these numbers have a range approximately between 10^{-308} and 10^{308} and a precision of $\sim 2^{-52} = 2.22 \times 10^{-6}$. Obviously this range is so large and the precision with which the numbers are expressed is so small that the numbers can be assumed to have almost "infinite precision." Once these digital filters and DFT-IDFT have been obtained by the procedures described so far, they can be further analyzed by mainframe computers, workstations, and PCs under "infinite precision." But when the algorithms describing the digital filters and FFT computations have to be implemented as hardware in the form of special-purpose microprocessors or application-specific integrated circuits (ASICs) or the digital signal processor (DSP) chip, many practical considerations and constraints come into play. The registers used in these hardware systems, to store the numbers have finite length, and the memory capacity required for processing the data is determined by the number of bits—also called the *wordlength*—chosen for storing the data. More memory means more power consumption and hence the need to minimize the wordlength. In microprocessors and DSP chips and even in workstations and PCs, we would like to use registers with as few bits as possible and yet obtain high computational speed, low power, and low cost. But such portable devices such as cell phones and personal digital assistants (PDAs) have a limited amount of memory, containing batteries with low voltage and short duration of power supply. These constraints become more severe in other devices such as digital hearing aids and biomedical probes embedded in capsules to be swallowed. So there is a

Introduction to Digital Signal Processing and Filter Design, by B. A. Shenoi
Copyright © 2006 John Wiley & Sons, Inc.

great demand for designing digital filters and systems in which they are embedded, with the lowest possible number of bits to represent the data or to store the data in their registers. When the filters are built with registers of finite length and the analog-to-digital converters (ADCs) are designed to operate at increasingly high sampling rates, thereby reducing the number of bits with which the samples of the input signal are represented, the frequency response of the filters and the results of DFT-IDFT computations via the FFT are expected to differ from those designed with "infinite precision." This process of representing the data with a finite number of bits is known as *quantization*, which occurs at several points in the structure chosen to realize the filter or the steps in the FFT computation of the DFT-IDFT. As pointed out in the previous chapter, a vast number of structures are available to realize a given transfer function, when we assume infinite precision. But when we design the hardware with registers of finite length to implement their corresponding difference equation, the effect of finite wordlength is highly dependent on the structure. Therefore we find it necessary to analyze this effect for a large number of structures. This analysis is further compounded by the fact that quantization can be carried out in several ways and the arithmetic operations of addition and multiplication of numbers with finite precision yield results that are influenced by the way that these numbers are quantized.

In this chapter, we discuss a new MATLAB toolbox called FDA Tool available[1] for analyzing and designing the filters with a finite number of bits for the wordlength. The different form of representing binary numbers and the results of adding and multiplying such numbers will be explained in a later section of this chapter. The third factor that influences the deviation of filter performance from the ideal case is the choice of FIR or IIR filter. The type of approximation chosen for obtaining the desired frequency response is another factor that also influences the effect of finite wordlength. We discuss the effects of all these factors in this chapter, illustrating their influence by means of a design example.

7.2 FILTER DESIGN–ANALYSIS TOOL

An enormous amount of research has been carried out to address these problems, but analyzing the effects of quantization on the performance of digital filters and systems is not well illustrated by specific examples. Although there is no analytical method available at present to design or analyze a filter with finite precision, some useful insight can be obtained from the research work, which serves as a guideline in making preliminary decisions on the choice of suitable structures and quantization forms. Any student interested in this research work should read the material on finite wordlength effects found in other textbooks [1,2,4]. In this chapter, we discuss the software for filter design and analysis that has been developed by The MathWorks to address the abovementioned

---

[1]MATLAB and its Signal Processing Toolbox are found in computer systems of many schools and universities but the FDA Tool may not be available in all of them.

problem[2]. This FDA Tool finite design–analysis (FDA) tool, found in the Filter Design Toolbox, works in conjunction with the Signal Processing (SP) Toolbox. Unlike the SP Toolbox, the FDA Tool has been developed by making extensive use of the object-oriented programming capability of MATLAB, and the syntax for the functions available in the FDA Tool is different from the syntax for the functions we find in MATLAB and the SP Toolbox. When we log on to MATLAB and type `fdatool`, we get two screens on display. On one screen, we type the `fdatool` functions as command lines to design and analyze quantized filters, whereas the other screen is a graphical user interface (GUI) to serve the same purpose. The GUI window shown in Figure 7.1a displays a dialog box with an immense array of design options as explained below.

First we design a filter with double precision on the GUI window using the FDA Tool or on the command window using the Signal Processing Toolbox and then import it into the GUI window. In the dialog box for the FDA Tool, we can choose the following options under the `Filter Type` panel:

1. Lowpass
2. Highpass
3. Bandpass
4. Bandstop
5. Differentiator. By clicking the arrow on the tab for this feature, we get the following additional options.
6. Hilbert transformer
7. Multiband
8. Arbitrary magnitude
9. Raised cosine
10. Arbitrary group delay
11. Half-band lowpass
12. Half-band highpass
13. Nyquist

Below the `Filter Type` panel is the panel for the design method. When the button for IIR filter is clicked, the dropdown list gives us the following options specifying the type of frequency response:

- Butterworth
- Chebyshev I
- Chebyshev II
- Elliptic
- Least-pth norm
- Constrained least-pth norm

---

[2]The author acknowledges that the material on the FDA Tool described in this chapter is based on the *Help Manual for Filter Design Toolbox* found in MATLAB version 6.5.

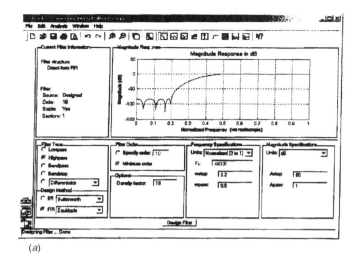

(a)

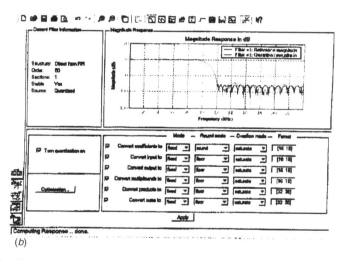

(b)

Figure 7.1 Screen capture of `fdatool` window: (a) window for filter design; (b) window for quantization analysis.

the following options are available for the FIR filter:

- Equiripple
- Least squares
- Window
- Maximally flat
- Least-pth norm
- Constrained equiripple

To the right of the panel for design method is the one for filter order. We can either specify the order of the filter or let the program compute the minimum order (by use of SP Tool functions Chebord, Buttord, etc.). Remember to choose an odd order for the lowpass filter when it is to be designed as a parallel connection of two allpass filters, if an even number is given as the minimum order. Below this panel is the panel for other options, which are available depending on the abovementioned inputs. For example, if we choose a FIR filter with the window option, this panel displays an option for the windows that we can choose. By clicking the button for the windows, we get a dropdown list of more than 10 windows. To the right of this panel are two panels that we use to specify the frequency specifications, that is, to specify the sampling frequency, cutoff frequencies for the passband and stopband, the magnitude in the passband(s) and stopband(s), and so on depending on the type of filter and the design method chosen. These can be expressed in hertz, kilohertz, megahertz, gigahertz, or normalized frequency. The magnitude can be expressed in decibels, with magnitude squared or actual magnitude as displayed when we click Analysis in the main menu bar and then click the option Frequency Specifications in the dropdown list. The frequency specifications are displayed in the Analysis panel, which is above the panel for frequency specifications, when we start with the filter design.

The options available under any of these categories are dependent on the other options chosen. All the FDA Tool functions, which are also the functions of the SP Tool, are called *overloaded functions*. After all the design options are chosen, we click the Design Filter button at the bottom of the dialog box. The program designs the filter and displays the magnitude response of the filter in the Analysis area. But it is only a default choice, and by clicking the appropriate icons shown above this area, the Analysis area displays one of the following features:

- Magnitude response
- Phase response
- Magnitude and phase response
- Group delay response
- Impulse response
- Step response
- Pole–zero plot
- Filter coefficients

This information can also be displayed by clicking the Analysis button in the main menu bar, and choosing the information we wish to display in the Analysis area. We can also choose some additional information, for example, by clicking the Analysis Parameters. At the bottom of this dropdown list is the option Full View Analysis. When this is chosen, whatever is displayed in the Analysis area is shown in a new panel of larger dimensions with features that are available in a figure displayed under the SP Tool. For example, by clicking the `Edit` button and then selecting either `Figure Properties`, `Axis Properties`, or `Current Object Properties`, the `Property Editor` becomes active and properties of these three objects can be modified.

Finally, we look at the first panel titled `Current Filter Information`. This lists the structure, order, and number of sections of the filter that we have designed. Below this information, it indicates whether the filter is stable and points out whether the source is the designed filter (i.e., reference filter designed with double precision) or the quantized filter with a finite wordlength. The default structure for the IIR reference filter is a cascade connection of second-order sections, and for the FIR filter, it is the direct form. When we have completed the design of the reference filter with double precision, we verify whether it meets the desired specification, and if we wish, we can convert the structure of the reference filter to any one of the other types listed below. We click the `Edit` button on the main menu and then the `Convert Structure` button. A dropdown list shows the structures to which we can convert from the default structure or the one that we have already converted.

For IIR filters, the structures are

1. Direct form I
2. Direct form II
3. Direct form I transposed
4. Direct form II transposed
5. Lattice ARMA
6. Lattice-coupled allpass
7. Lattice-coupled allpass—power complementary
8. State space

Items 6 and 7 in this list refer to structures of the two allpass networks in parallel as described in Chapter 6, with transfer functions $G(z) = \frac{1}{2}[A_1(z) + A_2(z)]$ and $H(z) = \frac{1}{2}[A_1(z) - A_2(z)]$, respectively. The allpass filters $A_1(z)$ and $A_2(z)$ are realized in the form of lattice allpass structures like the one shown in Figure 6.19b. The MA and AR structures are considered special cases of the lattice ARMA structure, which are also discussed in Chapter 6.

For FIR filters, the options for the structures are

- Direct-form FIR
- Direct-form FIR transposed
- Direct-form symmetric FIR

When we have converted to a new structure, the information that can be displayed in the `Analysis` area, like the coefficients of the filter, changes. We also like to point out that any one of the lowpass, highpass, bandpass, and bandstop filters that we have designed can be converted to any other type, by clicking the first icon on the left-hand bar in the dialog box and adding the frequency specifications for the new filter.

7.3 QUANTIZED FILTER ANALYSIS

When we have finished the analysis of the reference filter, we can move to construct the quantized filter as an object, by clicking the last icon on the bar above the `Analysis` area and the second icon on the left-hand bar, which sets the quantization parameters. The panel below the `Analysis` area now changes as shown in Figure 7.1b. We can construct three objects inside the FDA Tool: `qfilt`, `qfft`, and `quantizer`. Each of them has several properties, and these properties have values, which may be strings or numerical values. Currently we use the objects `qfilt` and `quantizer` to analyze the performance of the reference filter when it is quantized. When we click the `Turn Quantization On` button and the `Set Quantization Parameters` icon, we can choose the quantization parameters for the coefficients of the filter. Quantization of the filter coefficients alone are sufficient for finding the finite wordlength effect on the magnitude response, phase response, and group delay response of the quantized filter, which for comparison with the response of the reference filter displayed in the `Analysis` area. Quantization of the other data listed below are necessary when we have to filter an input signal:

- The input signal
- The output signal
- The multiplicand: the value of the signal that is multiplied by the multiplier.
- The product of the multiplicand and the multiplier constant
- The output signal

The object `quantizer` is used to convert each of these data, and this object has four properties: `Mode`, `Round Mode`, `Overflow mode`, and `Format`. In order to understand the values of these properties, it is necessary to review and understand the binary representation of numbers and the different results of adding them and multiplying them. These will be discussed next.

7.4 BINARY NUMBERS AND ARITHMETIC

Numbers representing the values of the signal, the coefficients of both the filter and the difference equation or the recursive algorithm and other properties corresponding to the structure for the filter are represented in binary form. They are based on the radix of 2 and therefore consist of only two binary digits, 0 and 1, which are more commonly known as *bits*, just as the decimal numbers based on a radix of 10 have 10 decimal numbers from 0 to 9. Placement of the bits in a string determines the binary number as illustrated by the example $x_2 = 1001_\triangle 1010$, which is equivalent to $x_{10} = 1 \times 2^0 + 1 \times 2^3 + 2^{-1} + 2^{-3} = 9.625$. In this discussion of binary number representation, we have used the symbol $\triangle$ to separate the integer part and the fractional part and the subscripts 2 and 10 to denote the binary number and the decimal number. Another example given by

$$x_2 = b_2 b_1 b_0 \triangle b_{-1} b_{-2} b_{-3} b_{-4} \tag{7.1}$$

has a decimal value computed as

$$x_{10} = b_2^2 + b_1^1 + b_0^0 + b_{-1}^{-1} + b_{-2}^{-2} + b_{-3}^{-3} + b_{-4}^4 \tag{7.2}$$

where the bits $b_2, b_1, b_0, b_{-1}, b_{-2}, b_{-3}, b_{-4}$ are either 1 or 0. In general, when x_2 is represented as

$$x_2 = b_{I-1} b_{I-2} \cdots b_1 b_0 \triangle b_{-1} b_{-2} \cdots b_{-F} \tag{7.3}$$

the decimal number has a value given by

$$x_{10} = \sum_{i=-F}^{I-1} b_i 2^i \tag{7.4}$$

In the binary representation (7.3), the integer part contains I bits and the bit b_{I-1} at the leftmost position is called the *most significant bit* (MSB); the fractional part contains F bits, and the bit b_{-F} at the rightmost position is called the *least significant bit* (LSB). This can only represent the magnitude of positive numbers and is known as the *unsigned fixed-point binary number*. In order to represent positive as well as negative numbers, one more bit called the *sign bit* is added to the left of the MSB. The sign bit, represented by the symbol s in (7.5), assigns a negative sign when this bit is 1 and a positive sign when it is 0. So it becomes a signed magnitude fixed-point binary number. Therefore a signed magnitude number $x_2 = 11001 \triangle 1010$ is $x_{10} = -9.625$. In general, the signed magnitude fixed-point number is given by

$$x_{10} = (-1)^s \sum_{i=-F}^{I-1} b_i 2^i \tag{7.5}$$

and the total number of bits is called the *wordlength* $w = 1 + I + F$. When two signed magnitude numbers with widely different values for the integer part and/or the fractional part have to be added, it is not easy to program the adders in the digital hardware to implement this operation. So it is common practice to choose $I = 0$, keeping the sign bit and the bits for the fractional part only so that $F = w - 1$ in the signed magnitude fixed-point representation. But when two numbers larger than 0.5 in decimal value are added, their sum is larger than 1, and this cannot be represented by the format shown above, where $I = 0$.

So two other form of representing the numbers are more commonly used: the one's-complement and two's-complement forms (also termed *one-complementary* and *two-complementary forms*) for representing the signed magnitude fixed-point numbers. In the one's-complement form, the bits of the fractional part are replaced by their complement, that is, the ones are replaced by zeros and vice versa. By adding a one as the least significant bit to the one's-complement form, we get the two's-complement form of binary representation; the sign bit is retained in both forms. But it must be observed that when the binary number is positive, the signed magnitude form, one's-complement form, and two's-complement form are the same.

Example 7.1

Given: $x_2 = 0_\triangle 1100$ is the 5-bit, signed magnitude fixed-point number equal to $x_{10} = +2^{-1} + 2^{-2} = 0.75$ and $v_2 = 1_\triangle 1100$ is equal to $v_{10} = -0.75$. The one's complement of $v_2 = 1_\triangle 1100$ is $1_\triangle 0011$, whereas the two's complement of v_2 is $1_\triangle 0011 +_\triangle 0001 = 1_\triangle 0100$.

The values that can be represented by the signed magnitude fixed-point representation range from -2^{w-F-1} to $2^{w-F-1} - 2^{-F}$. In order to increase the range of numbers that can be represented, two more formats are available: the floating-point and block floating-point representations. The floating-point representation of a binary number is of the form

$$X_{10} = (1)^s M (2^E) \tag{7.6}$$

where M is the mantissa, which is usually represented by a signed magnitude, fixed-point binary number, and E is a positive- or negative-valued integer with E bits and is called the *exponent*. To get both positive and negative exponents, the bias is provided by an integer, usually the bias is chosen as $e^7 - 1 = 127$ when the exponent E is 8 bits or $e^{10} - 1 = 1023$ when E is 11 bits. Without the bias, an 8-bit integer number varies from 0 to 255, but with a bias of 127, the exponent varies from -127 to 127. Also the magnitude of the fractional part F is limited to $0 \le M < 1$. In order to increase the range of the mantissa, one more bit is added to the most significant bit of F so that it is represented as $(1.F)$. Now it is assumed to be normalized, but this bit is not counted in the total wordlength.

The IEEE 754-1985 standard for representing floating-point numbers is the most common standard used in DSP processors. It uses a single-precision format with 32 bits and a double-precision format with 64 bits.

The single-precision floating point number is given by

$$X_{10} = (-1)^s (1.F) 2^{E-127} \tag{7.7}$$

According to this standard, the (32-bit) single-precision, floating-point number uses one sign bit, 8 bits for the exponent, and 23 bits for the fractional part

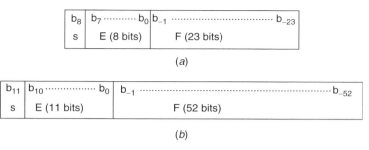

Figure 7.2 shows two bit-field diagrams:

(a) A 32-bit layout with fields: b_8 b_7 ········· b_0 | b_{-1} ····························· b_{-23}, labeled s | E (8 bits) | F (23 bits)

(b) A 64-bit layout with fields: b_{11} b_{10} ············· b_0 | b_{-1} ·· b_{-52}, labeled s | E (11 bits) | F (52 bits)

Figure 7.2   IEEE format of bits for the 32- and 64-bit floating-point numbers.

F (and one bit to normalize it). A representation of this format is shown in Figure 7.2a. But this formula is implemented according to the following rules in order to satisfy conditions other than the first one listed below:

1. When $0 < E < 255$, then $X_{10} = (-1)^s (1_\triangle F) 2^{E-127}$.
2. When $E = 0$ and $M \neq 0$, then $X_{10} = (-1)^s (0_\triangle F)(2^{-126})$.
3. When $E = 255$ and $M \neq 0$, then X_{10} is not a number and is denoted as NaN.
4. When $E = 255$ and $M = 0$, then $X_{10} = (-1)^s \infty$.
5. When $E = 0$ and $M = 0$, then $X_{10} = (-1)^s (0)$.

Here, $(1_\triangle F)$ is the normalized mantissa with one integer bit and 23 fractional bits, whereas $(0_\triangle F)$ is only the fractional part with 23 bits. Most of the commercial DSP chips use this 32-bit, single-precision, floating-point binary representation, although 64-bit processors are becoming available. Note that there is no provision for storing the binary point ($_\triangle$) in these chips; their registers simply store the bits and implement the rules listed above. The binary point is used only as a notation for our discussion of the binary number representation and is not counted in the total number of bits.

The IEEE 754-1985 standard for the (64-bit), double-precision, floating-point number is expressed by

$$X_{10} = (-1)^s (1.F) 2^{E-1023} \qquad (7.8)$$

It uses one sign bit, 11 bits for the exponent E, and 52 bits for F (one bit is added to normalize it but is not counted). The representation for this format is shown in Figure 7.2b.

Example 7.2

Consider the 16-bit floating-point number with 8 bits for the unbiased exponent and 4 bits for the denormalized fractional part, namely, $E = 8$ and $F = 4$. The binary number is represented as

$$X_2 = 0100000010_\triangle 0110$$

Then the exponent $E_2 = 100000010$; therefore $E_{10} = 130$, the denormalized mantissa $F_2 =_\triangle 0110$, which gives $F_{10} = 0.375$. Therefore the normalized mantissa $M = 1.375$. Finally $X_{10} = -(1.375)2^{130-127} = +(1.375)2^3 = 11$. Consider another example:

$$Y_2 = 100000111_\triangle 0110$$

Then $E_2 = 00000111$, $E_{10} = 7$, $F_2 =_\triangle 0110$, $F_{10} = 0.375$, and finally $Y_{10} = -(1.375)2^{7-127} = (-1.375)2^{-120}$.

The dynamic range of floating-point numbers that are supported by the FDA Toolbox as well as the SP Toolbox are listed in Table 7.1.

When the reference filter is quantized, we notice that the default value for the quantized data as shown in Figure 7.1b is the 16-bit signed magnitude, fixed-point binary number, and this is shown as format [16   15], which means that 15 bits are used for the fractional part and one bit is used as the sign bit. But note that the `quantizer` for the product and sum has the default format [32   30].

In the same panel showing the quantization of the different data, there are two other columns listed as `Round Mode` and `Overflow Mode`. When we click the button for the `Round Mode`, we get the following options in the dropdown list:

1. Round: `round`
2. Floor: `floor`
3. Ceiling: `ceil`
4. Fix: `fix`
5. Convergent: `convergent`

"Rounding" is the operation of choosing the value to the nearest quantized number. Negative values that lie halfway between two quantization levels are

TABLE 7.1   Dynamic Range of Floating Point Numbers Found in FDA Tool

Type of Floating-Point Data	Normalized Minimum Value	Normalized Maximum Value	Exponent Bias	Precision
Single precision	2^{-126}	$(2 - 2^{-23})2^{127}$	127	2^{-23}
	$\approx 1.18(10^{-38})$	$\approx (3.4)10^{38}$		$\approx 10^{-7}$
Double precision	2^{-1022}	$(2 - 2^{-52})2^{1023}$	1023	2^{-52}
	$\approx 2(10^{-308})$	$\approx (1.7)10^{308}$		$\approx 10^{-16}$
Custom precision	$2^{1-\text{bias}}$	$(2 - 2^{-F})2^{\text{bias}}$	$2^{E-1} - 1$	2^{-F}

rounded toward negative infinity, and positive numbers that lie halfway between
two quantization levels are rounded toward positive infinity. If the number lies
exactly halfway between two levels, it is rounded toward positive infinity. The
operation called 'floor' is commonly known as *truncation* since it discards all
the bits beyond the b bits, and this results in a number that is nearest to negative
infinity. These two are the most commonly used operations in binary arithmetic.
They are illustrated in Figure 7.3, where the dotted line indicates the actual value
of x and the solid line shows the quantized value x_Q with b bits.

The ceiling operation rounds the value to the nearest quantization level
toward positive infinity, and the fix operation rounds to the nearest level toward
zero. The convergent operation is the same as rounding except that in the case
when the number is exactly halfway, it is rounded down if the penultimate bit is
zero and rounded up if it is one.

Suppose that two positive numbers or two negative numbers in the fixed-point
format with b bits are added together. It is possible that the result could exceed

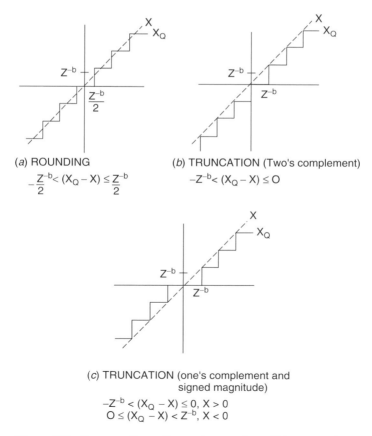

(a) ROUNDING
$$-\frac{Z^{-b}}{2} < (X_Q - X) \le \frac{Z^{-b}}{2}$$

(b) TRUNCATION (Two's complement)
$$-Z^{-b} < (X_Q - X) \le 0$$

(c) TRUNCATION (one's complement and signed magnitude)
$$-Z^{-b} < (X_Q - X) \le 0, X > 0$$
$$0 \le (X_Q - X) < Z^{-b}, X < 0$$

Figure 7.3 Process of rounding and truncation of binary numbers.

the lower or upper limits of the range within which numbers with b bits lie. For a signed magnitude, fixed-point number with wordlength w and fraction length f, the numbers range from -2^{w-f-1} to $2^{w-f-1} - 2^{-f}$, whereas the range for floating-point numbers is as given in Table 7.1. When the sum or difference of two fixed-point numbers or the product of two floating-point numbers exceeds its normal range of values, there is an overflow or underflow of numbers. The *overflow mode* in the FDA panel for the quantized filter gives two choices: to use `saturate` or to `wrap`. Choosing the `saturate` mode sets values that fall outside the normal range to a value within the maximum or minimum value in the range; that is, values greater than the maximum value are set to the maximum value, and values less than the minimum value are set to the minimum value in the range. This is the default choice for the overflow mode.

There is a third choice: to scale all the data. This choice is made by clicking the `Optimization` button. Then from the dialog box that is displayed, we can use additional steps to adjust the quantization parameters, scale the coefficients without changing the overall gain of the filter response, and so on. The coefficients are scaled appropriately such that there is no overflow or underflow of the data at the output of every section in the realization.

Before we investigate the effects of finite wordlength and the many realization structures, by using all the options in the dialog box in the FDA Tool, it is useful to know some of the insight gleaned from the vast amount of research on this complex subject. It has been found that in general, the IIR filters in the cascade connection of second-order sections, each of them realized in direct form II, are less sensitive to quantization than are those realized in the single section of direct form I and direct form II. The lattice ARMA structure and the special case of the AR structure are less sensitive to quantization than is the default structure described above. The lattice-coupled allpass structure, also known as "two allpass structures in parallel," is less sensitive than the lattice ARMA structure. We will determine whether realizing the two allpass filters $A_1(z)$ and $A_2(z)$ by lattice allpass structures has any advantages of further reduction in the quantization effects. If the specified frequency response can be realized by an FIR filter, then the direct-form or the lattice MA structure realizing it may be preferable to the structures described above, because the software development and hardware design of the FIR filter is simpler, is always stable, has linear phase, and is free from limit cycles.

We first design the reference filter that meets the desired specifications; then we try different structures for the quantized filter with different levels and types of quantization. Comparing the frequency response, phase response, and group delay response of the reference filter with those of the quantized filter, we find out which structure has the lowest deviation from the frequency response, phase response, and so on of the reference filter, with the lowest finite wordlength. The FDA Tool offers us powerful assistance in trying a large number of options available for the type of filter, design method, frequency specification, quantization of the several coefficients, and other variables, and comparing the results for the reference filter and the quantized filter, it allows us to make a suboptimal choice of the filter. This is illustrated by the following example.

7.5   QUANTIZATION ANALYSIS OF IIR FILTERS

Let us select the same fifth-order IIR lowpass elliptic filter that was considered in Example 6.17. Its transfer function $G(z)$ is given by

$$G(z) = \left(\frac{0.1397}{1.965}\right)$$

$$\times \frac{(1 + 1.337z^{-1} + 2.251z^{-2} + 2.251z^{-3} + 1.337z^{-4} + z^{-5})}{(1 - 1.629z^{-1} + 2.256z^{-2} - 1.597z^{-3} + 0.8096z^{-4} - 0.1866z^{-5})}$$

$$(7.9)$$

The frequency specifications for the filter are given as $\omega_p = 0.4$, $\omega_s = 0.6$, $A_p = 0.3$ dB, and $A_s = 35$ dB. The transfer function $G(z)$ was decomposed as the sum of two allpass filters $A_1(z)$ and $A_2(z)$ such that $G(z) = \frac{1}{2}[A_1(z) + A_2(z)]$, where

$$A_1(z) = \frac{0.5089 - 0.6763z^{-1} + z^{-2}}{1 - 0.6763z^{-1} + 0.5089z^{-2}} \tag{7.10}$$

and

$$A_2(z) = \left(\frac{0.8805 - 0.5368z^{-1} + z^{-2}}{1 - 0.5367z^{-1} + 0.8805z^{-2}}\right)\left(\frac{-0.4165 + z^{-1}}{1 - 0.4165z^{-1}}\right) \tag{7.11}$$

Recollect the following lattice coefficients used to realize the lattice structures for $A_1(z)$ and $A_2(z)$ computed in Chapter 6:
For $A_1(z)$:

$$K1 = \begin{bmatrix} -0.4482 \\ 0.5089 \end{bmatrix}$$

$$V1 = \begin{bmatrix} 0 \\ 0 \\ 1 \end{bmatrix}$$

For $A_2(z)$:

$$K2 = \begin{bmatrix} -0.2855 \\ 0.8805 \end{bmatrix}$$

$$V2 = \begin{bmatrix} 0 \\ 0 \\ 1 \end{bmatrix}$$

$$k3 = [-0.4165]$$

$$v3 = \begin{bmatrix} 0 \\ 1 \end{bmatrix}$$

Now we log on to the FDA Toolbox by typing `fdatool` in the MATLAB command window and enter the following specifications to design the reference filter under `infinite precision`. This is a lowpass, IIR, elliptic filter with sampling frequency $= 48,000$ Hz, $F_{pass} = 9600$ Hz, $F_{stop} = 14,400$ Hz, which correspond to the normalized sampling frequency $= 2$, $F_{pass} = 0.4$, $F_{stop} = 0.6$, respectively. The maximum passband attenuation is set as $A_p = 0.3$ dB and the minimum stopband attenuation, as $A_s = 35$ dB. When we design this filter, we find that the minimum order of the filter is given as 4, and therefore we increase it to 5 as the order of the filter so that we can realize the allpass networks in parallel and compare it with the frequency response of other types of filters. With this selection, the frequency response and phase response displayed in the `Analysis` area are as shown in Figure 7.4. The coefficients of the numerator and denominator of the IIR reference filter are given below.

Numerator coefficients (normalized to render the constant coefficient of the numerator as one) of this reference filter are

1.000000000000

1.337660698390

2.251235030190

2.251235030190

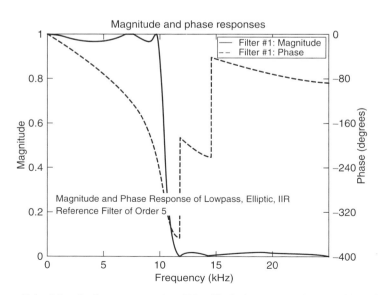

Figure 7.4   Magnitude response of an IIR elliptic lowpass (reference filter) filter.

1.337660698390
1.000000000000

The denominator coefficients are

    1.000000000000000
 −1.629530257267632
    2.257141351394922
 −1.598167067780082
    0.809623494277134
 −0.186626971448986

As expected these results match the coefficients in Equation (7.9) within an accuracy of four digits, because both of the filters were designed by the same Signal Processing Toolbox function `ellip`.

Next, we turn on the quantization, and click the `Set Quantization Param-eters` button. The quantization parameters are all set to the default values similar to those shown in Figure 7.1. We change the format for the fixed-point coefficients of the filter from [16   15] to [9   8] without changing the format for any of the other data—although most of the DSP chips currently available use 16 or 32 bits. The magnitude response of the cascade connection of two second-order sections and one first-order section in direct form II when we quantize the filter coefficients to 9 bit wordlength is shown in Figure 7.5, along with the magnitude

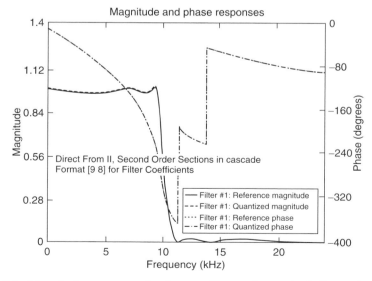

Figure 7.5 Magnitude response of reference filter and quantized filter with format [9   8] in cascade connection of second-order sections.

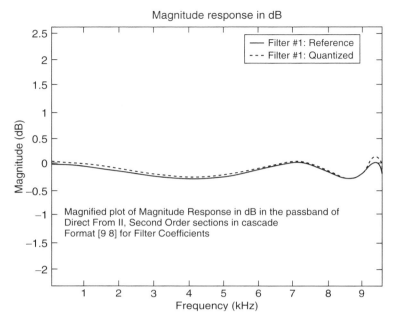

Figure 7.6   Magnified plot of the magnitudes (in decibels) of the two filters in Figure 7.5.

response of the reference filter. The Figure 7.6 shows a magnified plot of the magnitude in decibels in the passband, which gives the response of the quantized filter, which is very close to the response of the reference filter. But most of the DSP chips available on the market have a wordlength that is a power of 2 (wordlengths of 8, 16, 32, etc.). So we try a quantization of 8 bits, and the magnitude response of this filter is shown in Figure 7.7. But we see that the deviation of the magnitude from that of the reference filter is pronounced near the edge of the passband. Although we prefer to choose a wordlength of 8 rather than 9, this deviation is considered excessive, so we must choose other structures. As an alternative structure, we convert the direct form II structure to the ARMA structure with the same wordlength of 8 bits, and the resulting magnitude response is shown in Figure 7.8. A magnified plot of this response in its passband is shown in Figure 7.9. It does not produce a significant improvement over the response shown in Figure 7.7 for the quantized filter in the default structure of direct form II, with the same wordlength of 8 bits.

So we decide to convert the lattice ARMA structure to the lattice-coupled allpass structure; each allpass structure is realized by lattice allpass structures and starts with a 9-bit fixed-point quantization for the filter coefficients, and we get the result shown in Figure 7.10. Hardly any difference is seen between the reference filter and the quantized filter with the format [9   8], the same as the direct form

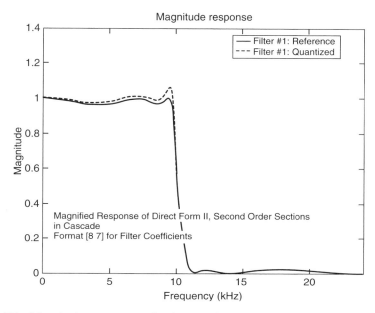

Figure 7.7 Magnitude responses of reference filter and quantized filter with format [8   7] in cascade connection of second-order sections.

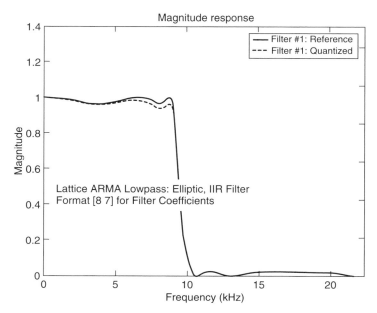

Figure 7.8 Magnitude responses of reference filter and quantized filter with format [8   7] and lattice ARMA structure.

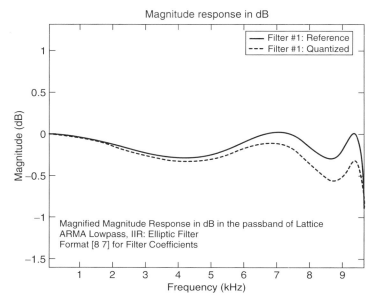

Figure 7.9 Magnified plot of the magnitude responses (in decibels) of reference filter and quantized filter with format [8   7] in lattice ARMA structure.

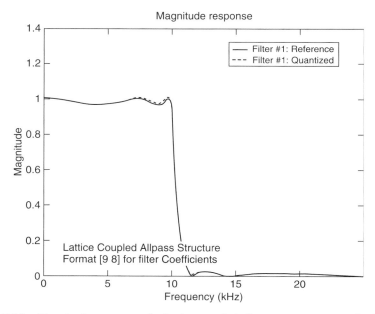

Figure 7.10 Magnitude response of a lattice-coupled allpass structure, quantized with a format [9   8].

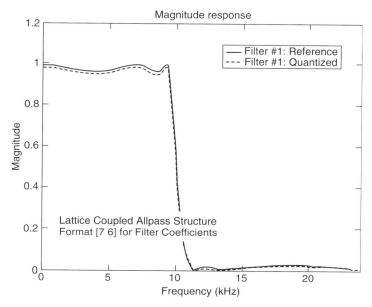

Figure 7.11 Magnitude responses of reference filter and quantized filter with format [7 6], in lattice-coupled allpass structure.

II structure with 9 bits. Next we try the 7 bit wordlength for this structure and the magnitude response shown in Figure 7.11. Again, we prefer to choose an 8 bit wordlength for this structure. The magnitude and phase responses of the filter with 8 bits are shown in Figure 7.12. A magnified plot of the magnitude in decibels in the passband of this 8-bit filter is shown in Figure 7.13. It shows that the maximum attenuation for the reference filter is 0.3 dB as specified, and the deviation from the specified passband magnitude, for the quantized filter is about 0.1 dB. This amount of deviation is less than that exhibited by the lattice ARMA filter in Figure 7.9 Therefore this lattice-coupled allpass structure for the IIR filter is chosen as a compromise.

The lattice coefficients of the second-order allpass filter $A_1(z)$ and those for the third-order allpass filter $A_2(z)$ realizing the reference filter are printed out and shown in the right column of Figure 7.14. The lattice coefficients for the two allpass filters displayed in Figure 7.14 match those given in the vectors K1, V1, K2, V2, k3 and v_3 given at the beginning of this section, within an accuracy of four digits. In the left column are shown the corresponding coefficients of the quantized filter with a 8 bit wordlength in the fixed-point, signed magnitude format [8 7].

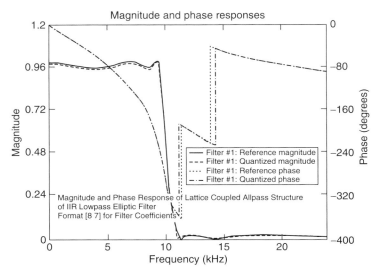

Figure 7.12 Magnitude and phase responses of reference filter and the quantized filter with format [8 7] in lattice-coupled allpass structure.

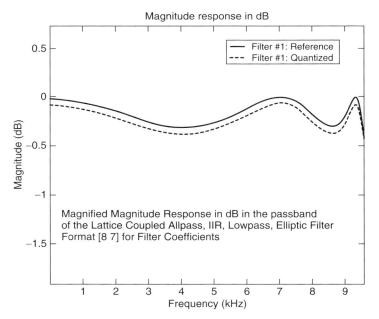

Figure 7.13 Magnified plot of the magnitude responses (in decibels) of reference filter and quantized filter with format [8 7] in lattice-coupled allpass structure.

```
Quantized Lattice coupled-allpass filter
Lattice1
     QuantizedCoefficients{1}      ReferenceCoefficients{1}
   (1)               -0.4453125   -0.448202538502541490
   (2)                0.5078125    0.508902517834580630
Lattice2
     QuantizedCoefficients{2}      ReferenceCoefficients{2}
   (1)               -0.3359375   -0.338701369319380500
   (2)                0.8750000    0.871154661800650490
   (3)               -0.3671875   -0.366724401842417720
beta
     QuantizedCoefficients{3}      ReferenceCoefficients{3}
 + (1)                0.9921875    1.000000000000000200

    FilterStructure = latticeca
        ScaleValues = []
   NumberOfSections = 1
   StatesPerSection = [5]
  CoefficientFormat = quantizer('fixed', 'round', 'saturate', [8   7])
        InputFormat = quantizer('fixed', 'floor', 'saturate', [16  15])
       OutputFormat = quantizer('fixed', 'floor', 'saturate', [16  15])
 MultiplicandFormat = quantizer('fixed', 'floor', 'saturate', [16  15])
      ProductFormat = quantizer('fixed', 'floor', 'saturate', [32  30])
          SumFormat = quantizer('fixed', 'floor', 'saturate', [32  30])
 Warning: 1 overflow in coefficients.
```

Figure 7.14   Coefficients of reference filter and quantized filter with format [8   7] in a lattice-coupled allpass structure.

7.6   QUANTIZATION ANALYSIS OF FIR FILTERS

Next we decide to investigate whether the alternative of designing a quantized FIR filter would give us a better result. Choosing the same frequency-domain specifications as for the IIR lowpass elliptic filter, we design an FIR lowpass filter with an equiripple passband and stopband. The reference filter with infinite precision uses the remez algorithm and yields a linear phase FIR (type I) filter of order 16. The magnitude response of this filter is shown in Figure 7.15. When we select the sign magnitude, fixed-point 7 bit wordlength and the 8 bit wordlength, the results are as shown in Figures 7.16 and 7.17, respectively.

It is apparent that there is not a significant difference between the two filters with 7 and 8 bit wordlength. In Figure 7.18 we plot a magnified magnitude in decibels in the passband of the FIR filter with 8 bits for the wordlength. The maximum deviation from the specified passband ripple of 0.3 dB is ~0.1 dB. The coefficients of the reference filter and the quantized filter are listed in Figure 7.19. It is noted that several coefficients of the quantized filter have an underflow as indicated by the digit 0 in the first column and have been rounded to zero.

Finally we compare the quantization effects on the IIR with the effect on the FIR filter by comparing the magnitude responses shown in Figures 7.18 and 7.13. It is easy to notice that the FIR filter has a lower sensitivity to quantization than does the IIR filter that we chose above. The IIR filter in the form of the lattice-coupled allpass structure and the FIR filter in the direct form have a wordlength

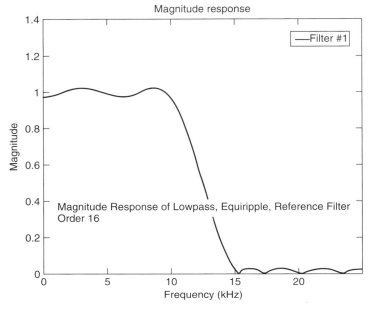

Figure 7.15 Magnitude response of a lowpass equiripple FIR (reference filter) filter.

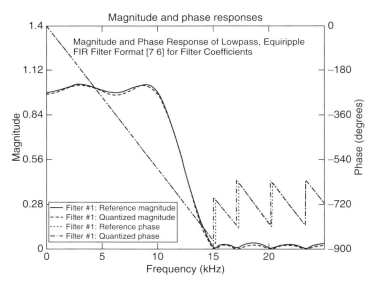

Figure 7.16 Magnitude and phase responses of reference FIR filter and quantized filter with format [7   6] for filter coefficients.

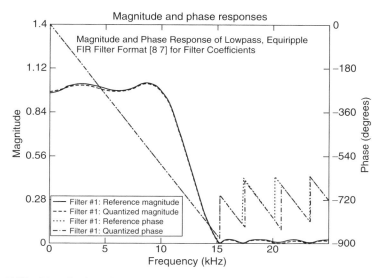

Figure 7.17   Magnitude and phase responses of FIR reference filter and quantized filter with format [8   7] for filter coefficients.

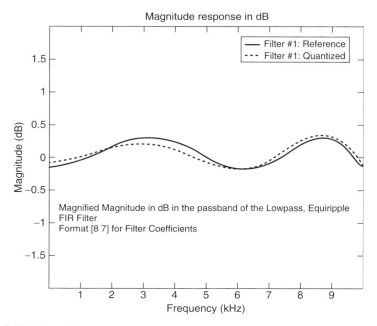

Figure 7.18   Magnified magnitude responses (in decibels) of reference FIR filter and quantized filter with format [8   7] for the filter coefficients.

```
Quantized Direct form FIR filter
Numerator
        QuantizedCoefficients{1}        ReferenceCoefficients{1}
  0 ( 1)                  0.0000000     0.000278615600941334
    ( 2)                 -0.0234375    -0.026495003913332794
  0 ( 3)                  0.0000000    -0.000221811497688629
    ( 4)                  0.0468750     0.044103186729025759
  0 ( 5)                  0.0000000     0.000251054558481910
    ( 6)                 -0.0937500    -0.093412121343936769
  0 ( 7)                  0.0000000    -0.000289785456229263
    ( 8)                  0.3125000     0.313920929416822760
    ( 9)                  0.5000000     0.500313133105531720
    (10)                  0.3125000     0.313920929416822760
  0 (11)                  0.0000000    -0.000289785456229263
    (12)                 -0.0937500    -0.093412121343936769
  0 (13)                  0.0000000     0.000251054558481910
    (14)                  0.0468750     0.044103186729025759
  0 (15)                  0.0000000    -0.000221811497688629
    (16)                 -0.0234375    -0.026495003913332794
  0 (17)                  0.0000000     0.000278615600941334


       FilterStructure = fir
           ScaleValues = []
      NumberOfSections = 1
       StatesPerSection = [16]
      CoefficientFormat = quantizer('fixed', 'round', 'saturate', [8  7])
           InputFormat = quantizer('fixed', 'floor', 'saturate', [16  15])
          OutputFormat = quantizer('fixed', 'floor', 'saturate', [16  15])
    MultiplicandFormat = quantizer('fixed', 'floor', 'saturate', [16  15])
         ProductFormat = quantizer('fixed', 'floor', 'saturate', [32  30])
             SumFormat = quantizer('fixed', 'floor', 'saturate', [32  30])
```

Figure 7.19   Data for reference FIR filter and quantized FIR filter with 8 bits of word-length.

of 8 bits. The number of multipliers required in FIR direct form is only 9 because of the symmetry in its coefficients, whereas the lattice-coupled allpass network requires 10 multipliers, which is not a significant difference. However, we know that the phase response of the FIR filter is linear, which is a great advantage over the IIR filter. Hardware implementation of the FIR filter is simpler than that of the IIR filter. Unlike the IIR filter, the FIR filter does not exhibit limit cycles and is always stable. This leads to investigate the 8-bit FIR filter further as a candidate for generating the code to program a DSP chip of our choice.

It must be pointed out that the specifications we selected for the digital filter may or may not meet typical application requirements. Also, we would like to point out that while we argued that a 8 bit wordlength may be preferable over a 9 bit wordlength, currently most of the digital signal processors (DSPs) are 16-bit or 32-bit devices. The design process using the `fdatool` is meant to illustrate only the different choices and decisions that an engineer may face before arriving at a particular digital filter that will be considered for further investigation as described below.

Now we assume that we have designed the digital filter and we have tested its performance using the `fdatool`, when the coefficients of the filter and the input samples are represented by a finite number of bits. We have also considered the effect of rounding or truncating the results of adding signals or multiplying the signal value and the coefficient of the filter and ascertained that there is no possibility of limit cycles or unstable operation in the filter. Very often a digital filter is used as a prominent part of a digital system like a cell phone, which has other components besides power supply, keyboard, or other I/O interfaces. So we have to simulate the performance of the whole system with all components connected together in the form of a block diagram.

7.7   SUMMARY

In this chapter we described the use of the MATLAB tool, called the `fdatool`, to design digital filters with finite wordlength for the coefficients in fixed-point and floating-point representations, and investigated several different types of filter structures and different types of magnitude response specifications. Once we narrowed down the choice of the filter that meets the frequency response specifications, we have to simulate the performance of the filter using Simulink, to check that the filter works satisfactorily under different types of input signals that will be applied in practice. In Chapter 8 we discuss this and other practical considerations that are necessary for hardware design of the filter or the whole digital system in which the filter is embedded.

PROBLEMS

The problems given in Chapter 4 can be assigned either as homework or as a term project only if the FDA Toolbox is available with MATLAB and Signal Processing Toolbox in the computer facilities of the school, college, or university. The students may be asked to investigate the quantization effect of the filters specified in Chapter 4 and arrive at the suboptimal choice, using these tools.

REFERENCES

1. S. K. Mitra, *Digital Signal Processing—A Computer Aided Approach*, McGraw-Hill, 1998.
2. E. C. Ifeachor and B. W. Jervis, *Digital Signal Processing, A Practical Approach*, Prentice-Hall, 2002.
3. A. Bateman and I. Paterson-Stephens, *The DSP Handbook, Algorithms, Applications and Design Techniques*, Prentice-Hall, 2002.
4. S. K. Mitra and J. F. Kaiser, eds., *Handbook of Digital Signal Processing*, Wiley-Interscience, 1993.
5. S. M. Kuo and B. H. Lee, *Real-Time Digital Signal Processing: Implementations, Applications and Experiments with TMS320C55X*, Wiley, 2001.

6. A. Singh and S. Srinivasan, *Digital Signal Processing*, Thompson Books/Cole Publishing, 2004.

7. N. Kehtarnavaz and B. Simsek, *C6x-Based Digital Signal Processing*, Prentice-Hall, 2000.

8. P. Lapsley, J. Bier, A. Shoham, and E. Lee, *DSP Processor Fundamentals*, IEEE Press, 1994.

9. S. M. Kuo and W.-S. Gan, *Digital Signal Processors: Architectures, Implementations and Applications*, Pearson Prentice-Hall, 2004.

10. R. Chassaing, *Applications Using C and the TMS320C6XDSK*, Wiley, 2002.

11. R. Chassaing and D. W. Horning, *Digital Signal Processing with the TMS320C25*, John Wiley, 1990.

12. The Mathworks, Inc., *Learning Simulink, User's Guide*, 1994.

CHAPTER 8

Hardware Design Using DSP Chips

8.1 INTRODUCTION

In Chapter 7, we used the `fdatool` to illustrate the analysis and design of a digital filter in which the coefficients of the filter and the input samples are represented by a finite number of bits. We also found the effect of rounding or truncating the results of adding signals or multiplying the signal value and the coefficient of the filter and ascertained that there is no possibility of limit cycles or unstable operation in the filter. In the example chosen we decided that an FIR filter would meet the frequency response specifications of a lowpass elliptic filter, with a wordlength of 8 bits. Very often, however, a digital filter is used as a prominent part of a digital system such as a cell phone, which has other components such as power supply, keyboard, or other I/O interfaces. So we have to simulate the performance of the whole system with all components connected together in the form of a block diagram.

8.2 SIMULINK AND REAL-TIME WORKSHOP

Simulink is the software that is available as a companion toolbox to MATLAB and is used to model and simulate the performance of dynamic systems, under varying conditions. Just as MATLAB works with a number of toolboxes, Simulink has access to a library of many additional tools called *blocksets*, such as the DSP blockset, fixed-point blockset, communications blockset, and control system blockset, as shown on the left side of Figure 8.1.

The Simulink browser library includes blocksets for simulation of aeronautical and mechanical systems, too, namely, are `aerospace blockset` and `simMechanics`.[1] Each of these blocksets contains a large number of blocks that are used to define specific transfer functions or algorithms and a variety of input signals.

---

[1]Depending on the version of Simulink, this may or may not contain some of the blocksets mentioned in this chapter.

Introduction to Digital Signal Processing and Filter Design, by B. A. Shenoi
Copyright © 2006 John Wiley & Sons, Inc.

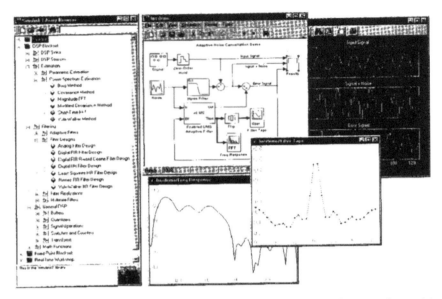

Figure 8.1 Screen capture of the Simulink browser and block diagram of a model.

The GUI interface is used to drag and drop these blocks from the blockset and connect them to describe a block diagram representation of the dynamic system, which may be a continuous-time system or a discrete-time system. A mechanical system model [6] is shown in Figure 8.1. Simulink is based on object-oriented programming, and the blocks are represented as objects with appropriate properties, usually specified in a dialog box. Indeed, the `fdatool` that we used in Chapter 7 can be launched from SIMULINK as an object or from the MATLAB command window because both of them are integrated together to operate in a seamless fashion. Simulink itself can be launched either by typing `simulink` in the MATLAB command window or by clicking the Simulink icon in its toolbar.

For the simulation of a digital filter, we choose the DSP blockset, which contains the following blocks in a tree structure:

```
DSP Blockset

→DSP Sinks
→DSP Sources
→Estimation
→Filtering              →Adaptive Filters
→Math Functions         →Filter Design         →Analog Filter Design
→Platform Specific I/O  →Multirate filters     →Digital Filter Design
→Quantizers                                    →Digital Filter
→Signal Management                             →Filter Realization
                                                  Wizard
→Signal Operations                             →Overlap-Add FFT filter
→Statistics                                    →Overlap-Save FFT filter
→Transforms
```

When we open Simulink window, and click `File→New→Model` in sequence, we get a window for the new model. Then we drag the block shown above as `Digital Filter Design` and drop it in the window for the new model. When we click on this object in the new window, it opens the same window as the one for the `fdatool` shown in Figure 7.1. After we have imported the parameters of the digital filter that we designed in an earlier session, or after we have completed the design of the quantized filter as explained in Chapter 7, we use the `Filter Realization Wizard` shown above under the `DSP Blockset` and get the realization structure for the filter. This serves as the model for the filter to which we can now connect different types of sources and observe the output on the scope connected to the filter, as the sink. Very often, we are required to design a whole system, in which case a digital filter is the only major block in the system, but there are other subsystems integrated with it. So it may be necessary to use the blocks for the adaptive filters or multirate filters or the blocks from the `Communication` blockset and `Controls` blockset, besides the `DSP Blockset`, and so on. After building the block diagram model for the total digital signal processing system, and using Simulink to carry out extensive simulation of the model under varying conditions, we check to ensure that it meets the specifications satisfactorily; if not, we may have to modify the design of the filter or tune the parameters. For example, we may simulate the total system with a finite number of bits in floating-point or fixed-point format, using the `Fixed Point` blockset to represent all data. We may have to change the design completely and simulate the new system.

8.3   DESIGN PRELIMINARIES

All the design and simulation of digital filters and digital systems done by MATLAB and Simulink is based on numerical computation of scientific theory. When this work is completed, we have to decide on one of the following choices:

1. Design a VLSI chip, using software such as VHDL, to meet our particular design specifications
2. Select a DSP chip from manufacturers such as Texas Instruments, Analog Devices, Lucent, or Motorola and program it to work as a digital system
3. Choose a general-purpose microprocessor and program it to work as a digital signal processor system.
4. Design the system using the field-programmable gate arrays (FPGAs).

In all cases, several design considerations have to be explored as thoroughly as possible before we embark on the next step in hardware design.

If we decide to select a DSP chip from one of the abovementioned manufactures, we have to consider the bandwidth of the signal(s) that the digital filter or the the digital system will be processing, based on which sampling frequency of the ADC is selected. However, the sampling frequency of the ADC may not be the same as the clock frequency of the CPU in the chip or the rate at which data will be transferred from and to the memory by the CPU (central processing unit). This in turn determines the rating in mips (millions of instructions per second). Depending on the amount of data or memory space required by the processor, the amount of power is determined. Other considerations are the I/O (input/output) interfaces, additional devices such as the power supply circuit, and the micro-controller, add-on memory, and peripheral devices. Finally the most important is the the cost per chip. We also need to consider the reliability of the software and technical support provided by the manufacturer; credibility and sustainability of the manufacturer also become important if the market for the digital filter or the system is expected to last for many years.

The selection of the DSP chip is facilitated by an evaluation of the chips available from the major manufacturers listed above and their detailed specifications. For example, the *DSP Selection Guide*, which can be downloaded from the TI (Texas Instruments) Website www.dspvillage.ti.com, is an immense source of information on all the chips available from them.

The DSP chips provided by TI are divided into three categories. The family of TMS3206000 DSP platform are designed for systems with very high performance, ranging within 1200–5760 mips for fixed-point operation and 600–1350 mflops (million floating-point operations per second) for floating-point operation. The fixed-point DSPs are designated by TMS320C62x and TMS320C64x, and the floating-point DSPs belong to the TMS320C67x family. The fixed-point TMS32062x DSPs are optimized for multichannel, multifunction applications such as wireless base stations, remote-access servers, digital subscriber loop (DSL) systems, central office switches, call processing, speech recognition, image processing, biometric equipment, industrial scanners, precision instruments, and multichannel telephone systems. They use 16 bits for multiplication and 32 bits for instructions in single-precision format as well as double-precision format. The fixed-point TMS320C64x DSPs offer the highest level of performance at clock rates of up to 720 MHz and 5760 mips, and they are best suited for applications in digital communications and video and image processing, wireless LAN (local area networking), network cameras, base station transceivers, DSL, and pooled modems, and so on. The floating-point TMS320C67x DSPs operate at 225 MHz and are used in similar applications.

The TMS320C5000 DSP family is used in consumer digital equipments, namely, products used in the Internet and in consumer electronics. Therefore these chips are optimized for power consumption as low as 0.05 mW/mips and speeds of ≤300 MHz and 600 mips; the TMS320C54x DSPs are well known as the industry leader in portable devices such as cell phones(2G, 2.5G, and 3G), digital audio (MP3) players, digital cameras, personal digital assistants (PDAs), GPS receivers, and electronic books. The TMS320C55x DSPs also deliver the highest power efficiency and are software-compatible with the TMS320C54x DSPs.

The TMS320C2000 DSPs are designed for applications in digital control industry, including industrial drives, servocontrol, factory automation, office equipment, controllers for pumps, fans, HVAC (heating–ventilation–air conditioning), and other home appliances. The TMS320C28x DSPs offer 32-bit, fixed-point processing and 150 mips operation, whereas the TMS320C24x DSPs offer a maximum of 40 mips operation.

More detailed information and specifications for the DSPs and other devices such as ADCs, and codecs (coders/decoders) supplied by TI can be found in the *DSP Selection Guide*. The amount of information on the software and hardware development tools, application notes, and other resource material that is freely available in this Website is enormous and indispensable. We must remember that DSP chips produced by other manufacturers such as Analog Devices may be better suited for specific applications, and they, too, provide a lot of information about their chips and the applications.

8.4 CODE GENERATION

The next task is to generate a code in machine language that the DSP we have selected understands and that implements the algorithm for the digital system we have designed. First we have to convert the algorithm for the system under development to a code in C/C++ language. This can be done manually by one who is experienced in C language programming. Or we simulate the performance of the whole system modeled in Simulink, and use a blockset available in it, known as the Real-Time Workshop [7] to generate the ANSI Standard C code for the model.[2] The C code can be run on PCs, DSPs, and microcontrollers in real time and non–real time in a variety of target environments. We connect a rapid prototyping target, for example, the xPC Target, to the physical system but use the Simulink model as the interface to the physical target. With this setup, we test and evaluate the performance of the physical target. When the simulation is found to work satisfactorily, the Real-Time Workshop is used to create and download an executable code to the target system. Now we can monitor the performance of the target system and tune its parameters, if necessary. The Real-Time Workshop is useful for validating the basic concept and overall performance of the whole system that responds to a program in C code.

An extension of Real-Time Workshop called the Real-Time Workshop Embedded Coder is used to generate optimized C code for embedded discrete-time systems.

Note that the C code is portable in the sense that it is independent of any manufacturer's DSP chip. But the manufacturers may provide their own software to generate the C code also, optimized for their particular DSP chip. However, programming a code in machine language is different for DSP chips from different manufacturers, and the different manufacturers provide the tools necessary to obtain the machine code from the C code for their DSP chips.

[2]Depending on the version of MATLAB/Simulink package installed on the computer in the college or university. software such as FDA Tool, Real-Time Workshop and others mentioned in this chapter may or may not be available.

8.5 CODE COMPOSER STUDIO

Texas Instruments calls its integrated development tool the Code Composer Studio (IDE). The major steps to be carried out are outlined in Figure 8.2. Basically, these steps denote the C compiler, assembler, linker, debugger, simulator, and emulator functions. It must be pointed out that the other manufacturers also design DSP chips for various applications meeting different specifications; their own software bundle follows steps similar to those mentioned above for the Code Composer Studio (CCS) from Texas Instruments (TI).

First the Code Composer Studio compiles the C/C++ code to an assembly language code in either mnemonic form or algebraic form, for the particular

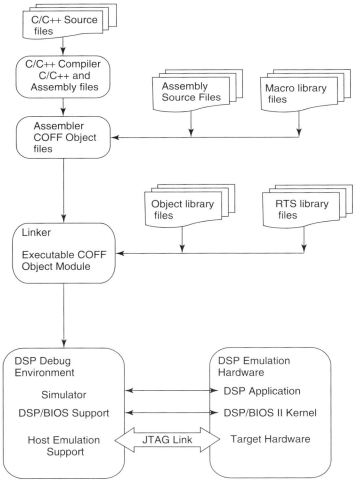

Figure 8.2 Software development flow for generating the object code from the C code.

DSP platform that we have chosen. If we choose the TMS320C55x DSPs to illustrate the software development cycle, then the command used to invoke the C compiler is of the form

```
c155[-options] [filenames] [-z[link_options] [object_files]]
```

The [filenames] list the C program files, and other assembly language files, and even object files with their default extensions .c, .asm, and .obj, respectively. The C language is not very efficient in carrying out a few specific operations, such as fixed-point data processing that are used in DSP applications. For this reason, assembly language files are added to the C language program files in order to improve the efficiency of the program in carrying out time-critical sections of the assembly language code delivered by the assembler. We can choose from many options in [-options] and in [link_options] to control the way that the compiler shell processes the files listed in [filenames] and the way that the linker processes the object files. For more details, students should refer to the TI simulator user's guide [25].

The next step is translation of the assembly language code by the assembler to the object code in binary form (or in machine language) specific to the DSP platform. The CCS command to invoke the assembler is of the form

```
asm55 [input_file [object_file] [list_file] [-options]]
```

Since there might be several C program files that implement the original algorithm in small sections, the assembler produces the output file in several sections. It may also collect assembly source files from an external library, which implement processes that are used again and again at several stages of the software and load them into the list of [filenames]. For example, Texas Instruments provides a large number of highly optimized functions in three libraries, namely, the DSP library (DSPLib), the image processing library (IMAGELib), and the chip support library (CSLib). Then there are assembly files that are long programs and therefore are shortened to a macro so that they can be invoked by a single or a few lines of instructions. All of these external files are added to the list of assembly language files and converted to binary form, under a single format known as the *common-object file format* (COFF). The object_file produces the object file in COFF format; the list_file shows the binary object code as well as the assembly source code and where the program and the variables are allocated in the memory space. But they are allocated in temporary locations, not in absolute locations. Therefore these relocatable object files can be archived into a library of reusable files that may be used elsewhere. There are many options in the assembler, and their use is described in Ref. 25.

The linker utility is invoked to combine all the object files generated by the assembler to one single linked object code, and this is done by assigning absolute addresses in the physical memory of the target DSP chip as specified by a memory map. The memory map is created by a linker command_xfile, which lists the various sections of the assembly code and specifies the location of the starting address and length of memory space in RAM and ROM (random access and read-only memory), and where the individual sections are to be located in the RAM and ROM, as well as the various options. Then the linker command is invoked as follows:

```
lnk55 command_file.cmd
```

The linker can call additional object files from an external library and also the runtime support (RTS) library files that are necessary during the debugging procedure. It also has many options that can be used to control the linker output, which is an executable COFF object module that has .out as its extension. Detailed information on the linker can be found in Ref. 17. Remember that information on compiler, assembler, and linker commands may be different for other DSP platforms, and information on these commands may be found in TI references appropriate for the DSP platform chosen.

8.6 SIMULATOR AND EMULATOR

After we have created the executable COFF object module, we have to test and debug it by using software simulation and/or by hardware emulation. For low-cost simulation, we use the development starter kits, for example, the TMS3205402 DSP starter kit for the TMS320C54x DSP, and for more detailed evaluation and debugging, we use an evaluation board such as the TMS320C5409. Finally, we have the emulator boards such as the XDS510 JTAG emulator, which are used to run the object code under real-time conditions.

The executable object code is downloaded to the DSP on the DSK board. The simulator program installed on the PC that is connected to the DSK board accepts the object code as its input and under the user's control, simulates the same actions that would be taken by the DSP device as it executes the object code. The user can execute the object code one line at a time, by inserting breakpoints at a particular line of the object program, halt the operation of the program; view the contents of the data memory, program memory, auxiliary registers, stacks, and so on; display the contents of the registers, for example, the input and output of a filtering operation; and change the contents of any register if so desired. One can also observe or monitor the registers controlling the I/O hardware, serial ports, and other components. If minor changes are made, the Code Composer Studio reassembles and links the files quickly to accelerate the debugging process; otherwise the entire program has to be reassembled and linked before debugging can proceed. When the monitoring and fixing the bug at all breakpoints is over, execution of the program is resumed manually. By inserting probe points, Code Composer Studio enables us to read the data from a file or written to a file on the host PC, halting the execution of the program momentarily, and then resume it. It should be obvious that simulation on a DSK is a slow process and does not check the performance of the peripheral devices that would be connected to the digital system.

In order to test the performance of the object code on the DSP in real time, we connect an emulator board to the PC by a parallel printer cable, and the XDS 510 Emulator conforms to the JTAG scan-based interface standard. The peripheral devices are also connected to the emulator board. A DSP/BIOS II plug-in is included in the Code Composer Studio to run the emulation of the software. It also contains the RTDX (real-time data exchange) module that allows transfer of data between the target DSP and the host PC in real time. The Code Composer Studio enables us to test and debug the performance of the software under real-time conditions, at full sampling rate. Without disrupting the execution of the software, the emulator controls its execution of the breakpoints, single-step execution, and monitoring of the memory and registers, and checks the performance of the whole system, including the peripheral devices. When the emulation of the whole system is found to operate correctly, the software is approved for production and marketing.

This is a very brief outline of the hardware design process, carried out after the design of the digital system is completed by use of MATLAB and Simulink. Students are advised to refer to the extensive literature available from TI and other manufacturers, in order to become proficient in the use of all software tools available from them. For example, Analog Devices offers a development software called Visual DSP++, which includes a C++ compiler, assembler, linker, user interface, and debugging utilities for their ADSP-21xx DSP chips.

8.6.1 Embedded Target with Real-Time Workshop

Simulink has been expanded to generate and simulate bit-true, timing-accurate code for directly designing DSP and FPGA targets and produce tests at system level. This software tool considerably reduces the design effort outlined above, as it facilitates the design of digital filters and systems obtained by the Signal Processing Toolbox and FDA Toolbox and generates executable machine code for hardware design.

8.7 CONCLUSION

The material presented above is only a very brief outline of the design procedure that is necessary to generate the assembly language code from the C code, generate the object code using the assembler, and link the various sections of the object code to obtain the executable object code in machine language. Then this code is debugged by using an evaluation board, simulator, and emulator; all of these steps are carried out by using an integrated, seamless software such as the Code Composer Studio that was used to illustrate the steps. Like any design process, this is an iterative procedure that may require that we go back to earlier steps to improve or optimize the design, until we are completely satisfied with the performance of the whole system in real-time conditions. Then the software development is complete and is ready for use in the DSP chips chosen for the specific application.

REFERENCES

1. S. M. Kuo and B. H. Lee, *Real-Time Digital Signal Processing; Implementations, Applications and Experiments with TMS320C55X*, Wiley, 2001.
2. S. M. Kuo and W.-S. Gan, *Digital Signal Processors: Architectures, Implementations and Applications*, Pearson Prentice-Hall, 2004.
3. R. Chassaing, *Applications Using C and the TMS320C6XDSK*, Wiley, 2002.
4. R. Chassaing and D. W. Horning, *Digital Signal Processing with the TMS320C25*, Wiley, 1990.
5. R. Chassaing, *Digital Signal Processing and Applications with the C6713 and C416 DSK*, Wiley, 2004.
6. The MathWorks, Inc., *Learning Simulink, User's Guide*, 1994.
7. The MathWorks, Inc., *Real-Time Workshop for Use with Simulink, User's Guide*.
8. P. Embree, *C Algorithms for Real-Time DSP*, Prentice-Hall, 1995.
9. The MathWorks, Inc., *Embedded Target for the TI TMS320C6000^{TM} DSP Platform, for Use with Real-Time Workshop$^{(R)}$, User's Guide*.
10. Texas Instruments, *TMS320C6411 Fixed-Point Digital Signal Processor* (SPRS196).
11. Texas Instruments, *TMS320C6000 CPU and Instruction Set Reference Guide* (SPRU189).
12. Texas Instruments, *Manual Update Sheet for TMS 320C6000 CPU and Instruction Set Reference Guide* (SPRZ168).
13. Texas Instruments, *TMS320C64x Technical Overview* (SPRU395).
14. Texas Instruments, *Code Composer Studio Tutorial* (SPRU301).
15. Texas Instruments, *Code Composer Studio User's Guide* (SPRU328).
16. Texas Instruments, *TMS320C6000 Programmer's Guide* (SPRU198).
17. Texas Instruments, *TMS320C6000 Assembly Language Tools User's Guide* (SPRU186).
18. Texas Instruments, *TMS320C6000 Optimizing C Compiler User's Guide* (SPRU187).
19. Texas Instruments, *TMS320C6000 C Source Debugger User's Guide* (SPRU188).
20. Texas Instruments, *TMS320C6000 DSP/BIOS User's Guide* (SPRU303).
21. Texas Instruments, *TMS320C6000 DSP/BIOS Application Programming Interface (API) Reference Guide* (SPRU403).
22. Texas Instruments, *TMS320 DSP Algorithm Standard Rules and Guidelines* (SPRU352).
23. Texas Instruments, *TMS320 DSP Algorithm Standard Developer's Guide* (SPRU424).
24. Texas Instruments, *TMS320C6000 Simulator User's Guide* (SPRU546).
25. Texas Instruments, *TMS320C55x Optimizing C Compiler User's Guide* (SPRU281).
26. Texas Instruments, *TMS320C55x Assembly Language Tools User's Guide* (SPRU380).
27. Analog Devices, *ADSP-21xxx Family: Assembler Tools and Simulator Model*, 1995.
28. Analog Devices, *ADSP-2106x SHARC User's Manual*, 1997.
29. Motorola Inc., *Motorola DSP Assembler Reference Manual*, 1994.
30. Motorola Inc., *DSP56xxx Digital Signal Processor: User's Manual*, 1993.

CHAPTER 9

MATLAB Primer

9.1 INTRODUCTION

MATLAB is a very powerful and well-known software package[1] that is used in science and engineering disciplines, for numerical computation, data analysis, and graphical visualization. It is available in almost all platforms such as personal computers, and workstations running under several operating systems. When you begin a session by typing the command `matlab`, the first window displayed on the monitor is the command window with the prompt `>>`, which is waiting for your command.[2] Use the command `exit` to end the session.

MATLAB contains a large collection of built-in functions and commands that are used in an interactive mode, when you are in the command window. As soon as the name of a function or a command is typed at the prompt in the command window, with the proper syntax, the answer is displayed immediately. But there are two other windows, the edit window and graphics window, which will be discussed later. The software package is designed to use additional sets of functions that are more applicable in particular disciplines such as control systems, digital signal processing, communications engineering, and image processing. There are more than 20 sets known as "toolboxes" (e.g., control toolbox, digital signal processing toolbox, communication toolbox, image processing toolbox). All of them run under MATLAB and implement the functions on the basis of matrix manipulation of numerical data, and that is why the software is called *MATLAB* (*mat*rix *lab*oratory). Simulink is another toolbox that is used to simulate the performance of the systems, when the systems are built by connecting individual blocks representing different subsystems and the output is obtained when the systems are

---

[1]The software is available from The MathWorks, Inc., 3 Apple Hill Drive, Natick, MA 01760-2098, phone 508-647-7000, fax 508-647-7001, email `info@mathworks.com`, Website `http://www.mathworks.com`.

[2]If you are logging on a workstation connected to a computer network, you may have to set the proper environment by typing `setenv DISPLAY network number:` or some other command before launching MATLAB.

---

subjected to different kinds of input signals. MATLAB allows us to construct new functions using the enormous number of built-in functions, commands, and operations in MATLAB and in the many toolboxes, without having to know how to compile, link, load, and create executable code, because MATLAB uses its own language to carry out all these steps, which are invisible to the user. It carries out the steps and gives the answer very fast! In most versions of MATLAB, there is a "symbol" toolbox, which performs does symbolic operations such as differentiation, integration, matrix inversion, and solution of differential equations when the operations are expressed in their symbolic form. In more recent versions of this software, new toolboxes such as Filter Design Toolbox and DSP Blockset, which are based on the object-oriented programming features of MATLAB, have been added. These have been treated in some chapters of this book.

9.1.1   Vectors, Arrays, and Matrices

Vectors and scalars are special cases of a matrix—all of which are represented as arrays in MATLAB. A *scalar* is an array of 1×1 dimension, whereas a *row vector* is an array of $1 \times n$ dimension, and a *column vector* is an array of $n \times 1$ dimension. When elements of an array are typed in a row within square brackets, with a space between the elements, MATLAB displays it as a row vector. For example, when you type

```
>>A = [1 2 0 3 1 5]
```

it displays

```
A = 1   2   0   3   1   5
```

If the array is typed without assigning a name for the array, `>>[1 2 0 3 1 5]`, MATLAB responds with

```
ans = 1   2   0   3   1   5
```

When you type elements with a semicolon between them, the elements are displayed in a column vector, for example

```
>>B=[1 2 0; 3 1 5; 0 4 -2] displays the 3 -by-3 matrix
B= 1   2   0
   3   1   5
   0   4   -2
```

If a semicolumn is entered at the end of an array or a command, then the array and the output of the command is not displayed on the command window, but the command as well as the output variables are saved in a buffer known as the *workspace*. The workspace saves the variables, data, contents of arrays and matrices, and other elements as well as a record of the commands typed by the user. It is recommended that at the beginning of the session, you change the directory to the disk drive `a:` if you have one in your computer so that the contents of the workspace are saved in the floppy disk in that drive. Instead of using the semicolumn between the elements, you can type the element on the next line or by leaving one space, type three dots at the end of the line and continue on the next line as shown below; this is useful when the array is very long and extends beyond the end of the line:

```
>>C=[1 2 0
3 1 5
0 4 -2]
or
>>C=[ 1 2 0; 3 1 5; ...
0 4 -2]
displays the answer
C = 1    2    0
    3    1    5
    0    4    -2
```

9.1.2   Matrix Operations

It is now obvious that a column vector can be created by typing the elements with a semicolumn separating them or creating a row vector and transposing it. In MATLAB, the transpose of a matrix or a vector is carried out by the operator, that is, the command x' gives the transpose of the vector or matrix x. Since the vectors and matrices listed and described above have been saved in the workspace, if we type `>>A'`, we get

```
ans
1
2
0
3
1
5
```

and `>>D=C'` yields

```
D =
1    3    0
2    1    4
0    5    -2
```

If we type `C(:)`, we get a column vector with the columns of C arranged in a vertical vector:

```
ans =
  1
```

```
 3
 0
 2
 1
 4
 0
 5
-2
```

When a scalar, vector, or matrix is multiplied (or divided) by a scalar c, every element of the scalar, vector or matrix is multiplied (or divided) by c. When c is added to matrix, it is added to every element of the vector or matrix. For example, `x = 5; F=x*C` gives the output

```
F=   5   10   0
15   5   25
0   20  -10
FF=x+C gives the output as
FF=  6 7   5
     8 6 10
     5 9   3
```

Addition and subtraction of two matrices (and vectors) is carried out by MATLAB, according to the rules of matrix algebra, when they have the same dimension. Multiplication of a vector or matrix by a vector or matrix is carried out according to the rules of algebra when they are compatible or commensurate for multiplication. The matrix operations and their corresponding notations available in MATLAB are given below:

Addition	+
Subtraction	–
Multiplication	*
Power or exponent	^
Transpose	'
Left division	\
Right division	/

Note that the command `x=M\b` gives us the solution to the equation `M*x=b`, where M is a square matrix that is assumed to be nonsingular. In matrix algebra, the solution is given by $x = M^{-1}b$. The left division is a more commonly used operation in application of matrix algebra. (The command for the right division `x=b/M` gives the solution to the equation `x*M=b`, assuming that x and M are compatible for multiplication and the solution in matrix algebra is given by `x=bM`$^{-1}$.)

When we use the same variables used above but define them with new values, they become the current values for the variables, so we define and use them below as examples of the operations described above:

```
>>A=[1 2 1;0 1 1;2 1 1];
>>B=[2 1 0;1 1 1;-1 2 1];
>>C=A+B
C=
3   3   1
1   2   2
1   3   2
>>D=A*B
D=
3   5   3
0   3   2
4   5   2
>>M=A;
>>b=[2;4;4];
>>x=M\b
x = 0.0000   -2.0000   6.0000
```

Whereas the addition and subtraction of matrices are carried out by the addition and subtraction term by term from the corresponding positions of the elements, we know that the multiplication and "division" of matrices follow different rules. MATLAB gives the correct answer in all the preceding operations. It has another type of operation that is carried out when we use a dot before the sign for the mathematical operation between the two matrices. The multiplication $(.*)$, division $(./)$, and exponentiation $(.^\wedge)$ of the terms in the corresponding positions of the two compatible matrices are the three *array operations*.

Instead of multiplying the two matrices as D=A*B, now we type a dot before the sign for multiplication. For example, the answer to >>D=A.*B is

```
D=
2    2   0
0    1   1
-2   2   1
```

It is easy to see the result of the command >>A$^\wedge$2 = $A * A$ as

```
ans =
3   5   4
2   2   2
4   6   4
```

Let us define a matrix

$$X = \begin{bmatrix} 1 & 2 \\ 3 & 4 \end{bmatrix}$$

Now we compute $U=X.\hat{\ }2$ and $V=2.\hat{\ }X$ and get the following outputs:

```
>>U=X.^2
```

$$U = \begin{bmatrix} 1^2 & 2^2 \\ 3^2 & 4^2 \end{bmatrix}$$

```
>>V=2.^X:
```

$$V = \begin{bmatrix} 2^1 & 2^2 \\ 2^3 & 2^4 \end{bmatrix}$$

A matrix can be expanded by adding new matrices and column or row vectors as illustrated by the following examples:

```
>>F=[A B]
F=
1   2   1   2   1   0
0   1   1   1   1   1
2   1   1  -1   2   1
>>b=[5 4 2];
>>G=[A;B;b]
G =
1   2   1
0   1   1
2   1   1
2   1   0
1   1   1
-1  2   1
5   4   2
```

The division operator ./ can be used to divide a scalar by each of the matrix element as shown below, provided there are no zeros in the matrix:

```
>>W = 12./X produces the result
W= 12   6
    4   3
>> WW= [6   2; 2   3];
```

W./WW divides the elements of W by the elements of WW term by term:

```
ans = 2   3
      2   1
```

The element in the (i,j) position of a matrix G is identified by typing >>G(7,2), and we get ans = 4, and we can change its value by typing >>G(7,2)=6, so that now we have

```
G =
   1    2    1
   0    1    1
   2    1    1
   2    1    0
   1    1    1
  -1    2    1
   5    6    2
```

The colon sign : can be used to extract a submatrix from a matrix as shown by the following examples:

$$>> Q = \begin{bmatrix} 2 & 5 & 6 \\ 3 & 2 & 4 \\ -3 & 1 & 8 \end{bmatrix}$$

$>>Q(:,2)$ gives a submatrix with elements in all rows and the second column only:

```
ans =
     5
     2
     1
```

The command $Q(3,:)$ gives the elements in all columns and the third row only:

```
ans =
    -3   1   8
```

The command $Q(1:2,2:3)$ gives the elements in the rows from 1 to 2 and in the columns from 2 to 3:

```
ans =
     5   6
     2   4
```

There are many other operations that can be applied on a matrix, such as A, as listed below:

MATRIX OPERATIONS

rot90(A)	Rotates the matrix array by $90°$
fliplr(A)	Flips the columns left to right
flipud(A)	Flips the rows up to down
triu(A)	Gives the upper triangular part of the matrix
tril(A)	Gives the lower triangular part of the matrix

There are a few special matrices; we will list only three that are often found useful in manipulating matrices:

ones(m,n), which gives a matrix with the number one in all its m rows and n columns `zeros(m,n)`, which gives a matrix with zeros in all its m rows and n columns

`eye(m)`, which gives the "identity matrix" of order $m \times m$.

We note that the inverse of a matrix A is obtained from the function `inv(A)`, the determinant of a matrix A is obtained from the function `det(A)` and the rank from `rank(A)`.

Since this is only a primer on MATLAB, it does not contain all the information on its functions. You should refer to the user's guide that accompanies every software program mentioned above or any other books on MATLAB [1–3]. When you have logged on to MATLAB or any of the subdirectories for the toolboxes, there is an online help readily available. You type `help functionname`, where `functionname` is the name of the function on which detailed information is desired, and immediately that information is displayed on the command window. So there is no need to memorize the syntax and various features of the function and so on. The best way to learn the use of MATLAB and the toolboxes is to try the functions on the computer, using the `help` utility if necessary.

9.1.3 Scalar Operations

If $t = (0.1\pi)$ radians per second, the MATLAB function `sin(t)` gives the answer as 0.3090. To compute and plot `v = sin(0.1`πt`)`, in the time interval $[0 \quad 2\pi]$ we have to choose discrete values for the continuous variable t and compute v at these values. To do so, we create an array `t=[0.0:0.1:2.0]`; this gives the sequence of 21 values within $t = 0.0{-}2.0$ in increments of 0.1. Now if we type the function `v=sin(pi*t)`, the result is a sequence of 21 values. The command `stem(v)` immediately plots these values for v in a "graphics window" as shown in Figure 9.1.

We have used the command `figure` to create a new window and the command `plot(t,v)` to get the plot as a continuous plot joining the discrete values of v (see Fig. 9.2). If we did not use the command `figure`, the second figure would replace the first one on the graphics window. Typing the command `grid` on the command window results in the plots having grid lines shown in these figures. Next we use the commands for adding a title and the labels for the y and x coordinates with the commands `title`, `ylabel`, and `xlabel`.

So the commands entered on the command window to get the two figures are as follows. Since MATLAB chooses the scales for the x and y coordinates, depending on the range of their values, we may have to change the literal arguments in the `ylabel` and `xlabel`:

```
t = [0.0:0.1:2.0];
v=sin(pi*t);
stem(v);grid
title('Values of sin(pi*t)')
ylabel('Values of sin(pi*t)')
xlabel('Values of 10t')
figure
```

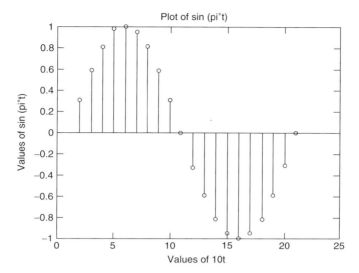

Figure 9.1   Plot of sin(pi*nT).

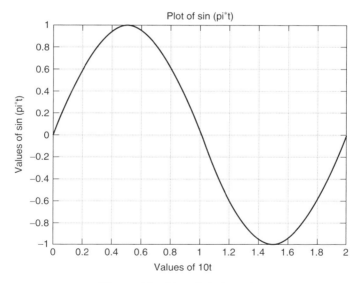

Figure 9.2   Plot of sin(pi*t).

```
plot(t,v);grid
title('Plot of sin(pi*t)')
ylabel('Value of sin(pi*t)')
xlabel('Value of t')
```

9.1.4 Drawing Plots

Additional arguments can be added in the command `plot(t,v)` to specify the color of the curve; for example, `plot(t,v,'g')` will show the curve in green color. The arguments for other colors are as follows:

y	yellow
m	magenta
c	cyan
r	red
b	blue
w	white
k	black

The next argument that can be added is a marker used to draw the curve. For example, `plot(t,v,'g','+')` will plot the curve with the + sign instead of the line curve, which is the default marker. Other markers that are available are

o	circle
.	point
*	star
-	solid line
:	dotted line
--	dashed line
-.-	dash−dot−dash

One can plot several curves in the same figure; for example, we can plot both v and y versus t by the command `plot(t,v,'g','-'t,y,'r','*')`. Another way of plotting more than one variable in the same figure is to use the command `hold on` after plotting the first variable and then typing the command for plotting the second variable:

```
plot(t,v,'g');
hold on
plot(t,y,'r')
```

The use of the MATLAB commands `subplot grid`, and `axis` have been described and used earlier in the book. The commands `gtext` and `ginput` are also very useful in plotting. There is a tool called `fvtool` (filter visualization tool) in the more recent versions of the Signal Processing Toolbox, which offers several other features in plotting the response of digital filters. You may type `help gtext`, `help ginput`, or `help fvtool` to get more information about them.

9.1.5 MATLAB Functions

The other functions, in addition to `sin`, that are available in MATLAB are given below:

TRIGONOMETRIC FUNCTIONS

sin	sine	cos	cosine
tan	tangent	asin	arcsine
acos	arccosine	atan	arctangent
atan2	four-quadrant arctangent	sinh	hyperbolic sine
cosh	hyperbolic cosine	tanh	hyperbolic tangent
asinh	hyperbolic arcsine	acosh	hyperbolic arccosine
atanh	hyperbolic arctangent		

MATHEMATICAL FUNCTIONS

abs	absolute value or magnitude
angle	phase angle of a complex number
sqrt	square root
real	real part of a complex number
imag	imaginary part
conj	complex conjugate
round	round toward nearest integer
fix	round toward zero
floor	round toward $-\infty$
ceil	round toward ∞
sign	signum function
rem	remainder
exp	exponential base 2
log	natural logarithm
log10	log base 10

9.1.6 Numerical Format

We can specify the format in which MATLAB displays numbers. If the number is an integer, then by default, it is displayed as an integer. If it is a real number, it is displayed with approximately four digits to the right of the decimal point (e.g., 12.0945), and this is the default format `format short`. If the number has many more significant digits, we specify other formats, using the scientific notation. For example, let the number be 12.094567832155321. If we type the MATLAB command `format long`, this number will be displayed with 16 digits as 12.09456783215532. If we declare the `format short e`, the number will be displayed with five digits and an exponent in the form 1.2094e+01, whereas the command `format long e` selects 16 digits and an exponent: 1.209456783215532e+01.

Remember that these formats are used for display on the monitor, the result of commands, functions, and operations. But the numerical computations that implement the functions and scripts are done by MATLAB with a higher degree of precision if and when it is necessary, for example, when we use the functions and scripts in the Signal Processing Toolbox.

9.1.7 Control Flow

Three functions are used to control the flow of command execution that depend on decisionmaking statements. Such functions are found in other programming languages and also in MATLAB. They are `for loops`, `If-elseif-end loops` and `while loops`, which will be illustrated below.

The statement

```
>> for n=1:10
 x(n )=n^2+4*n
end
```

produces a vector containing 10 values of $x(n) = n^2 + 4n$, for $n = 1, 2, 3, \ldots, 10$.

One can define an array such as `n=3:-0.5:-1.0`, in which the increment is -0.5 and the result is an array `n = [3.0 2.5  2.0  1.5  1.0 0.5  0.0 -0.5 -1.0]`. The default value for the increment is 1.

To define a two-dimensional array, and a function `H(i,j)=0.1^i+0.2^j`, we use the statements

```
for i =1:20;
  for j =1:20;
      X(i,j) = 0.1^i+0.2^j
  end
end
```

An example of the use of the `if` statement is

```
>>n=-10:10
if n<0
      x(n)=0;
elseif 0≤n≤5;
      x(n)=(0.8).^n;
else
      x(n)=0
end
```

Note that an error message will be shown if we use the statement `x(n) = (0.8)^n` without the dot before the exponent.

The `while` loop is executed step by step as long as the relation holds true. An example of this is

```
>>n=1
while n<8
x(n)=0.5^n;
n=n+1
end
```

If the values of $x(n)$ when n takes the maximum value of 7 is desired, we type x after the `end` statement and get the result

0.5000   0.2500   0.1250   0.0625   0.0313   0.0156   0.0078

But this problem is solved more easily by the following two statements to get the same values for $x(n)$, $n = 1, 2, 3, \ldots, 7$, but we have to insert a dot before the exponent (^) since n is a row vector of seven elements. It is very helpful to find the order of a matrix or a vector A by using the statement S= size(A) to know when to use the dot for the term-by-term operation—particularly when we get an error message about the dimensions of the matrices:

```
>>n=1:7;
x(n)=(0.5).^n
```

9.1.8 Edit Window and M-file

So far we have introduced a few of the common functions and operations of MATLAB that are used in the command window and the graphics window. When we are in the command window, we are in an interactive mode, where each command is executed immediately after it is typed and the answer is displayed. If we wish to make a change in any one of the previous statements or the input data, we have to trace it back one line at a time using the ↑ key and edit the line, then use the ↓ key to get to the line where we had stopped. If that statement is very many lines before the current line or if we want to make major changes in the program, or if we wish to find the output of the program for different values for the input parameters, this is not a convenient procedure. So we create a program or a script by clicking File-Open-New-M-file and use a text editor that is built-in MATLAB or any other text editor and save it in the current directory as a file with a name and an .m extension. We can write this script using the MATLAB functions and operations; we can even use other functions or functions that we have written. Such a file is called an M-file, and after it is saved, we click the command window and type just the name of the M-file without the extension. The entire script is executed if there are no bugs in it and the results displayed. If there are any error messages, we go back to M-file in the edit window and make corrections, save it, get back to the command window, and then type the name of the M-file to run it again. Either we enter the values of the input variable(s) in the M-file or add the following command in the M-file:

```
input('Type in the input parameters for xyz')
```

When the script is to be executed, the program displays the statement Type in the input parameters for xyz and waits for the input from the keyboard. We may have requests for input for several parameters, and when the data for all the parameters are entered by us from the keyboard, the program is executed.

This is helpful when we wish to find the response (output) of the program with different values for the input parameters.

Similarly, when we add the statement

```
disp('Values of the parameter xx')
disp(xx)
```

the program displays the values for the parameter after the script has been executed, which may not be otherwise displayed as the output from the program.

When any statement is preceded by the % character, the statement is not executed by the program; it is used only as a comment for information or explanation of what the program does. It is a good practice to add a few lines with this % character at the beginning of any script that we write and include the name of the file also.

Example 9.1

We click `File, Open, New` from the menu bar when we are in the command window and then choose M-file. An edit window appears next. Now we give an example of a M-file that we write using the built-in text editor:

```
>>clear  %clears all the variables in the Workspace
%This program we call Ration.m computes the value of a
%  rational function f(x) with a numerator 2x+0.5 and a
%  denominator x^2+0.1x+0.05 and plots it over the interval
%  0 ≤ x ≤ 1.0.
>>x=0.0:0.01:1.0;
>>num=2*x+0.5;
>>den=x.^2+0.1*x+0.05;    %Note the dot in the first term on
                          %  the right side expression
>>val=num./den;
>>plot(x,val);grid
title('Plot of the function f(x)')
ylabel('Value of f(x)')
xlabel('Value of x')
```

This file is saved with a name `Ration.m` on the current drive, and then we get back to the command window, in which we type `>>Ration`. All the statements of the M-file `Ration.m` are executed immediately, and the plot is shown in the graphics window (see Fig. 9.3). If there are any error messages, we launch the file in the edit window, then edit and correct the statements where necessary. This example is a simple one, but we have many examples of M-files as well as files used in an interactive mode discussed earlier in the book.

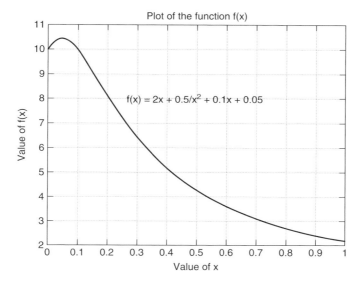

Figure 9.3   Plot of $(2x + 0.5)/(x^2 + 0.1x + 0.05)$.

9.2   SIGNAL PROCESSING TOOLBOX

The Signal Processing Toolbox is a collection of about 160 functions that are extensively used for the analysis, design, and realization of discrete-time systems and tasks or operations such as modeling, detection, filtering, prediction, and spectral analysis in digital signal processing. They run under MATLAB, which has about 330 functions and operations. By typing `help function` in the command window, where `function` is the name of these functions, detailed information about them is displayed. By typing `help signal`, we get a complete list of all the functions in the Signal Processing Toolbox, when this has been installed as a subdirectory of the MATLAB directory. If we know the name of the function that does the numerical processing but not the syntax and other details, we can type `help function`. But when we have to carry out numerical processing but don't know the name of the MATLAB function, we may have to go through the list of all MATLAB functions and choose the appropriate one for the purpose. The list of all MATLAB functions in the Signal Processing Toolbox is given in Section 9.2.1, and students are encouraged to use the `help` utility and become familiar with as many of the functions as possible. That should improve their efficiency in calling up the appropriate function immediately when the need arises while they write and edit the script. Note that we can use any of the thousands of functions found in all other toolboxes and in the simulation software called *Simulink* that runs under MATLAB, which makes this software extremely powerful and versatile.

9.2.1   List of Functions in Signal Processing Toolbox

```
>>help signal
  Signal Processing Toolbox
  Version 6.0 (R13) 20-Jun-2002

  Filter analysis.

  abs - Magnitude.
  angle - Phase angle.
  filternorm - Compute the 2-norm or inf-norm of a digital
    filter.
  freqs - Laplace transform frequency response.
  freqspace - Frequency spacing for frequency response.
  freqz - Z-transform frequency response.
  fvtool - Filter Visualization Tool.
  grpdelay - Group delay.
  impz - Discrete impulse response.
  phasez - Digital filter phase response.
  phasedelay - Phase delay of a digital filter.
  unwrap - Unwrap phase.
  zerophase - Zero-phase response of a real filter.
  zplane - Discrete pole-zero plot.

  Filter implementation.

  conv - Convolution.
  conv2 - 2-D convolution.
  convmtx - Convolution matrix.
  deconv - Deconvolution.
  fftfilt - Overlap-add filter implementation.
  filter - Filter implementation.
  filter2 - Two-dimensional digital filtering.
  filtfilt - Zero-phase version of filter.
  filtic - Determine filter initial conditions.
  latcfilt - Lattice filter implementation.
  medfilt1 - 1-Dimensional median filtering.
  sgolayfilt - Savitzky-Golay filter implementation.
  sosfilt - Second-order sections (biquad) filter
    implementation.
  upfirdn - Up sample, FIR filter, down sample.

  Discrete-time filter object.

  dfilt - Construct a discrete-time, filter object.
  (Type ''doc dfilt'' for more information)
```

FIR filter design.

cremez - Complex and nonlinear phase equiripple FIR filter
  design.
fir1 - Window based FIR filter design - low, high, band,
  stop, multi.
fir2 - FIR arbitrary shape filter design using the frequency
  sampling method.
fircls - Constrained Least Squares filter design - arbitrary
  response.
fircls1 - Constrained Least Squares FIR filter design - low
  and highpass.
firgauss - FIR Gaussian digital filter design.
firls - Optimal least-squares FIR filter design.
firrcos - Raised cosine FIR filter design.
intfilt - Interpolation FIR filter design.
kaiserord - Kaiser window design based filter order
  estimation.
remez - Optimal Chebyshev-norm FIR filter design.
remezord - Remez design based filter order estimation.
sgolay - Savitzky-Golay FIR smoothing filter design.

IIR digital filter design.

butter - Butterworth filter design.
cheby1 - Chebyshev Type I filter design (passband ripple).
cheby2 - Chebyshev Type II filter design (stopband ripple).
ellip - Elliptic filter design.
maxflat - Generalized Butterworth lowpass filter design.
yulewalk - Yule-Walker filter design.
IIR filter order estimation.
buttord - Butterworth filter order estimation.
cheb1ord - Chebyshev Type I filter order estimation.
cheb2ord - Chebyshev Type II filter order estimation.
ellipord - Elliptic filter order estimation.

Analog lowpass filter prototypes.

besselap - Bessel filter prototype.
buttap - Butterworth filter prototype.
cheb1ap - Chebyshev Type I filter prototype (passband
  ripple).
cheb2ap - Chebyshev Type II filter prototype (stopband
  ripple).

```
ellipap - Elliptic filter prototype.
Analog filter design.
besself - Bessel analog filter design.
butter - Butterworth filter design.
cheby1 - Chebyshev Type I filter design.
cheby2 - Chebyshev Type II filter design.
ellip - Elliptic filter design.


Analog filter transformation.

lp2bp - Lowpass to bandpass analog filter transformation.
lp2bs - Lowpass to bandstop analog filter transformation
lp2hp - Lowpass to highpass analog filter transformation.
lp2lp - Lowpass to lowpass analog filter transformation.


Filter discretization.

bilinear - Bilinear transformation with optional
  prewarping.
impinvar - Impulse invariance analog to digital conversion.


Linear system transformations.

latc2tf - Lattice or lattice ladder to transfer function
  conversion.
polystab - Polynomial stabilization.
polyscale - Scale roots of polynomial.
residuez - Z-transform partial fraction expansion.
sos2ss - Second-order sections to state-space conversion.
sos2tf - Second-order sections to transfer function
  conversion.
sos2zp - Second-order sections to zero-pole conversion.
ss2sos - State-space to second-order sections conversion.
ss2tf - State-space to transfer function conversion.
ss2zp - State-space to zero-pole conversion.
tf2latc - Transfer function to lattice or lattice ladder
  conversion.
tf2sos - Transfer Function to second-order sections
  conversion.
tf2ss - Transfer function to state-space conversion.
tf2zpk - Discrete-time transfer function to zero-pole
  conversion.
zp2sos - Zero-pole to second-order sections conversion.
zp2ss - Zero-pole to state-space conversion.
zp2tf - Zero-pole to transfer function conversion.
```

Windows.

bartlett - Bartlett window.
barthannwin - Modified Bartlett-Hanning window.
blackman - Blackman window.
blackmanharris - Minimum 4-term Blackman-Harris window.
bohmanwin - Bohman window.
chebwin - Chebyshev window.
flattopwin - Flat Top window.
gausswin - Gaussian window.
hamming - Hamming window.
hann - Hann window.
kaiser - Kaiser window.
nuttallwin - Nuttall defined minimum 4-term Blackman-Harris
   window.
parzenwin - Parzen (de la Valle-Poussin) window.
rectwin - Rectangular window.
triang - Triangular window.
tukeywin - Tukey window.
wvtool - Window Visualization Tool.
window - Window function gateway.

Window object.

sigwin - Construct a window object.
(Type ''doc sigwin'' for more information)

Transforms.

bitrevorder - Permute input into bit-reversed order.
czt - Chirp-z transform.
dct - Discrete cosine transform.
dftmtx - Discrete Fourier transform matrix.
digitrevorder - Permute input into digit-reversed order.
fft - Fast Fourier transform.
fft2 - 2-D fast Fourier transform.
fftshift - Swap vector halves.
goertzel - Second-order Goertzel algorithm.
hilbert - Discrete-time analytic signal via Hilbert
   transform.
idct - Inverse discrete cosine transform.
ifft - Inverse fast Fourier transform.
ifft2 - Inverse 2-D fast Fourier transform.

Cepstral analysis.

cceps - Complex cepstrum.
icceps - Inverse Complex cepstrum.
rceps - Real cepstrum and minimum phase reconstruction.

Statistical signal processing and spectral analysis.

cohere - Coherence function estimate.
corrcoef - Correlation coefficients.
corrmtx - Autocorrelation matrix.
cov - Covariance matrix.
csd - Cross Spectral Density.
pburg - Power Spectral Density estimate via Burg's method.
pcov - Power Spectral Density estimate via the Covariance
  method.
peig - Power Spectral Density estimate via the Eigenvector
  method.
periodogram - Power Spectral Density estimate via the
  periodogram method.
pmcov - Power Spectral Density estimate via the Modified
  Covariance method.
pmtm - Power Spectral Density estimate via the Thomson
  multitaper method.
pmusic - Power Spectral Density estimate via the MUSIC
  method.
psdplot - Plot Power Spectral Density data.
pwelch - Power Spectral Density estimate via Welch's
  method.
pyulear - Power Spectral Density estimate via the
  Yule-Walker AR Method.
rooteig - Sinusoid frequency and power estimation via the
  eigenvector algorithm.
rootmusic - Sinusoid frequency and power estimation via
  the MUSIC algorithm.
tfe - Transfer function estimate.
xcorr - Cross-correlation function.
xcorr2 - 2-D cross-correlation.
xcov - Covariance function.

Parametric modeling.

arburg - AR parametric modeling via Burg's method.
arcov - AR parametric modeling via covariance
  method.

armcov - AR parametric modeling via modified covariance
    method.
aryule - AR parametric modeling via the Yule-Walker method.
ident - See the System Identification Toolbox.
invfreqs - Analog filter fit to frequency response.
invfreqz - Discrete filter fit to frequency response.
prony - Prony's discrete filter fit to time response.
stmcb - Steiglitz-McBride iteration for ARMA modeling.

Linear Prediction.

ac2rc - Autocorrelation sequence to reflection coefficients
    conversion.
ac2poly - Autocorrelation sequence to prediction polynomial
    conversion.
is2rc - Inverse sine parameters to reflection coefficients
    conversion.
lar2rc - Log area ratios to reflection coefficients
    conversion.
levinson - Levinson-Durbin recursion.
lpc - Linear Predictive Coefficients using autocorrelation
    method.
lsf2poly - Line spectral frequencies to prediction
    polynomial conversion.
poly2ac - Prediction polynomial to autocorrelation sequence
    conversion.
poly2lsf - Prediction polynomial to line spectral
    frequencies conversion.
poly2rc - Prediction polynomial to reflection coefficients
    conversion.
rc2ac - Reflection coefficients to autocorrelation sequence
    conversion.
rc2is - Reflection coefficients to inverse sine parameters
    conversion.
rc2lar - Reflection coefficients to log area ratios
    conversion.
rc2poly - Reflection coefficients to prediction polynomial
    conversion.
rlevinson - Reverse Levinson-Durbin recursion.
schurrc - Schur algorithm.

Multirate signal processing.

decimate - Resample data at a lower sample rate.
downsample - Downsample input signal.

interp - Resample data at a higher sample rate.
interp1 - General 1-D interpolation. (MATLAB Toolbox)
resample - Resample sequence with new sampling rate.
spline - Cubic spline interpolation.
upfirdn - Up sample, FIR filter, down sample.
upsample - Upsample input signal.

Waveform generation.

chirp - Swept-frequency cosine generator.
diric - Dirichlet (periodic sinc) function.
gauspuls - Gaussian RF pulse generator.
gmonopuls - Gaussian monopulse generator.
pulstran - Pulse train generator.
rectpuls - Sampled aperiodic rectangle generator.
sawtooth - Sawtooth function.
sinc - Sinc or sin(pi*x)/(pi*x) function
square - Square wave function.
tripuls - Sampled aperiodic triangle generator.
vco - Voltage controlled oscillator.

Specialized operations.

buffer - Buffer a signal vector into a matrix of data
  frames.
cell2sos - Convert cell array to second-order-section
  matrix.
cplxpair - Order vector into complex conjugate
  pairs.
demod - Demodulation for communications simulation.
dpss - Discrete prolate spheroidal sequences
  (Slepian sequences).
dpssclear - Remove discrete prolate spheroidal
  sequences from database.
dpssdir - Discrete prolate spheroidal sequence
  database directory.
dpssload - Load discrete prolate spheroidal sequences
  from database.
dpsssave - Save discrete prolate spheroidal sequences
  in database.
eqtflength - Equalize the length of a discrete-time
  transfer function.
modulate - Modulation for communications simulation.
seqperiod - Find minimum-length repeating sequence in a
  vector.

sos2cell - Convert second-order-section matrix to cell
  array.
specgram - Spectrogram, for speech signals.
stem - Plot discrete data sequence.
strips - Strip plot.
udecode - Uniform decoding of the input.
uencode - Uniform quantization and encoding of the input
  into N-bits.

Graphical User Interfaces

fdatool - Filter Design and Analysis Tool.
fvtool - Filter Visualization Tool.
sptool - Signal Processing Tool.
wintool - Window Design and Analysis Tool.
wvtool - Window Visualization Tool.

See also SIGDEMOS, AUDIO, and, in the Filter Design Toolbox, FILTERDESIGN.
If we type help functionname, we get information about the syntax and
use of the function and so on, but if we type type functionname, we get
the program listing also. An example of this given below; one can modify any
function, save it with a different name and run it:

```
>> type kaiser
function w = kaiser(n_est,beta)
%KAISER Kaiser window.
% W = KAISER(N,BETA) returns the BETA-valued N-point Kaiser
%    window.
%
% See also BARTLETT, BARTHANNWIN, BLACKMAN, BLACKMANHARRIS,
%    BOHMANWIN,
% CHEBWIN, GAUSSWIN, HAMMING, HANN, NUTTALLWIN, RECTWIN,
%    TRIANG,
% TUKEYWIN, WINDOW.
% Author(s): L. Shure, 3-4-87
% Copyright 1988-2002 The MathWorks, Inc.
% $Revision: 1.15 $ $Date: 2002/03/28 17:28:33 $
error(nargchk(2,2,nargin));
[nn,w,trivialwin] = check_order(n_est);
if trivialwin, return, end;
nw = round(nn);
bes = abs(besseli(0,beta));
odd = rem(nw,2);
exind = (nw-1)^2;
n = fix((nw+1)/2);
xi = (0:n-1) + .5*(1-odd);
```

```
xi = 4*xi.^2;
w = besseli(0,beta*sqrt(1-xi/xind))/bes;
w = abs([w(n:-1:odd+1) w])';
% [EOF] kaiser.m
```

REFERENCES

1. D. Hanselman and B. Littlefield, Mastering MATLAB 5, Prentice Hall, 1996.
2. The MathWorks, Inc., *MATLAB User's Guide*, 1993.
3. D. M. Etter and D. C. Kuncicky, *Introduction to MATLAB 6,* Prentice-Hall, 2002.
4. W. J. Palm III, *Introduction to MATLAB 6 for Engineers*, McGraw-Hill, 2001.
5. J. N. Little and L. Shure, *Signal Processing Toolbox for Use with MATLAB, User's Guide*, The MathWorks, Inc., 1994.
6. S. K. Mitra, *Digital Signal Processing Laboratory Using MATLAB*$^{(R)}$, McGraw-Hill, 1999.